The Confucian Mind

The Confucian Mind

❖

A Historical and In-depth Look at
Asian Culture and Psyche

Daniel Wang

Copyright © 2006 by Daniel Wang.

Library of Congress Control Number: 2006905495
ISBN: Hardcover   1-4257-2209-1
                     Softcover   1-4257-2208-3

All rights reserved. No part of this book may be reproduced or transmitted in any form or by any means, electronic or mechanical, including photocopying, recording, or by any information storage and retrieval system, without permission in writing from the copyright owner.

This book was printed in the United States of America.

To order additional copies of this book, contact:
Xlibris Corporation
1-888-795-4274
www.Xlibris.com
Orders@Xlibris.com

35138

Contents

CHAPTER 1: BACKGROUND 7

CHAPTER 2: THE BIRTH OF CONFUCIANISM 37

CHAPTER 3: MORAL AWAKENING: MENTIUS' REVISION 58

CHAPTER 4: TOWARDS PRAGMATISM:
XUN'S INTERPRETATION 75

CHAPTER 5: RUTHLESS EFFICIENCY: LEGALISM 83

CHAPTER 6: MYSTICISM AND THE FIRST SYNTHESIS:
IMPERIAL CONFUCIANISM 101

CHAPTER 7: BUDDHISM 118

CHAPTER 8: JAPAN: THE ADVENT OF CIVILIZATION 134

CHAPTER 9: ZEN, EN AND THE SECOND SYNTHESIS:
NEO-CONFUCIANISM 152

CHAPTER 10: CONFUCIAN CHILD REARING AND
FORMATION OF THE CONFUCIAN MIND (1) 175

CHAPTER 11: ZEN, EN AND THE BIRTH OF
JAPANESE CIVILIZATION: BUSHIDO 191

CHAPTER 12: JAPANESE CONFUCIANISM 214

CHAPTER 13: TOTAL HYPOCRISY 237

CHAPTER 14: MEIJI RESTORATION AND REFORM 257

CHAPTER 15: CONFUCIAN CHILD REARING AND
FORMATION OF THE CONFUCIAN MIND (2) 277

CHAPTER 16: REVOLUTION 287

CHAPTER 17: COMMUNISM AND THE
THIRD SYNTHESIS: MAOISM 312

CHAPTER 18: A CAPITALIST DEMOCRACY? 342

CHAPTER 19: A NEW ERA 356

CHAPTER 1
BACKGROUND

Before starting our inquiry into the Confucian civilization, I must stress that it is difficult to find simple and accurate expressions for most of its cultural values in English or any other Western language. A dictionary can give a translation of any word, and it would be good enough when the subject is purely material. For abstract ideas, however, a translation, though closest one can find in English, can still be so far away from its essence in Chinese/Japanese that it is downright misleading. Take the word power. In Western context it generally does not imply ownership of other people's lives. In Asia, power means ownership. If a person does not own another, he would be considered powerless, although in the Western eye he can still be all powerful. A modern Western corporate manager, for example, is seen as powerful. He can dismiss any employee. But that alone does not constitute power in Asia, because it is not enough to generate fear. To a Japanese employee, getting fired usually means the end of his career, possibly his livelihood. It attaches a stigma to him. No other reputable corporation will hire him. It is more accurate to say a Japanese worker is owned than to say he is employed, by his company. The discrepancy between Eastern and Western conceptions of power does not stop there. The idea of slavery is also different. In Western history it is a legal term. There used to be, dating back to ancient Greece, two classes of people, namely free men and slaves. A slave exists in contrast to a free man, without any rights, under the law. Outside the West in general and in East Asia in particular, there has never been a class of free men, or a similar legal tradition that grants any rights to any man. No one has ever been free in the Western sense. Thus the experience and perception of slavery—an altogether different kind of slavery than the Western version—can not be found in Western history. As late as early twentieth century all Chinese including high ministers were slaves

7

(奴才) of the emperor, a social condition that never existed in the West. Many other Western ideas like justice, freedom, human rights, as well as concepts implying a free man status, such as a stakeholder, all run into a similar problem: they have no equivalent in Confucian civilization.

Notwithstanding the difficulty in analyzing Confucian tradition in English, it does not follow that the subject can be better handled in Chinese or Japanese (written Japanese language shares its cultural core with Chinese, as most of its culturally significant terms were imported from China in ancient times and still rendered in Chinese characters, though some of these have acquired different connotations). Without the benefit of an analytical tradition like that of classical Greece, the Chinese language is more suited for poetry, emotions and summary moral judgments than for reason. In fact the term logic was not introduced until nineteenth century by the British, and its scope and application remain limited even today, only to the material realm, such as natural science and technology. When it comes to analyzing ethics, human relations and the human mind, its reason and psychology, the Chinese language quickly becomes murky and a logical minefield. Newly minted words in modern times (mostly by Japanese) that describe foreign ideas Asians had never experienced, like freedom, carry dramatically different, often opposite meanings from their Western origin. In other cases Chinese words long in existence were stretched to denote Western concepts that are related but not at all the same, such as justice, power, rights, slave, reason, religion, love, and loyalty, due to incomprehension of the profound differences. The incompatibility between these two civilizations is far greater than most people realize. What Westerners consider common sense would often look absurd in the Confucian eye, and vice versa. Social science theories born out of Western history, such as feudalism, capitalism and democracy, can not be applied here without straining these terms beyond recognition, which means in a study like this many of the ready made notions and tools Western historians take for granted have to be avoided, often without a good replacement. Readers are advised to set aside all high level philosophical constructs of human society, whether political, economical or religious, and Western perceptions regarding justice, religion, power and so on for the moment, focus on the basics of human existence, and imagine it under a whole new set of circumstances that had never appeared at any point in recorded Western history. The difference between East and West is at any rate not philosophical, but psychological, for philosophy in the narrow sense of the word presupposes freedom of thought, which is a condition unique to the West.

So where do we find a common starting point shared by all civilizations? It is my observation that most peoples of the world in their evolution from early primitive hunting and gathering communities in the wild to modern civilized societies have gone through a critical transition period somewhere in their history, before which they were all very much alike (savages and barbarians are the terms often used for them), but after which each people acquired a distinct set of values fitting their particular conditions, geological, environmental and political. Firm establishment of these initial cultural values was often accompanied by the first widespread usage of a written language, which facilitated the conception of abstract ideas. Once these values were accepted by the society in written form, they became the cornerstones of a civilization, making it difficult for the passing of time to fundamentally alter them, as later generations were brought up with the same values impervious to collective memory losses that plagued earlier oral traditions. The moral/ethical core of a culture is in my judgment the single most significant factor in shaping the character of a people. The first Western moral principle, justice, was formed in classical Greece and though there have been subtle changes to its interpretation since then its essence survives today, and it is still the cornerstone of Western civilization. The same is true with values of the Confucian civilization. A sensible approach would then be to start with a careful examination of this transitional period when a civilization lays its intellectual foundation: physical circumstances, social conditions, preconceived ideas and prejudices carried over from earlier oral traditions, as well as political dynamics of the time.

For primitive human beings, whether they were hunters, gatherers, herders or farmers, survival and propagation of the species were the only concerns. In a short life they were often subject to wild animal attacks, hunger, disease and the elements, not to mention brawls and wars with other people, with little power or knowledge to defend themselves, while at the same time trying to raise their young. Death was as natural and common place as everyday routine, and so taking the life of a fellow human for material gain would not necessarily be frowned upon, in fact it was often taken as a sign of strength and glory. Survival of the fittest was a fact of life. One who possessed superior physical prowess and ruthlessly cut down his competitors, most of whom innocent victims by modern standards, would be worshiped as a hero instead of condemned as a felon. People might have strong senses of pride, glory and shame, but little or no sense of guilt. There might be accepted customs as to what was and was not appropriate conduct, but these were observed only by necessity of the circumstances, not out of a moral conviction. Once upon a time the entire humanity fit this description; they were pre-moral, or amoral.

One example of pre-moral peoples would be ancient Greeks at the time of the Trojan War. They lived in tribes of varying sizes, often engaged in raiding, killing and pillaging others, and took pride in their pirating activities. The heroes of this time of whom the Greek gods are prototypes were individualistic, highly conscious of themselves, in possession of many human feelings, such as envy, anger and shame, but showed no concern for human lives. There were customs and norms in these communities. Theft was not considered the right thing to do. But if the thief was stronger than his victim he would simply kill him, and if the victim had no relatives to avenge him, the theft as well as the slaying would be accepted by the community. Similar attitudes were prevalent regarding other offenses such as rape. By the time of Socrates the Greek society was moral, as the killing of a free man was no longer accepted without him first being convicted in a public trial judged by his peers. The transition period from pre-moral to moral culture took place somewhere in between.

Another example of pre-moral peoples would be Western Europeans before the advent of the Roman Empire and/or Christianity. Aptly called barbarians these were marauding hordes constantly in battle with each other for survival. Their view on human life can be gleaned from the custom of dueling. Though later on the duel evolved into a ritual primarily centered on honor, in its earliest form it was a common way to settle disputes. Regardless of merits of their arguments two men would fight it out, and in the end the winner of the brawl won the argument, while the loser was likely wounded or dead. Two women in dispute would go through the "ordeal", whereby they would plunge their arms in boiling water, to see who was tougher. What was easily acceptable to all primitive peoples was that the physically stronger ones would naturally win, which is a plausible condition of natural selection. The moral sense of right and wrong, just and unjust did not register with them yet. As late as the tenth century the Vikings were still living such a lifestyle. By sixteen century Martin Luther were questioning Church practices and authority out of his understanding of justice. Luther's argument on what leads to salvation—that being not good deeds, which can be forced or feigned, but genuine repent of the heart—is a clear indication of the maturation of a moral people.

In identifying a pre-moral people we have to be careful in distinguishing customs, rules and ethics from morals. In common usage both words—ethics and morality—are often interchangeable, but I shall distinguish them as follows. Ethics means conformity to an accepted code of conduct, and morality means goodness in character. One concerns outward behavior, the other inner conscience. This definition is somewhat arbitrary, but I can not find better alternatives. Whatever words we may choose, this distinction between outward conduct and inner conviction is critical in understanding the Confucian civilization, in which the freedom to act according to one's real intensions is severely limited.

A pre-moral people can have elaborate rules governing the appropriateness of conduct, they just do not have a moral conviction. They can be shamed by violations in front of others, but they lack an inner conscience to feel guilty in the privacy of their hearts. This point may present difficulty to some readers. In the West, civilization began with a moral concept, namely justice. All other social constructs like political and legal systems were built on top of it. It is perhaps hard to imagine a highly developed political machine and an extensive system of administrative rules governing every human conduct in a pre-moral society. But that was how the Confucian civilization began.

The area that gave birth to this civilization was the Great Northern Plains of China, roughly the size of Western Europe, with most ancient tribes living along river banks. In southern China the terrain is rugged, people tended to live in small tribes largely separated from each other by mountains, marshes and forests. With no natural barrier in the Northern Plains, population growth over millenniums eventually forced many tribes to interact with each other, in trade as well as in wars, spreading agricultural technologies and organizational skills. The North would develop into an empire, with a written language and an elaborate political system, while the South would remain barbarous and irrelevant for much of Chinese history.

By about 5000 BC (?) there were farming communities and domesticated animals in China. Early legends paint a picture of peace, harmony and a relaxed lifestyle for this period (the land was vast, fertile, full of various games, and sparsely populated). People traded their possessions in free markets. There was allegedly no war, no theft, and no anxiety. Nor was there an idea of family as we know it today. Men and women met in large parties outside and picked their own partners for a one night union. These parties were a regular happening and continued for commoners until Confucius' time in sixth century BC. Children never knew who their fathers were, and were raised by their mothers.

We don't know how long this blissful life lasted for the people of northern China. By the time King Huang (黄帝) entered the stage at around 3000 BC (?), however, tribal warfare had become the predominant activity.

The legends give no detail about what happened in the two thousand years between 5000 BC and 3000 BC that would explain why the society turned from peace to violence, but we can conjecture that it probably had a lot to do with population growth. These early farming communities settled along river banks, as population grew over time all prime estates with easy access to water might have come to dispute. Inter-tribal theft, robbery and skirmishes ensued, tensions built up, until one death would ignite war.

By 3000 BC (or sometime in the third millennium BC) China had entered a new era as King Huang defeated the only other major competitor, laid waste to numerous smaller tribes and became undisputed king of the land (at this time his domain—the area directly under his control—was only a small fraction of the Northern Plains, large parts of which were still wilderness). From here on there was always a king, and the Chinese tradition took a different path than that of Greece.

In antiquity when a tribe defeated another in an all-out battle, members of the losing tribe were either slaughtered or enslaved, usually depending on how much they resisted. Naturally brave and defiant men were killed and timid ones as well as women and children were kept as slaves. Among members of the winning tribe, the chief would get the lion's share of the loot, and others would get diminishing shares corresponding to their ranks or contribution. Regardless of how much booty one received, there was at least a clear distinction between the conquerors and the captives, which would constitute the group of masters and the group of slaves. This was true in ancient Greece and everywhere else. What happened next had a lot to do with geography and lifestyle.

In the rocky and barren land of Greece people could not grow high yield crops in large quantities. They typically herded sheep and planted olives to supplement their diet. In such a lifestyle it took at least several acres of land to feed one family, compared to only about a quarter of an acre in high yield farming cultures. In other words density of human population was much lower in Greece than other ancient communities (Egypt, Mesopotamia, China, India, etc). The city of Athens, for example, had only about three thousand inhabitants in 1200 BC, and it was one of the largest population centers in Greece. Rugged terrain also hindered transportation between the tribes, who often found it easier to reach each other by sea than by land, even if they were on opposite sides of the Greek mainland. This further limited the potential size of any tribe by preventing multiple tribes from merging into one through warfare. When warriors from one tribe sailed into the sea and raided another along the shore or on another island, they would either take the loot and go home, or settle down as new masters of the conquered land, in which case they would become politically independent from their original tribe. Triumphant warriors could not take large number of slaves back home, for there was not enough land to support a sudden doubling or tripling of its population. Regardless of who won the tribal wars that went on incessantly, in the end the geological conditions dictated that there would be a number of independent small tribes dotted over the landscape, where each was limited in the growth of its population by lack of fertile plains. These tribes remained within striking distance of each other, at least by water, which meant that defense was always an issue. For a tribe of limited size defense calls for a whole hearted effort from every able bodied man, therefore slaves could not account for the bulk of the population—slaves typically do not make enthusiastic fighters for their masters. From the poem "Works and Days" composed somewhere in eighth century BC by Hesiod we know that the average Greek like him had no slave of his own and had to plow the fields himself. Under such circumstances camaraderie between tribesmen was essential for the survival of the community. If a tribal chief started to abuse his fellow men, they would rebel, run away, or ally with a rival—in any case the abusive chief would not last long. Indeed there were probably tribes and chiefs of this kind but they did not survive. What eventually emerged from the Greek condition was a culture where power of a chief was quite limited, and every tribesman was not just a warrior, but a stakeholder in his community, an equal to the chief in that sense. From there the idea of the free man was born, as well as the concept of justice, not only in contrast to slaves, but also in recognition of each individual's rights, such as the right to a public trial.

In the Northern Plains of China when a tribe conquered another it simply swallowed up the latter's territory and turned its members, or what was left of them, into slaves. Unlike the Greeks they did not have to bring the slaves home, instead they kept them where they were, farming the same fields. The winning tribe would then be freed from food production, weapons manufacturing and other chores, and concentrate on warfare. Their training would improve, as well as their technology. King Huang was said to have invented the wheel, which may have been the beginning of chariots in China, and must have given his tribe a great advantage over rivals. After a series of conquests the situation became such that all defiant enemy fighters within reach were killed and the winning tribe ended up with a huge number of slaves many times more than its own population.

This was a turning point. The result of these conquests was an empire. Unlike the Greek Empire which was really a coalition of city states spread around the coast of Aegean Sea, where each city was politically independent, the only thing binding them together being a common culture, and most residents were free citizens, the Chinese empire was ruled by a single authority, the vast majority of residents were slaves, and there was no well defined culture or written language yet. Since the king had eliminated all major rivals in reachable distance, the empire was beyond challenge for a long time to come. Without outside challenge camaraderie between warriors lacked sustaining power. At this point relationship between the king and his warriors was still egalitarian, similar to Greek warriors. They had fought in battles together; they were brothers in blood; the king in a sense was just another warrior. But from there on, over the course of many centuries, as the empire went unchallenged, its culture would gradually change.

The conquerors/warriors and their descendents were permanently relieved from manual labor. They lived in a main settlement, something like a city. They did not have private farm land, the way Greeks did, since management of such property was time and energy consuming. Farm fields were spread along river banks in a large area, plowed by peasant slave communities (descendents of conquered people). Warriors could just swing by every year at the time of harvest, and take what they want, or have peasants in each village send in their tribute. So the economy was not based on private property, but collective farming by slave labor. The warriors would each get a number of family slaves to do household chores. Thus the slave population was divided into two parts. A small percentage of them were family servants. They lived in the family compounds of their masters and were deemed private property: they could be bought and sold, and were generally not allowed to marry. The bulk of the slave population retained a semblance of free lifestyle. They lived in farming villages as they used to, there may be village elders who settled disputes among them, and for much of the year they went about their own business unfettered. They were also allowed to marry and encouraged to reproduce. Despite all that their lot was not necessarily better than that of family servants; the opposite was often true. In addition to producing food, peasants also had to work on hydraulic works, defense fortifications, manors and other buildings, and whatever their masters may want them to do. At the end of the year they could be exhausted, physically abused or maimed, only to find that their masters left barely enough food for their families. On large construction projects many were worked to death. The work for family servants was of less physical intensity. What was required of them were loyalty, intelligence, and over all a servile mentality. A servant who had gained the trust of his master could be promoted to an official role such as a tax collector, in other words family servants due to their vicinity to the masters enjoyed some upward social mobility.

I do not like to call goods and services rendered by peasants in this scenario "tax", because that distorts its meaning. It was masters coming to collect what belonged to them, not representatives selling some kind of service to a constituency. But their actions did look like collecting tax, and there is no good term in English for such a scenario, so I may have to use "rent" or "tax" when I can not avoid it. The peasant slaves were by nature the same as family slaves, except that they lived in their own communities far away from their masters. Their harvest, their labor and their lives all belonged to their masters. All slaves—family or peasant—lived precarious lives, as they could be killed at whim by the warriors. Their children grew up knowing and mostly accepting their station. The few defiant ones were of course killed. Loyal servants were promoted. Peasants would raise their own children to be obedient. Over many generations a slave culture and mentality was inculcated in the populace.

In the next development, when peasants had become compliant, and population increased, they were ordered into battle as foot soldiers, while members of the warrior class fought in chariots. Descendents of the original warriors provided generals and colonels, and peasant slaves made up the bulk of the army, some of them promoted to captains and lieutenants by virtue of military merits and loyalty (armies of most ancient civilizations, such as Egypt, Assyria and Persia, were also of this nature, with the notable exception of Greek city states whose army was primarily made up of free men). At this point the empire was so large and wars, if waged at all, grew to such a scale that individual valor on the part of the officers was no longer a major factor. Size of the army, their training, technology and tactics decided the outcome of wars. Moreover, peasant slave soldiers who accumulated enough merits on battlefields were promoted to higher ranks, and their families had a chance to become hereditary officers as well, and family servants of the king could become high priests, if they had served him well.

For the slaves, the prospect of being promoted by the king out of their miserable lives provided a reason for loyalty. They were reminded everyday that their lives were worth nothing unless the king bestowed favor on them. Since many of them had combat experience and they far outnumbered descendents of the first group of warriors who founded the empire, political dynamic of such a society was dramatically different from the Greek condition. A king who carefully manipulated the slaves to his advantage no longer depended on the officers for survival. As his power grew with his empire, he started to purge the ranks of those who showed the slightest disloyalty or disobedience. Moreover, slaves who were newly promoted to high ranks on the basis of their servile loyalty inevitably brought with them a corruptive influence on the free spirit of other hereditary officers. Because they were used to being ordered and abused, they tended to stay blindly obedient to the king in his political maneuvers against other hereditary nobles. In addition, the king did not have to worry about his political enemies running away to help foreign tribes because he had no serious rival. In the first Chinese imperial dynasty—the Xia Dynasty (夏, ~2000 B.C.?~1600 B.C.?)—which lasted hundreds of years the imperial house had ample time to put down any political opposition and reduce the entire warrior class to dependents on his good will, with the help of slavish peasant soldiers. By now the initial class of warriors who eventually turned into the class of free men in Greece had in China completely lost their leverage with and independence from the ruler. The society became hierarchical, and no one was free.

The desire to insert more and more grades in social hierarchy was rooted in the gigantic gap between the original group of conquerors and the original group of captives. When decades or centuries later some slaves were promoted to the official rank, say by military merits, they wanted to be part of the ruling class, while descendents of the conquerors wanted to draw a line between themselves and the pretenders with slave blood in them. Thus a half way grade was created. But the newly promoted officers might be respected leaders of the peasant army and therefore had the king's ear on important matters. Families of purer noble blood but declining influence might find it profitable to broker marriages with these officers to gain power and influence in the court. There were also other possible scenarios for this kind of marriages to happen. Descendents of these hybrid marriages would likely get another new grade just for them. Generations later there were multiple grades, each claiming a higher percentage of noble blood (meaning from the original conquerors) than the next. Something similar happened among the slaves. Demoted officers filled their ranks, injecting noble blood to the pool. Over time many would claim to be a descendent of some officer in the near or distant past. As lower ranking official positions were open to slaves in peaceful times, such as court clerks, tax collectors and family stewards, which would create yet more grades, the line between conquerors and captives eventually disappeared completely. The society was organized in a continuous social hierarchy from top to bottom with many ranks in between, and it assumed a pyramid structure: less and less people towards the top, more and more towards the bottom. The identity of every person in such a society was his position in the pyramid, a position given by the ruler, who was the pinnacle and anchor of that pyramid. If the ruler was a strong willed man, he could easily take advantage of servile loyalty from the peasantry (bottom of the pyramid) and turn the top portion of the pyramid into his slaves as well.

To sum up this evolution which happened over many centuries, the turning point was when an unchallenged empire emerged with a relatively small number of warriors in possession of a huge number of slaves. Prior to this point the culture developed in line with natural selection: the strongest and fittest in combat always won. After this point a man-made environment took over, and the fittest of this environment were not the strong willed, but the most servile. At first this rule of artificial selection only applied to the slaves, but since their numbers dominated the population, over time the ruling house would use them to crush resistance from descendents of the warriors, gradually remove the line between warriors and slaves, and eventually reduce nobles to servile dependents as well. This long process was not designed by any particular king, of course, but it was, shall we say, a natural development under the circumstances, given that it was repeated by many ancient civilizations from Asia to South America. I call the process counter-evolution.

Between 3000 BC and 2000 BC kingship did not always stay in one bloodline. One time a king handed the crown to a capable minister, a practice which centuries later Confucius cited as a standard bearer of high virtue, though the same event if looked at objectively can be easily construed as the powerful minister forcing the king to resign while staging shows to legitimize his own ascension. In one of these shows the minister, having been the real ruler for years, finally crowned himself at the death of the old king, and then ordered the entire population to mourn the late king for three years—an act that supposedly proved his loyalty—while at the same time exiled the king's son, the legitimate heir. This was the legendary beginning of an important Chinese tradition, the Three Year Mourning, which Confucius later made an important rule of his ethics.

There is no direct physical evidence to support the existence of Xia Dynasty, but archeological findings of a large palace dating back to this era are consistent with a highly concentrated power that ruled at minimum hundreds of thousands of people. Xia's political structure carried by word of mouth was inherited by following dynasties. Power of the imperial court radiated from the capital, decreased as the distance increased. It reflected the way Chinese rulers and consequently Chinese people viewed the entire world, up until late nineteenth century, both culturally and politically. For many Chinese it even persists today in the cultural sense, that all people are categorized as to how close they are to the Chinese culture—the superior culture of the Central Kingdom (which is what China literally means in Chinese), the center of the universe.

Some four hundred years later the Xia Empire was overthrown by Shang (商), one of the tribes in the eastern barbarian territory, which started the Shang Dynasty (~ 1600 BC?~ 1100 BC?). We owe much of our knowledge about Shang Dynasty to the ritual of divination and the first evidence of written Chinese language. The following is a typical procedure. Before a proposed activity, such as a hunting trip, the king would order a religious inquiry to decide whether it bodes well to proceed. The question is carved on a tortoise shell or an animal bone to be asked of the gods, thought to reside somewhere in heaven (or sky, as the two words are one and the same in Chinese). The shell or bone is then heated from underneath for awhile, until lines and patterns appear. A religious official would then read and interpret the divine message, and give an answer to the question, which in this case would be either yes or no, but in other cases depending on the question could be more complicated. The message from gods was not always followed, as it was weighed against several other factors, such as the king's preference, court officials' opinion, and public sentiment, and there was a formula to arrive at a final decision based on all these factors. Tens of thousands of pieces of these shells and bones survived today, which are collectively termed "oracle bones", and their content "oracle inscriptions".

This divination was performed before virtually every royal activity, important or trivial. They include rituals, battles, hunting, journeys, sacrifices, king's movements, wellbeing during the coming week or coming evening, informing ancestors, misfortune, harvests, solar and lunar eclipses, births, deaths, illnesses, dreams, rains and requests for fair weather. Unlike Greek gods who resemble their heroes in every way except immortality, Chinese gods are not humanized (Individual qualities like courage, prowess and character were not at all important for the Chinese king, who had no competitor). The water god lives somewhere in the river or the sea and makes floods; the earth god lives somewhere under ground and causes earthquakes. Other gods—of wind, lightening, thunder and rain—are thought to live somewhere in the sky. There have been no attempts to depict images of these gods, or how they relate to humans, instead they are distant and indifferent, having their own mysterious ways. In addition to these there are also ancestral gods.

A former king who had conquered far and wide would become a god after death; his spirit is thought to always protect the interest of his clan. There is also the Heaven god, thought to be the most powerful, possibly because it plays host to many other gods who live in the sky (heaven).

Placating the gods had been a long standing tradition dating back to time immemorial, whether through consultation or sacrifice. In primitive kingdoms with a small population that have stone tools and limited knowledge about what lies on the other side of the forest, a king though dominant can not be assured of perpetual rule. Heaven may strike with lightening or floods and destroy the kingdom. There is always a chance that some other tribe in the distance may become a serious challenger all of a sudden. The feebleness of small human groups in the face of almighty nature keeps a sense of fear and awe. Towards the end of Shang Dynasty, however, the king could summon an army of hundreds of thousands of soldiers from the peasantry armed with bronze swords and arrows, natural disasters like floods were no longer a threat and no longer seen as actions of angry gods, as people learned how to effectively deal with them after ample experience building large scale hydraulic works. With secular power on such a scale the gods became less feared. In fact one of the last Shang kings openly challenged the Heaven god. He made a clay statue of Heaven (we don't know what it looked like), had a bag filled with blood hung above it and shot the bag with an arrow, allowing blood to pour unto the statue in a ritual slain of the deity. The point was not to prove himself a deity, but that as a secular king he was more powerful than gods.

The fact that this king did not suffer any consequence from his blatant blasphemy must have cast a great shadow of doubt over these gods. Rituals of divination and sacrifice would continue to be performed for a long time, but with diminishing earnestness. Over the following centuries the attitude of many worshipers had changed from that of a sincere believer who would obey any sign of the gods and diligently live his life according to the perceived divine instruction, to that of a casual and skeptical practitioner who would reluctantly do ritual services just because it was a tradition.

Shang Empire started off not much larger than Xia, but over its five hundred year history it expanded to half of the Northern Plains. At its end population was probably several million. By all accounts its later kings were brutal rulers. One of the rules of the legal code stipulated that those who dumped ashes on the road were to be executed. Other gruesome punishments, mostly various kinds of body mutilations, were meted out for the most trivial offences, such as larceny. Some of the kings killed people including high ministers just for fun, displaying their mutilated bodies over a banquet. One king asked a minister what he would do to his most hated enemy. The minister replied: put him in a big jar and heat it from underneath. The king then ordered the minister to try the new jar himself. It is quite clear that towards the end even the highest ranks were treated like slaves by the king.

Shang history played out the counter-evolution process once more. The last king of the previous dynasty (Xia) was an abusive figure. His mistreatment of neighboring tribal chiefs earned him many enemies, and his excesses alienated his own people. The Shang tribal chief took full advantage of widespread malcontent and organized an alliance to overthrow the Xia Empire. In his own reign the first Shang king was quite conciliatory. Those chiefs who helped him were given autonomy in their own domains, so were his own generals. Abusive practices of Xia were abolished. Five centuries later the last Shang king was even more atrocious than the last Xia king. He invented all sorts of hideous ways to torture and kill people. He had a garden full of human flesh hung everywhere, in which he liked to have parties with his women, that was his favorite pastime.

What happens in a dynasty is the gradual weakening of the egalitarian spirit that it took in a revolt to topple the previous dynasty, the encouragement and nourishment of a servile mentality, the strengthening of imperial power, until the ruler feels so safe that he can do whatever he wants to other higher ranks. In his campaign to depose the old regime the first king and his generals are invariably comrades who treat each other as brothers. But once his power is safe the new king or his successors will always try to undermine the power of these generals and their descendents. Low ranking officers and servants who have proved their loyalty are promoted, who would gradually replace descendents of the founding generals. If some of the newly promoted turn out to be less devoted than desired by the king, there is never a shortage of faithful servants waiting in line. As long as slaves who make up the vast majority of the population are encouraged to be more and more slavish (and the generals are helping the ruler in this regard), the long term trend is always in favor of the ruler, regardless of short term advantage or disadvantage he may have against the generals. Counter-evolution is a process where independence of nobility from the king continues to diminish and servility is gradually solidified as the cultural norm. It is a process that automatically starts when the turning point (vast majority are slaves) is reached, and no one can stop it.

We do not know when exactly the Chinese written language came into being, but we do know that by the end of Shang Dynasty in eleventh century

BC it was still largely restricted to court usage. This writing system, not alphabetical but pictorial, was devised by the court for its administrative purposes, quite different from Greek, which was first borrowed from other Indo-Europeans and then developed by members of the free men class to express themselves, as in Homer's epics. Thus in the earliest Chinese documents there was no mention of human mental activities, like feelings and emotions, no one was angry or jealous or anything else (these words did not exist yet), just an inanimate recording of things and major events, with an utter indifference. No plots, no reasons, it was like a computer recording mechanical operations, although by this time all of the words used for the various social ranks, legal code, administrative apparatus and military affairs were already invented.

With a language reflective of a mind not yet capable of abstract ideas, or in any case not widely known, and a social hierarchy continuous from top to bottom, it was impossible to develop the Greek idea of a slave as opposed to a free man who did not exist. The way the society looked to Shang people was not a clear division between free men and slaves, but a finely graded vertical hierarchy. As the official class completely lost their independence from the king, the idea of rights which has independence as a necessary condition was prevented by reality before having a chance to be conceived. In its place there was only the idea of privilege, granted by the crown. And this privilege in turn was indistinguishable from power or authority, for the higher one ranked in the pyramid social structure, the more power and authority he had over more people underneath him. As a consequence the Chinese language (and Japanese) still can not distinguish between the four ideas of right (as in human rights), privilege, authority and power. All four are rendered in the same word: quan (权). In the Asian context privilege, authority and power are combined into one, and right remains a foreign idea unintelligible to Asians even today.

Around the same time the Trojan War was waged, a semi-barbarian tribe at the western edge of the Shang Empire was making moves against its overlord. The Zhou tribe had a colorful history. They were allegedly descendants of Xia Dynasty driven from prime estates to barbarian territory in the northwest, where they had to switch back and forth between farming and herding to eke out a living, as they suffered defeats by farming settlements to the south and nomads to the north (barbarians) and were pushed around looking for a home. When they sought protection by Shang, the Shang court ordered them to fight the northern nomads, which they obliged. After losing many of their men and winning Shang's proxy war, they were abused and humiliated as their leader was executed by the Shang king, after which they still had to pledge allegiance to Shang just to secure its blessing. This being typically how the Shang court dealt with other tribes, it came as no surprise that in the end many tribes allied themselves, behind the leadership of Zhou, in an epic campaign that eventually toppled the mighty Shang Dynasty. It was said that in the final decisive battle hundreds of thousands of Shang soldiers gave up fighting for an abhorrent king they did not like in the first place, making history what had seemed impossible to most at the time, since the Shang Empire was much larger than all of the rebel tribes combined.

Circumstances surrounding the establishment of Zhou Dynasty (周, ~ 1100 BC?-481 BC) were somewhat different from the Shang, which led to a break from tradition and a different political system. The relatively small Zhou tribe conquered the giant Shang many times its size in one major battle with the help of "eight hundred states" (numerous other even smaller barbarian tribes). Politically Zhou founders were in a weaker position than Shang founders; they had to adopt an extremely conciliatory posture to hold the empire together. Moreover, the first Zhou king died shortly after the triumph over Shang, and the nascent dynasty was effectively ruled for six years by his brother, the Duke of Zhou (周公), who acted as regent to the underage heir apparent. By tradition or by agreement, the Duke was to return power to the new king when he came of age, a condition that must have also figured in the consideration when the Duke framed political structure of the new dynasty.

Barbarian and semi-barbarian tribes that allied with Zhou were granted autonomy. That still left the huge Shang population many times that of Zhou to be ruled. In the past Shang kings had used ancestral deities to legitimize their rule, claiming that royal bloodline was specifically blessed by the gods. To explain why now the gods favored the Zhou bloodline to the masses (conquered Shang people), and drawing from the prevalent feeling that the last Shang kings were excessive in their oppression and exploits, the Duke of Zhou advanced a theory that Heaven was upset by the atrocities of the Shang king and made a decision to replace him. The Heaven deity was established as the governor of universe, to be feared by the king, who was now the chosen son of Heaven. Heaven was constantly watching over the world, ready to punish a harsh ruler and replace him with a more lenient one, who he would call his son. So the king now had Heaven's Mandate to rule, but was at the same time subject to Heaven's sanctions if he stepped out of bound. What constituted that boundary in the mind of the Duke was whatever was deemed appropriate by the masses. Actions that were accepted without much resistance would be appropriate, and measures widely resented and particularly those violently protested would be inappropriate. Though not articulated in the records as such, this approach actually took account of long standing traditions and customs observed by Shang people. Peasants were taxed at a level that they could live with.

In order to avoid concentration of power in the hands of the king, which the Duke intuitively understood as the root cause of despotic behavior, he cleverly created a power balance by redistributing the peasant slave population. The Shang Empire was set up in such a way that the area surrounding the capital where the king had direct control had the lion's share of the total population (a third to a half), leaving the outside states starved for manpower and defenseless against barbarians, and the king unchallengeable domestically. By the Duke's design the Zhou capital had a much lower percentage of total population though still being the largest town, and important states headed by prominent members of the royal clan (the dukes) were strongholds in their own right. This setup solved the domestic problem beautifully, in fact a few generations later an erratic king was successfully dethroned and exiled by the combined effort of two powerful dukes. With populations—and therefore military forces—that could rival the king, the princes gained a great deal of independence. The Zhou Empire was a confederation of semi-independent states.

To prevent excesses and keep everything in order meticulous rules were written. The sizes of the walled towns had to correspond to the prince's title, the capital being the largest, followed by the dukes', then by the marquises', etc. Organization of the imperial government from how many ministers and officers in what positions, duties of each position, to how many guards at each gate, imperial activities such as what to do in each season and when to hunt, what, how and when to eat at court, how to treat guests and arrange a party, what kind of musical instrument to play, everything that they could think of there was a rule on paper describing in detail the proper way to do it. The logic was apparently that if everyone behaved in a proper way, excesses on the part of all nobility including the king would be detected and curbed at the earliest moment, instead of being indulged and allowed to get out of control. As princes periodically visited the king's court, and saw for themselves whether the proceedings strictly followed the book and how the king carried himself in his manners, they could at least detect early signs if the king was going crazy.

These rules were collectively called *li* (礼). Its purpose was to define what was appropriate for the ruling elite in terms of how they should rule and interact with each other. It provided a blueprint for the Zhou administrative organs as well as guidance on personal conduct for kings and princes. It crystallized a hierarchical order, since proper behavior was defined according to one's rank. By laying out a code of conduct on paper it also preempted the king's arbitrary power over the princes. Now if a king wanted to execute a prince he needed a good reason, such as violation of the code. When these rules were observed they cultivated a mild temperament in the king and the princes which would make them much less likely to act like ruthless savages that characterized Shang kings. *Li* therefore represented an attempt by Zhou ruling class to leave the barbarian past behind. It marked a growing distaste for violence and desire for peace and order. The Duke obviously realized that *li* alone would not be enough to keep the king in check, which was why he carefully redistributed the slave population in such a way that made it impossible for the king to wield arbitrary power. Unfortunately this most important power balancing mechanism was not written in *li* as a rule, which would later have a major consequence.

Li can be translated to rules or rites of propriety and hierarchy, for it regulates everyday human behavior, but we must remember that it was not merely etiquette, though it did induce a culture of civility as opposed to the sword waving brutes of the past. It was the written part of a political system designed for long lasting peace and order, and sometimes functioned like a legal code (though only applicable to the ruling class) the violation of which had serious consequences. Since every prince could be called to the king's court, no member of the nobility could afford to ignore *li*, as improper behavior would often lead to more than embarrassment. Princes would in turn employ experts of *li* for instructions, who often became close confidants and high ministers in state courts. Over time new rules were added to the collection by the king's court.

In a few centuries the ruling elite were no longer warriors in their outlook. Music, poetry, literature, wine, feast and rituals became routines of the day, hunting was reduced to a rare pastime, sword a decoration or collectible item, and whether one carried oneself according to *li* was the defining criterion that separated a civilized noble from a savage. From the king's court to states' courts, nobility assumed a new cultural identity, which was called wen, or "of the letter", as opposed to wu, or "of the sword". They wore capes made of fine silk, hats and shoes. They had expensive musical instruments (big bronze suspending bells each making one note when stricken) and books (written on bamboo strips tied together with leather strings). They moved about in such a manner that exuded civility and politeness. *Li* had ensured a long term domestic peace and with it prosperity. The ruling class now looked at bare footed half naked ill-mannered illiterate barbarians with condescension. Wars with these tribes were no longer just to pacify a potential enemy, but to bring them into the civilized world. Ethnicity was never an issue. As long as a tribe swore loyalty to the king and adopted *li*, it was part of the civilized Zhou Empire like any other.

It was in this spirit that the court declared "Everywhere under Heaven all land belongs to the king; to the borders of all those lands everyone is the king's servant". At this stage Zhou kings truly believed they were sons of Heaven and their enlightened rule represented Heaven's will. They could hardly be blamed for their confidence because every direction they looked, theirs was the highest form of civilization by far. The king's domain was declared to be all-under-heaven. Due to the isolation of East Asia from the Middle East and Indian civilizations this perception would last through much of Chinese history, and consequently Chinese was never a racial or ethnic term but always a cultural term until the twentieth century.

This same set of rules that established order and brought about civility also solidified hierarchy. The general spirit at the time was that the inferior should always show obedience, by prostrating, by bowing, by standing aside, by keeping quiet, and that the superior should show courtesy by acknowledging these gestures of submission, treating the inferior with politeness and forgiveness, and most of all, refraining from acting erratically in a fit of rage. In the past a Shang king could kill a chief of any tribe for no apparent reason. *Li* was designed to prevent such senseless violence among the ruling class. A Zhou king ought not to punish a prince without a good reason, such as the prince committing treason. Though there was no such thing as the right to a trial or a moral ideal like justice to serve as a basis for the practice, these conventions were collectively observed by the ruling class, their authority coming from an ancestral sage, the Duke of Zhou. On a human level the princes obviously preferred these rules to the Shang practice or any other barbarian alternative they might have knowledge of, thus both the Book of Rites (*li*) and ancestral worship which had always existed gained wide acceptance.

To examine that hierarchy and what it meant for the bulk of the people we need to look beyond the ruling class at the entire Zhou society. The origin of many states can be illustrated by the Lu State (鲁), founded by none other than the Duke of Zhou himself, where centuries later Confucius was born. After serving six years as regent and laying the foundation for the Zhou Empire, the Duke of Zhou returned power to the young king who just came of age, was given six clans of Shang people (slaves), a thousand horse carriages and various other items of value, and set out in one of the largest entourages assembled at the time to establish his state on the eastern edge of the empire close to sea. This seeding population of the Lu State consisted of the Duke and his family, perhaps a few dozen guards, and six clans of Shang slaves totaling a few thousand. The clan was the predominant kinship organization of Shang society with its own internal hierarchy often headed by a patriarch, but it disintegrated under Zhou rule so we need not concern ourselves with its internal structure.

Thus from the very beginning a state including all of its inhabitants was given by the king to a prince, in this case the Duke. Therefore the term "state" in Chinese (and Japanese) is GuoJia (国家), literally "state-family", because the state belonged to the prince, it was his enlarged family. Descendents of the prince's family would form the hereditary ruling class of the state, descendents of the guards would be low ranking officials, and in the counter-evolution process (slaves being promoted to these positions) become indistinguishable from the conquered Shang people, who were the vast majority of the population. In fact most inhabitants did not have individual names; they were identified as "a man from Lu" or "a woman from Lu".

When Zhou defeated Shang all the people of Shang were immediately enslaved in theory. But that did not constitute a dramatic downfall in the lifestyle of most Shang people—they were slaves in the Shang Dynasty to begin with. Only the top ranking ones lost their privileges. Lower ranking officials such as tax collectors and accounting clerks were still needed and would often keep their old job since few from the Zhou tribe were even literate. In addition, Shang religious rituals were largely kept at state courts, providing comfortable jobs for those familiar with the rules. Since the bulk of the population were still Shang people, their customs and traditions survived intact, including their view of the social hierarchy, that it being a continuous grading system from top to bottom.

A state would be organized as before. The prince's family and servants lived inside a walled town. The bulk of Shang people—peasants—lived outside, working on farmland. Also inside the town were officials performing various duties, their family servants, and other Shang slaves who plied the trades of metal work, horse feeding, cloth weaving, and so forth. Just like before peasants would make up the bulk of the army in times of war, and some of them would be promoted to the official class. For townspeople there were also opportunities for promotion, particularly those who could read, write and recite rules of *li*, and in case of competition for a job precedence was given to those from a noble family.

Peasants worked in the newly devised "well-field" system. Arable land of a state was carved into equal-sized squares separated by straight roads wide enough to allow horse carriages to pass. Each square was then divided into nine equal smaller squares separated by narrow pathways that allowed peasants to walk through. The eight squares on the peripheral were assigned to eight peasant families respectively, and each was allowed to keep the entire yield of their own field. Work on the square in the middle was to be shared by members of these eight families, and its yield was collected as rent. This was one of two parts of taxation; it amounted to a rate of 1/9 on crops. In addition to this, peasants were also required to give free labor in other projects as usual, such as hydraulic works, construction of their ruler's mansions, city walls and other defensive fortifications, and in times of war, each family was required to provide one or two soldiers and their own weapons and food. What's really taxing was the second part, and a good ruler should refrain from fighting unnecessary wars or building too many mansions, according to the Duke.

The well-field system was critical in forming the social psychology that would last till this day with regard to the idea of equality. The ruler owned all land and all peasants in his state. In order to efficiently manage his properties, he treated every peasant as the same, and assigned each family an equal amount of land. A peasant did not own the land assigned to him; rather he had temporary usage rights to it. He could easily forfeit his lot by anything other than absolute obedience to his prince. Between peasants every family had the same sized lot. Centuries of such practice had formed in them a specific sense of equality, that people of the same social station should be treated equally by the ruling authority. This was not the idea of equal opportunity for a free citizen of Athens, who could choose to engage in any business, and whatever the outcome due to one's ability, effort or pure luck was considered fair. Western equality is between free men, and it means the *absence* of state intervention on the basis of one's social status. Asian equality is between slaves, and it *requires* the ruler/state to make sure that opportunity and pay for everyone in the same social ranking are the same. Because lot assignment was dictated from above, outside his control, the peasant could only accept equal outcome as fair, whereas free citizens of Athens were responsible for their own success or failure, making it psychologically easier for them to accept different fortunes.

An equally important Asian value can be traced to as early as the well-field system. Since crop yield of the middle square went to the state, it was called "public field". The other eight squares were called "private fields". Given the abundance of land in the Northern Plains, each square was made sufficiently large so that peasants needed to work very hard to cover all the ground. By human nature every peasant would like to spend his limited energy on his private field rather than the public field. But if none of the eight families worked on the prince's share they would all be severely punished. Regardless of what kind of work sharing scheme they employed between themselves, their predicament necessarily put their private interest against the interest of their neighbors. Among these eight families (and peasants of the entire empire were all grouped in such a way) those who spent most of their energy in the public field, in other words for the community, were naturally liked and appreciated, while those who cared more about their private fields thus leaving little energy for the community were despised. Over time peasants developed a distain for all private interests. In Chinese (and Japanese) the two words "private" and "selfish" are one and the same (私).

In this context "public" (公) and "private" (私) do not concern property ownership at all. It is quite clear that the real owner of both public and private fields in the well-field system was the prince. Over the course of history the well-field system would be replaced by other schemes similar in nature but different in detail and the same sense of private vs. public remained. Here "private" simply means private interest, and "private property" means a property entrusted—often for a specific purpose—to a particular person or family by the state. The sense of "private" exists only against other slaves but not against the owner. Nothing can be held private against the state. "Public" means that which is not entrusted to any private party. Both "private" and "public" ultimately belong to the state/ruler.

It is debatable whether the negative connotation attached to everything private is a moral value. Private interests such as self preservation are basic human instinct. People who have a moral conviction against anything private simply can not survive. Part of the underlying dynamic here, not specific to the well-field system but generally applicable to all master-slave relations, is that by definition any private interest of a slave is against the interest of his master. A master wants his slave to work harder; a slave wants to save energy and loaf off—his master may not do well financially as a result but what does he care? The genius of the well-field system and other mechanisms that hold a group of slaves collectively responsible is that it redirects the conflict from between master and slave to between slaves. It sanitizes the nature of exploitation by turning the master into "public". Although "public field" really belongs to the prince, he is not there in person. In the meantime work is shared by the group everyday; in that sense it *is* public as far as the community is concerned.

Cultural development in the towns, dominated by the ruling class, was a little more complex. For centuries the multi-centered power structure and rules of *li* kept a high degree of civility in the polite society, which not only included the king and the princes, but also their court ministers, family stewards, other high ranking officials, and anyone aspiring to be a member of this elite club. The spirit of *li* is peace and order, but it does not provide mechanisms for negotiations between disputing parties, rather it dictates solutions to various scenarios. By *li* a prince who coveted a precious stone owned by one of his ministers, for instance, could not simply order it surrendered, even though in theory everything in his domain belonged to him. Rules like this had nothing to do with justice, in the sense that private property was recognized as inviolable. They were put in place under the reasoning that unrestraint use of (legitimate) power would lead to resentment and eventually downfall of the ruling house. The way these rules were enforced was not by courts or specified penalties, but by reputation and implied sanctions. Since *li* established a universal standard of what was and was not appropriate, violators would first suffer a bad word of mouth, and these words would slowly but surely travel. Depending on the nature of the offense, an infamous noble could lose his social standing and livelihood, a reckless prince could lose his domain, by order of the king's court, and an erratic king could lose his crown, by rebellion of princes. All this was possible mainly because of the delicate power balance and consensus on proper conduct.

Under this scheme life was safe and pleasant for a noble. The way state ministers were paid was by receiving a piece of farmland and a number of slaves from their prince. This was not the same thing as a fief in feudal Europe. A fief was legally owned by a knight provided that he paid an annual fee to his lord or prince, it was private property. In China all land in a state was owned by the prince, some of it was temporarily given to a minister for stipend, usually for the duration of his service, but since in many cases the son would succeed the father's position this land could have the misleading appearance of private property. It naturally follows that no fee or taxes were collected from these stipend properties. Lower ranking officials were paid in grains, cloth, meat, and other items. This "ownership" of land and slaves by a minister, which was in legal sense temporary but in practice very close to permanent, as high ranking positions were mostly hereditary, provided both security and opportunity for his family. A shrewd manager of farm, cattle and slaves could accumulate a lot of wealth. Interstate trade provided a venue. Cloth, silk, swords, cattle, wild game, gold, jewelry and indigenous products were traded across the entire empire. A minister could be richer than his prince.

The blissful life of nobles was made possible by lasting peace, which in turn owed itself to a delicate power balance between the king—son of Heaven—and hundreds of princes each ruling a state. However, unlike thirteenth century British nobility who had the principle of justice (inherited from Roman culture) behind their Magna Carta, this Zhou balance was the result of wise conventions, and a conservative temperament among nobility. It lacked a moral foundation, which made it vulnerable to a change of circumstances, which came around 770 BC, when the king's army suffered a major defeat at the hands of barbarians. The king himself barely escaped with his life, had to abandon his capital in northwest China, and was rescued by a vassal state to the east, which now played host to the king's new court. Losing his own domain irrevocably weakened the king's authority. It triggered a series of events over time. The state hosting imperial court gradually took hostage of the crown, and imperial decrees started to reflect interest of that state. Other states, particularly the larger ones, stopped paying homage to the court, insinuating that the king was hijacked. The king's order began to lose authority, and was increasingly met with nothing more than lip service. Sensing a weakening of central control, larger states began to gobble up smaller ones and expand their territory as well as population. A situation emerged where in theory the empire was still ruled by a king, but in practice it was each state for itself. An imperial edict would only be carried out by the strongest states, and only when it suited them.

At the beginning of Zhou (~1100 BC?) when most states—or state-families—were founded, they typically had a population anywhere between a few hundred and a few thousand. Centuries of peace and stability brought about a population boom. Annexation since eighth century BC fueled growth of the strong states. By sixth century BC the largest states each had hundreds of thousands in head count, and the rest a few dozen smaller ones—most of whom were themselves perpetrators of aggression against now defunct weaker princes—were just buying time. Annexation usually happened by intrigue, such as luring a prince of a small state into a trap whereby he forfeited his state on a wager or promise, although force was always threatened, in case the loser did not honor his word. There were occasional incursions and wars as well, though most of these tended to be small scale and quick, and the aggressors would usually deny these actions, to keep a proper veneer to the world. Meanwhile violent domestic power struggles broke out within many state ruling houses. Princes were frequently assassinated, by their own brothers, their own sons or high ministers. In fact only a small percentage of princes lived to their natural death, and they were very lucky, for the same could not often be said about their family members left behind. While all this was happening the appearance of peace and order was maintained between the largest states. The king was still recognized, though in name only. Princes were still singing the tones of appropriate conduct and courtesy to each other, though *li* was gradually ignored and eventually forgotten by most courts. In some states the rulers had completely reverted back to brutal practices of the barbarian past that the civilized Zhou ruling elite had long despised, now that there was no one to hold them accountable for their actions and the sanctions of shame though still existent lost teeth.

The previous *li* based order was enforced by a network of princes united around the king. If one state minister usurped his lord, for instance, the king would issue an edict denouncing his action, and nearby princes would send troops to remove him, carrying out the king's order. With demise of the king's power and authority, domestic affairs in large states were free from outside interference. At this time there were no significant standing armies in the states. In occasional inter-state wars the prince would order peasants into battle, but other than that he only had a limited number of family servants and guards. Under the circumstance rich ministers or merchants could stir public opinion in the towns against the prince or vice versa, to great effect. With *li* no longer being the code of conduct observed by all and nothing else to replace it, what kept a resemblance of peace among the ruling class was the sense of appropriateness inculcated over time. Depending on the particular state, and the situation varied a lot from one to the next, that peace was often fragile. A wealthy minister envied by his prince or other officials might find rumors circulating around town that his riches were ill-gotten, such as through excessive exploitation of his slaves, thus violating propriety. Having been thus demonized he was a ripe target for brutal attacks from his enemies, often helped by a looting mob. A minister with a reputation of generosity could be envied for his fame, and accused of hypocrisy, if he did not capitalize on his good name and depose the prince first. Since propriety or the perception of it often had a tremendous effect on public opinion in the towns, every man of any consequence felt pressured to profess it. When crooked murderers started doing charity work and successfully buying a good name, and upright gentlemen not corrupted enough to play these games of deception were lynched by the mob, the once honest nobility turned hypocritical.

Declining social order meant increasing social mobility. In more tranquil times family background was the primary consideration in promotion. Now most states had to worry about their own survival. A prince needed competent advice on how to strengthen his state against potential aggression, and perhaps take over a weaker neighbor. As a result restrictions on family linage were loosened in favor of talent. Competent managers of state affairs emerged, many of whom had a humble pedigree. As the talented and ambitious climbed the social hierarchy with spectacular success, the rest of the slave population often watched with jealousy. They were used to a culture where everything was equally assigned to them by the authority, such as their family lot, and promotions being based on servile loyalty. With their sense of fairness it was hard to accept the fact that any individual could take initiative and change his own fate dramatically in a short period of time, because they never had that opportunity. This sentiment was intensified by the distain for self interest, a value rooted in the well-field system.

Another ingredient of popular sentiment was anger. Slaves—the vast majority of the population—were born into their social station. They grew up being taught to be unconditionally obedient to their superiors, and they accepted it under coercion. But no one liked being a slave; it did not feel good to be abused without recourse. However, this master-slave hierarchy had always been there since time immemorial, and it was reinforced by all components of the culture: social customs, ethical codes, and a written language with all these embedded. The condition was not humanly desirable for the slaves, and yet it was defined as the only proper way. Thus people were left in a state where they had accumulated a great deal of anger but could not find any expression for it. Whatever happened was ultimately the decision of the ruler, who owned the state including all its inhabitants. It would look as though resentment was unjustified. Without a proper outlet anger brewed inside and turned into hatred of those who were better off.

That hatred was *always* there, waiting to be aroused. When authority started to weaken, as was the case in many states of sixth century BC China, it often manifested in mob behavior. Most individuals were not brave enough to do anything that would make him stand out, but if everyone started looting it felt safe. Mob activity was both a discharge of pent up frustration and a rebellion to authority, albeit in a cowardly way. Some opportunists with humble pedigrees took advantage of the sentiment and branded themselves champions of the people/slaves, but when they gained power and wealth on the back of public support they would become just as hated if they stopped handing out favors to the crowd. Sometimes when those in power were too strong to be within reach of the mob, a relatively rich merchant could be a convenient target, especially one who liked to flaunt his wealth. A rich merchant without strong political backing was a sitting duck.

In many states of sixth century BC China the situation was semi-orderly. On most days and for most people it was business as usual. The officials did their job and individual criminals were captured and punished, but every once in a while power struggles in the court would spill over into the streets, often in the form of two gangs dueling it out. Some of the gangsters—the organizers—were family servants of each side, while others were unrelated townspeople convinced that the opposing side had ill-gotten wealth, and lots of it, which they were keen to get a piece of. Over time the seemingly powerful and wealthy had fallen one after another. On a more pedestrian level the same rule seemed to apply as well. Every peasant was assigned the same amount of land regardless of their ability. The physically stronger ones had no advantage, quite the contrary, they were much more likely to be commandeered for state projects or drafted into wars, which made them on a whole less likely to live long.

From this social background came the first recorded Chinese thinker, Lao (老子), and the idea of Dao (also rendered as Tao), or literally the Way. Lao concluded from reality of his time what he considered to be a universal law, that the weak and cowardly would consistently outlive the strong and strong-willed (柔弱胜刚强), because they were not noticed and unlikely targeted. In other words natural selection favored the weak, the kind of people who had no ambitions, easily gave in to others' demands, did not mind being kicked around, avoided all disputes and remained anonymous.

This was the starting point of Chinese intellectual development, and by then Chinese common sense was already the opposite of that of Greece. In a Greek community a stronger man holding an advantage was as natural as a stronger lion having a better chance to survive in the African jungle. In a pyramid culture that logic was reversed. The well-field system turned peasants against self-interest. The ruling class for their own utility used and abused the able bodied more than the weaklings. Master-slave style hierarchy in the urban setting permanently acidified the lower ranks who could not articulate their resentment, because the language was invented by the ruling class specifically for the glorification of this hierarchical rule, and therefore could only vent their frustration on individuals who happened to be more fortunate.

This is another aspect of counter-evolution. We have discussed the first aspect, which is that the servile in the long run triumphs over the independent or defiant, which in turn forces the individual to be ever more slavish. Now in order to avoid being the target of public rage, which is always present though most of the time latent, the individual is forced to avoid competition or confrontation, to be a coward, yielding, anonymous, or even pathetic if necessary, just to stay alive a little longer. If the first process instills fear of authority in the individual, the second instills fear of standing out from the crowd in any way. Following all official rules is not enough to stay safe; one also has to take good consideration of public sentiment, or popular pathology.

Trying to explain this counterintuitive idea of the weak always triumphing in the end over the strong, Lao looked to nature for an answer.

"Water gives life to everything, yet it does not compete with anything; it stays at the lowest places disliked by all men. With this quality water is close to Dao. A sage lives at low places (to avoid competition); he lives a quiet life with a calm heart; he gives generously without expecting anything in return; he does not lie and always keeps his promises; he fulfills his official duties with fairness and no selfish concerns; he acts according to the natural timing of things. He does not compete, therefore no one finds fault with him." (The Book of Lao, 道德经)

The idea is to keep a low profile, don't fight for anything, don't get noticed, be content with your station, don't try to get away with cheating, don't harbor any malice in your heart, don't compete with anyone or desire anything, and no one will have any reason to hate you or to harm you. This is the essential Daoist argument. It is a passive acceptance of reality in order to find safety.

There is a fundamental difference between the ways early Greek and Chinese thinkers looked at the world. Greek thinkers were free men. They were in control of their own destiny. The challenge before them was to understand the material world, so that they could better deal with it, for their own benefit. To them there is a clear line between human society and the material world. Materials are inactive. There seem to be rules governing their movement (such as water always flows down to lower places). Materials can not control themselves so they always follow these natural laws of physics. Humans are active. Humans make choices. Thus human behavior is arbitrary, out of free will, not passively following laws of physics. Chinese thinkers on the other hand were slaves. Their mindset reflected that of the whole population. Anyone could be ordered to do anything by the ruler, for reasons they did not know and did not dare ask.

An able bodied man was likely to be sent to front lines and die in a war waged by the ruler, often for unstated personal reasons, such as over a woman, a piece of property or simply out of spite for a rival prince, while a cripple was more likely to be overlooked for any such duty and end up living longer. This was just like tall, straight, beautiful trees were cut down for furniture, while short, crooked, deformed trees were left standing. People felt like inanimate objects, being moved for reasons they did not know, and in ways they could not control. Thus in the Chinese mind both natural phenomena, like water flows to lower places (we now know it is due to gravity), and hidden rules of human society, such as the weak always end up the survivor, are both manifestations of nature's Way, or the Dao. There is no distinction between material world and human society. They both follow the same mysterious rules. Dao is the sum total of all nature's rules that also govern human society.

As discussed earlier, the pyramid social structure was gradually formed over many generations by power dynamics in an unchallenged empire initially consisting of a relatively small number of warriors and a large number of slaves. Formation of this structure took place long before there was a written language, or the ability to conceive abstract ideas. Once the structure was there, internal power dynamics would force the entire population in the direction of more servility, which further strengthened the structure itself. Long before first thinkers of the culture could emerge and articulate their ideas, the entire population had already adopted cultural values and common psychology of slaves. This had two immediate effects on the minds of a nascent civilization awakening from a primitive and naïve past. First, common values and psychology were taken as a constant of the world (just like the sun rises from the east every morning), because they had *always* been there. People would not even contemplate why they were there; let alone whether they ought to be there. Second, just like in Western civilization the first abstract idea was a sense of appropriateness regarding inter-human relations; only here it was based on slave values and psychology. This sense of propriety was not a moral value. It was not a choice. It was a necessity, the violation of which implied severe sanctions by the society. This same sense of propriety, called *yi* (义), has remained largely intact even today, twenty five hundred years later, and in modern times has been used to interpret the Western idea of justice, in the entire Confucian world.

Like other Chinese thinkers Lao's real interest was to study human society, which is understandable—survival is always the ultimate human concern. Studying nature's Way was to discover its rules, and use them for the purpose of guiding one's actions in human society. Regardless of their specific situations in life, those who followed Dao, according to Lao, would be successful, and those who were ignorant about it or worked against it would be smashed by nature's unchallengeable laws. He observed that people often fought for a good reputation (in order to get office) and for valuables (gold, jewelry), which eventually led to much of the fighting in the world. After contemplation he concluded that the following is the Dao on how to deal with rivalry (which leads to violence), theft and disorder:

"(advise to the ruler) Do not value a good reputation (give office to people with such fame), then people will not fight among themselves; do not prize articles difficult to procure (gold and jewelry), then people will not steal; do not show them what is desirable, then they will have a peaceful mind. Therefore the sage (the wise ruler) governs this way: he empties people's mind (give them nothing to think about), fills their bellies (so that they are content), weakens their wills (so that they are obedient), and strengthens their bones (so that they can work hard for you). He (the wise ruler or sage) keeps the people ignorant and without desires, and tightly controls the few who are knowledgeable (so that they dare not act on their knowledge). Since no one does anything tricky (the masses are ignorant and without desires, the knowledgeable are intimidated), order is sure to return." (The Book of Lao, 道德经)

This may sound cruel but since each state belonged to one ruler despotism was the appropriate way. Suggestions like this were not made cynically; they were thought to benefit both ruler and ruled because they reflected Dao, according to which people should live more like sheep herded by the ruler. Sheep have no desire for power, wealth and fame. They are simple minded and that is why they are happy. To Chinese thinkers it was not an opinion, but a fact, that human beings are helpless animals at the mercy of the ruler and nature's laws. Tempt them with wealth, they'll steal; tempt them with power, they'll kill; they may be born with a pure humanness (Dao) but it is easily corruptible by worldly temptations; they are not fundamentally different from a herd of sheep: they'll be docile and content if you (the ruler) treat them according to the Way or their nature.

Dao being the first abstract idea in Chinese history quickly gained acceptance far beyond the Daoist school. As nature's law, it was thought to be deep, mysterious and universal. Later Chinese thinkers of different schools applied the idea of Dao to human society in different ways, though they all claimed a better understanding of it than others.

Chapter 2

THE BIRTH OF CONFUCIANISM

By sixth century BC the Zhou Empire was in crisis. Wars and annexation had reduced the number of states from several hundred to a few dozen. States entered into alliances at moments of convenience, only to turn on each other at the next opportunity. For a precious stone or a pretty woman many a prince did not hesitate to wage all out war, gambling the fortune of his state and people, which of course was his private possession. Traditional code of conduct was paid lip service in formal settings but largely abandoned in practice. The once honest and polite ruling class took a giant step back into barbarism and developed a new habit of deception. The king was reduced to irrelevancy in a desolate court that was once the power center of all-under-heaven.

An anecdote in the superpower state of Qi may shed some light on the culture at the time in many states. The duke liked exotic food. He had tasted everything except human flesh, so one of the servants killed his own infant son and presented the delicacy to the pleased duke. The duke also for some reason liked feminine man, so another servant castrated himself to get close to him; this was the precursor of eunuchs in later Chinese dynasties. These two servants were so favored by the duke that they moved themselves into powerful positions and eventually usurped him in his old age and gained real control of the state, leaving the duke to die in wretched poverty. Despite all this the duke was hailed as one of the greatest rulers of the time, because under his tenure his state became the first dominant state. He wasn't seen as a cruel man at all. Compared with some other princes who used servants to test food poisoning, who tried their new swords on their subjects' necks, and who shot at towns people with real bow and arrow just for fun, he was merely eccentric. Chinese at this stage, after centuries of civilized life, were still amoral (showing no concern for human life).

Ascension of Qi State was mainly due to bold economic and political measures taken by a capable prime minister, a leading thinker a century before Confucius. Located at the eastern seaboard the state had a sizable coastal industry of salt manufacturing that provided steady revenue, as salt was traded all over the empire. At the time many states were curtailing commercial activities because it was seen to promote greed and violence. Qi did not see anything wrong with greed, though it stepped up enforcement of its penal code, one of the harshest of the time, to curb violence. Qi was also the earliest to abolish the well-field system and levied taxes according to the natural size and fertility of different fields. People were then less bound to their families; adult children could move out and get their own assigned lot. At a time when China was still sparsely populated this practice greatly enhanced productivity as more and more young people were able to break away from their parents and start their own lives. The prime minister also separated the ruler's ownership of the state and its actual management. Having been sold this idea the prince gave him sweeping power, thus enabling smooth execution of state affairs under his decades-long stewardship, insolated from power struggles within the prince's family. By seventh century BC the business friendly and prosperous state of Qi became the first super power, with the largest population and economy of the land.

Directly to the south of Qi was the State of Lu, founded by the Duke of Zhou himself. The Duke built Lu into a model state by demanding all his officials to strictly follow the rules of propriety and hierarchy (*li*). Any officer who neglected his duty was severely punished. His fairness and discipline brought order, and gained him allegiance of his subjects. The tradition of self-discipline by following *li* was carried on by his descendents, making the State of Lu the most peaceful albeit rigid society of the empire. Compulsory education for the ruling class consisting of the Six Skills (*li*, music, archery, chariot driving, writing and math) was kept alive with unyielding devotion while these skills died out in other states. Subsequent dukes carried on the legacy and all ruled with moderation. Amidst a world where bloody in-house succession battles were the norm and brute force was increasingly the dominant language, the state of Lu seemed determined to be the last stronghold of civility.

The Six Skills that constituted Zhou civilization should not be understood in Western terms. Music, for example, was not a free expression of human feelings, but part of the rites performed at court. Here is an excerpt from the Book of Rites (*li*) concerning the definition and function of music:

"All the modulations of the voice arise from the mind, and the various affections of the mind are produced by things external to it. The affections thus produced are manifested in the sounds that are uttered. Changes are produced by the way in which those sounds respond to one another; and those changes constitute what we call the modulations of the voice. The combination of those modulated sounds, so as to give pleasure, and played by shields and axes (in case of war), and plumes and ox-tails (in case of peace), constitutes what we call music." (Book of Rites, 17:1:1)

"Music is thus the production of the modulations of the voice, and its source is in the affections of the mind as it is influenced by external things. When the mind is moved to sorrow, the sound is sharp and fading away; when it is moved to pleasure, the sound is slow and gentle; when it is moved to joy, the sound is exclamatory and soon disappears; when it is moved to anger, the sound is coarse and fierce; when it is moved to reverence, the sound is straightforward, with an indication of humility; when it is moved to love, the sound is harmonious and soft. These six peculiarities of sound are not natural; they indicate the impressions produced by external things. On this account the ancient kings were watchful in regard to the things by which the mind was affected." (Book of Rites, 17:1:2)

"And so they instituted li to direct men's aims aright; music to give harmony to their voices; policy to unify their conduct; and punishments to guard against their tendencies to treachery. The end to which rites, music, punishments, and laws conduct is one; they are the instruments by which the minds of people are assimilated, and good order in government is made to appear." (Italics mine) (Book of Rites, 17:1:3)

The first part can be seen as the Dao of music. People make six distinct sounds in cases of sorrow, pleasure, joy, anger, reverence and love. A combination of these sounds when played by instruments is music. But these sounds are not "natural" to human beings, in the way that food and sex are. In other words these sounds can be controlled and regulated, unlike the urge to eat and have sex which can not be fully controlled. Therefore ancient kings instituted four things to bring people's minds into conformity: rites, music, administration and punishments (penal code). Music was an instrument through which people's minds were controlled and regulated. There was an official melody for joy so everyone should express their joy by the same melody. During court rituals it was played as a cue for participants to get in the joyful mood. The same was true for other emotions. Through music people learned how to express the six kinds of emotions, all in the same way, just like through rites people learned how to behave themselves under various situations, all in the same way. These were all efforts for the same end: to bring people into harmony by conformity. Music was commissioned by the ruler, not as a free expression of human emotion, but the exact opposite of it: to control and regulate expressions of human emotion.

So how did rulers make music? Here is another excerpt:

"When a ruler's aims are small, notes that quickly die away characterize his music, and the people's thoughts are sad; when he is generous, harmonious, and of a placid and easy temper, the notes are varied and elegant, with frequent changes, and the people are satisfied and pleased; when he is coarse, violent, and excitable, the notes, vehement at first and distinct in the end, are full and bold throughout the piece, and the people are resolute and daring; when he is pure and straightforward, strong and correct, the notes are grave and expressive of sincerity, and the people are self-controlled and respectful; when he is magnanimous, placid, and kind, the notes are natural, full, and harmonious, and the people are affectionate and loving; when he is careless, disorderly, perverse, and dissipated, the notes are tedious and ill-regulated, and the people proceed to excesses and disorder." (Book of Rites, 17:2:9)

"Ancient kings established schools for teaching their music, and different grades for the learners. They marked most fully the divisions of the pieces, and condensed into small compass the parts and variations giving beauty and elegance, in order to regulate and increase the inward virtue of the learners. They gave laws for the great and small notes according to their names, and harmonized the order of the beginning and the end, to represent the doing of things. Thus they made the underlying principles of the relations between the near and distant relatives, the noble and the mean, the old and young, males and females, all to appear manifestly in the music." (Book of Rites, 17:2:11)

The first paragraph here was meant to remind a ruler that his character was inevitably reflected in his music, and the music in turn would mold the character of his subjects, so he should be careful what kind of music he made. The second paragraph gives a rough idea of how music was learned back then. Music notes were given specific meanings, as the grading in the hierarchical social order, between high and low, near and far (in terms of blood relationship), was incorporated in them. It was not a liberal art by any stretch of the imagination. Here we can see that music was an integral part of the ruling apparatus, along with rites (*li*), administration and penal code. People were seen as so malleable that their characters could be easily shaped by the ruler's music.

In seventh century BC there was a power struggle in the ruling family of Lu. The end result was that real power passed from the prince to the families of his three brothers, who built their own walled towns in the expanding state. In areas close to their towns they advertised themselves as benign rulers and implemented favorable policies to attract peasants from the prince's domain. Strictly speaking peasants were slaves bound to their princes and couldn't just move from one master to another. But since the three families had blood ties to the ruling house rules became murky in this case.

By the middle of sixth century BC these Three Families (三桓) had controlled the state of Lu for a century. They divided its resources (mainly peasants) between themselves: one of them got half, the other two a quarter each. Chiefs of these families were the three high ministers of the state, and they took turns to rule. The duke was a puppet. While in other states a powerless ducal house was not likely to continue for generations, the duke of Lu not only kept all his ritual and ceremonial roles but was consulted on all important matters of the state, as all official decrees still bore his seal. The high ministers observed all court rites and maintained a cordial relationship with him.

This particular power balance in the state of Lu lasted many generations, maintaining a civil and polite culture that was increasingly hard to find elsewhere in the empire. But the practice was unscripted. When Duke of Zhou laid the foundation for the empire, he paid special attention to the power balance between the king and the states, but he did not say anything about governance within a state, which was to him merely a family matter. At the time of its founding Lu had several thousand inhabitants but by sixth century BC it had several hundred thousand. With a weak prince and three powerful barons the political landscape of Lu resembled that of Zhou Empire.

In the state capital lived the duke's family and high ranking officials, who constituted the privileged class, called the *shi* (士) class, as well as descendents of Shang slaves performing various servile duties. By sixth century BC one could count at least ten ranks in the vertical hierarchy of the urban society. For peasants outside town the main venue for promotion was military merit. For urban slaves it was to study *li* and become a court official in charge of rituals. *Shi* (the ruling class) would include high and middle official ranks which were largely hereditary, and male members of their families, but probably not petty officers. Members of the ducal family and the Three Families were of the highest rank, followed by other ministers without blood ties to the duke, then military officers, then tax collectors, then officers enforcing the penal code, then accounting clerks, and so on. Non-officials were ranked as well. First there was the peasantry, who lived in the fields outside the walled towns. They were a distinct class altogether. The servants who lived in town were divided into many ranks.

Stewards of the families of ministers were of a high grade, followed by those who drove horse carriages, then guards, then those who fed horses, then those who made carriages, then other manual laborers, such as metal workers, cloth weavers, etc.

This was when and where Confucius stepped on the historical stage. Born around 551 BC in the capital, he was a descendent of Shang slaves. His father was a low ranking officer serving a noble family, but died when he was only three. His mother brought him up alone, weaving cloth for a living, which was one of the lowly occupations in town. Hard as it was, she was determined to give her son proper education so that he could get out of their social station. Confucius started to learn the Six Skills very early and eventually became an expert of Zhou rites (*li*). In that sense he was lucky, for by his time most of the written material was lost due to movements of the Zhou Court and chaos in other states, and the State of Lu was the only place one could still find copies of these "books", which were bulky bamboo strips tied together with strings. A 500 page book today would have weighted 100 pounds back then, thus the Chinese phrase for erudition is "five horse carriages worth of knowledge".

Confucius' mother passed away when he was a teenager, so he moved in with his relatives. Around this time there was a party hosted by one of the three high ministers, and all the *shi* were invited. Confucius thought of himself as a *shi* because his mother told him that his distant ancestors back in Shang Dynasty were nobles. Apparently the guards did not agree and he was scornfully rejected at the gate. This must have hurt him deeply. A strong desire to get in the ruling class motivated him as he thought that was where he belonged.

Confucius got married around nineteen years of age, and soon afterwards had a son. At this point he was apparently known to the duke by name, most likely because of his erudition and mastery of *li*, for the duke sent him a carp to commemorate the occasion, and Confucius named his son Carp. Some time later he was given low ranking positions, such as a granary keeper and inventory clerk, and he worked diligently. These positions paid very little and did not become stepping stones to higher places as he might have hoped.

When Confucius was thirty five the duke mounted a military attack on one of the Three Families in an attempt to take back control of the state. He was soundly defeated as the other two unexpectedly got the news and joined the fray. The duke subsequently left Lu for Qi, and rejected repeated calls from the Three Families to return to his ceremonial role as head of state. It is not clear why after over a century of peace in the state of Lu under the same power structure the duke all of a sudden wanted to change it. We do know that Confucius was firmly in the duke's corner in this battle. He went to Qi immediately following his master, perhaps thinking that his high hopes of a glorious political career in Lu died with the exile of the duke. The situation in Qi proved unsafe and ultimately forced Confucius back home, where he started teaching in his forties.

Confucian teaching was not the Socratic idea where teacher and students would reason and debate at will. A hierarchy had to be established between teacher and students before any teaching could start, just like in any other social activity at the time. Since most of Confucius' pupils were poor slaves they treated him as their master. They lived with him, did all the chores of daily life and served his needs, perhaps in lieu of a tuition that they could not afford. They would learn rules of conduct (*li*) and whatever other ideas Confucius chose to tell them, but teacher's words were not debatable. Occasionally they could ask questions when they did not understand an idea, but it was a serious matter. They had to enter his room, one at a time, and present the question in reverence. After getting an answer they had to quickly get out. Casual conversations between teacher and students apparently did not exist. If the same question was asked by different students Confucius would give different answers to each of them, and they were often left puzzled and guessing what the teacher really meant. What they got from Confucius were often instructions on how to behave. Since each had a different character, each got different instructions so that they would all conform to a single standard. To Confucius a teacher was a saint, as he built an aura of mystery around himself, and claimed to be born with all his knowledge (生而知之). That became an Asian tradition. A teacher is really a prophet, with a divine gift. Others will never even come close no matter how hard they try—therein lies his brilliance, atop an intellectual hierarchy not to be dethroned by mere mortals, and being his student is just to get a small fraction of his knowledge, which is to be faithfully followed without question or even comprehension. Hence in Chinese (and Japanese) the three words teaching, indoctrination and religion are one and the same (教).

His teaching practice became another long lasting Asian tradition, that knowledge and skills of any kind are passed down in a master-apprentice relationship that is in nature a master-slave relationship, where in exchange for knowledge one has to submit years and perhaps decades of his life in slavish service to his teacher/master. Debating with the teacher is simply out of the question. It is also absurd. Since knowledge is considered a valuable commodity the obtaining of which could bring you power and/or wealth, and you paid a dear price in money or labor for it, why would you question it? You should learn as much as you can and secretly hope others wouldn't do the same so that you have a clear advantage. This view of knowledge as a static collection of rules persists in Asia today. The relationship between teacher and students even in modern schools still has traces of the old tradition. For example, respecting the teacher means one must not under any circumstances question the teacher's view.

The former duke of Lu died in exile; his successor was chosen by the Three Families and this time they wanted no more shenanigans from their prince so the three chiefs/high ministers all moved in the state capital, monitoring every move of the duke, leaving their three walled towns each to a trusted family steward. Within years these three stewards gained full control of the armies of their respective families. The steward from the most powerful family staged a military coup by putting the young heir under house arrest when his father the high minister died. Thus a family servant of a high minister took actual power and control of the state.

It took three years for the nobles to wrestle back power from the usurper, after a long war that nearly torn the state apart. Shortly thereafter Confucius was appointed high minister of the state (chief of law enforcement). He then started to push for his vision of governance. The biggest problem was to him the fact that real power lay in the hands of the Three Families and not the duke, which upset the right order. However, it was difficult to tackle the problem because their family guards were stationed in three walled cities, well protected from any potential attack from the duke—the former duke tried once but failed. For the duke to have any chance their city walls must be demolished, and that required their own cooperation. Confucius came up with a trick. He argued in court to the three ministers that the walls should come down for their own good, to prevent their family stewards from making these towns their own stronghold and usurping their power again. With fresh memories from horrifying recent events the Three Families agreed. But when two of the three cities were laid bare they finally realized what Confucius was up to. At this point Confucius persuaded the duke to send in troops to forcefully take down the last city wall, but the attempt failed. Not long after that Confucius lost his high ranking job and spent the rest of his life teaching, spreading his ideas and unsuccessfully seeking office in other states.

These are snapshots of Confucius' life and the world he lived in. It was a time when a long standing social order was destabilized. The pyramid was still there, both in reality and in people's minds. But who got to occupy top positions in the pyramid was less certain. The throne of many a state was successfully usurped by a minister, who might not have come from nobility at all. Unprecedented social mobility both up and down encouraged adventurism and risk taking, delivering irresistible opportunities to the bold and clever, while at the same time disrupted order and tranquility. In fact Confucius himself benefited from this more vigorous culture. Had he been born one century earlier, he would have stood no chance to make it to high minister, given his humble pedigree. Yet he dreaded uncertainty and disorder. He preferred the rigid and orderly past, only with a relaxation of promotion rules, allowing people like him with no noble blood to advance through diligent study of a standard curriculum.

The core of that curriculum was *li*, a set of rules that defined proper conduct for every member of the ruling class according to their ranks, and Confucius was the undisputed leading expert on *li* of his time, when most state courts had long abandoned these rules. His political view was that order must be restored, and it can only be done by restoration of *li*. His ultimate objective was to return to the past, restore an orderly hierarchical society. The broken vase should be put back together, with every piece in its proper place.

That sentiment was not shared by most of his peers. Many princes enjoyed the new found freedom, now that the Zhou king was no longer a check on their power. For centuries *li* was forced on them and they were gladly rid of these cumbersome and restrictive rules. Some state courts were turned into perennial parties and orgies. Between food, wine, music and women these princes were having a good time like never before. Sure conspiracies were brewing and danger was looming behind the scenes, but to give up all that pleasure for potentially more security, which was by no means guaranteed, was not an appealing idea. Looking at the big picture, declining social order not only created unprecedented opportunities, it gave birth to a new can do spirit. For the strong willed entrepreneurs, nothing seemed out of reach anymore. Interstate trade was on the rise due to lack of a central authority to control it, which generated scores of rich merchants, improved and hastened the spread of agricultural and other technologies, and lifted overall material standard of living. In short, many were too busy exploring the new vibrant world and celebrating their new found riches to complain.

Among complainers there were different views as well. Lao saw the decline of order as a result of human nature being corrupted by temptations of power, wealth and fame, therefore deviating from the Dao. In earlier times people were honest and content, much like sheep, and much closer to Dao. But now people were liars each scheming for profit, many did not hesitate to resort to violence. These people were trapped in their own greed and not wise enough to realize that the very thing they were craving would be their own undoing. Thus his solution was for the princes to not value the commonly valued (reputation, gold, etc.) so that no one would fight over these, not let people know what they should not know (how they are ruled, how it feels to rule, etc.) so that they would remain ignorant, and let them have enough food so that they would be content, in short, to return human nature (of slaves) to the primitive and naïve state.

Confucius could not agree with this approach. He had been a high minister. He was a respected teacher with scores of faithful followers. He had tasted power, privilege, and material comfort including service from his lifelong disciples, understood the pull of these temptations, and was not under any illusion that human nature could be turned back to that legendary primeval state. Seeing no other alternatives, he insisted on restoring old rules. But the clock of history could not be turned back just by human will. Conditions that brought about the first installment of a civilized society no longer existed. The power balance between Zhou court and the states that gave birth to the polite culture was irrevocably ruined. The subsequent problem was not as he first thought that the knowledge of *li* was lost therefore enough teaching would do the job, but that the culture of nobility had shifted away from it, and even if a ruler was willing, he was often powerless to force his ministers into these strict rules. Confucius' first conclusion was then a ruler must have absolute power over his ministers.

Philosophically this is an erroneous reading of the Zhou political system. When Duke of Zhou laid its foundations, he deliberately redistributed the slave population in a more even fashion, so that the king could not summon a dominant force from peasants directly under his control. This set up gave power to the dukes and helped maintain a balance. It was within the frame of such a balanced structure that the rules of propriety (*li*) were observed by all parties. These rules required everyone to behave, including the king. Confucius only saw that rules were observed in the past, but did not realize that it took checks and balances to bring about that condition.

If we stick to the letter of the rules laid out by the Duke of Zhou, then Confucius was right. One thing Duke of Zhou did not anticipate was the scale of population growth in five centuries. It was doubtful that an eleventh century BC man, smart as he was, could even comprehend a time span of five centuries. When he founded the State of Lu, all he had was a few thousand private servants. By Confucius' time in sixth century BC it had hundreds of thousands in head count. In the original design a state was just a family. One could argue, as Confucius did, that even with a few hundred thousand people a state was still the family of its ruler. The Duke of Zhou did not anticipate a condition where three members of the ducal family shared power, either, and no script was provided for this scenario.

Power balance within Lu State resembled that of the Zhou Empire. The duke played a ceremonial role, but his status as head of state was never challenged. The Three Families shared power through rotating regency between them. Although one of the three was as strong as the other two combined, that family never tried to conquer the other two, or to take away the duke's symbolic role. There was of course the aforementioned mishap where a steward of that family put his master under house arrest and assumed regency of the state, which caused political turmoil, and it eventually took a war to restore the old structure. But it was a flaw that with some adjustments the system could and proved that it was able to handle.

Confucius' objection to the set up was not just about potential instability. He did not think it was right. The state in theory belonged to the duke, and so in practice he should have absolute power; it was his family. Even though the Three Families were his close relatives, they had no legitimate claim to any piece of the pie. In other words, since a state started five centuries before as the family of a prince, it should remain so forever, regardless of how many inhabitants there might be. The three high ministers were in theory family servants of the duke. Family servants naturally should not have real control over state affairs and resources.

This argument was reasonable enough for his time, but an erroneous reading of the Zhou design. Just as it took a power balance to maintain mutual respect between the king and the princes, it would also take a power balance within a state for a duke to even bother receiving his ministers. As a matter of fact in Confucius' time many state rulers simply killed their ministers and abolished state courts altogether, let alone subjecting themselves to rules of courtesy, proving that absolute control did not bring civility back. His state was the only one where these rules were still followed, albeit not quite as precisely as he liked, exactly because of an existing power balance. Confucius strenuously adhered to the letter, but utterly failed to see the invisible power sharing part of the Zhou design, and its indispensability to peace and order. He advocated a political theory where he wanted absolute power in the hands of one ruler *and* for that ruler to treat his ministers with courtesy, according to rules.

Believing that he and only he understood the Zhou system, which to him was all about rules of propriety (*li*), he became a *li* fundamentalist. At the time old records of *li* were all but destroyed in wars and chaos, and he was in possession of the only remaining copy. He then proceeded, with the help of his disciples, to significantly revise the rules, adding and deleting as he saw fit. Most rules in this thick book (Book of Rites) before us today were clearly added either by him or his successors. This was akin to someone holding the only copy of bible in the world, editing and changing its content to his liking, while at the same time preaching to the world that everyone must live their lives according to rules in the bible.

After his editing the rules reflected a strict social hierarchy modeled after a family. Since a state was the family of its ruler, and ministers his family servants, the ruler-minister relationship, according to Confucius, must be the same as father-son relationship. By popular culture at the time, which was a slave culture, children were trained to be obedient to parents. This was necessitated by the predicament of slaves. Adults knew that the defiant ones among them would invariably be cut down by masters sooner or later, as that kind of character contradicted their social station. For the safety of one's own children a parent had no choice but to curb their free spirit as they grew up. Obedient sons had a far greater chance to survive. By modeling ruler-minister after father-son, Confucius significantly downgraded the position of ministers relative to the ruler.

At the time except the very top of the social pyramid most people were slaves. They shared the same psyche, articulated by Lao. When it came to high ministers, however, the situation became murky and varied from state to state. Some high ministers managed to get super rich and turned their wealth into political power, even replacing their princes. Some amassed great power but chose to keep their princes as puppets. Some managed to forge a cordial relationship with their princes on more or less equal footing. Some were dominated by their princes and lived in constant fear. Some were downright slaves to their princes and willingly so. Each state had its own story and Chinese culture was in flux.

The three high ministers of Confucius' home state obviously treated the prince like princes treated the Zhou king, as common sense would dictate, because they were close relatives of the prince, just like many princes were relatives of the king. Their interactions followed court rituals that respected the prince's higher rank, though real power was not in his hands. Hierarchy among nobility was more like deference between equals. After Confucius' interpretation, however, social hierarchy took a giant step in the direction of master-slave. His body language in court and particularly in front of the duke, when he was high minister, vividly depicted in the Analects (his words and anecdotes recorded by his students), gives the impression of a servile character trembling in the presence of his master. He was consequently ridiculed and scorned by other ministers for being obsequious. To the hereditary nobles who were used to treat the duke as one of their own, and felt quite relaxed and safe around him, Confucius' demeanor probably reminded them of a lowly servant at home. To Confucius who grew up among slaves, the duke's high court was a place of reverence, the duke's trivial requests were weighty responsibilities, and the duke's small favors were divine blessings. To other ministers a father-son relation with the duke would have been an insult; to Confucius it was an honor.

By applying a hierarchical family model universally, Confucius developed his political theory into a worldview. Now the family holds prototypes of all inter-human relations, the most important of which is the father-son relation, and it is explained in detail in the Confucian bible, the Book of Rites.

"For all sons it is the rule: in winter, to warm the bed for their parent, and to cool it in summer; in the evening, to adjust everything for their repose, and to inquire about their health in the morning; and when with their companions, not to quarrel." (Book of Rites, 1:1:2:1-2)

"When a son sees an intimate friend of his father, not to presume to go forward to him without being told; nor to address him without being questioned: this is the conduct of a filial son. A son, when he is going out, must inform his parents where he is going; when he returns, he must present himself before them. Where he travels must be a fixed place; what he engages in must be some reputable occupation. In ordinary conversation, he does not use the term 'old' (with reference to them)." (Book of Rites, 1:1:2:4-6)

"A son should not occupy the south-west corner of the apartment, nor sit in the middle of the mat, nor walk in the middle of the road, nor stand in the middle of the doorway. He should not take the part of regulating the quantity of rice and other viands at an entertainment. He should not act as personator of the dead at sacrifice. He should be as if he were hearing his parents when there is no voice from them, and as seeing them when they are not actually there. He should not ascend a height, nor approach a cliff; he should not indulge in reckless reviling or derisive laughing. A filial son will not do things in the dark, nor attempt hazardous undertakings, fearing lest he disgrace his parents. While his parents are alive, he will not promise a friend to die (with or for him), nor will he have wealth that he calls his own. A son, while his parents are alive, will not wear a cap or other article of dress, with a white border (because it is the color worn in funerals)." (Book of Rites, 1:1:2:9-15)

What transpires here goes far beyond obedience. A son can not have any wealth of his own, because everything he has belongs to his parents. He can not risk his own life unless sanctioned by his parents, because his life belongs to them. He has to always report his whereabouts to the parents, lest they can't find any help in case of need. He has to take it upon himself to make them always comfortable day and night, servicing and anticipating their every need. He has to always think about them, even when they are not present. He has to fill his mind with their voices and their faces, so that they have full control of his heart. He can not make any important decisions without getting their permission first. In a word, his body, mind and soul belong to his parents until they die. Thus a son is defined as a fully owned slave of his parents. Unlike with just another slave, such as a family servant, the gist of this relationship is not service, but mentality. Confucius had many servants, but only one son. What he looked for in his son was filial loyalty (孝). But instead of earning it, he wanted to force it by rules, by training, and by indoctrination. Therefore this is not the Western sense of loyalty, which implies a choice. This is the loyalty of a slave to his master.

It is not immediately obvious why obedience was not enough for Confucius in defining the father-son relation. Obedience to parents was part of social mores in a slave society since time immemorial, something taken for granted. We can conjecture that political implications surrounding ruler and minister probably figured prominently in his consideration here, having equated the two relations of ruler-minister and father-son. Loyalty is even more important than obedience for a ruler, who can afford a moderately defiant subordinate who means no harm, but not a servile character insidiously plotting his downfall. Confucius' articulation combined elements of two otherwise unrelated human relations, forging a new type of relation that he thought perfect both at home and in government. Unperceived by him, and understandably so, is the intrinsic contradiction between obedience, which is coerced, and loyalty, which is voluntary. Forcing loyalty onto someone who is already obedient inevitably leads to slavery, not that slavery was such a horrible idea for Chinese of Confucius' time. Thus loyalty was no longer a choice or a judgment; it became a psychological condition, which we shall discuss at length in the coming chapters. Parallel to filial loyalty, which is directed at parents, there is what I would translate to servile loyalty (忠), directed at the ruler. The two are conceptually the same idea.

Strong aversion to even the slightest disorder led Confucius to see everything in the world in a hierarchical view. The elder brother-younger brother relation was defined as: younger brother must be unconditionally obedient to elder brother. In general younger people must obey older people. Reciprocity applies only between friends and strangers: what you do not want yourself, do not give or do to others. To Confucius a friend is an outsider, one who occasionally comes for a short visit, and is not part of one's immediate circle. A friend is not that different from a stranger. The relationship between friends is not important. Relations within the family, on which the society is modeled, must all be hierarchical. Ruler-minister, teacher-pupil, master-apprentice, and government official-plebian subjects, all follow the father-son prototype. To illustrate how extreme he really was in his insistence of hierarchy, in one episode he named the hierarchy of plants, placing rice above peach, to the bewilderment of the duke and court officials.

What pushed Confucius to hierarchical extremism was the nature of a pyramid society. As the first theorist to develop an intellectual conception of such a society, he was naturally limited by that historical context. In a Greek city state the bond between free men was the common interest in protecting themselves from foreign invasion. They each had private property and were masters of their own domain. If conquered by another state they would turn into slaves. They were stakeholders. Loyalty to the state was in essence loyalty to one's own interest; it was a choice and a logical one. Social order would have to be based on justice, which implied equality between stakeholders. In Confucius' state the only real stakeholders were members of the royal family, everyone else was their servant. If a state was conquered by another, most inhabitants would not be affected. Peasants would keep working the same well-fields, just for a different master. Loyalty to the state, meaning to the ruling house, was not a logical choice at all. Order in such a society had to be enforced by a hierarchy, with brute force.

At a time when authority was weakened, amidst spreading political adventurism, and brute force alone was no longer adequate, as rulers often feared rebellion, Confucius devised a doctrine that if absorbed by the masses would keep the hierarchical order intact without much use of force. The doctrine first instills fear for disorder. Then it claims that order can only be maintained if everyone accepts a strict social hierarchy and behaves according to his station in it. The nature of that hierarchy was defined even harsher than convention or reality warranted, just so that it left no room for negotiations and uncertainty. To mitigate inevitable repulsion to this scheme by some, Confucius did advocate upward social mobility, regardless of family origin, but in a very restricted way: through mastery of his bible, the Book of Rites (*li*).

He could not be blamed for the hierarchical scheme, as that was the only visible way to bring order in his social context, if order was the overriding objective. To overdo in righting a disorder and trying to pull back people's increasingly unfettered minds is understandable, if he felt like all hell broke loose and Armageddon was coming. The extremely harsh definition of hierarchy can also be expected, given the still underdeveloped Chinese language, and his desire for unambiguousness. Nevertheless, he completely missed the indispensable role of power balance in the Zhou system, and his theory equates statecraft with family affairs, which is an over simplification that would encounter enormous problems in later Chinese history.

In his time the theory was not well received. Events on the ground had moved way past the point where a prince could single handedly restore the old culture, not that any of them was even interested in that. What the princes wanted from advisors were theories and policies that if implemented would strengthen their states, such as how to raise revenue and how to build military prowess. Publication of penal code (to enhance credibility of the state), promotion of trade (to raise revenue and economic capacity), land reform (to motivate the younger generation), all of which Confucius strongly objected to because they disrupted the old order even more, were the kinds of practices that led to some success stories, though managing sweeping policy changes was by no means easy for even the most capable minister. Confucius' theory had no answer on economic, military or diplomatic strategy. Moreover, these rules of propriety and hierarchy (*li*) that he held sacred are exhausting. Here are some of them regarding how to receive a guest.

"Whenever a host has received and is entering with a guest, at every door he should give place to him. When the guest arrives at the innermost door leading to the feast-room, the host will ask to be allowed to enter first and arrange the mats (on the floor to sit on). Having done this, he will come out to receive the guest, who will refuse firmly to enter first. The host having made a low bow to him, they will enter together. When they have entered the door, the host moves to the right, and the guest to the left, the former going to the steps on the east, and the latter to those on the west. If the guest be of the lower rank, he goes to the steps of the host (as if to follow him up the steps). The host firmly declines this, and he returns to the other steps on the west. They then offer to each other the precedence in going up, but the host commences first, followed by the other. They bring their feet together on every step, thus ascending by successive paces. He who ascends by the steps on the east should move his right foot first, and the other at the west steps his left foot." (Book of Rites, 1:1:2:7)

All these rules apply just for entering the room and sitting down, there are a lot more to come before, during and after dinner. No wonder there were few volunteers. To diligently observe *li* requires a great deal of self-sacrifice, of suppressing the born human instinct for freedom. It takes a strong conviction to overcome inconveniences and sometimes accept humiliations, for the perceived good of a hierarchical social order. It is exactly because it is tiresome and humiliating that makes the conviction to follow through all the more precious and admirable. It is perhaps not humanly possible to observe the entire mountain of rules that is *li*, but one has to at least observe filial loyalty to parents and obedience to elder brother, to be called a good man.

"Those who have filial loyalty to their parents and obedience to their elder brothers, seldom show a disposition to resist the authority of their superiors. Such men have never engaged in violent uprisings. A ruler starts with fundamentals. When fundamentals are firmly in place, the Dao (Way) grows. Filial loyalty and obedience to elder brother are the fundamentals of *ren*." (Analects, 1:2)

The above short paragraph contains the gist of Confucian ethics. The cause of social disorder, in Confucian understanding, is subordinates rebelling against superiors, violating hierarchy. Thus the objective of Confucian indoctrination is to make everyone obedient and willingly so. Those who have filial loyalty and obedience in their character are not prone to rebellion. They and only they are good people.

Ren (仁) is a core Confucian principle. It can be loosely translated to goodness. What constitutes goodness to Confucius is first and foremost a disposition, a demeanor, a temperament, a psychological profile. A good man is obedient, willingly servile, and selflessly devout to parents. He is stubborn and obstinate in following rules of propriety and hierarchy (*li*), diffident, cautious and concerned in serving his superiors, taciturn and reticent in front of peers, diligent, serious, meticulous, and punctilious in discharging his duties, all of which are practically a portrait of Confucius himself. On the other hand, confidence, eloquence, pride, defiance, free spirit, and independence, are all marks of a bad person. For a ruler there is a different standard disposition: goodness means moderation (This is for his own sake, since excessive exploitation and oppression could lead to his own downfall). So there are two prototypes of goodness, one for the ruler, another for the rest.

The prototype disposition can and is often achieved passively, through family training as one grows up under abusive parents, a psychological process we shall discuss later. For a grown up who has not been well trained by his parents, goodness (*ren*) means to have a strong conviction and force himself into that disposition, or in Confucius' words, "steadfastly following *li* by suppressing all human tendencies (to the contrary)" (克己复礼). Thus Confucius' *ren* is not a moral concept. Most people who were by Confucian definition *good* were merely acting out of fear and/or forced habits. Chinese at this stage were still amoral, as they did not have the necessary condition to develop a moral sensibility: choice. Confucius did not want to give people (slaves) choices, and then tell them what a moral choice would be. Instead he wanted to control people's actions and emotions. To him an orderly society is a fully controlled society.

Emotions are controlled through their expressions. A good example of this can be found in rules regarding mourning practices. The three-year-mourning was an ancient tradition practiced by descendents of Shang at the time, but it was not a Zhou tradition and not adopted by the Zhou ruling class. The custom is very demanding, as it dictates that during the three years immediately after the death (say of a father), the chief mourner (his son) has to abandon all his activities and live in a tent at the grave to concentrate on mourning. He can not take office or any other job, visit friends or attend parties. He can not drink, eat any meat, have sex, or even laugh. For three years he not only has to perform duties of mourning, which is mainly howling at the grave and uttering eulogies of the deceased, but also has to appear grieved. Confucius' reasoning of the duration of that period is simple enough: for the first three years of your life you could not walk and completely depended on your parents, and so the least you can do is to give three years of your time back to them (Analects, 17).

"When the mother of BoYu (Confucius' son) died, he kept on wailing for her after the year. Confucius heard him, and said, 'Who is it that is thus wailing?' The disciples said, 'It is BoYu.' The Master said, 'Ah! Such a demonstration is excessive.' When BoYu heard it, he forthwith gave up wailing." (While his father is still alive, a son should not wail for his mother beyond the year) (Book of Rites, 2:1:1:28)

"There was a man who wept like a child on the death of his mother. Confucius said, 'This is grief indeed, but it would be difficult to continue it. Now the rules of *li* require it to be continued and carried on. Hence the wailing and leaping are subject to fixed regulations." (Book of Rites, 2:1:2:37)

Wailing has to be regulated. It has to be kept on for three years for the father, and one year for the mother (if the father is still alive, otherwise three years). It has to be performed in different places according to one's relationship with the deceased: depending on the near/far and high/low of that relationship. The volume of wailing has to be just right; too loud, people know you can't keep it up for the time required; too low, you don't look truly in grief; too long you break the rules; too short you botch the job. Regulated to such an extent wailing ceases to be a natural expression of sorrow, it becomes a performance, and only an expert can do it with perfection.

What this tells us is that the value of making a free choice did not register with Confucius. He wanted people to weep when they were supposed to, and stop in a fixed time. He wanted conformity not just in actions, but in feelings. If one was not in the mood to cry when he was supposed to, he should cry anyway, and try to force himself into that mood. This was the same attitude he had for gods. He did not believe in the gods. But since worship was an ancient tradition, therefore part of the rules, he earnestly carried out the rituals, and acted as if the gods were present. End result is the only concern; there is nothing wrong in forcing others and oneself to conform.

Confucius accepted Lao's opinion on human development from primeval times, namely a decline or corruption of human nature, and worked it into his own historical view, which basically breaks history into two parts: the ancient stage (before Xia—the first dynasty), and the dynastic stage. It was thought that in ancient times people were happy and peaceful because they had no selfish concerns. They helped all elders like they helped their own; they loved all children like they loved their own. Officials and even rulers were chosen according to their virtue and ability. No one accumulated any wealth, they all shared everything; no one saved energy for his own enterprise, they all worked for the community. Every man had a job, every woman had a home, every senior had security and every child was taken care of. No one was rich, no one was poor, every one was equal, and this was called the world of Grand Equality (大同), a utopian vision of the distant past. With the advent of Xia Dynasty the kingdom was kept under control of one family as a private property, people started to place selfish interest of their own families above the collective. Princes kept their states to their own descendents the same way kings did with the empire, and no one gave power to the virtuous and capable. Everyone cared only about his own family members, and worked only to enrich himself. Thus *li* was introduced as a necessity to keep the society from disintegrating, for unchecked selfishness could only lead to chaos and total destruction. But even that did not stop people from fighting each other driven by their private ambitions, hence we need virtuous rulers to take control and cultivate all with the values of *ren* (goodness). The new dynastic world was called Small Wellbeing (小康). This is the Confucian high level view of history.

In this view ancient people did not need any rules because they lived by the Dao, or the Way, which meant a state of ignorance and desirelessness, like animals, closer to nature. Every one voluntarily worked for the community and the community provided security and insurance for them, so that no one had to worry about anything, and there was little incentive to steal, to rob, or to cheat. It may sound like communism in some respects, and to early Chinese thinkers it was not a system imposed by authority but rather a natural state of early humans who were pure and simple, like Adam and Eve before eating an apple from the knowledge tree. Since then Dao was lost to self interest. Lao proposed going back to the Grand Equality by abolishing all human desires saving the two most basic—to survive and to reproduce, but Confucius did not see it as possible and judged that people had irreversibly lost their innocence. So to deal with the situation at hand the best one could, in a world of Small Wellbeing, he advocated a system governed by rules of *li*, where everyone was trained or indoctrinated to be a good man, with a disposition of filial loyalty and obedience to elders.

However, recorded history up until then did not always support Confucius' argument. Peace and order did not always follow implementation of *li*; a usurper was sometimes a competent and successful ruler, earning universal praise. Confucius thought that was wrong. To return to the old order people had to set their minds straight. They needed to be indoctrinated the sense of right and wrong (proper and improper). If history stood in the way, then history had to be changed. Prior to his time history was faithfully recorded by court appointed professionals of each state. Because there was no sense of right or wrong, rulers had no reason to manipulate the records one way or another. In order to convince future rulers of his plan, he altered historical records to show that in the past those rulers who followed *li* enjoyed peace, order and prosperity, and those who did not ended up in failure. He invented a new verb, Shi2 (弑), meaning to kill (a ruler). There had always been the verb, Sha (杀), which means to kill. But Sha could be used in the slaying of anyone, while Shi2 could only be used in the killing of one's parent or ruler. The new verb was intended to build the idea that killing one's owner was always wrong into the language. Thus a successful usurper who in the past was admired as a hero would in the future be condemned as a criminal.

Confucius' thought is not in the Western sense a philosophy. It can not stand up to vigorous logic and reason. It was not meant to convince free thinking citizens like those in Athens, but devised as a tool for the ruler—owner of a state—to bring about a desired order. The underlying assumption was that a ruler could do anything to control his subjects/slaves. That assumption was not even conscious. It was just a simple fact, part of the social background, like a river that had always been there. His views are undoubtedly draconian to modern readers, but quite benign to his contemporaries. However, he did try to push the culture in the direction of an increasing degree of servility. That was also expected given the nature of a pyramid society. The only way to climb social hierarchy was to gain favor of the ruler; any theory that appealed to a ruler would have to help him prevent possible defiance of the masses. In that light Confucius was part of the counter-evolution process. Had he not done it, someone else would have advanced a similar theory sooner or later.

Chapter 3

MORAL AWAKENING: MENTIUS' REVISION

In the two centuries after Confucius, reality on the ground changed dramatically. China stepped into the iron-age, though weaponry was still largely made of bronze. Cows began to plow the fields with iron farm tools, greatly enhancing productivity. Population grew rapidly, as well as living standards and life expectancy. On the political front, the last Zhou king died in 481 BC, marking the end of a dynasty and the beginning of what is called the Warring States Period (481 BC-221 BC). The year 481 BC was not significant in terms of power balance. In that sense Zhou court had been irrelevant for a long time by then. But it was significant symbolically as it officially gave the states total independence, and their rulers started to call themselves kings. Annexation of weaker states by stronger ones intensified. As most small states were gobbled up, superpowers began to turn on one another for hegemony. Armies grew in size with population; training and tactics of warfare gained sophistication. The famous SunZi's Art of War represented but one of many military schools of thought available. Up until Confucius' time wars were short, usually completed in a few hours with minimum casualty; time of war was usually picked by both sides to avoid interfering with agricultural work; rituals were often observed on battlefield, such as to wait till the other side was ready in its formation before charging, not to kill the enemy ruler, not to kill elderly or wounded enemy soldier, etc. Wars between states were once a show of courage and strength—those were the good old days when one could afford to lose, the defeated party usually conceded some land and slaves and that was it. Gradually the situation became such that for all but the few largest states losing a war often meant total annihilation, and even sizable states with tens of thousands of troops could perish in a single battle. Wars became longer (some lasted years), more fiercely contested (many with orders to fight to the last man), and much larger in scale. Old rituals were thrown away. All kinds of tricks, maneuvers, deceptions, psychological operations became fair game. No state was immune to attacks either, as each of the five (and later seven) superpowers suffered devastating defeats at some point from which it took decades to recover.

In rural areas the well-field system was replaced by a new tax system where a percentage was collected from each acre for higher efficiency and lower risk. The state cared less about who was plowing which field as long as taxes were paid. Land became tradable and ministers, officials, rich merchants bought vast amount of it. Commerce prospered as traveling and even relocating between states became easier. Huge interstate free markets were formed where commodities from four corners of the empire were traded. Different state had different copper currencies though gold was also widely used. Commercial activities provided a way out for many peasants. Instead of working on land that did not really belong to them, which entailed not only fees but other services whenever required, they could work for their rich merchant boss (often a high minister) and avoid military service. The wealthiest merchants gained a great deal of independence from their kings, as their trade networks crossed state boundaries. The culture of commerce and profit seeking was in vogue.

Due to this land reform and commercial vibrancy many members of the ruling class had gathered so much wealth that they no longer depended on their kings. A few of them were rich enough to finance wars. They had vast amounts of land, large numbers of slaves from which they could draw a sizable private army, and sometimes close ties with foreign rulers, making it difficult for their kings to fully control them. They would recruit leading thinkers of the time for their own private think tanks, to argue for their interest and interpret rules and traditions in their favor. They became semi-independent even though in name each state still belonged to its ruler as his state-family. Among this group there was a growing antagonism to the old hierarchy, and Confucian values which exuded servility certainly did not sell well.

Meanwhile the primary concern for kings was no longer domestic order. The remaining states were large, with sizable forces, which made it hard to dethrone the ruler. The challenge now was how to build military prowess. In this brutally competitive world, standing still meant slow suicide. Military power in turn was not just about training a professional army. In any major war the bulk of the forces were not professional, but directly recruited from peasantry. The strength of a state was thus a comprehensive indication of its social cohesion, population size and economic output. Because they had sweeping powers over their subjects, kings could implement practically any policy. No idea was too bizarre to try as long as a king was convinced it had a chance to succeed. This was an unprecedented experimental ground for any and all social theories. Capable thinkers/ministers were eagerly sought. To meet the market for such talent numerous strategists and schools of thought emerged. These thinkers came from all possible backgrounds. Some were sponsored by rich merchants. Some were recruited into academies set up by kings. Some were fully independent financially. They traveled freely between states trying to sell their ideas for high office. A king may like your idea and put you in charge of his state for a few years, if things do not turn out well he'll simply replace you with other self-claimed experts and try different ideas. You are then free to sell yourself elsewhere. In Confucius' days these positions were largely hereditary and openings were rare. By fourth century BC hereditary families were mostly pushed aside to give room for active management. Ministership was no longer a nobility title. It was merely a job with a high turnover rate.

This situation gave birth to a new class. It was still called *shi* class, but no longer the largely hereditary class of nobles of Confucius' time, who were mostly members of royalty. It included all current and former high ministers, as well as scholars, some of whom had retired from government service, some were in between jobs, some were new upstarts looking for the first political opportunity, some were content to remain scholars for life. I would translate it to the scholar-official class. A new social theory would be proposed by a member of this class once in a while, and its merits would be debated by others, regardless of which states they lived in. They formed an informal international community. Fierce competition between states for talent gave the scholar-official a lot of bargain power and they gradually assumed a sense of self-worth that was unprecedented in Chinese history. For the first time anyone with a humble birth could say 'I want to change the world' and actually accomplish it. The talk of the world was not which king was a great ruler but which minister was so capable that he turned a state into a superpower in just a few years. To be a great *shi* was the inspiration for all.

From time immemorial the bottom bulk of a pyramid society—peasants, laborers and low ranking officers—had always been slaves. Position of those close to the top—high ranking officers—was conceptually and practically uncertain. Confucius argued that these be slaves to the ruler as well, following the father-son prototype. Events on the ground, however, moved in the opposite direction. Since his time, the official class had expanded to include scholars, and many gained financial independence. A renowned scholar could be super rich just by teaching. There was no shortage of wealthy merchants who wanted to be prime ministers some day, and they wouldn't mind paying a hefty tuition to get there. Because they no longer depended on kings for a living, some scholars started to think beyond the issues that concerned the kings the most. They were able to take a higher up view at the society as a whole, and examine everyone's place in it, including that of the king. All conventions became questionable and were indeed questioned. They were the first thinkers in Chinese history to have a real choice on how to live their lives and how to see the world, and with that choice came a moral awakening.

Among a plethora of ideas the Confucian school was the earliest and best established academically. They had eight different denominations, thousands of followers and a complete set of written works. But Confucianism was devised for order and stability through total control of domestic masses, not for rapid growth to meet external challenges. The spirit of *li* was to discourage competition and disable individual creativity sorely needed at a time of fierce competition. Many of its rules became impractical because the slow paced largely pressure free culture of Confucius' time was gone. For example, at a time when a state needed all its manpower to feed and defend itself, spending three years crying at the grave of one's parents as a national tradition for all grown men seemed excessive. Indeed the great thinker Mo (墨子) sharply criticized Confucian mourning practices as wasteful. He observed the best timbers were used for coffins and the best clothes were put on corpses when survivors were in rags, not to mention time and energy spent in these filial loyalty shows. As mourning rituals—the most important according to Confucius—came into question Confucian values behind them also looked suspicious to Mo. The idea that one must love one's parents more than anyone else regardless of circumstances—that is why you should spend your last penny on their funeral services—and particularly not love any non-kin, contradicted the experience of many peasant soldiers who through prolonged wars grew strong emotional ties with their comrades in the ditches. Mo was one of these soldiers. With empathy to the lowest of the low in social standings he argued for universal love as opposed to the Confucian hierarchical love.

To Mo the problems of the world are rooted in lack of love. Sons do not help their fathers in their old age because they do not really love them; fathers do not treat sons with care because they only use them and do not really love them; thieves steal because they do not love their victims; states fight because people do not love foreigners. If there were love between people all-under-heaven, the world would have been paradise. It is clear that to Mo love is voluntary. To Confucius parents' love for their children is unquestionable by virtue of their ownership. They may use and abuse their children but that does not put their love into question, just like one would whip his sheep or even kill it for food but that does not diminish one's love for his sheep (you love it simply because it is your possession); for the same reason one can not love someone else's children because they do not belong to him. On the other hand children's love for their parents means filial loyalty, the forced love of a slave to his master. From Confucius to Mo, the concept of love evolved from ownership and forced servility to a voluntary human emotion.

Mo was also concerned about equality and plight of the peasantry. He realized that wars were waged in a ruler's private interest, with no regard given to how many people would die for him. He was against aggression. He devised military equipment (he was a genius engineer as well) and strategy to help a weak state's defense, but never offense. He proposed an equivalent of the United Nations' non-aggression clause, though superpowers did not sign on to it. His arguments were quite sensible and down to earth, which stated that centuries of warfare had shown that no state was invincible and it would be wise for the superpowers to agree to a peace treaty. The problem though was that such treaties were made between states many times before and always broken, therefore no state had any credibility left. Having failed at that, he and his followers, who were all fearless fighters ready to die at any moment for their conviction, tried to use their own firepower to discourage wars, with limited success.

Mo asserted that self interest should serve collective interest which was the only way it could be guaranteed in the end. When Confucius talked about self-interest, he was thinking about officials and rulers who tried to amass wealth and power by any and all means. Therefore he advocated moderation. Self-interest to him was not improper in and of itself if it did not interfere with one's service to parents and ruler, and there was no such thing as collective interest—a state was private property of its ruler. Without directly challenging that idea Mo suggested that everyone had a stake in defending his state, and therefore everyone should unite not just in actions but also in thought, and self-interest would damage that bond.

Another influential thinker, Yang Zhu (杨朱), had the revolutionary idea that self-interest was the highest virtue. Confucian moderation was widely known by then, as well as Mo's selfless solidarity, but in the end what was apparent in the real world was that everyone was ultimately concerned with their own interest far above anything else, regardless of what they professed, so why not be truthful and recognize people's natural instincts? "Public" interest was actually private interest of a king, so why couldn't the average person put his own interest first? Yang challenged a deep rooted Chinese value born out of long lasting slavish conditions simply by being brutally honest. His school acquired a large following and along with the Mo school became two of the most dominant intellectual forces, gaining ground on Confucianism which was seen as the authoritative representation of Zhou culture. Yang claimed that wars occurred because people were unwisely willing to fight for their kings, if everyone put their self-interest front and center, no one would be stupid enough to die for their states which weren't theirs to begin with.

Yang touched on an important point which had so far eluded Chinese: rulers owned everything and all their subjects were by definition their slaves. It had been that way so long it became subconscious. A state started in eleventh century BC as a state-family of its founder. If for the first few centuries that was simply accepted as a fact, by fourth century BC most of the rulers were either usurpers or descendents of them and not offspring of the original Zhou princes, and their claim to ownership of the state and its population became theoretically tenuous. Though few people were brave enough to directly challenge that notion for fear of repercussions, it dawned on a significant number that this ownership was not necessarily the right order of things, even if it had been an ancient tradition. When even a king's ownership of his state was questioned, Confucius' carefully designed family style hierarchy anchored by the king looked absurd.

Another great thinker, Zhuang (庄子), successor of the Daoist school after Lao, attacked Confucius' cherished rules of propriety and hierarchy, *li*. He argued that the natural state of human beings was the same as that of animals: free of rules. Being a nature lover he was totally disgusted by all the rules human beings made for themselves in the name of social order, particularly Confucian rules that were so suffocating. He observed that large birds could fly miles without stopping while small ones could barely jump from one tree to the next. They do not all follow the same rules so why should humans? Diversity is the natural state of affairs in the world and so it would be against Dao to force conformity. In addition, people are born with a given nature, which is a manifestation of Dao, and it is wrong to make them follow rules against their nature. For example, *li* says that when one entertains his friends the dinner party should follow standard rules on where to sit, what to serve, in what order, etc. Zhuang says I just want to have a good time, why should I care if I am using the correct utensils or following the prescribed procedure? *Li* says that one must cry for the entire mourning period of his deceased relative. Zhuang says I do not want to force myself to cry if I do not feel like crying, it would be disingenuous.

"True grief is not crying, true anger is not shouting, true love is not smiling. What is true inside one's heart is what makes it precious." "Treat your family the way you feel about them, do not use excuses (*li*) for your actions; drink and feast for happiness, do not mind the utensils (*li*); mourn if you are sorrow, forget about the rules (*li*)." (The Book of Zhuang, Miscellaneous 31)

In the face of this borage of well reasoned rebuttals Confucianism was in serious trouble, when a great thinker came to its rescue. Born around 372 BC, Mencius was a descendent of one of the Three Families of Lu State, which were by then out of power. Like Confucius he grew up with his mother alone (his father's circumstances unknown). He studied Confucianism all his life following the school of Confucius' grandson who specialized in filial loyalty, and took office only for a short period of time, around the age of fifty. He left a detailed written account of his arguments. His views however showed a major departure from that of Confucius in many ways, despite his orthodox Confucian training. He clearly realized that these ancient rules of propriety and hierarchy (*li*) were obsolete, therefore could no longer serve as the rigid backbone of Confucianism. Chinese intellect by fourth century BC had also developed past the point where a set of concrete rules of conduct could define a worldview. Confucius' idea of goodness of man was directly derived from social hierarchy; it meant servility for subjects and moderation for rulers. By Mencius' time any definition of goodness must apply to all men, kings and slaves alike. Confucius' goodness was not a moral concept; it was an ethical standard, something to be trained or forced on people. By Mencius' time two talented people could choose to live their lives in different ways, unencumbered by any rules, and both be successful. Goodness was for the first time the result of a choice, a moral choice.

What marks the beginning of human moral awakening is the sense that a human life is precious. This usually happens at a historical stage when food production is secure, starvation is no longer a constant threat, and social conditions have stabilized so that random death is uncommon. People then slowly develop an aversion to mortal threat. For an ancient Greek farmer, who is self sufficient on his own property, the main threat to his livelihood is aggression from others in the community, such as a stronger neighbor.

In pre-moral times the strong would kill the weak in a dispute, and that was taken for granted. As members of a tribe gradually assume a spirit of cooperation and camaraderie through wars against other tribes, a natural feeling follows that any member of the tribe, regardless of how strong he is, can not survive without the help of others. They understand that they depend on each other. Then for a strong man to kill his neighbor in peace time for material gain would offend the community, because consequently they are one member weaker than before, not to mention that member has helped win battles in the past. As security and prosperity last (no threat of starvation, no need to kill), taking the life of a fellow for material gain becomes unacceptable. From here the idea of justice is born. It is based on fundamental equality between members of a community.

In a pyramid culture everyone is owned by the ruler. The ruler imposes laws on his subjects. He forbids his slaves to kill each another in random brawls, which would be a loss to him no matter who wins. Thus the masses face no threat from physically stronger members of their community, but they fear their ruler, who by fact and by law can arbitrarily take their lives. Lasting security and prosperity have extended life expectancy and made random death uncommon. The masses are then naturally repulsed by the ruler's decision to send them to reckless wars or hard-to-survive duties. They hope, and increasingly expect, that their obedience deserves mercy from their ruler. This, in a nutshell, explains why the first moral principle of a pyramid culture is mercy, while the first moral principle for ancient Greeks is justice.

Mencius redefined goodness (*ren*) as mercy, commiseration and benevolence. This new idea reflected moral sensibility of the time, and quickly gained wide acceptance. In comparison the old Confucian *ren* was too ambiguous an idea for people to grasp, because Confucius wanted to incorporate in it all the character traits and dispositions of a model man like himself. Mercy (*ren*) became the cornerstone of Mencius' worldview, replacing rules of propriety and hierarchy (*li*). He gave the word *li* a new meaning, an abstract idea that describes a character that is always non-competitive, yielding and accommodating to others. He thought that was the spirit of some rules in the Book of Rites, while other rules that contradict this spirit were now deemed wrong (非礼之礼). Just like the new moral principle of mercy, the new idea of *li* is about individual character and applies indiscriminately to everyone. It is no longer a code of conduct in various situations, but a temperament and a conviction not to fight over desirables, and to always put others first.

To build a new worldview based on *ren* (mercy), Mencius first claimed that *ren* is a born human instinct, that everyone is born a moral being. He illustrated the point by observing that strangers who see a child about to fall into a well would rush to the rescue, not to gain any favor from the child's parents or seek praise of neighbors, but because they "can not bear to see the suffering of others", which is the nature of *ren*. That begs an explanation for all the evils of the world, which Mencius attributed to lack of learning and self-cultivation. In other words the benign human nature is vulnerable to temptations, bad examples and idleness. A man succumbs to corruptions of the world during the day, but in the calm of night his benevolent nature reclaims lost moral ground. Because nature is on the side of good, it is not too much to ask *ren* from everyone.

Thus a ruler can no longer be free of responsibilities. *Ren* requires him to commiserate with his subjects, to feel their pain, and to share their joy. A commiserating ruler has no problem ruling a kingdom, because in his heart and mind he has united with his people. Statecraft is not about policies, rules, or cynical manipulation of the masses; it is about conscience. The ancient idea of Heaven's Mandate, invented by Zhou founders to legitimize their overthrow of the previous Shang Dynasty, was applied by Mencius to the newly independent states. A king who rules harshly and causes suffering to his subjects loses Heaven's Mandate to rule. "If the king has great faults, the ministers ought to remonstrate with him, and if he does not listen to them after they have done so again and again, they ought to dethrone him." (Mencius, 5:2:9) A king who conquers the hearts and minds of all-under-heaven will unify the world, without waging war, because people from other states will all flock to his kingdom. One king asked: I treat my people better than other kings, why aren't their people coming here? Mencius replied: you are a robber just like other kings; the difference is only in degree. To commiserate means you really feel what your people feel, only then will you put their interest before yours.

In his view a king still owns his state and people (excluding the scholar-official class), but that ownership is conditional. A scholar-official, on the other hand, is an independent who can work for the king as a shepherd, to herd his masses like sheep. Thus the right relation between ruler and minister should be that of the modern employer-employee, not Confucius' father-son relation. "When the ruler regards his ministers as his hands and feet, they regard him as their belly and heart; when he regards them as his dogs and horses, they regard him as a stranger; when he regards them as dirt and grass, they regard him as a robber and an enemy." (Mencius,

4:2:3) Obviously new found financial independence of the scholar-official class fostered a sense of pride. They were shedding the last pretences of servility and poised to bargain hard with kings, while the kings for necessity prized strategic acumen above submission. In this new culture the slavish demeanor of Confucius would incur shame, and the Confucian value of servile loyalty (to the ruler) would look ridiculous. A scholar-official was no longer a mere servant of the ruler: he was an independent critic, a champion of the masses. He might choose to serve a sovereign but he had his dignity. Certain lines could not be crossed or else he would quit in protest or even take revenge against the sovereign. The ideal scholar-official (*shi*) was a proud and moral man who sought no profit but demanded respect. Mencius declared the virtue of a *shi*: "Riches and honors can not tempt him; poverty and mean conditions can not swerve him; power and force can not bend him." (富贵不能淫, 贫贱不能移, 威武不能屈, Mencius, 3:2:2) This was the high watermark of individual dignity in Chinese history, not to be matched ever since.

Confucius' hierarchical system was completely abandoned by Mencius. Ruler-minister relation was no longer modeled after the father-son prototype. However, filial loyalty was adopted intact. We may recall that Confucius' reasoning for filial loyalty was to bring up obedient sons not given to rebellion. Now that Mencius practically advocated rebellion under certain conditions, a new line of reasoning was offered, again based on mercy and commiseration. If adult children do not take care of their aging parents, the latter will likely live in misery. A merciful heart can not let this happen, thus serving one's parents in their old age is a necessity.

But having mercy on one's aging parents is not the same as being obedient and slavishly loyal to them. Here Mencius became incoherent, as he wanted to secure both a voluntary emotional tie between parents and children, based on mercy and benevolence, as well as filial loyalty, which could only be forcefully trained. Realizing this problem, he advocated a bizarre solution.

"One of Mencius' disciples said, 'Why is it that the superior man does not himself teach his son?'

Mencius replied, 'The circumstances of the case forbid its being done. The teacher must inculcate what is correct. When he inculcates what is correct, and his lessons are not practiced, he becomes angry. When he becomes angry, then, contrary to what should be, he is offended with his son. At the same time, the son will think, "My master inculcates on me what is correct, and he himself does not proceed in a correct path." The result of this is that father and son are offended with each other and their relationship turns sour.'

The ancients exchanged sons, and one taught the son of another.

Between father and son, there should be no reproving admonitions to what is good. Such reproofs lead to alienation, and than alienation there is nothing more inauspicious." (Mencius, 4:1:18)

There is no evidence that Confucius exchanged his son with someone else for teaching him proper manners. He or his disciples would have mentioned it given the importance of filial loyalty to Confucianism. Moreover the rationale for that practice did not exist for Confucius. Mencius apparently understood that human emotion can not be forced. Yet he wanted sons to serve his parents, voluntarily. That is the dilemma. He did not want sons to have the choice not to serve their parents, and he wanted the service to be voluntary. So he tried to ensure the first requirement through family training, since he knew properly trained sons have the disposition to be obedient. That training itself is abusive (or else it would not succeed), consequently the trainee hates the trainer. To preserve an emotional tie between father and son, satisfying the second requirement, the trainer is preferably not the father. Better hate someone else than one's own father, thus the exchange.

One might wonder why Mencius, who espoused commiseration, had so little concern for children's feelings. Shouldn't parents commiserate with their own children? Why keep doing things to them that make them hate you? This had a lot to do with the necessity to bring up obedient sons, since the masses were slaves. A defiant slave was not likely to survive for long. It also had to do with the livelihood of seniors. There was no social security back then.

In the West this problem was not quite as acute, again, due to the presence of a class of free men and consequently legally protected private property. In early Greece each free man owned a piece of land which he could explore whichever way he wanted, and engage in various trades. By the time his children grew up, if they did not move away from home in pursuit of their own career, it would be in their interest to take care of the old and inherit his property. Moreover, if all the sons stayed home there was tension between them to divide the limited inheritance. It would be much more preferable to the father himself if some of his sons went out and established themselves in the society, who would then be more capable of helping the aging parents financially. Out there in the society a man had to compete, and a servile disposition trained from childhood could not possibly help him. In the pyramid society of China no peasant owned the land he plowed; it was assigned to him by the ruler and for the ruler. An old man no longer able to work would be replaced by a younger man, and left with nothing. Because there was no such thing as private property protected by law (the ruler owned everything), the only retirement plan most people could possibly have was the loyalty of their children. On the other hand, adult children did not depend on their parents for a living at all nor could they inherit anything from their slave parents. As soon as one came of age and was physically able, the ruler would make him clear some virgin land and start plowing—the deaf, the mute, the retard, as long as one was able to work the fields he would get his share of land from the ruler, not from his parents. Thus senior slaves were always in a precarious position. They had no property, and they were useless to the ruler, who wouldn't mind if they all dropped dead the day they stopped working.

Mercy drove some adult sons to take care of their parents. But for many, parents were just not lovable figures that they liked to help. In the process of bringing up obedient sons, parents inevitably abused them. That emotional tear was too much especially for teenagers to overlook. Given a chance they would rather leave home for good. In all pyramid societies there was this dilemma between a merciful heart that could not bear to see suffering of the entire senior generation, and their battered sons who wanted to get away from them. This would offer a plausible explanation as to why Mencius kept filial loyalty, which he knew had to be forced on children, in his otherwise benevolent worldview.

Although on paper Mencius never directly challenged anything Confucius said, his dramatic reinterpretations of all the important ideas had given Confucianism a totally new appeal. The ownership type hierarchy is undermined: rulers no longer own the scholar-official class, and their ownership of the peasantry becomes conditional. Criticism of a king is no longer offered only as an advice; it can be a moral condemnation and a stern warning. The ultimate goal is no longer a hierarchical society with absolute order, but a moral society where everyone is concerned about the plight of the downtrodden, has sympathy for the weak and poor, a society permeated with tender hearts that can not bear the sufferings of others.

In this system the role of the scholar-official class undergoes a subtle but profound change. They still occupy a high place in the pyramid, between the ruler and his helpless subjects. They are still advisors to the ruler on various state affairs. But they are no longer necessarily defenders of the existing social order, or protectors of the ruler's interest. Instead they assume two primary roles, both of which are new. One is to define morality for the Chinese civilization, to cultivate the population with moral values, and to make judgments on right or wrong. This can be loosely called moralism. The other is to address grievances of the masses, to bring care to the illiterate, obedient and silent majority—the slaves. This I shall translate to peopleism (民本主义).

The two are of course closely related. As we have shown, the first moral principle of the Chinese civilization was mercy/commiseration, and that was a direct reaction to the predicament of the slaves. What is moral has to be beneficial to the masses. One can no longer claim, as Confucius' did, that a particular social hierarchy is good just because it brings peace and order. Excessive exploitation of the masses is immoral, even if it is done in peace and order. Playing the role of advocates of people's interest gives the scholar-official class a moral mandate, a sense of righteousness, as well as courage to defy cruel rulers. At the same time, "people" are slaves. They do not have an independent will. They are used to being controlled and if control is loosened, they might indulge in erratic ways. They must be taught, cultivated, trained, to understand good from bad, to behave in a civilized manner. A scholar-official is a shepherd, and the masses are sheep. Peopleism is not Western populism. It does not give in to popular sentiments if these are deemed immoral. It does not treat the masses as equals or respect their opinion. But it does advocate mercy on their behalf.

Moralism here goes far beyond moralizing in the modern Western sense. Perhaps the role of the Medieval Church comes close. Although making judgments is part of the equation, the main focus is on cultivation. That is somewhat different from education/indoctrination. In Mencius' view a man is born a moral being. Nature is on his side in his battle against corruptive influences of the world. Thus every man is obligated to maintain his moral fiber, by self-cultivation, which can be done through practices like meditation, quietly observing the world, studying the nature of things, self-monitoring and self-discipline.

This was the transition period in Chinese history from a pre-moral "shame" culture to a moral "guilt" culture. There had always been social customs and a widely accepted sense of appropriateness, the violation of which in front of others would incur shame. People did care about how they were perceived by the community, for their livelihood depended on it. But they did not have an internal reasoning that told them a certain action was wrong in and of itself. With a new found concern for life that led to a moral awakening, leading thinkers like Mencius realized that a moral person was one who had mercy in his heart, who would never take a life even if he could get away with it, and not necessarily the one who obeyed all rules and behaved properly in public. A moral man was careful about his actions when no one was watching (慎独).

With these two new roles, as practitioners of moralism and peopleism, the scholar-official class had found a permanent and indispensable place in the pyramid structure. Their obligation is first to Chinese civilization and second to the masses. Even their advisory role to the ruler must help those two purposes. If a ruler rejects sound advice and behaves in an immoral manner, the upright scholar-official is obligated by conscience to quit.

Now we have two distinct doctrines under the same banner of Confucianism (Mencius' school was the only surviving Confucian school by late fourth century BC). One is a stern hierarchical doctrine based on a set of strict rules meant to train a character of total submission, aiming at peace and order, from Confucius. The other is a moral doctrine based on assumed benevolent human nature that only needs a call to conscience in order to stay the moral course, aiming at a merciful and harmonious society, from Mencius. The two are contradictory in spirit. A Confucian good man is defined as a faithful servant, which filial loyalty helps to bring about. A Mencian good man is defined as a benevolent and strong willed independent, in the spirit of "power and force can not bend him". Yet in Chinese understanding they both belong in the same school of thought. The contention between these two doctrines, one insisting on an obsequious character, the other striving for independence, laid the seed for a hypocritical Chinese culture.

Despite their differences, Confucius and Mencius had three important things in common. First, both wanted an ideal society. Second, both saw goodness of the individual as the foundation for an ideal society. Third, neither tolerated other views/doctrines. In Confucius' case demanding perfection was the direct result of his incomprehension of the Zhou system. As discussed earlier, social disorder in Confucius' time was caused by collapse of the long lasting power balance between the king and the princes. Confucius saw it as all due to people not following rules. But some people observing some rules did not bring about peace and order. Therefore he concluded that all people must obey all rules. Only in that ideal society can there be peace and order. In Mencius' case demand for perfection had to do with his moralizing worldview. When mercy/commiseration was the only principle guiding both personal conduct and statecraft, it eliminated the need for any rules. When a king asked why he was not successful when his tax was only half of the other states, Mencius' said he was like a deserter who had run fifty steps mocking another who had run a hundred steps. But what is merciful rule? Mencius said 10% tax was maximum, which was simply impractical, if one wanted to have any national defense at all. For a ruler to be truly merciful in Mencian standard, he can not enjoy a higher living standard than any of his subjects. Only in such an ideal case will the masses feel that their ruler truly commiserates with them.

Thus it is easy to see why every individual must be turned into a good person. If only some people are good others are bad, the ideal society can not happen, and all is lost. Social order is not just about political philosophy; morality is not just about an individual's soul. Everything is part of the whole picture; every piece must fit. When scholar-officials approach the moral/ethical issue, they do not look at it as saving one soul at a time. They do not bother with individual cases. They just want to issue a universal standard and demand everyone comply. It is about peace and order, and civilization for all-under-heaven. An ideal society dictates conformity.

That means dissent is nothing but poison. When scholar-officials debate other views/doctrines, in addition to the sense of self-righteousness that their view is the only truth, they are also apprehensive that the existence of competing views on the moral issue would inevitably lead to confusion and weaken the moral fiber of society. Therefore the most vile language and harshest condemnation are often used on dissidents, whose theses may be just as sensible to an unbiased ear. In response to intellectual challenges from the aforementioned Mo and Yang schools Mencius commented:

"Yang's principle is "each one for himself", which amounts to denial of the sovereign. Mo's principle is "to love all equally", which amounts to denial of one's father. Denying both ruler and father makes one an animal." (Mencius, 3:2:9)

An animal in Confucian parlance is an immoral being, either because it can not be made to follow rules, or because it does not seem to have mercy, particularly a predator. If a Greek saw a tiger devouring a deer alive, he would probably identify with the tiger, admiring its physical prowess, just like he worshiped warrior heroes. For Chinese, a people who had lived at the mercy of their rulers since the beginning of time, it was more natural to see themselves as the deer, living perpetually at the mercy of tigers and without any hope of getting out of that predicament. What they hoped for was an orderly society free of Darwinian survival battles, thus they despised animals for their lack of order and compassion. Both Confucius and Mencius captured that sentiment in their doctrines. As a result the most derogatory terms in Chinese that can be used on a person are ChuSheng (畜生, domestic animals) and QinShou (禽兽, wild beasts). Moreover, Chinese language can not distinguish between "immoral" and "amoral", because to both Confucius and Mencius, both ideas represented bad people. To Confucius it was those who did not follow the rules, in other words those who failed to develop a good habit. For Mencius it was those who had a corrupted nature, in other words those who lost their born moral sense.

Unlike other thinkers of the time who argued in more practical terms, as in examining the pros and cons of each assertion in detail, the Mencian argument above is moral and categorical. Confucius was against all debates, but Mencius was forced to defend Confucianism against attacks from these two schools that by then achieved dominance. Since this is the only record of debate left from the two Confucian saints, its style established the Confucian debate tradition, which is not to focus on merits of the opponent's argument, but on their moral character, and it always ends with sweeping moral condemnation and character assassination. We can get a daily dose of such debates in the Taiwan parliament.

For all the differences between Confucius and Mencius, and between Confucians and many other schools, they were all trying to advance a theory of social values, a way of governance and a certain course of action for the scholar-official class in order to bring about a desired society, they were all pro-action. The Daoist school took exception. Its founder Lao—a contemporary of Confucius—made some insightful observations of both nature and human society, which Chinese thought both function under the principle of Dao, or the invisible Way, and gave his advice on how to best survive, which is to harbor little desire, avoid competition and keep a low profile—go to the low places where no one wants to go, like water.

In keeping with that spirit but also taking advantage of a new found independence, the fourth century BC Daoist thinker, Zhuang, a contemporary of Mencius, pushed Lao's argument in a slightly different direction. Lao saw man-made rules and ethics as a restraint made necessary only by failure to follow Dao. A sage does not care about man-made values like *ren*, or follow man-made rules like *li*. Because he follows Dao, he is naturally benevolent and free of wickedness. Two centuries later it became clear to Zhuang that human morality was not even good for a contingency plan, because people would just fake it. A king may broadcast the one time he opened his granary for flood victims, while covering up the extraction on his subjects on a daily basis. A minister may be a perfect gentleman with nothing but love and care for others, while in private plotting the downfall of his enemies. What *ren* (mercy) had done was nothing but turning everyone into cheaters. The world would have been better off without any moral values at all.

What Zhuang advocated is primitivism as a way of life. A sage lives like ancient peoples before the corruption of knowledge, greed, and sophistication. He does not chase after power, wealth or fame, he sees beyond all secular desires, he stays away from the fray, he lives a life that is pure, simple, free and in harmony with nature. True happiness can only be obtained by returning to nature, drawing inspiration from it, following the example of animals, and living an unrestricted life free of the bonds of social conventions. To live such a life, one ideally would need his own land and be independent, which meant he must be a retired official or merchant, a member of the *shi* class. Failing that, if one had to serve his king for a living, he would be wise to lay low and stay out of all political entanglements. Other officials may engage in debates and try to advance their theories, or work hard to accumulate merits, or form alliances with each other and jostle for positions, the Daoist would be the one with no strong opinions on anything, no real merits to cause jealousy or even attention, and no political affiliations. He simply does not care. All he wants to do is get the pay, go home and enjoy life. By secretly rejecting the official doctrine, whatever it is, the Daoist manages to keep his spiritual independence, and spends his energy on the only thing that is real to him: to live a long and healthy life. The study of Dao, or the Way, is now focused on its manifestation in the human body, its inner workings, health, strength, energy and disease. This shift changed the course of Chinese medicine, which from here on emphasized how to better a healthy person more than curing an ailment.

In sixth century BC the founders of Daoism and Confucianism, Lao and Confucius, were both prudent and fearful in character. Lao was yielding, and Confucius was servile. By fourth century BC their successors, Zhuang and Mencius, were both much more daring in their temperament. Mencius professed the unbendable dignity of the *shi*, abandoning servility. Zhuang transformed the Daoist character, from one who was quiet and withdrawn, who would give in to any opposition and endure any abuse (弱则活，曲则全), to a free spirited dissenter who could not have cared less about moral values coming from state authority, or the state for that matter, and just to flaunt his spiritual rebellion, he would be obsessed with his own health, wellbeing, and living a long and enjoyable physical life (逍遥，养生). In other words he traded cowardice for escapism, though the two are not mutually exclusive.

CHAPTER 4
TOWARDS PRAGMATISM: XUN'S INTERPRETATION

As a moral principle mercy differs from justice in a fundamental way. Justice is symmetrical; it presumes equality. Mercy is asymmetrical; it is expected from masters by slaves. If accepted by a community justice is automatically observed, because violators will be punished by peers. Mercy, on the other hand, is hard to enforce; to a large extent it depends on the master's good will. If slaves can enforce merciful rule they are not slaves. Mencius tried to sell the principle to a king on practical grounds: a merciful ruler will attract peasants from all-under-heaven to his domain, leaving his rivals with no one to rule. That reasoning is flawed. No matter how much concern and care a ruler showers over his subjects, it does not change the fact that they are his slaves, not real stakeholders. If one is not starving, the next thing he wants is security, dictated by human nature. The only way for a slave to get any security is to gain so much wealth and power that the ruler can no longer disposed of him easily. Lenient rule did not bring about loyal slaves willing to fight their king's wars in third century BC China; it resulted in emboldened self seeking, which became a prevalent culture of the time. Power struggles between aspiring scholar-officials intensified, and the successful was usually the bold, cold blooded, and greedy.

Any honest advisor to a king would have to draw the conclusion that merciful rule simply did not work to the ruler's advantage. What actually worked were hard nosed discipline, cold hearted calculation, and cynical manipulation. Mencius thought that human nature is virtuous (i.e. non-confrontational, yielding, sympathetic, and benevolent); if treated nicely slaves will be docile and grateful. Reality was the opposite: give them an inch, they'll take a yard. In the cutthroat competition for power and security a virtuous man was nowhere to be found. The third century BC Confucian scholar Xun (荀子) commented:

"Man's nature is evil; goodness is the result of conscious activity. The nature of man is such that he is born with a fondness for profit. If he indulges this fondness, it will lead him into wrangling and strife, while all sense of courtesy and humility will disappear. He is born with feelings of envy and hate, and if he indulges these, they will lead him into violence and crime, and all sense of loyalty and good faith will disappear. Man is born with the desires of the eyes and ears, with a fondness for beautiful sights and sounds. If he indulges in these, they will lead him into license and wantonness, and all ritual principles and correct forms will be lost. Hence, any man who follows his nature and indulges his emotions will inevitably become involved in wrangling and strife, will violate the forms and rules of society, and will end as a criminal. Therefore, man must first be transformed by the instructions of a teacher and guided by ritual principles, and only then will he be able to observe the dictates of courtesy and humility, obey the forms and rules of society, and achieve order. It is obvious from this, then, that man's nature is evil, and that his goodness is the result of conscious activity." (Xun, Book 23, "Man's Evil Nature")

It was assumed by Chinese thinkers that any indulgence in natural human desires—food, sex, etc.—will inevitably lead to conflict with others, and the only remedy is to force restraint on everyone, implying a despotic authority. This again has to do with the pyramid culture, as compared to the egalitarian Greek culture. When each Greek farmer had his own property, justice meant that one could not encroach on his neighbor. The fence between private properties provided a boundary for human desires. One could enjoy food, sex, and other pleasures so long as he did not run over that fence or hurt other people. The principle of justice laid the foundation for a civilized society where every citizen was free but at the same time knew where the limit was—"your freedom to swing your arms stop at my nose". In a pyramid culture private property never existed in the legal sense, except for the ruler. The evolution process from savagery to civilization was one of increasing control by the ruler over his slaves, forcing everyone to stop their brawls and obediently follow whatever rules handed down to them. Over time laws devised by the ruler for his own purpose formed the foundation of conventions and values, of what was or was not deemed appropriate by the masses. There was order and civilization, but the sense of propriety in the mind of the average person was not based on a moral principle like justice, rather it was based on social customs and psychology developed from a slave culture.

When the old order was on the brink of collapse in third century BC, that sense of propriety was challenged, but it could not find an easy replacement. One minister claimed a fee for his service to the king; another drew a big salary, both from state coffer. With limited funds and unlimited greed, interests of the two would clash. But where was the proper boundary? It was impossible to define because neither of them owned anything in theory. The ruler would be the judge. Ministers would then either fawn over him or fortify their positions and force the ruler's hand, for example by allying themselves with foreign enemies. Without private property, without a natural boundary like a fence between private properties, there was no way to define fairness. In the mean time people did prefer peace and order as they were used to it; they hated to see bloodshed over money, they did not want to start from barbarism all over again, even if they could have imagined an alternative culture. Thus they concluded that human desires inevitably lead to strife (no natural boundary), and therefore have to be restrained by the ruler.

Moreover, since the ruler can not be the arbiter in every single civilian dispute, rules must dictate who wins the argument in any given case. Again here we run into the same problem of not having an objective value like justice, whereby any two equals would make the same judgment in any situation as to what is fair. The easy alternative is, as Confucius proposed before, to have a social hierarchy. In any given situation the older person has authority, if the two are of the same social rank; otherwise the higher ranking individual wins. If people are equals, then because there is no basis to make fair judgments on disputes, there can not be peace. This is why there must a hierarchy between any two persons in the world. Now we have a better articulated reason for *li*.

"What is the origin of *li*? I reply: Man is born with desires. If his desires are not satisfied for him, he cannot but seek some means to satisfy them himself. If there are no limits and degrees to his seeking, then he will inevitably fall to wrangling with other man. From wrangling comes disorder and from disorder comes exhaustion. The ancient kings hated such disorder, and therefore they established ritual principles in order to curb it, to train man's desires and provide for their satisfaction. They saw to it that desires did not overextend the means for their satisfaction, and material goods did not fall short of what was desired. Thus both desires and goods were looked after and satisfied. This is the origin of *li*." (Xun, Book 19, "A Discussion of *Li*")

This line of reasoning still accurately reflects Asian worldview today. It is a three step argument: A. Human beings have desires. B. They will inevitably fight each other to satisfy their desires. C. Therefore rules are needed to curb their desires. There is no distinction here between a desire for something, which is a thought, and an effort to seize it, which is an action. Rules are designed not just to regulate actions, such as prohibiting robbery, but also to "train" human desires. Xun observed that by human nature a man desires to eat when he is hungry, and yet a hungry man will not dare be the first to eat if he is in the presence of his elders, because he knows that he should yield to them. That means his nature is evil, but rules like filial loyalty has trained his nature, so that now he is good—his born nature is contained by his acquired nature. *Li* is meant to inculcate in people an acquired nature, a post-natal psyche. Love, for instance, must be regulated. Universal love—proposed by Mo—is condemned as overly indulging in love. Just like indulgence in food and sex will ruin one's health, unrestrained love will exhaust one's love (seen as in limited quantity). If you love your spouse or friends, it will undermine your love for your parents, resulting in less time and care given to them. Therefore one has to ration one's love, so as to keep its spending in balance with its supply, and spend it only when appropriate.

It is quite rational in a pyramid culture to come to the conclusion that both a strictly defined social hierarchy and a set of rules aiming at curtailing human desires are needed for peace and order. Xun presented a convincing case. For a third century BC thinker, he was nothing short of brilliant. Once the secrets of social dynamics were discovered, however, the idealism of Confucius and Mencius was gone, replaced by a calm calculating pragmatism. To Confucius everyone should be indoctrinated into docile beings, which would lead to peace and order, and filial loyalty was the instrument of that indoctrination. To Mencius peace and order would naturally come if rulers followed their conscience, since everyone was born a moral being. The focus of filial loyalty was love, and he wanted to preserve it while at the same time make children accept hierarchy, hence the practice of sending children away for the training. Xun addressed that inconsistency by declaring the truth: Confucian family hierarchy is against human nature. A son is not naturally obedient to his parents, but without that obedience he can not be controlled. *Li* is absolutely necessary for social stability, hence filial loyalty, the most important rule of *li*. It is human nature that must be condemned. The purpose of learning is not to safeguard man's innate benevolence, which does not exist, but to acquire a goodness, or obedience, that is not in human nature. Mencius' incoherence is rectified with austere clarity. The ruler-minister relation is likewise outlined.

"When the king has excessive plans and actions that will likely damage or ruin the state, and as a senior officer one has the capacity to address the king concerning these matters, then staying when one's advice is implemented and leaving when it is not is called 'remonstrance';

Staying when one's advice is implemented, but continuing to argue one's case before the king, to the point of threatening suicide with real intensions to carry it out if one's advice is not heeded, is called 'fighting;

To assemble the wise and gather all ministers and officials in a chorus of remonstrance, so that even though the king is unwilling he has to listen, the state is then saved from the greatest of calamities, and in the end the king's honor is upheld and his state made secure, is called 'assistance';

In case the king is stubborn in his ill fated pursuit, to temporarily seize power from him and act against his order, to secure the state from danger and deliver the king from disgrace, is called 'opposition'.

Men who remonstrate, fight, assist and oppose in these manners are the state's protector, and the king's treasure.

In the service of a sage king, one should follow orders and carry them through, not remonstrate or fight. In the service of a mediocre king, one should remonstrate and fight, not flatter or toady after his wishes. In the service of a cruel and violent king, one should quietly do damage control (of the mess created by the king's willful acts), not directly confront him. If one happens to be in a chaotic age, forced to live in the state of a cruel king without any means to escape, then one should promote its refinements and extol its goodness, avoid its ugliness and conceal its failures, and habitually speak of its virtues but never refer to its shortcomings. This is the way to survive." (Xun, Book 13, "The Dao of Ministers")

Here Xun wrote the Confucian manual on how ministers should conduct themselves, mixing in a healthy dose of Daoist survival techniques, while throwing away all pretenses of moral concerns. The Mencian doctrine that when faced with a cruel and violent king ministers not only have the right but moral obligation to overthrow him or even kill him is rejected. The king is clearly the owner of his servants—the ministers. Loss of moral ideals means the loss of potential judgment on the ruler, which inevitably leads to abject slavery of the scholar-official class. Xun probably did not see that. Or maybe he did not care.

Confucius advocated indoctrination by *li*. Habitual observance of the rules, he thought, would foster the desired character. When everyone becomes a good (obedient) person, there is no need for brute force. Xun restored *li* to the prominence of Confucianism, after a Mencian diversion to mercy, for a similar purpose Confucius intended it to serve: to shape human character (curtail human desires). At the same time, Xun did not believe that indoctrination alone would be able to transform the entire populace. Therefore laws are still needed for the lower classes, who can only understand straightforward reward and punishment. *Li* is no longer the sole instrument that leads to an ideal society, it is part of a two pronged approach, the other being legal code, for a ruler to bring about peace and order in his kingdom. To Confucius everyone including the ruler has to follow *li*; to Xun *li* is a tool in the hands of the ruler. That means the ruler does not need to believe in it himself, but he does need to make the masses believe. He singled out five objects of worship as the foundation of all the rules of *li*: the Heaven deity, the Earth deity, the ruler, ancestors, and teachers (天地君亲师). In paying tribute to these, the ruler understands that it is for indoctrination purposes, in other words to let it become a shame in public culture for anyone to show the slightest disrespect (disobedience) to them. Scholar-officials as loyal servants to the ruler practice such worship as their duty, their habit, and their lifestyle. Only then will the masses truly believe that these are powerful deities, and disloyalty/disobedience to them would incur divine displeasure. This cynical tactic would enjoy overwhelming success in later Asian history. As late as early twentieth century, virtually every Chinese and Japanese household had a memorial tablet for these five deities, and the masses truly believed that emperors, ancestors/parents and teachers were not to be defied, for fear of divine punishment.

For indoctrination to work, alternative views must not be allowed to confuse the minds of the masses. To make that point Xun conjured up the following story of Confucius, as Confucius was by then already an ancient saint thus more convincing. Though the story was historically untrue, prior to nineteenth century Chinese all believed it was true, and throughout Chinese history legal thinking and practices all followed this example, so for our purpose of studying Confucian culture we have to treat it as though it were true.

When Confucius was teaching for a living, another low ranking official, Shao Zheng Mao (少正卯), opened his own private school and taught different views. The two became rivals competing for students and it was a real tug of war. Years later when Confucius finally became a minister of the state (in charge of law enforcement), the first thing he did, on the seventh day after taking office, was to execute his former rival teacher. His students asked him: "Shao was a renowned teacher in the state, but you executed him as soon as you had power, will you not lose people's hearts and minds?" Confucius said: "Sit down and let me tell you my reasons. Man has five sins besides theft. (1) He knows everything (about *li*) but he doesn't believe it; (2) He stubbornly defies the rules; (3) His speech is false (meaning different from official doctrine) yet he is rather convincing (so he is able to attract a large audience); (4) He remembers a lot (about history) yet they are all ugly events (meaning they tend to undermine the official doctrine) (5) He not only agrees with all the wrong views but make them more eloquent. One should be executed with any one of these five sins, but Shao committed all five, that's why large crowds gather at his home, his sophistry is able to deceive them, his courage and resoluteness enables him to establish a different school outside the correct one. He is the brave and outstanding among the Little Men (bad people), that's why we have to kill him."

Shao was apparently a dissident, and an eloquent and brave one. Had he been less courageous, less knowledgeable and less convincing, so that he would not have attracted a large audience, his sins might have been excusable. But he had to be a hero. So what choice do I have? The reasoning here is straightforward enough. The presence of a competing view is a menace to indoctrination, particularly if it is a convincing one. When people start to doubt the official doctrine they'll resent the fact that it is forced on them, and start to disobey, and subsequently cruel punishments will have to be used by the state to keep them in control, which will further antagonize them and even harsher measures become necessary to maintain order, thus the degree of violence will escalate and the society will begin to unravel. A sage anticipates this chain of events at the earliest sign, and puts out the fire before it spreads and causes any serious damage. You don't like the restive sheep constantly jumping over the fence and defying your orders, particularly if they are leaders among the herd. You kill the few trouble makers not because you enjoy killing, but because you hate it, so you kill a small number before every sheep starts to jump fences and you'll have to kill a large number.

This story set the foundation for Confucian legal tradition, according to which it is the spirit of law rather than the letter of law that should be enforced. Shao did not violate any penal code; in fact he was doing exactly what Confucius was doing: teaching. But from the Confucian point of view, all penal codes serve a single purpose—to maintain hierarchical order in society; the purpose is more important than the means to achieve it; therefore, all actions that serve the purpose are not only justified but should be enthusiastically carried out, including prosecution of crimes not defined by and not included in the penal code; for the same reason even the officially sanctioned penal code should be treated with flexibility, the ultimate criterion being social order, the purpose; and order in the long term can be fully achieved only by indoctrination. To reduce crime and punishment everyone must think alike and feel alike, in other words to have the same heart, mind and ethics.

Actually it is awkward to call this a 'legal' tradition, for the term 'legal' implies a process strictly based on written rules. What we know in the modern world as a legal system was divided into two parts back then. One part of it—the penal code—was not applicable to kings and high ministers. For this elite group only *li* applied. The penal code itself was often poorly written, nothing more than a few rules describing various punishments, and a guideline of what constituted certain crimes. The officials in charge had almost arbitrary power in handing out judgments on inferiors. So the Confucian legal tradition was based on ideas not rules, yet it was a 'legal' tradition in the sense that it set a precedent that was to be followed by later rulers. The five reasons given by Confucius in Shao's case imply that you can be convicted of a capital crime just by what you think. Western readers who consider the darkest periods of their history as when people can be prosecuted just for what they say need to fasten their seatbelts for what is to come in the following chapters.

Xun's reasoning revealed the nature and power dynamic of a pyramid culture. His interpretation remained true to the gist of Confucius' original design: peace and order based on hierarchy, only that he articulated it far better than Confucius. However, such a straightforward rendition of a cruel reality offended the growing Chinese moral sensibility, which yearned for mercy. As a result he was never canonized as a Confucian saint, although his theory quietly dominated subsequent political and legal thinking. In addition to the Confucius-Mencius contention on what constituted a good man (an obedient servant espousing self-restraint or a self-righteous moralist championing the people's cause), there was now an added dispute of political philosophy of whether the ruler ought to achieve peace and order by any and all means, or strive for a moral ideal for all-under-heaven. These are permanent fixtures of Chinese thinking under the broad umbrella of Confucianism, between a servile and an assertive character, between pragmatism and idealism.

CHAPTER 5

RUTHLESS EFFICIENCY: LEGALISM

When most thinkers of various schools were debating their social theories during the pivotal historical period of the Warring States, several capable administrators made their impact in the real world, on the balance of power between these states. The most consequential of them was ShangYang (商秧), a contemporary of Mencius, who served as prime minister in the state of Qin (秦) in fourth century BC.

Qin started off as a tiny state at the northwestern corner of the Zhou Empire, not far from the initial Zhou capital. By virtue of its location Qin was constantly at war with northern nomads when most other states were enjoying relative peace in early Zhou Dynasty, although it managed to win most of the times and gradually expanded its territory. When the Zhou king was himself defeated by barbarians and moved his court to the east in eighth century BC, Qin was left surrounded by western and northern barbarians, essentially cut off from the rest of the empire. In isolation its culture did not develop along the same lines of the other Zhou states, and remained a mixture of Shang culture and barbarism. In 746 BC, for instance, it enacted the capital punishment of "termination of three clans", meaning for a serious crime not only the culprit, but his family, his father's clan, his mother's clan and his wife's clan were all executed. In other words anyone who was related to him in blood ties could not escape, and dozens of innocent people could die for the crime of one. Common practice in other states was to limit punishment to the individual except for the most serious crime like attempted usurpation of the throne, in which case it was limited to the immediate family and female members were often spared. In 678 BC, Qin reinstated the Shang practice of live burials (a large number of servants/officials of a deceased king were buried alive with him) which was deemed uncivilized and long abandoned by other states. It was little wonder that Qin was seen as cruel and backward and shunned by the rest of the empire. Qin culture remained decidedly pre-moral when other states became increasingly moral.

Qin rulers rarely shared power with members of their own royal house; they had total control most of the time. Thus large hereditary aristocratic families did not emerge to play a big role. This condition made it easier for drastic and sweeping measures to be taken by the ruler. In 361 BC the king, eager to improve his political standing against other states, issued a decree to recruit capable ministers for his government. ShangYang, a native of a neighboring state, answered the call and quickly gained the king's trust. In 359 BC he was made prime minister and initiated his first major reform with the following measures:

A. Group all peasant households into small units. Every five or ten households were grouped into one identifiable unit. The unit was required to report crimes committed by any of its members, failure to do so would incur punishment for the whole group.
B. Break up large clans and families. If there were two adult sons in a family, one of them had to move out and start a new household, otherwise tax would be doubled for the family.
C. Clear rules for promotion. The official class was divided into twenty vertical grades like a military organization. Promotion depended entirely on meritorious military service. Taking one enemy head in battle would advance you one grade. This system defined social hierarchy and replaced hereditary aristocracy.
D. Prohibition of private feuds. Fighting was allowed only with permission of the state, mainly on battle fields against enemies. Physical violence between families and individuals was banned. No brawls, fist fights, no gangs.
E. Encourage agricultural production and ban trade. Those with outstanding production in grain or cloth were exempt from forced labor. All merchants and jobless wanderers were thrown in labor camps. Scholars and sophists who could freely travel between other states were rejected at the border.
F. Dismantle hereditary nobility. All nobility titles were replaced by the twenty grades and were no longer hereditary. The aristocracy class lost all power and privileges and was treated no different from commoners in status, except their land holdings and other possessions were left intact. New privileges were assigned according to the new grades, and everyone including the old aristocracy had to gain it through military service.

Two principles reflected here deserve our special attention: collective liability and a meritorious grade system that determines one's social rank. Grown out of the well-field system, collective liability takes another step by this reform. It is not just about taxes anymore, but political administration, information gathering and law enforcement as well. In order to build a strong state the society is organized like an efficient military force. Civilian families are grouped into fives and tens just like soldiers are assembled in squads and platoons. The group functions as a tight unit, taking and carrying out orders. They are to think themselves as soldiers in a perpetual war, and they are to be trained in discipline like soldiers throughout their lives. A populace so trained makes management of a state effortless and low cost. There won't be any crimes, for no crime can escape detection of the prying eyes of everyone in such tight knit communities. Hence no bureaucracy is needed to keep track of each individual—their local group takes care of that. Every civilian is effectively an agent of the state, disseminating its decrees, enforcing its laws, educating their young with state doctrine, organizing themselves for state projects, and monitoring each other for state control, all without being paid a penny by the state. Life for the individual is under a lot of restrictions, and there is no privacy to speak of whatsoever, but as long as one follows the rules he can rest assured that he won't be killed by a willful master for no reason or harmed by street thugs—these are eliminated. It is not free, but it is safe.

In addition to security one who lives in such a system can see a clear path to promotion, for the social ladder in the form of a grade system and how to climb it are published and well known. Promotion by merit implies equal opportunity, a point made even clearer with termination of all hereditary privileges for members of the royal clan. The society is still hierarchical, even more so than before, because ways to get out of the structure, such as by becoming a merchant or a scholar, are blocked. It is a simple society, and highly organized. One's position and therefore worth is determined solely by his rank in the grade system, and military service is the only way to raise it. Stipend in the form of land and slaves are given by the king according to one's rank, which can be just an honorary title, in which case the person does not hold office and does not have any real power. The same rank can also be an official position with real power. But regardless of which is the case, people with the same rank are considered social equals. In addition, a rank once achieved stays with the person forever, until he gets further promoted for new accomplishments or demoted for serious mistakes, and it becomes the most important part of his identity.

The aristocrats—mostly relatives of the king—were not happy, and the prince openly denounced the new policy. This kind of dissent would have been routine in other states at the time but to ShangYang it was a crime. He threw away the Confucian doctrine "physical punishments do not apply to ministers and up", and stressed that the penal code applied to everyone with the only exception of the king himself. Since the prince was the heir, his body was spared, but his two private teachers/mentors were tattooed on the face—a permanent mark of shame. This action silenced all criticism and the new laws were put into practice smoothly. Within just ten years the policy had achieved overwhelming success, as far as the king was concerned. There was no theft, no robbery and more honesty; everyone had a job and was happy doing it knowing the certainty of rewards; men were brave on battle fields but timid in their own community; and the state left its fumbling past in the dust, becoming one of the superpowers.

In 350 BC right on the heels of such impressive success ShangYang released a second wave of legal reform with the following measures:

A. Establishment of a state-wide prefecture system. The state was divided into 41 prefectures, each assigned a prefect and an assistant to him. With this law the long standing tradition of building new towns in the wilderness as homes for aristocrats and having them manage the surrounding area came to an end. The king now had direct control over the entire state through his magistrates.
B. Unification of measurements for length, capacity and weight throughout the state. This was made easy by the first reform in which the state took over all commercial activities from private merchants and monopolized markets. It greatly simplified management of state affairs, in calculating taxes, payments and agricultural production, in building roads and making maps, and in planning military equipment supply and other logistics.
C. Further division of the family. The first reform had limited the number of adult males in one household to two, this law made it one. Father and son had to separate, as well as brothers.

These reforms demolished the only form of social and political structure Chinese had ever known: the king ruled the area around the capital, other nobles with kinship ties to the king ruled their own territory scattered around the state or empire. ShangYang saw this structure as the root cause for the demise of Zhou Empire, because the princes eventually grew stronger than the king. His new highly centralized system abolished fiefdom-like practice and put the king's magistrates in direct charge of the districts. These officials reported directly to the king, operated under strict rules and could be rotated between different jurisdictions to prevent a buildup of personal loyalties and local strongholds. The aristocracy was completely stripped of power and privilege.

The official (*shi*) class also lost arbitrary power (prosecutor, judge and jury all in one) over the plebian. They were mostly promoted from the peasantry as military officers. This system provided upward social mobility to the average peasant through military service, something other states did not have. Moreover, since Qin officials had to follow strict rules too, it afforded the plebian a sense of security and fairness. As they accumulated credits on battlefields and saw their social standing visibly rising, for the first time in history they had some control of their own destiny, and became assertive in their outlook. Peasants of other states were passive subjects living in perpetual fear and anxiety, and dreaded war (they were hardly ever rewarded for risking their lives), Qin never lacked volunteers. In fact many a man could not wait for a chance to advance themselves. By liberating young men from the arbitrary control of local masters, such as a hereditary noble or a clan patriarch, and putting them in a system where they had real hope for a better life, ShangYang unleashed a human energy that proved unstoppable.

Toughness and fairness were both critical to success of the reform. Peasants and officers alike were all tightly controlled. In a culture where blood ties were by far the strongest human relations, large families had to be broken up to prevent concentration of power and wealth, in addition to increasing agricultural productivity. Civil associations of any kind were banned, as they could potentially turn political. Peasant families were registered village by village—they could not move without official approval—and grouped into fives and tens, with a head designated for each group who would constitute the lowest ranking state officials. Blacksmiths, ceramic makers and other craftsmen living in towns were all gathered in kind, so that there was a blacksmith street, shoemaker street, etc. Their families too were grouped into fives and tens and registered.

That leaves traders and scholars, and both were banished. Scholarship was prohibited and scholars were all exiled. The laws of the state were not to be challenged or debated; violators were either ostracized or executed. The state also mounted large scale education (indoctrination) campaigns, aiming at making everyone know every single law on the books. Unification of the mind, so that it was not contaminated with other ideas, and concentrated on the goals set by the state, was key for a king to harvest the power of his people with maximum efficiency. The trade profession could not survive the three strikes against it: profit-seeking as the main motive, which had a negative connotation to it among the peasants; accumulation of wealth in the hands of a few, which was deemed subversive; distraction for peasants and officials alike who could be lured away from their duty to serve the king, which was seen as corruptive. All professions other than the production of food, clothing and weapons were considered unnecessary and harmful, and consequently banned. Everyone was to concentrate on the "useful" trades, and organized in their efforts. Hence a total transformation of not just the political system but the entire society was implemented. The king now had total control over everyone and everything, down to the last person and the last detail, with their conscious cooperation.

Within just one generation of the start of these reforms Qin State became such a dominant power that the other six superpower states, collectively called the eastern states, had to scramble for solutions, and an alliance of all six was proposed in the face of the Qin threat, though eventually to no avail.

Success of Qin reveals a third aspect of the counter-evolution process. In addition to triumph of servility and cowardice, the mechanism to motivate slaves is also counter-intuitive. In a free state like Athens, citizens are real stake holders. The state is created by themselves for their own benefit. It provides protection for their private property and their freedom from foreign enemies. Their motivation to fight for the state is rooted in the desire to protect their own property and way of life. Thus the strength of the state lies in its role as the protector of property and freedom of its citizens. If the state begins to encroach on their rights, they will cease to identify with it or defend it. In a pyramid society like China people other than the kings are not real stake holders, so it is hard to motivate them to fight for the state. A king may follow Mencius' advice by lowering taxes and treating his subjects with leniency. But this hardly changes their mentality since it does not change ownership. Lower tax means the king has to sacrifice his own interest. What he loses in revenue this year he may be inclined to get back next year. It does not take a genius to figure out that the master always wins in this zero sum game. The Mencian approach is not practical because it contradicts the owner's interest. Motivation has to be found elsewhere—climbing the social hierarchy. In other words by dividing slaves into many ranks in a vertical hierarchy. Everyone is a master of his inferiors and a slave to his superiors at the same time. The higher one climbs, the less masters above him, and the more slaves below him. Stipend also corresponds with one's rank. There are three keys in making this mechanism work. One is to block all escape routes. No one is allowed to make a living in any private activities outside state control, or else the hierarchy loses some of its coercive power. Everyone has to be ranked in the same state controlled system. Another key is transparency of promotional rules. Now that there is no escape everyone wants to climb that ladder, but if promotion is arbitrary the subjects would lose motivation, for they wouldn't know what to do to advance themselves. To make sure the system is airtight a high degree of conformity and state control is indispensable, which brings us to the third key, turning everyone into eyes and ears for the ruler, by way of collective liability. Individual freedom as well as privacy has to be sacrificed. Increasing state control at the expense of individual rights weakens a free state, but it strengthens a slave state.

For this system to work perfectly no mercy can be allowed, in other words the culture is preferably amoral. If an officer is required to report to duty the next day, for instance, than the failure to do so would mean his execution, regardless of uncontrollable circumstances such as bad weather or injury that made it impossible for him to comply. To accept exceptions the state would have to device moral guidelines for the bureaucracy to adjudicate all these cases, which not only bogs down the system but also leaves openings for various abuse and corruptions. By making simple practical rules and then sticking to them dogmatically, the system is able to be fair in most cases and retain high efficiency, provided that the populace has no moral principles against it, which fit the culture of Qin. In the other states, however, this system could not be successfully copied. There the *shi* class was too independent to subject themselves to such draconian measures. They enjoyed their privacy and private enterprises, whether it was trade or scholarship. They had long abandoned collective punishment and saw it as barbarian. They got used to prosperity and demanded independence.

By third century BC it became increasingly clear that Qin's dominance was unshakable, regardless of what the other states did in terms of tricks and sabotage. Thinkers had to react to the reality and provide an explanation for the meteoric rise of this semi-barbarian state. Two of the most obvious features of Qin were absolute control by the king and a clear and transparent legal code that applied to all. It dawned on some that however good the Mencian moral doctrine sounded, what actually worked in strengthening a state was not a virtuous king who governed with moderation, but a clear set of rules that enhanced efficiency and motivated the peasantry. On battlefields of the warring states, hard nosed pragmatism trumped moral idealism.

From there it only took a small step for one of Xun's pupils, HanFei (韩非子), to push the pragmatic interpretation of Confucianism one step further, and arrive at a completely amoral worldview. HanFei argued that validity of many conflicting moral theories proposed by different thinkers was indeterminable, and therefore meaningless, since each was based on an unsubstantiated version of events in the distant past. He had a valid point. Confucius altered history books of his home state to prove his thesis; later thinkers followed his example by making up tales of ancient sages and kings. So why not leave aside the moral debate and focus on real and pressing issues of the day, like the rising Qin State on a conquering spree, while in other states rich and powerful ministers could not be counted on for loyalty. What actually mattered to a king was how to effectively strengthen the military and his power to control it, not to try or pretend to be virtuous, only to be taken advantage by his own ministers, and watch his state devoured by a more disciplined, no frills and no nonsense Qin.

"Kings of enemy states may recognize our righteousness, but we can not lay them under tribute as vassals; lords within our state may disapprove our doings, but we can always make them pay tribute to our court. . . . Therefore the enlightened ruler strives for might (and not virtue).

Indeed, the strictly kept household sees no fierce servants, but a compassionate mother has spoilt children. From this I know that authority and power are able to suppress violence, but that virtue and favor are not sufficient to stop disorder.

Therefore, the sage king does not count on people's doing him good, but forbids them to do him wrong. If he counts on people's good will, he may not find more than a few dozen of such people in the state; if he forbids people to do him wrong, he can bring the entire state into conformity. Governance should be geared towards the many instead of the few. Hence he governs by law not by virtue." (HanFeiZi, Book 19, "Learned Celebrities")

This may sound like the Machiavellian "safer feared than loved", seventeen hundred years before the Italian philosopher, although HanFei was not merely observing the real world, with as keen an insight as Machiavelli's, but adamantly pushing for a master-slave style social order that Renaissance Italians could not have dreamed of. From the reasoning above it is clear that the value-free political ideology of HanFei was a direct result of the futility of proposed moral values at the time. No matter how much mercy kings had for their subjects and parents had for their children, their ownership of the latter meant that those being owned would not likely return such kindness with willing devotion, but rather try to escape from total control of parents and kings, and strive for independence. For as long as that ownership relation was upheld, moral overtures were but a ploy for immoral objectives. What a pragmatic king or parent should do then, was to declare his claims outright and demand compliance. Here laws, instead of purported virtues, were much more effective. Laws were decreed from on top to achieve order and strengthen the ownership hierarchy, so that parents could enjoy undivided devotion from their children, kings could harvest unconditional loyalty from their subjects, all without pretension to virtue. Confucius would have disagreed with this approach, for he preferred indoctrination to harsh punishment. But he certainly would have appreciated its amazing effectiveness.

"In the old days it was the custom in Qin for ruler and ministers to ignore state laws and engage in private dealings, wherefore the country was disorderly, the army weak, and the sovereign not respected. Thereupon ShangYang persuaded the king to alter its governance and tradition by making rules clear and open, rewarding informants of culprits, discouraging trade and encouraging farm production. In those days the people of Qin were used to the beaten track that men guilty of crimes could be pardoned and men of no merit could be honored. Therefore, they were very apt to violate the new law. In the meantime, however, censure on offenders of the new law was strict and resolute; reward for informants of culprits was generous and real. Hence no culprit was missed. As many people were punished, they resented it, grumbled and protested. Lending no ear to all these, the king enforced the Law of ShangYang to the utmost, until at last people came to know that men guilty of crimes would infallibly be censured and informers became many. Eventually people dared not violate the law and penalty was rare. Therefore, the state became orderly, the army strong, the territory expanded, and the sovereign respected. The cause of all these was nothing other than heavy punishments for sheltering criminals and big rewards for informing on culprits. Such was also the way to make all-under-heaven to see and hear on the ruler's behalf." (HanFeiZi, Book 4, "Wicked Ministers")

Part of ShangYang's reform was to turn the entire nation into spies for the state. Everyone was monitored by neighbors, friends and family. All actions against state law were to be reported to authority, with rewards for the informer, and failure to report would incur severe punishment often equal to the crime not reported. No one was to have any privacy. It was a transparent society. The ruler could see and hear everything without stepping out of imperial palace. That guaranteed order and conformity, and a nation built like an army ready to mobilize and fight at any time. ShangYang's reforms had other economic elements, but coming from a Confucian upbringing, HanFei's main concern was order and control. Three centuries after Confucius, HanFei saw with clear hindsight that the Confucian goal of strict order and hierarchy could only be achieved with Legalist means—by openly declared rules backed up by physical punishments. It has to be stressed here that the draconian measures in Qin were not seen as cruel but fair, especially when the end result was an orderly society where people could enjoy peace and safety, which was more than could be said about the conditions for the vast majority of peasants elsewhere.

In the implementation of laws such as those of Qin the sovereign has to first overcome resistance from the officialdom. As HanFei pointed out, their interests do not match those of the king. A totally transparent society would doom the prospects for many ministers and independent minded *shi*, and their resistance is therefore inevitable. A major part of HanFei's thesis deals with the issue of how a king can reign in these renegade officials, or at least identify and do away with them.

"In general, the right way to listen to the ministers is to take what they utter as the measure of what they accomplish (and make sure they match)."

"To remain tranquil and stay quiet is the real nature of Tao. . . . Make the inferiors feel uneasy. Improve their actions by practicing inaction. When you show your approval of them, they will toady and get emboldened in their shenanigans; when you show your disapproval, they will resent it and neglect their duties. So do not harbor any strong emotions to them and make your empty mind the abode of Tao." (HanFeiZi, Book 2, "Wielding the Scepter")

Here HanFei incorporated many Daoist ideas in his system. Daoism teaches that human emotions are often results of ignorance of nature's ways. People cry incessantly at their parent's death, but to Daoists natural death is part of nature's cycle and there is nothing sad about it. People resent it when their friends do not return their courtesy in accordance with *li*, but to Daoists these artificial rules of propriety mean nothing and human nature would not conform to them. To people who understand Dao, everything happens according to nature's design, and there is no reason to be overly excited or anxious about it. So the Daoist demeanor is one of indifference, calm and inaction, as if the mind is empty. This emptiness is not ignorance, quite the contrary, it is a state of mind with full knowledge of nature and the universe. Human affairs that largely centered on power and wealth, and human emotions that revolve around dubious man-made conventions, seem petty and idiotic in the grand scheme of things. HanFei applied this empty-mindedness and inaction to the art of controlling ministers. The ruler should not reveal his personal habits, lest the ministers will tempt him in a way he can not resist; he should not give away his preferences, lest the officials only say what he wants to hear and shield him from the truth; he should not say much at all and stay detached, lest he becomes an unwilling participant of court intrigues by developing emotional ties to any official; he should not personally attend to state affairs, but delegate them to his officials according to their specific talents, letting the cats catch mice and roosters cry dawn; he should stand from a distance, in the background, observing everything objectively, applying rewards and punishments as the laws warrant. This not only ensures fairness, but puts an aura of mystery over the ruler, making him a god to be revered and feared, not a man of flesh and blood to be seduced and manipulated. Confucius urged that for officials to be feared by peasants they should not be restricted by open rules but should have arbitrary power and remain unpredictable. HanFei completely inherited that idea, but treated the officialdom and peasants as the same, limiting arbitrary power to the king only, in effect turning the scholar-official class into total slaves.

As far as governance is concerned, it was a natural evolution from Confucius to Xun to HanFei, dictated by reality on the ground, if we stay on the ultimate objective of Confucianism: peace based on a hierarchical social order. The only two significant changes in that evolution were the role of the officialdom and open rules. Confucius wanted the ruler to delegate both duty and authority to the officials, without providing a way to keep them on a short leash except perhaps through conformity on *li*. So the ruling class including the officialdom, the polite society as it were, would be governed by *li*, and others would be governed by the penal code. As events unfolded in the three centuries after him—many ministers became almost as powerful as their sovereigns, some even took over their states, *li* was widely ignored and sometimes ridiculed—it was evident that his approach did not work. Indoctrination of *li* required an unchallenged authority which was long gone. In addition the officialdom became less and less a hereditary class, as social mobility increased dramatically with competition between states and blossoming trade. The line between officials and commoners was blurred, as the cultural barrier between a refined lifestyle based on rules of propriety and one of insolent ruthlessness disappeared. It made a lot of sense then, if one was to stay on the original Confucian objective, to treat the officials and commoners as one class. Since it was a fact that officials could no longer be trusted with any authority, the only workable solution was the HanFei or Qin approach: open rules, do not trust officials with much discretion.

Naturally in HanFei's thesis legal codes replaced *li* as its cornerstone. He commented that *li* was only appearance, while its substance was the master-slave hierarchy between ruler-minister and father-son. To emphasize appearance created a culture where everyone became a cheat. In other words people might seem obedient in front of their king or their parents, but they really did not have unconditional loyalty and filial loyalty at heart. Confucius intended these rules to cultivate a servile character but they failed to achieve that end. Reality was that many officials were doing things damaging to their state, which in theory still belonged to the king, and this polite society under the guises of civility was rotting with corruption and deception. HanFei observed:

"A high powered minister takes over all matters of the state into his own hands, hence everybody, whether outside or inside the court, is bound to become his tool. Thus, without his cooperation, lords from abroad can not accomplish any negotiation, wherefore even enemy states praise him; without his help, no official in government service can advance their career, wherefore all officials do his bidding; without his approval, the courtiers can not approach the sovereign, wherefore the courtiers conceal his vices; and, without his good opinion, the allowances of scholars will decrease and treatment accorded them will deteriorate, wherefore the learned men speak well of him. These four assistances are means whereby wicked ministers embellish themselves."

"Ruler and minister always have different interests. How is it known? I say: The sovereign's interest is in appointing able men to office, the minister's interest is in securing office with no competent abilities; the sovereign's interest is in awarding rank and bounties for distinguished services, the minister's interest is in obtaining wealth and honor without merit; the sovereign's interest is in having heroic men exerting their abilities in service to the state, the minister's interest is in having his friends and partisans effect self-seeking purposes." (HanFeiZi, Book 4, "Solitary Indignation")

This is perhaps a fair appraisal of the interests of different parties involved in state politics at the time. But given the fact that kings owned their respective states, and ministers were mere servants whose potential independence could only come in the way of amassing great personal wealth, they could not be blamed for putting their own interest before that of the state. The idea of a king's ownership of all his subjects was implicitly challenged by Mencius and others, not in direct and articulated statements but in tone. These thinkers realized that there was something wrong about the fact that rulers could arbitrarily kill, maim and exploit their subjects, but the historical circumstances that never allowed the emergence of a free men class denied them the language to challenge that ownership. When each state started as a state-family of its ruler and people had always been slaves since time immemorial, there was no way of forming the idea of individual rights in a morally acceptable manner. Thus many thinkers including Confucians, Mohists and Daoists ended up proposing some moral judgments on bad rulers hoping they would be considerate of their subjects, or total escapism as the only form of dissent, instead of a political compromise that might have given the *shi* class a permanent stake in the state. They all looked back at ancient sages for guidance, claiming that the chaotic world they lived in was a result of degeneration from a perfect era in the past. Confucius exalted Zhou founders for their implementation of *li*; Mo advocated Xia founders for their service to the people (hydraulic works); Mencius praised ancient kings for their voluntary handover of throne and the value of mercy; Lao and Zhuang referred to distant primitive times as the ultimate paradise in total harmony with nature. They all bought into the notion consciously or subconsciously that perfect order and harmony was the only way to happiness, without realizing that previous order was maintained by a power balance. Pragmatists like Xun and HanFei were the first to discover that ancient harmony was due to low human population, and took a realistic approach to governance, while at the same time abandoning the moral issue.

Evolution of Chinese thought from eleventh to third century BC is illustrative of the struggle of a people trying unsuccessfully to shed the baggage of their slavery past. From their humble beginnings as family servants in the state-families, the *shi* (scholar-official) class had come a long way in their search for a proper place between rulers and peasant slaves. Towards the end of the period many of them had gained a great deal of independence from their kings thanks to fierce interstate competition and trade. However, Chinese history never afforded them a condition where each man could own a piece of property legally and permanently; instead all-under-heaven came in the form of many states, each owned by a king. Whatever moral or political theory they proposed had to be accepted and implemented by a king to have any real impact. Thus the more independent minded of this class found themselves in a dilemma: trying to gain a king's approval for the right to oppose him. Their efforts in this direction had to be carried out clandestinely under the banner of peace and compassion, as a hidden motive behind proposed morality. In the end none of them was able to directly refute the deeply rooted tradition that a king owned his state and inhabitants, or clearly establish independence as a virtue. As a result the idea of a free man in the Greek sense proved elusive, and the position of the *shi* class was left at the mercy of political circumstances.

In the Confucian view (both Confucius and Mencius), indoctrination of the masses is the only way to the ideal society, and the scholar-official class, playing the role of teacher/mentor, must be afforded respect by the ruler. In HanFei's Legalist view, indoctrination is ineffective and unimportant, and there is no distinction between a scholar-official and a peasant, they are all possessions of the ruler. An open and fair legal code eliminates the culture of lying. Your loyalty is what you do on battlefield, not what you profess in court. Legalism seriously undermines the privileged position of the *shi* class, and was passionately condemned by them. As a result it became known as a distinct school of thought, even though philosophically it can be easily construed as just another interpretation of Confucianism.

Having borrowed from Confucianism its main principles and objectives, from Qin culture its harsh rules and unapologetic ruthlessness, from Daoism its practical and cynical manipulation, from other schools of thought their straightforward reasoning, and putting everything together in an amoral pragmatic approach to despotism, Legalism was the culmination of Chinese political theory, a Confucian pragmatism philosophically. Completely adopted by Qin, it enabled the culturally less sophisticated if not technologically backward state to accomplish the unthinkable task of unifying the Chinese Empire of twenty million, in an area greater than Western Europe, through large scale wars fought by hundreds of thousands of soldiers on either side, across the entire landscape of mountains and rivers, some over a thousand miles apart. The discipline, efficiency and dedication of every soldier and officer were not matched in later Chinese history.

Politically the main difference between Legalism and Confucianism is the role of the scholar-official class. In the Confucian system scholar-officials are a privileged class. They are interpreters of the moral order. They are indoctrinators to the masses. They define the civilization and through their work all-under-heaven will be turned into moral beings, in a process similar to domesticating wild beasts. Only then can there be lasting peace and order. In the Legalist system officials are preferably military men. They are to be promoted from foot soldiers. Their job is to faithfully carry out orders.

They do not form a class; everyone is equal under the ruler. The way to turn the masses into loyal soldiers is not through indoctrination, but fair and harsh rules. The two approaches to statecraft advocated by Confucianism and Legalism are not mutually exclusive. A scholar-official can be both an indoctrinator and a faithful warrior for the ruler. Indoctrination can be done with the help of rules/laws.

Legalism was the intellectual end product of political theories after centuries of trial and error. It fully captured the power dynamic and psyche of a pyramid culture. Its well articulated statecraft (tight control/no escape route; tough and open rules; collective liability; ruler's behind-the-scenes approach) amounted to a precise and effective social engineering. However, its draconian rules and callous treatment of human lives were an affront to the principle of *ren* (mercy) and unacceptable to a majority of the scholar-official class, who considered Legalism downright barbarous. Not being able to directly challenge the reasoning (if one acknowledges that the ruler does own his state and subjects) or undisputed effectiveness of this theory, scholars had to use the well established intellectual authority of Confucianism (the Mencian interpretation) as a feeble attempt at putting a check on the ruler's arbitrary power, by insisting a moral order (Heaven's Mandate) that they had exclusive rights to interpret.

Like other schools of thought at the time HanFei's Legalism was presented to a king as a systematic political strategy. Selling an idea to a single ruler is quite different from selling it to, say, a crowd of free thinking citizens of Athens. In order to pass the test of open ended questioning Greek thinkers developed a vigorous logic, namely deduction. If one says A implies B he has to clearly define A and B, and show the intermediate steps, in other words connecting the dots, until each step is immediately obvious. This is the only airtight logic that human beings have ever developed and it is the foundation of modern science. A Chinese thinker's objective was to convince a ruler in private. One has to first identify the ruler's interest against that of all others. One must also take careful note of the ruler's character, emotional disposition and idiosyncrasies, and skillfully use it to his advantage. Logic of the argument is much less important than inter-personal rapport. Confucius and later thinkers commented on their experience of such attempted persuasion, and left remarks like "do not try when the ruler is not in a good mood", "do not repeat the same thing too many times" and "do not be too eager to give your opinion, speak only when asked". Once the argument is accepted by the ruler it is to be enforced and the slaves do not get a chance to debate it. However, government policy does need a plausible reason, at least superficially, if for nothing else than to make it easier to swallow, particularly for the official class who have so far been left out of the process. Thus every argument made public comes with a seemingly impeccable reason, though the mental process is not that of a logical deduction. Here is an important quote from Confucius.

The Master said: "There are not two suns in the sky; nor two rulers in a state; nor two masters in a family." (Book of Rites, 27:5)

If in Confucius' time Dao—nature's Way—was still believed to be human's way as well, by HanFei's time some thinkers began to doubt it, including HanFei. However, the same style of reasoning had always been there, and thinkers still felt obliged to justify their social theories with natural phenomena. Thus what appears simple on paper often implies a far more complex mental process. There are three statements in the above passage. There is only one sun in the sky—that is a fact. There was only one ruler in a state—that was a fact in the sense of nominal ownership but not necessarily in the sense of real control. There was only one master (patriarch) in a family—that was not universally true at all back then when women could and did have real power in some households (depending on the social ranking of the wife's family relative to that of the husband) and in many families adult sons were in control instead of their aged parents. This passage preaches that there ought to be just a single ruler with undivided power in every state or family. The fact that there is only one sun in the sky was used as the sole argument for that thesis, because it was viewed as an indication of nature's laws, a revelation of Dao. But in the mind of the preacher the process often went backwards. He might have had the conclusion first (one ruler), which was what he wanted to sell, then he set out to search for a good reason, and nothing was more authoritative than nature's law, or Dao. From one sun in the sky it really takes an analogical leap of faith to come to one ruler in a state or one master in a family, but no one was allowed to question it because the conclusion once enacted by the ruler would be as unchallengeable to the ruled as its reasoning. So we have two statements, one is a natural phenomenon easily acknowledgeable and the other is a political argument to be enforced by the ruler and accepted by the population. The intension behind linking the two together is to give the latter a kind of legitimacy as if it is an indisputable law of nature. The statements laid out in parallel forms deliberately leave a great deal of ambiguity, so that each person can accept it in different ways privately.

The ostensible line of reasoning assumes that human values have to comply with nature's laws. The fact that there is only one sun reveals one of nature's principles that there should be one master and one master only.

That being the Way is then the only correct course to follow. To defy it would be to defy Dao. It would also be unwise since harm would follow, just like not planning farm work around the rhythm of seasons would bring poor yield. In stating the natural phenomenon and finding a visually plausible link to the human phenomenon that few had ever thought of before, the preacher also wants to impress that he has carefully studied nature and is an expert of Dao, to enhance his own credibility. So here is a wise man telling you the ways of the world, laying them out in plain comparison so that you can understand and warning you at the same time that it would be wrong to offend nature and you would inevitably suffer if you do. One can be convinced of the credibility of the preacher by the genius of his observation and ignore merits of the claim. There is also an egotistical temptation for one to quickly identify with a sage, claiming full comprehension of his profound thoughts, leaving the ignorant masses in the dust.

If you happen to be a confident and independent thinker, and not impressed with the authoritative reasoning, the message to you is that the conclusion is not entirely predicated on the argument (there are unstated enforcements that will make you accept it anyway), but to smooth the shove down your throat, or to reduce the pain it inevitably inflicts on your honor, the preacher has deliberately omitted the real reason you are accepting it, namely coercion, and provided an impeccable excuse so that you can feel less violated, and convince yourself to accept the logic "why not one ruler, after all there is only one sun". Still, the process leaves your pride bruised if not destroyed, if you were a free spirited person to begin with, and that is its intended purpose. Once you have come thus far (accepting one ruler), the third part (there is only one master in the family) and subsequent parts if any will go down much more smoothly. Although you know for a fact it is not true that every family have one master nor do you believe it ought to be that way, but to seriously question it would reopen your psychological wounds for you know the prior process has already compromised your intellectual integrity. To avoid shame and reopening an old scar a defense mechanism in human biology kicks in and relieves you of the pain as well as the desire to ever reason again in such matters.

These two distinct lines of reasoning, one ostensible and one insidious, which we might call authoritative persuasion and coercive persuasion, always coexist in Chinese political arguments. In any given case the preacher may intend to stress one or the other with the same statements. If he is advising the ruler, he may intend to be entirely persuasive; if he is debating an opponent, he may intend to be entirely coercive; in other cases such as indoctrinating the masses there can be a mixture of both.

The beauty of it is that a lot is left unsaid and both the preacher and the audience have ample room to position themselves without being seen as unprincipled or coerced. The argument may have convinced the ruler and then been forced on the subjects, but both the ruler and the preacher can look benign and moral as if they have persuaded all, and insomuch as the subjects are convinced it is a persuasion; but if they become skeptical, the coercive interpretation will be stressed by actions, without changing a single word of the argument. A listener may have been forced to accept it, but he can pretend that he accepted it on principle so as to save face. The purpose of this type of argument is to sell one's ideas, both to superiors (individually) and to inferiors (collectively), and the two are not separated since the ruler has to sell it to his countrymen, albeit by coercive persuasion if necessary—coercion dressed like persuasion. Because ultimately it is going to be implemented by force anyway, the analogy part (one sun) does not aim at proving the argument beyond reasonable doubt, but rather to provide a plausible excuse, a psychological way out for the oppressed, of course it doesn't hurt if the excuse is itself obvious, looks like it might carry a deep meaning and comes from an intellectual authority.

Coercive persuasion could have been called brainwashing, which is the term Westerners invented when they first came in contact with the Chinese experience, but they have not fully understood it, and the term has since been used in Western context and in a shallow sense, akin to propaganda bombardment, information control or indoctrination. To avoid confusion I shall not use the term. The coercive persuasion process has two steps. First there is a subtle but unmistakable coercion. An unstated but clearly present threat achieves better results than a bluntly uttered one, for no one likes to admit cowardice; furthermore, the entire argument can be legitimately interpreted as reason, and the threat nonexistent. Second there is one follow up argument that by itself is hard to accept, sometimes obviously untrue, but the subject will find a reason to convince himself, in order to avoid shame of being coerced into accepting the first one. By this time the subject is persuaded, not just of the current argument, but also of any future argument from the authority, regardless of how ridiculous they may sound to someone without such training. It is an ingenious design.

Chapter 6

MYSTICISM AND THE FIRST SYNTHESIS: IMPERIAL CONFUCIANISM

It seemed like a cruel joke on Chinese that just when the scholar-official class had largely turned into moral beings with a merciful heart, all their states were conquered by the one semi-barbarian state with an amoral culture at the northwestern corner of their known world. The triumph of Qin was also a victory for Legalism. It proved once and for all that when it comes to warfare, the scholars and their moral doctrines were ineffective in motivating the peasantry to fight. With Qin's unification of the Chinese Empire in 221 BC, the Zhou style political system where each prince had his own domain was gone for good, along with the era of blossoming schools of thought. The official class who previously achieved semi-independence, where they had a choice between allying themselves with one king or another, being a champion for the peasantry, or simply playing all sides for their own benefit, now lost all bargain power and found themselves at the mercy of the only ruler under heaven, who now styled himself under the new title of emperor.

The Qin military machine did not stop after unification; they embarked on ambitious civil projects. Each state used to have slightly different written languages (pictographs); these were simplified to a common form. Their currencies as well as measurement of length, weight and area were all unified. A network of wide and straight roads were built and reworked to the same width, which reached all parts of the northern plains and western basin. In the south large water ducts were constructed which in addition to rivers formed a web of waterways. Within a decade or so an impressive transportation system over the entire empire was completed that lasted through the nineteenth century without much change. In its territorial size the Qin Empire was then as large as Europe, with a population around

20 million. Politically former states were replaced by hundreds of counties which were then grouped into forty provinces; magistrates and their offices were set up and staffed in each county; rich families of the defeated states were uprooted, moved to new locations, their land holdings were confiscated and redistributed to peasants. Expeditionary forces were sent to conquer barbarian territory, as far south as present day Vietnam.

A comprehensive legal code was devised based on the code of former Qin State. In its complexity and consistency it surpassed Chinese legal system today. It included everything thought to be in need of regulation, and given the nature of Qin Legalism, practically no human activities—social, economic and political—were left out. From the structure of the government, descriptions of official positions, duties and stipend on all levels, to appointment, dismissal, promotion and demotion of officials, to civil and criminal law, to taxation and military conscript, to industrial standards, agricultural practices, currency minting and exchange, domestic and international trade, everything.

In addition to the main body of code there were Q&A passages explaining the letter and intention of each rule, which carried the same legal authority as the code itself; previous cases that were supposed to provide guidance for future practice, although case law had limited significance in the Chinese legal system (for reasons to be discussed later in the chapter); and provisions for how new laws should be written. The main body was not supposed to be changed by even a single word, but should situations arose that the existing code did not address, the emperor could issue decrees nationally, and officials could do the same in their own jurisdiction. Administratively county chiefs and provincial governors also functioned as judges for their jurisdictions, and a judicial office was set up on the national level. Cases could be appealed up that chain. These officials were in turn subject to periodical reviews by their superiors against specific criteria. This system also lasted through the nineteenth century.

As if all of the above was not enough achievement, several gargantuan construction projects were undertaken. There was the Great Wall project, where an estimated half a million men worked to build and link up previous constructions to form a 4,000 mile long continuous defensive barrier against northern nomads. There was the tomb project, where 700,000 war captives and other criminals labored for a future resting place for the emperor that was 150 meters high above ground, deep into the ground, and one squire mile in area. Finally there was the imperial palace project, where 1.5 million men were employed to build a stone structure that was about 500 meters long and 150 meters wide.

It is a testimony to the efficiency of the Legalist Qin system that all these were accomplished in just fifteen years. The other states were advanced in moral theories and intellectual development, but Qin was light years ahead of them in large scale organizational skills and engineering. Without Qin many of these projects could not even have been imagined. Being amoral certainly has its benefits: there is little restraint on how things ought to be done; whatever works is adopted. While an amoral culture makes it possible, Legalism owes its success to the fact that it has uncovered the mechanism to motivate slaves, by forcing everyone into the same social/military hierarchy, by making promotion fair and transparent, and by holding peasants collectively liable for their actions, which leads to a high degree of conformity.

Ruthless efficiency can bring fantastic results, but by itself is not enough to rule a conquered people who expect mercy from their ruler. In all these construction projects a total of no less than three million men, fifteen percent of the entire population, were forced to labor for the emperor, years on end, with little or no pay. The emperor treated all conquered people with contempt, but they were accustomed to a much more lenient rule. Under the whip of Qin soldiers resentment was growing. Meanwhile, former scholar-officials of the conquered states were stewing in their own bitterness. To the Qin emperor Zhou culture was corrupt, decadent and should be abolished. He rejected advises from Confucians to grant domains to members of the imperial house following Zhou tradition, to leave the two largest industries—salt and iron manufacturing—in private hands, or to exercise leniency and moderation. In fact he was irritated by criticism from these learned men. He ordered all books in private possession to be burned. In a fit of rage he buried four hundred sixty scholars alive.

This was total savagery the likes of which the civilized scholar-official class had never seen in their lifetime. Losing their home, land and privileges was a devastating blow, but to add insult to injury, their customs, rituals and music, their poetry, prose and chess games, their clothing, courtesy and demeanor, their values, culture and whole lifestyle were spurned by the new regime. From high up on the social ladder with considerable independence and pride, to a group deemed stupid, rotten, and useless, in just one decade, these people had seen a free fall of their fortunes and were humiliated beyond measure.

All these tensions simmered under the surface, but against the mighty Qin military machine there was little anyone could do, until that is, cracks developed inside the system. A brigade of the Qin army was sent to a remote post some six hundred miles away. They were delayed by severe weather and lost any chance of reporting to the destination on schedule. Facing certain death under Qin code they rebelled by taking over a local government and occupying a few counties. This set off an avalanche of uprisings across the empire, as former scholar-officials and their subjects revolted in droves, including Confucius' own eighth generation grandson. Just when the empire needed its officers the most, many of them turned their back on it. One general commanded a large army and conquered what is now Northern Vietnam, but when the emperor ordered him to come back and rescue the empire, he refused, declaring himself an independent king (this was the origin of Vietnam as a political entity). Within just fifteen years of its inception, the mighty Qin Empire came to a violent and abrupt end. It was hated so much that its record setting palace, in size, luxury and grandeur, was burned to the ground. It took three full months for the fire to subside.

Just as Qin's meteoric rise propelled Legalism to the top, its precipitous fall exposed the weakness of this political philosophy. Having done away with morality altogether, there is no place in this system for traditional values like moderation or mercy. There is nothing in Legalism that tells the ruler when he has driven his subjects over the edge, he has to rely on the masses as his eyes and ears to detect early signs of widespread malcontent, and take action accordingly. In Qin State this was done by collective liability laws, which over time worked into the culture. But people of other states were not used to spying on each other for the state, or being collectively punished for the crime of one. The scale of the territory was also a major factor. Officers who would not dare rebel in Qin State could do so in Qin Empire, particularly in times of crisis, knowing that they had plenty of room to maneuver or simply run out of reach of the emperor. In fact independent Chinese kingdoms were founded in both Vietnam and Korea during this time. In short, two of the three keys to the success of Legalism were missing: tight control/no escape route and collective liability.

Trying to draw lessons from Qin's demise, the Han Dynasty (206 BC-220 AD) that followed reverted to the Zhou system at first, where relatives of the emperor were enfeoffed with their own kingdoms. There was a common feeling that Qin's totalitarian rule was unacceptably harsh. However, military technology and tactics at this time were far more advanced and population was far larger than a millennium before when the Zhou system was founded, and a power balance was no longer tenable. Within a couple of generations the Han imperial house annihilated all the kingdoms and reinstated the Qin style administrative structure (magistrates appointed by and serving the imperial house as opposed to lords with independent domains).

The Han regime now faced an intellectual challenge. It fully adopted the Qin political system, with all powers concentrating in the hands of the emperor. Yet it was apparent to all that harsh legal code or coercion alone was not enough to rule a moral people, particularly in an immense empire. Thus an intellectual marriage between Confucianism and Legalism was needed to make sure that the legal code reflected widely accepted Confucian (Mencian) principles, such as mercy, and in case there was a conflict between the two, the presiding officials had the discretion to act out of conscience, rather than being required to strictly follow the letter of the law. Moreover, the Confucian worldview was to be adopted as the only official ideology, with its emphasis on turning the masses into moral beings through indoctrination.

Key rules of propriety (*li*) made it into the legal code. For instance, laws were added/changed such that a father would have total control over his grown children, including the right to take their lives, and the state were to enforce these laws at the request of the father. The old Qin practice where a grown son was forced to move out and start a new household was abolished. Now a grown man was forbidden to move out unless his father agreed. A grown daughter could only marry with her father's approval, to the man of her father's choosing. The family was given a prominent place in society. Just like Confucius observed, sons trained to be filially loyal were unlikely to rebel, and peace was achieved without much coercion from the imperial authority. No standing army was even needed to rule an empire. In a true story a group of convicted felons were told to go home and help out farm work (there was a shortage of labor), and report to the execution ground after harvest time in the autumn. By the designated date all of them came back, not one run away or into hiding—they all believed they were guilty and deserved capital punishment. The emperor was so moved he pardoned all of them. Legalist totalitarian rule did not hamper moral convictions at the time.

The synthesis between Confucian moral indoctrination and Legalist administrative practices was smooth, because both schools of thought acknowledge the ruler as owner of the universe. There is, however, a significant difference between Confucius' and Mencius' view on ruler-minister relation. Confucius preached a ruler's ownership of his ministers as slaves: they should admonish him at times for his own good, but always remain loyal and obsequious to him. Mencius preached independence in relation to the ruler: help him when he is benevolent for the purpose of the people, criticize, leave, or even kill him when he is stubbornly wicked. These two positions could not be really reconciled, but given the reality of unchallenged imperial power in the unified empire, the scholar-official class had to give up the principle of independence, at least on paper, in exchange for a privileged position. What they did not want was to outright condemn themselves into perpetual servitude to the emperor. The architect of this synthesis, prime minister Dong Zhong Shu (董仲舒), resorted to mysticism and ambiguity to resolve or at least suspend the impasse.

Here the Yin-Yang theory came in handy. Carried in the ancient Book of Changes (易经), it was part of an elaborate system of mysticism combined with some mathematics explaining the workings of the universe. It states that there are two opposite sides or properties to everything, such as up and down, left and right, interior and exterior, before and after, anger and joy, hot and cold, day and night, etc. The two opposites combine to make the universe a whole, without either the universe could not exist. The two sides take turns to dominate: it gets hot in the summer, but beyond a limit it starts to cool down, until it gets to the other extreme in winter, when it will start to warm up again. When one side grows the other diminishes, as their sum remains a constant. But there is a limit to the growth of either side beyond which it will start to shrink while the opposite side starts to grow. Nature balances itself by preventing extremes in either direction in such a manner. The two sides seem to be engaged in constant struggle against each other for dominance, yet they have to form a harmonious whole for the universe to work. One can not at the same time look at two different things, or listen to two sounds, or draw a circle with one hand and a square with the other. That proves the two sides have to work together and be ultimately unified as one. Nineteen hundred years later the German philosopher Friedrich Hegel apparently adopted this theory in his dialectic, where every situation is said to contain within itself two conflicting elements, the thesis and antithesis (Yin and Yang), that eventually work themselves out to achieve a resolution—a synthesis, or a new situation with its own set of two conflicting elements, and this is the mechanism of change in the world.

The Yin-Yang dichotomy had long been associated with the relationship between man and woman, in particular between husband and wife, seen as two sides in constant conflict but also complemented each other to hold society together and propagate the species. Dong expanded it to include two other relationships in addition to husband-wife: ruler-minister and father-son. Yang is said to always dominant Yin. Therefore the ruler, the father and the husband are the Yang, while the minister, the son and the wife are the Yin in their respective relations. Yang commands, Yin obeys, that is the natural state of their relationship. From there either side can grow, but within limits. Yin can not grow as far as to be equal with Yang, and Yang can not completely deny Yin, beyond these limits the other side will strike back. That is the nature of things, the Dao of the universe. Since Yang is defined as higher than Yin, usurpation is then interpreted as upsetting the natural way and offending Heaven, therefore evil. On the other hand, Yang has to watch out for his own excesses, for beyond a certain limit nature will interfere and restore the relationship to its proper state. What it essentially says, is that the ruler naturally dominates his ministers, and they should obey him, on the other hand, if he goes too far in oppressing them, nature will find a way to punish him.

This may sound like a rephrasing of the Heaven's Mandate doctrine, but it is more flexible and can be interpreted as either for or against the master-slave relation of ruler-minister. The key here, is that neither the nature of the Yin-Yang relationship, nor the moral doctrine on which the ruler is to be judged, is clearly spelled out. Confucius used the father-son relation as the model for ruler-minister relation. By tradition a father did own his children; he could abuse them, abandon them, sell them, or even kill them with impunity. Dong used the husband-wife relation instead as a standard bearer for the ruler-minister relation. In those days a husband did not own his wife; their relative power position within the family had a lot to do with the social status of the husband's and the wife's original families. In general a husband could not physically abuse his wife, or else her family would raise hell. By shifting the model from a clearly ownership relation to a traditionally non-ownership relation, Dong in effect tried to gain some ground or at least leave some breathing room for the scholar-official class, albeit in a subtle way. However, by stressing that Yang should always dominate Yin, he left room for other interpretations, such as that a husband should indeed own his wife, in which case the three relationships would be realigned to master-slave again. So the ruler could be satisfied that his command if not ownership was secure under the scheme, and he could readily assume ownership should reality on the ground one day lend itself to that; and the scholar-official class could take comfort in the fact that the theory in tone opposed total domination of them by the ruler as extreme. The most unfortunate outcome of this synthesis was that the relationship between man and woman got tangled up in the political debate, and it marked the starting point of a long and hard decline in the social status of Asian women.

That leaves the question of how much dominance by the ruler over his ministers and exploitation of the masses is excessive. How much should Yang dominate Yin? What defines excess? Dong turned to the natural world for an answer. If the ruler stepped out of his bounds, he said, nature would give a sign, an earthquake, a flood, a drought, a heavy storm, a meteor, or something else—to be interpreted by knowledgeable ministers and scholars. Heaven became a thinking deity constantly watching over everything under him. The change of seasons, weather patterns and epidemics—every natural event represents a message from Heaven, who not only cares but is intimately involved with the world, though not to the extent of communicating with each individual. Important rules of propriety (*li*) were then reinterpreted in terms of the Yin Yang dichotomy and the Five Elements—gold, wood, water, fire and earth—that everything in the universe can be reduced to. Thus Heaven, *ren* and *li* all come together in a coherent system, each being a manifestation of the Dao and representing it, which is the ultimate power and source of the universe. As such the new Confucian doctrine added a strong dose of mysticism to the plain and earthly rules of propriety (*li*) and mercy (*ren*).

In the intellectual jostling between ruler and scholar-official class this was a solution vague enough for both sides to accept. There were no real objective restrictions on the ruler the breaching of which would render him immoral; on the other hand, ministers had the prerogative to use natural phenomena for their political argument. Should the ruler's control firm up over time, he could appoint ministers who would see things his way; should his control weaken, the scholar-official class and their representatives in court could press for more breathing room.

Dong went on to mandate by law Confucian training for officialdom. Six Confucian classics were singled out (The History of Lu State written by Confucius, five early Zhou documents including the Book of Rites, all edited by Confucius and his followers); official appointments at many high positions were based solely on the mastery of these classics. The court set up a school (the first Chinese university) in the capital, later to be duplicated in the provinces, where students were trained on these Confucian works, and took graduation exams by which they were graded and assigned to various official posts accordingly. With this practice mastery of the six books became the inside track up the social ladder for young upstarts. The best and brightest of learned men all set out to write their thesis showcasing their understanding of ancient classics, hoping to achieve Dong's fame and fortune. Volumes were written in what came to be known as a distinct discipline of scholarship (经学, literally scripture scholarship); one of these books took hundreds of pages just to explain a single word in the classics. In addition middle and low ranking officials were chosen on the basis of filial loyalty, sparking a mass movement to Confucian family values. The three year mourning that was hitherto rarely observed suddenly spread like wild fire. Men competed with each other for regional and national filial loyalty championships. One could literally hear the constant squall echoed from graves all over the continent.

Once the official ideology was settled, what followed was a ban on all competing ideas, in keeping with Confucian teaching. Though the newly synthesized state ideology had loopholes that could in theory be explored by independent minded thinkers, its monopoly in the Chinese consciousness over time precluded that possibility, because the effect of Confucian values such as filial loyalty on the mind was not philosophical but psychological and debilitating. By installing Confucianism as state ideology the scholar-official class had cemented a permanent privileged status for themselves, but as a consequence also lost their intellectual independence forever. What is worse, as imperial power inevitably grew stronger in the counter-evolution process that was temporarily stalled in the Warring States period, the scholar-official class often found themselves compelled to enforce conformity and crush dissent, in order to prove their worth to the ruler.

Confucianization of the legal code of course started with the family. Physical violence against one's parents used to deserve face shaving (to incur shame, akin to face tattooing) in Qin code, but death in Han code. In fact death penalty was attached to all acts against filial loyalty, which if judged by the principles stated in the Book of Rites, would mean whatever the father wanted it to mean. Thus the Han code effectively gave fathers the right to kill their sons, or to have their sons killed by the state. In Qin code husband and wife were basically equal. A husband caught in the act of adultery could be killed on spot with impunity; a husband who physically abused his wife was punishable by face shaving; women could divorce their husbands. In Han code these rules were gone. A wife could no longer divorce her husband on the grounds of his wrongdoing. Divorce was granted only if the husband agreed. This was the first step down for Chinese women, and it would get much worse later on.

Li in the form of Confucian family values made it into law, but it was interpreted in the Mencian way, in other words there was a merciful side to it. The very young (under eight), the very old (over eighty), pregnant women and the disabled were all entitled to some leniency, specified in the Han code. Because Confucius said that father and son should cover each other's crimes, Han code allowed family members to not testify against each other, reversing the Qin priority of loyalty to the crown before the father. It spared Chinese the indignity of having to spy on their own family for the state. The process of turning rules of *li* into law was accompanied by a parallel process of interpreting both *li* and law as not just rigid hierarchical rules and cold blooded penal code, but living documents embodying moral sensibility of the time.

The next change came in the practice of law. In keeping with Confucianism, Dong repeated that morality ought to be the primary force behind social order, the Yang of governance, while penal code was a supplement, a contingency for failures of moral indoctrination, the Yin of governance. Legalists focused on the letter, while Confucians emphasized the spirit. Weakness of the Legalist approach was already exposed in the case of the first open revolt against Qin, where rules required that the army brigade be punished for failing to report on time due to no fault of their own. But spirit of the law was not something easy to define. Confucianism could be used as the principle when interpreting the law, but with the Confucian-Mencian rift settled in ambiguity it was not suited for the job: Heaven will not make a noise every time a case is misjudged. In order to find out how any specific rule should apply to a specific situation, Dong personally presided over 232 cases, using the Confucius-written History of Lu State as a guide, hoping to establish a broad-based case law system for the future. There was a case where a man went out fishing and drowned in the open sea, his widow remarried four months later at her mother's request and arrangement, and was charged for violating the rule that a dead husband had to be formally buried before his widow could remarry, a crime punishable by death. Dong released the woman on the grounds that her action was in accordance with filial loyalty and not a sign of promiscuity.

Most of Dong's rulings were aimed at leniency, or the Confucian (Mencian) value of *ren*. However, his approach has three inherent problems that a Confucian political and legal system is incapable of solving. One is the tendency to convict people by what they think. The Confucian judgment is less about a particular violation of the legal code and more about the moral character of the suspect. The above case of the remarrying widow can be seen by Westerners as case dismissed for lack of criminal intent or physical impossibility to comply with the law, but that is not how Dong or other Confucians see it. Had the woman remarried by her own decision, Dong would have convicted her, even though the circumstances relating to the law at issue here remain exactly the same. The key question Confucians ask is whether or not she was a moral person, i.e. a good Confucian. Following her mother's order showed that she was, and as long as her actions were reasonable for a moral person she should be excused. Ruling on the basis of morality may have turned out benevolently in this particular case, but it also opened the door, or more precisely reopened the door after Confucius' purging of Shao Zheng Mao, to convict anyone on serious charges based on their character alone, real or perceived.

It had long been a capital crime to denigrate the ruler in Qin code. When enforced by Legalists violation of the rule had to involve someone saying something that could be construed as vilification. After Confucianization the Han code had a rule for "belly smearing" (腹诽), or silently badmouthing the ruler in one's belly (the stomach was thought to be where human mind is, instead of the head). Any facial expression or body language that could be interpreted as a sign of restiveness became criminal. Again the point is not the action, but the moral character of the person in question. If someone harbors resentment of the ruler, that is a capital crime in and of itself. Countless court officials were executed by their political opponents throughout Chinese history on this charge, which needed no evidence and could not possibly be disproved by facts. You can be convicted for what the authority thinks that you think.

Another problem with Dong's approach is that the Confucian political system precluded any significance of case law. All laws ultimately draw legitimacy from imperial power. At the beginning of every dynasty the founding emperor would release a new version of legal code, often copied from previous versions. Then there were decrees issued by the sovereign and local officials, these had legal authority only as long as their issuers were still in power. Subsequent rulers could very well change previous laws and often did. A ruler could change the rules between morning and afternoon. Dong's case law had legal power only as long as he was prime minister, and even then it did not have the authority of imperial edicts. Officials who did not fear Dong personally had no reason to follow his example. Legitimacy of any law always accurately reflects the power of the person behind it.

The third and perhaps the most devastating flaw of a Confucianized legal system, in terms of its impact on Chinese historically, is that the standard of moral judgments is not a fixed target. In Han Dynasty (206 BC-220 AD) a widow could remarry and live happily thereafter, but by late Song Dynasty (960 AD-1279 AD) and afterwards a remarrying widow would have ended up on the burning stake, for such betrayal of a deceased husband was no longer morally acceptable under any circumstances. As a result of the counter-evolution process, by which the ruler gains more and more power, his subjects become more and more servile, ethics tends to develop in the direction of increasing self-sacrifice. Moral values based on Western justice have a limited demand on the individual, because justice ultimately serves each individual. If I always believed in helping and never harming anyone, I would be considered moral. It would be injustice to require me not to harbor any selfish ideas (like pursuit of happiness) or to slavishly serve anyone else. But values based on master-slave relations like filial loyalty have no limits in terms of demand on the individual. A man is a good son if he gives all his possessions to his parents. But he can do better. Instead of partying with his friends he could spend his spare time massaging his parents, do household chores, run errands, and think of ideas to make them happy. He can do still better. Always kneel in their presence, speak in subservient tones, carry out their every order with zeal, and take all the blame for their mistakes and punishment for their crimes. He can do still better. In times of hardship he can bury his own three year old son alive, so that the toddler wouldn't compete with his aging parents for food (this true story was canonized as a model of filial loyalty in the book of "Twenty Four Stories of Filial Loyalty"). And it does not stop there. As long as one is still alive, more self-sacrifice is always possible (sacrificing one's son, who is considered one's property, is self-sacrifice). If moral requirement rises, and there is no limit to how high it can get, people can find themselves running afoul of the law just by staying alive.

Of all the legal changes that came with the establishment of this new imperial Confucianism, culturally the single most significant was enforcing filial loyalty by state coercion. It was not uncommon in ancient traditions the world over to grant fathers sweeping rights over their underage children. Classical Greece had similar laws. But to extend those rights throughout the entire lifespan of the father, thus covering a good portion of the son's adulthood, would completely change dynamics of the father-son relationship and child rearing practices. A young Greek man upon reaching adulthood becomes independent of his father, which affects the mental state of even a teenager in anticipation of the incoming independence. The Oedipus complex and father-son rivalry are part of the Western psyche. A Western parent who abuses his children can expect no affection from them later if not revenge. Love from children has to been earned. An Asian father on the other hand has full ownership of his children for life, backed by the state under the threat of death penalty should a grown son disobey. Hence he treats his son like a tool for his own benefit. Whatever he invests in his son, whether it is time, energy or money, he intends to reap the greatest reward later. Love from his children is demanded, and father-son rivalry is simply unimaginable. We shall come back to Confucian child rearing practice and its effect on the human psyche in more detail.

Once adopted by the imperial court as part of the legal code, Confucianism had the exact effect on the population anticipated by Confucius—"Those who have filial loyalty to their parents and obey their elder brothers, seldom show a disposition to resist authority of their superiors. Such men have never engaged in violent uprisings." The Han Dynasty lasted four hundred years (206 BC-220 AD), thanks in large part to Confucian indoctrination. In terms of perpetuating imperial rule, there is just one flaw in the system, that filial loyalty is directed at parents and it comes before servile loyalty (to the emperor), in other words the family and private bonds come before the state and public duties, which is a reversal of the Legalist tradition. The official class, having seized the position of interpreters on the state ideology, vehemently upheld family loyalty over state loyalty, as they badly needed breathing room under the emperor's autocracy.

The legal code had a provision that required a review of the performance of all officials periodically, in order to weed out the corrupted and incompetent, promoting the capable and meritorious. That was easier done in war times when military merits were plainly visible, by counting the number of enemy heads or ears each soldier collected from battlefield. In peace time there was no objective measure of accomplishment and the process was prone to manipulation. The court appointed inspectors were supposed to review the performance of local magistrates and report back to the emperor, instead they took bribes from and covered up for local officials, who then pledged loyalty to their inspectors instead of the crown. Adroit players of the political game of corruption, deception and cronyism were promoted, while the straightforward and diligent officers loyal only to the emperor's interest, the kind of people the legal system was designed to promote in the first place, were systematically weeded out of officialdom.

Confucian family values in the Han code added fuel to this silent erosion. With absolute power in the family a father would either forbid his adult sons to move out or keep them under his tight control, and given the fact that people back then married and reproduced as soon as they were biologically capable, and a man could have as many female consorts as he could afford, some super families emerged, with a patriarch commanding hundreds of kin members and thousands of slaves or more. Many prominent families from high ministers in court to local magistrates and clerks were linked to each other through a network of marriages and blood ties. As a whole the scholar-official class was supposed to form a nation-wide bureaucracy working for the crown but in reality they built strongholds in their own jurisdictions, made their power permanent and hereditary by gobbling up large shares of arable land and controlling an increasing portion of the peasantry, essentially becoming military governors.

Given that these super families had near arbitrary rule on their own turf, few helpless peasants were able to remain independent of them. One common practice for the peasantry was to simply give up their land and become their retainers, in exchange for the promise to be allowed to work on it and keep a portion of the harvest. By voluntarily pledging loyalty and submission to them, these peasants/retainers enjoyed security and exemption from tax and services, since officials and their family servants were non-taxable. They also formed the backbone of private militias, to fight for their master in turf wars. Over time the most powerful clans snowballed in size, wealth and power, and controlled most towns and counties. The empire was in essence divided up by the scholar-official class, who collectively took a large portion of the peasantry under their wings and thus reduced the tax and military base for the imperial house, weakening its power little by little until it finally collapsed in 220 AD, by which time the largest of these clans boasted a private army of one hundred thousand soldiers.

The Empire was broken up from within, and years of warfare that ensued reduced the number of factions to three, in the form of Three Kingdoms, which coexisted for sixty years before they were reunited for a short while, only to be shredded into more pieces by various ethnic groups of invading northern nomads shortly thereafter. China would stay divided for nearly three centuries, from early fourth to late sixth century. The northern nomads were efficient fighters, spending most of their time on horsebacks, but coming from illiterate herding tribes they could neither manage an agricultural state nor even conceive dimensions of the Chinese Empire. It would take nearly three centuries of ruling a Chinese population, marrying with them, learning Chinese language and culture, for descendents of these nomadic kings to grasp the genius of Confucianism and use it to their advantage, in which process they gradually shed their primitive warlike past and disappeared into the melting pot that was China.

After the demise of Han Empire various contenders for power used mysticism in the state ideology to advance their own political agenda. Somewhere a big rock would turn up with the name of a hitherto obscure warlord carved in it, purportedly a revelation of Heaven's mandate. White clouds considered auspicious were said to be present during a future king's birth, while the head of his rival faction was rumored to look like a hideous ghost, supposedly a product of divine displeasure. Repeated claims of this sort by various characters who for the most part did not last long on the historical stage eventually took a toll on the credibility of Dong's synthesized imperial Confucianism. With ample empirical data accumulated in these three centuries clearly in sight, it did not appear that Heaven conveyed any message through natural phenomena over the behavior of any king. As a result imperial Confucianism was largely stripped of its mystical aura, and reduced to practical political strategy. The dichotomy of Yin/Yang was discredited as a basis for Confucianism among Confucians, though it was picked up by Daoists and continued to circulate in the lower ranks of the population.

Loss of faith in Heaven, the fact that the Chinese domain was largely ruled by primitive northern nomads who did not understand their moral theories and could not have cared less, and a sense of helplessness about the situation, all contributed to growing cynicism in the official ranks. Since Confucius' time the scholar-official class had always been a dynamic force and history makers. Regardless of their schools of thought each believed that he could reshape the world. But now with the empire carved up and dominated by uncivilized nomads with no end in sight, a sense of futility began to spread. The scholar-official had lost his ambition and purpose. Instead he sought refuge in material comfort of his private life. Poetry, music, literature and painting became not just favorite pastimes but the whole point of life for many in this polite society who spurned physical labor and warfare, turning themselves to pale weaklings "without enough strength to tie a chicken", which was considered a sign of civility. Herbal medicine, food recipes, sexual techniques, along with astrology, magic and sorcery—all professed by Daoist priests—were in high demand. By and large they turned away from ideologies and political affairs, adopting the Daoist tradition of escapism, and focused on their own personal wellbeing. Life was not about utopian ideals anymore, but all about fine cuisine, carnal lust, longevity, and literary expression of human feelings.

China was reunited again by a single ruler in late sixth century when a system was finally worked out that effectively broke the back of the powerful clans and prevented them from forming again. Land was redistributed equally among peasants, according to how many men, women and ox each family had. It could no longer be traded. Ownership of private slaves was curtailed. A different system of recruitment was introduced to prevent peasants from abandoning their assigned lots and seeking protection from officials (hiding their existence from state registry by serving officials' families privately) just to avoid military service. Every six peasant families were to support one designated soldier, including his horse, food and weapon. Soldiers were exempt from other taxes. They would work on their land, keep all crops, and train for battle in the off season. This was an ingenious plan. First, soldiers were identified beforehand; others did not have to worry about military service. Second, soldiers were given something in return for their service, such as tax exemption. Third, they were trained in formations and tactics every year, giving them a battle readiness hard to obtain for a peasant army. In addition, peasant families were grouped into units of five, for each group was appointed a leader, typically an elder, who was to help local officials to control the population and prevent their free movement. So the Qin organization of peasants returned with a modification, this time not for collective liability, but for low cost management.

These effective measures of increasingly tight control enabled the Tang Dynasty (618-907 AD) to last three centuries, ruled by a family of mixed Chinese and northern nomadic blood. Learning from the failure of many short-lived previous nomadic kings, as well as the successful Han Dynasty, this family though not totally converted to Confucian moral values themselves, fully understood the power of Confucian doctrine in turning the masses into obedient slaves. They took the process started by Han Dynasty rulers to incorporate *li* into the legal code (以礼入法) to the extreme—now all laws must follow *li* (一准乎礼). In the meticulously compiled Tang Code the Confucian family with all its internal hierarchy is set in stone. Not just the father-son relation, but every person in a family has a fixed place in that hierarchical order and must behave accordingly. Elder brother beating younger brother, for example, is perfectly legal, but younger brother beating elder brother is a crime. Grown children are prohibited from moving out when their parents are still alive, regardless of what their parents want. They can not sue their parents or grandparents for whatever abuses inflicted on them; those who try commit the capital crime of "disrespect" (不敬) punishable by death.

The political system is now seen as a continuation of the family. Local officials of all levels become "parent officials" (父母官) of their respective jurisdiction, a village, a district, a county, a province. The emperor is the parent of all-under-heaven. Servile loyalty is filial loyalty directed at the emperor. The empire is the family of the emperor, and human relations in society are modeled after the family hierarchy. Because the father-son relation is well defined by Confucius, unaltered by Mencius, which leaves no room for ambiguity, the establishment of emperor as father of all essentially reduced the scholar-official class to sons, or slaves. The emperor now legally owns all-under-heaven as his private property, and the long struggle of the scholar-official class to find independence has lost legitimacy for good.

Chapter 7

BUDDHISM

Although India was populated by many dark skinned tribal groups quite early, it was the late coming Aryans, a light skinned nomadic Indo-European race, who dominated its civilization. When these migrants conquered northwestern India and parts of what is now Pakistan, they faced a similar scenario common to the beginning of other pyramid cultures: a small group of warriors in control of a huge number of slaves. The same counter-evolution process outlined in chapter one would ensue. What makes the Indian condition different is its racial dimension.

In the eyes of the earliest civilized peoples, barbarian groups were always repugnant due to their savage customs such as brutal human sacrifices and incest. Where there was no discernable racial difference, like the case of China, these abominable traits were thought to be correctable by indoctrination, after which the barbarians would become civilized. When there was a stark contrast in racial identity, however, all the social norms tended to be associated with skin color itself and deemed irreversible. That was how Aryans saw aboriginal Indians.

Conquered Indians were of course slaves, and divided in similar ways like Chinese into family servants, peasants and urban laborers. Some Aryan men had children by slave women, creating mixed races. In time a vertical social hierarchy—the caste system—emerged, with a strong racial undertone, where light skinned people were of higher castes and dark skinned lower in the pyramid. However, the line between the original group of conquerors (Aryans) and captives (aboriginals) was not as easy to erase as in China. How much noble blood one had was visible in this case even centuries later. Therefore the caste system eventually became rigid, and mobility from one caste to another was all but impossible. Gradually it multiplied from four to hundreds of castes, making it an even more finely graded and prohibitive web of barriers between people than found in other pyramid cultures.

Because of this rigid system Indian civilization lost much of its vitality at the very outset. Everyone was born into a certain caste, which defined his entire life: how he should be brought up, what he should learn, what rules to follow, what occupation to take, what kind of woman to marry, and what to do in retirement, down to every detail. All of this was preached by the dominant state ideology: Brahmanism (Brahman being the highest caste). Other ancient traditions typically employed a deity to justify kingship for a particular blood line, leaving the rest to chances, while Indian tradition pigeonholed everyone into a fixed position in society by birth.

Brahmanism was adopted in the entire northern India, as Aryans spread east and established many kingdoms, large and small. Mountain ranges and primitive conditions, perhaps also Aryan traditions, prevented unification of India in ancient times and these kingdoms coexisted for centuries in peace, solidifying a common Indian culture. At the very top of each tribe or kingdom the chief was often elected among a small group of Aryans, did not rule for life, and was by no means despotic. However, the caste system defined every aspect of Indian society from politics to economics to civil relations, and whoever was elected chief did not matter all that much, as far as the vast majority of Indians were concerned. The chiefs for example could not initiate sweeping social changes the way Chinese kings did in the Warring States period without dismantling the caste system first, which was impossible. For pre-moral peoples a restrictive society like this was alright—their only concern was survival. After long term peace and prosperity, when unnatural death became an exception rather than the rule, Indians began to develop a moral sensibility, and the caste system needed a justification.

At some point an anonymous genius came up with the idea of transmigration. We all live multiple lives, one after the next, with no end, even though we do not remember what happened in our previous lives. In each life the totality of our actions becomes our moral credit, known as karma, to be passed on to the next life. With good karma you will be a member of higher castes in your next life, with bad karma you will end up at the bottom of the pyramid, maybe even reincarnate in the form of a pig. As the birth-death-rebirth life cycle continues forever, so does the causal relation of actions-karma-social station.

This theory does far more than giving a plausible explanation for the otherwise hard to justify caste system. It eases anxiety associated with misery. I maybe a lowly slave living in squalor, but when I look at the Brahmans I am able to have some peace at heart, because I know my current predicament is caused by my own actions in a previous life, which I can not blame anyone else and there is nothing I can do now to change it. Moreover I remain hopeful for the next life. My body may die but my soul lives on forever. It also curbs the urge to revenge, to rebel, or to vent frustrations on others. I may be abused by my master, with whom I am naturally angry. But in order to earn good karma I can not afford to let loose of my emotions, instead I have to suffer through it all without complaint, and remain a caring and giving person. Returning abuse with love certainly helps my karma. Finally it provides a wonderful dream for the oppressed. If my life is miserable in this cycle, I may have better luck in the next one, where my current master may end up being my slave. I feel much better already. The genius of the theory is that it is about morality, in a way it does address the caste system, and yet it conveniently circumvents the issue of social justice altogether.

To escape from harsh reality—not necessarily starvation but lack of possibilities and a sense of hopelessness—some Indians also resorted to extreme asceticism, through techniques like meditation and yoga. The idea is to cleanse evil karma accumulated in past lives by extreme penance, which begs the question, what am I to repent if I do not even know what sins I committed in my past lives? On a more practical level, if this life is not enjoyable for me and there is nothing I can do to change it, why not find a way to minimize my suffering, and just sleep walk though it. If I sit still and think about nothing all day, I consume little energy, I need very little food which I can beg, and if I am lucky enough to fall into a trance, I might even taste the ultimate bliss, albeit for a brief moment.

Transmigration was incorporated into Brahmanism as the intellectual foundation of the caste system, making it a state religion. By sixth century BC it was well absorbed by the masses and became an integral part of Indian culture. In the last two centuries long standing peace was shattered by tribal warfare, possibly due to population growth. Some smaller states were conquered by more powerful ones, and the defeated nobility, chiefs and Brahmans (priests), were killed or enslaved. For the first time in memory many members of the nobility were under considerable stress. In this new era of uncertainty the highest ranked castes found that the rigid system which had long guaranteed a privileged life for them also hindered their mobility in times of distress.

In the Warring States period of China, kings of every major state were eagerly looking for talents who could enhance his strength. A prince whose state was teetering on the edge of destruction (such as HanFei) could go seek high office in another state, if he had some good ideas and was able to convince another king. The Chinese mind was focused on new social and political ideas, as that was the way to fame and glory. By sixth century BC the Indian caste system had developed to such an extent that occupations were fixed as well even for the highest ranked. A prince whose state was about to fall had no visible path to a privileged position in another state, for all high positions were occupied. Thus the stressed Indian nobility had no perceivable way out; there was nothing they could do to improve their security, and their attention naturally turned inward, onto lamentations of uncertainty of the world and suffering of the heart. The dominating mood in India was pessimism, due not to famine or poverty, but to lack of choices, while the mood in Warring States China was optimism, despite military strife.

It was around this time that two obscure members of Indian nobility left their families for a life of wandering in the world. One of them founded Jainism, the other Buddhism; both are basically offshoots of Brahmanism. According to the legend, Buddha—the Enlightened One—finally became enlightened after years of wandering and days of meditation under a tree. He then started preaching and gathered a following, and went on to sell his ideas to several important heads of state, who became patrons and built temples for his new religion (making him the highest priest—Brahman—in a powerful state), similar to what many Chinese thinkers did with their ideas.

The basic Buddhist view is that everything in this world including life is of a fleeting nature and not real. Unlike Greek thinkers whose observation that "one can not step into the same river twice" only prodded them to search for the ultimate truth, Buddha's purpose was to find peace in the human heart, not knowledge of the world. Since the only thing certain is uncertainty, life is inevitably sorrowful, for we all crave security and comfort. The purpose of Buddhism is total relief of pain and anxiety for people who feel helpless to control their own lives. It proclaims the "Four Noble Truths": 1) that all life is inevitably sorrowful; 2) that sorrow is due to craving; 3) that it can only be stopped by the stopping of craving; 4) that this can only be done by a course of carefully disciplined conduct, culminating in a life of concentration and meditation.

Buddhism inherited transmigration from Brahmanism, only that it is interpreted in a more pessimistic way. A better next life used to offer people some hope, however remote it was. But in Buddhist view even the life of a high caste member is still suffering, so there is nothing really to hope for in this world. The cycle of birth-death-rebirth becomes an unending ordeal, and the only way to permanently escape from it is through "enlightenment", by voluntarily renouncing all humanly desires. In the real world an Indian Buddhist would be happy to be a lifetime beggar. He would not intentionally starve himself like the ascetics, and he would be equally happy regardless of what conditions he found himself in, whether in the high seat of a splendid temple or in the most despicable slum, because all traces of the ego as part of humanly desires had been cleansed out of his system.

This new view on the life cycle leaves the original logic behind transmigration out of kilter. It takes hope for many to adhere to good behavior—good karma has a material reward in the next life. But when all hope and purpose are taken away, life itself becomes meaningless. Indeed Buddhism teaches that not only everything comes from dust and eventually goes to dust, what happens in between is a big nothingness as well. Human beings are seen to be stuck helplessly in an eternity of suffering without any moral significance, and the ultimate objective of human endeavor is nirvana, a total annihilation of the self in which life is ended in such a way that no rebirth will take place, thus finally delivering the individual from the vicious life cycle. One can not simply commit suicide, for self-extraction from pain is not nirvana; instead he has to find true enlightenment first, enduring all the suffering if necessary.

If the original logic of transmigration was clever, this new one is tortured. When life is nothing but suffering and utterly meaningless, the logical conclusion is to end it. Preserving such a life, thus lengthening the suffering, for the sole purpose of keeping alive the possibility to end suffering in the next life, is almost a contradiction of terms, because of which the philosophical side of Buddhism remains somewhat incoherent. One message is that human life is a big void, which leads to the conclusion that it can be easily taken without any moral consequence, as we shall see in the case of Japanese culture. The other message is that we should find a way to lessen suffering, which tends to resonate with sensibilities of a moral people, who are not disposed to accept the nihilistic view on life, as we shall see in the case of Chinese. In both cases these two messages can not be reconciled: if life itself is meaningless, why is suffering so important as to be the focal point of Buddhism?

Since everything in this world is but a temporary assembly of dust in one form or another, it is erroneous to attach human feelings to them. Wealth, power, fame, ambition or moral conviction may be the focus of many individual lives. But seen from the grand scheme of things—over many life cycles—all human endeavors are frivolous and trivial. The ideal Buddhist temperament is one utterly without concern for all things this-worldly and concentrating on the inner self. It takes more than a leap of faith for a person who cares not only about his material wellbeing but also his reputation and relative standing in his community, who has senses of pride and shame, to voluntarily metamorphose into a state of no care, no want, no emotion and no feelings. The first thing one need to comprehend is that regardless of fate and fortune life itself is sorrowful, because of cravings for among other things sex, then attachment to woman, then giving birth to a new cycle of sorrow, before old age and death exacerbates grief and lamentation and turns them into despair.

The inconsolable pessimism testifies to the brutality of Indian life back then, when peasants should have had a higher material standard of living than their contemporary counterparts, who are plagued by overpopulation and exhaustion of soil. If we compare Buddhism with the Chinese version of escapism, namely Daoism, we find that the Indians went far down the road of despair. The Daoists were content with a simple life and not interested in wealth or power and sought to avoid competition. Nevertheless they were happy as the abundance and beauty of nature afforded them joy and calm. To them going back to nature and the natural state of human existence in it was to find freedom and happiness away from control of the state, not to avoid pain. Their criticism on the Zhou establishment and its defender Confucianism may have been muted in tone at times but always pungent in substance. And Daoists were certainly not among the most courageous—YangZhu and Mo schools mounted frontal attacks on the official doctrine, though eventually unsuccessful in dethroning Confucianism they did help forcing it to address the issue of social justice. But we find no such criticism on the Brahman establishment and the caste system from Buddhism or any other Indian school. Buddhism preaches that all people as well as all living things are equal, but equality is understood either in the sense that in suffering from insecurity we are all equal, or averaging over many life cycles we are all equal. One can not hope to find equality by equating a human to an ant (a possible reincarnation of a human), or harboring total despair of life itself.

The only way to break the vicious cycle of birth-death-rebirth is to deny the self of all desires, through meditation, concentrating on cleansing of the mind of all thoughts, until one achieves the state of nirvana, leaving no traces of the individual personality or ego to be reborn. Man has various desires, innate or acquired, which all have to be eliminated before he can achieve nirvana, including the desire for sex. It is not merely self-control, but teaching the body through years of training to give up all cravings so that without any conscious effort it still has no wants. Man has various emotions, temperament and character that others identify him with, that constitute his humanity. Those have to be extinguished. Achieving nirvana is to go from human to non-human, non-entity and non-existence. However, this is not considered a fundamental change of the nature of human existence, which is thought to be transient and soulless to begin with. The human body is a composite of elements that changes every minute from birth to death. You are not who you were yesterday. The transient nature of human existence leaves no room for an eternal self or soul. Man is but a pile of dust temporarily put together by fate to suffer a meaningless life. This world that we live in is a world of dust.

How does the accumulative moral credit pass from a man to his next reincarnation then, if upon death nothing exists of him, body or soul? In other belief systems the soul is the carrier of a man's spirit; it does not die with the body and keeps on living as the immaterial part of a man's existence, whether in another world or in this one. Without a soul how does rebirth actually work, especially given that something does pass through between death and rebirth? Buddhism explains it with an analogy: it is like lighting one lamp with another, nothing of the first migrated to the second except the flame, and yet the second is a reincarnation of the first.

This is not the only example where analogies were the main vehicle of explanation. In fact most of Buddhism was explained in the same manner. Because truth and objective reasoning were precluded by a rigid political system, analogy was the dominant way of reasoning in India, just like it was in China. The analogies can not be pushed too far, nor are they meant to be. Yet no alternative is offered to provide the student, the layman and other inquirers with a clear comprehension by way of logic and reason. In addition to not being able to elaborate on everything for fear of obvious contradictions, Indian and Chinese teachers also took advantage of the situation by deliberately keeping a mystic aura around themselves, to let it be known that no matter how brilliant and hardworking a student is, he can never surpass his teacher/master. Sometimes words are invented not to articulate an idea, but to shroud it, to mystify it, and to elevate it beyond the reach or reproach of mere mortals.

The philosophical side of Buddhism is not our focus, nor was it ever for Buddhist teachers and monks alike. The actual message of Buddhism is psychological. Its spirit is to give up. You must give up everything—power, wealth, all your earthly possessions, your desires, your emotions, your thoughts, and every fiber of your existence. But it is not just about giving up, for you can not do it by committing suicide. You have to suffer through this life and the next and perhaps many more until you achieve nirvana.

You have to first use your mind to conquer your body and bring it into total submission, and then destroy your mind, leaving a void of yourself, a state of emptiness and nothingness. An "enlightened" mind is not a thinking mind, but to get there one has to think very hard about everything. If sex drive becomes hard to suppress, think about something ugly and disgusting, and concentrate on it for as long as it takes for the urge to pass. Other desires can be dealt with similarly. Buddhism is a life long mission to combat what the human animal is born with naturally. Once all humanly desires are exterminated, one may learn or perceive the "truth", which is not some abstract knowledge, but a particular state of mind.

Short of achieving nirvana, which is beyond the reach of all but a few saints, mere mortals can still find an effective way through Buddhist teachings to alleviate anxieties. By giving up and diminishing your very existence, you can gradually reduce your needs without feeling shortchanged. You are not what you eat, what you wear, or other things that you consume or possess; you are nothing, just like everything else in the world. So the less you eat, the less you possess, the closer you are to the true nature of all existence—nothingness. The less you desire, the less your concern and anxiety. You will become happier because you have less to worry about. In the end you need so little to survive that your safety is guaranteed. Having no quarrels with this world you can achieve peace and calm regardless of what is happening around you. And that was what turned many aching souls into believers.

In the first or second century AD, there emerged a new Buddhist school, who called their new brand of Buddhism Mahayana, or the Greater Vehicle (to enlightenment), and contemptuously termed the older Buddhism Hinayana, or the Lesser Vehicle. In the proceeding centuries, northwest India was invaded by Greeks (Alexander the Great), Scythians, Parthians, and other central Asians. These invasions opened up trade routes and cultural exchanges between India and the West. In the Buddhist sutras there are many recorded conversations between Indian Buddhist masters and Greek kings who occupied northwestern India. Western philosophies and religions including Christianity may have reached this region. Perhaps influenced by all these, Mahayana Buddhism differs from Hinayana in two important respects: its theistic tendency and its goal of life.

The Buddha was originally a great teacher, a thinking prince, revered for his wisdom, like Confucius, but still thoroughly human; now he was worshiped like a semi-deity, although given his well known life stories and Asian tradition he was not seen as god the way Jesus is to Christians. He was a perfect human, a status achievable by few others though still possible. He did not possess any special power but his teachings became unchallengeable to the followers. Portraits and sculptures carved in the Greek style were made in his image, and began to appear front and center in many temples, which became places not just for monks and lay Buddhists to meditate, but for the general population to worship and to pay tribute. Moreover the Great Vehicle declares that there are many Buddhas, not just in the past but in the future as well. In fact some of them may be living among us, helping the poor and saving the weak. They do not have to suffer the cycle of birth-death-rebirth, but they nevertheless choose to stay in this world, to sacrifice themselves in order to ease our pain and deliver more of us from the cycle of life (there is a hint of Christian influence here).

The Buddhist life of meditation, concentration, gaining knowledge through introspective examination of the self, and ultimately transcend the sorrowful secular world, was deemed inadequate and selfish by Mahayana Buddhism. According to the new creed, a Buddhist should not look away from other people's suffering, but spend his lifetime helping them. Cleansing of all humanly desires from his system, living many lives of virtue, learning the truth and eventually achieving nirvana, is only the first step, the Lesser Vehicle. A saint also has a loving heart, an ultimate concern for the wellbeing of others, and lives an altruistic life of self-sacrificing for even the trivial interest of others. There is a story where a Buddha (an enlightened priest) unhesitatingly gave both of his eyes to a lay person who needed them for medicine. And this is the way to achieve true enlightenment, the Greater Vehicle.

By first century AD Buddhism established itself as the dominant religion in central Asia, and a few Buddhist priests found their way to the Chinese court through the "silk road" built not long ago. By second century AD this road was already bustling with trading caravans and evangelical Buddhist monks. Several Han Emperors expressed interest in Buddhism and helped build the first few temples in China, but since Confucians and Daoists who filled the court were strongly against this invasion of foreign religion, Buddhist infiltration in China was an insignificant trickle in Han Dynasty. The main Confucian contention with Buddhist practice in the early stages was that the Buddhists temple chiefs refused to prostrate before the emperor. This was against rules of propriety (*li*) and by implication would put Buddhist priests above everyone else in the social hierarchy since others all had to kneel to the ruler. The Buddhists maintained that they were out of this world, that once a person joined a temple, shaved his head, put on the yellow robe and took the vow of celibacy and sobriety he had given himself to Buddha, and he no longer belonged to his parents or his ruler. To Confucians one who did not obey his father or his ruler was an immoral animal and should be put to death, this was the corner stone of their doctrine. To the Buddhists, however, caving in to these secular rules would be negating the purpose of their conversion to Buddhism, named literally "getting out of the family" (出家), following the example set by Buddha himself. To become a Buddhist monk was to abandon one's family and secular life, as well as all the rules that govern such a life. Han rulers allowed Buddhists to keep their own ways, though their existence in China was limited to just a few temples.

If Confucian objection to Buddhism was its potential erosion of social hierarchy, Daoists were fighting an invading religious rival. Daoism established itself as the authority on medicine, astrology, magic, witchcraft, and other knowledge of the universe and man. On the one hand their priests performed religious rituals that prognosticated fate and fortune and advised patrons on how to steer their lives to an auspicious path, on the other they provided medical help and counseled on food recipes and bedroom techniques to enhance man's health and enjoyment of life. They had settled their disputes with the Confucians and found a niche in society for themselves: Confucianism dominated political ideology, moral values, and social hierarchy, while Daoism offered a meaning of life for the individual—longevity, physical wellbeing and indulgence of the senses. Buddhism was trespassing on their turf. Its teachings dismissed material meaning of life as this-worldly and unenlightened, rendering many of Daoist services irrelevant; and it had its own way of looking at the future, through transmigration, making Daoist fortune telling erroneous. Thus Daoists mobilized their entire establishment to combat Buddhism, and initially they were able to win concessions from the Buddhists, like accepting the claim that the founder of Daoism, Lao, went to the west and became the teacher to Buddha, thus elevating Daoism above Buddhism intellectually (a teacher is always higher in hierarchy than his students/disciples). But in the end they could not stop the spread of this foreign religion, largely due to social conditions of the following period.

It was not until the fourth century, after the demise of Han Dynasty, when China was overrun by various tribes of northern nomads, who then proceeded to divide China into many states, that Buddhism found enthusiastic patrons among these kings and began to pour into China. Social conditions under which Buddhism and its priests were imported on mass were three fold. First, breakup of the empire and invasion of nomads seriously weakened the Confucian state ideology, since there was no centralized authority any more, and these new foreign kings (nomads) were of different ethnic groups who spoke different languages, they were not Confucians and did not necessarily like Confucianism or even understand it. With these kings the Confucian and Daoist scholars lost much of their clout and were not effective in mounting an assault on Buddhism, though some of them managed to gain prominent positions in these newly founded states. Second, the nomads who were now masters of the land wanted to rule ethnic Han Chinese for the long term. They knew they had to adopt at least some Confucian practices, but they feared that complete dominance of Confucianism would give Han Confucian officials too much power, for they alone had the knowledge to interpret Confucianism. A foreign religion would provide a counter balance to Confucian influence, and give the kings leverage to play the two factions against each other—or three factions if we count Daoism. The early Buddhist priests were foreigners—Indians and various ethnic central Asians—who had no roots in China and could not possibly pose any threat to the kings. Third, teachings of Buddhism are even more favorable to the ruler than Confucianism. Confucians are required to be loyal to the ruler, but the ruler is also required to be lenient and merciful, otherwise the populace will judge him immoral, and rebellion is sanctioned by Mencius under such a condition. Buddhists on the other hand will never resort to violence no matter how badly abused; they would rather starve to death, which may be good karma.

For those Chinese who did suffer for whatever reason or personal circumstance nothing in the Chinese civilization could give them comfort or internal peace. Chinese schools of thought are all materialistic, or to put it in Chinese language, "this worldly" (入世). There is no god or any other spiritual force to give meaning to life other than gratification of the senses. The idea of permanently relieving human being from all pain of this world is against Confucian principles, because it abdicates responsibility of the individual for his parents and ruler. For the suffering heart there is no relief. Into this void came Buddhism, which offered Chinese a form of psychotherapy, something they had never known before, that could quickly put their mind to peace. Some of them shaved their heads and became monks, fleeing oppression, war and uncertainty of life in general. Others continued to toil, but at least found the idea comforting that sufferings in this life will be rewarded in the next.

By the advent of Buddhism Chinese intellectual development had been through vigorous debates of the Warring States period, the trials of several forms of government in collective memory from Shang to Zhou to Qin to

Han, and the test of doctrines from heaven's mandate, to rules of propriety, to mercy and commiseration, to heaven's mysterious signs related to a ruler's behavior in unknown ways. As the Han Empire collapsed and the continent entered three and a half centuries of civil wars, short-lived dynasties and political chaos, imperial Confucianism lost some of its credibility. In other words, none of the proposed political and moral theories was left unscathed as the increasing volume of recorded history smashed all the rules previously thought to manifest nature's way, or Dao. For a people with an inquisitive mind apt at grand schemes and all-encompassing theories that cover all-under-heaven, Chinese found that none of their attempts stood up to the test of time, and were left bewildered and confused. Intellectual stagnation was set in contrast with ever changing realities on the ground. The principled, dignified and independent scholar-official of Mencius' time was no longer appreciated or approved, what worked was in some cases memorization of some ancient text whose meaning no one really cared about, but more often simply corrupt political deals and toadyism. The high achievers were lying sycophants in court. True benevolence was hardly ever rewarded although ruthless cruelty (by nomadic barbarians) often was. Imbued in a moralistic worldview after centuries of Confucian indoctrination, the Chinese mind was frantically grasping at an unresponsive Heaven or Dao to make sense of it all, and the idea of karma as moral credits on which one will eventually be judged was to many simply irresistible. The judge was believed to be Heaven, though Indian Buddhism never posited such deity. The judgment could come in the next life, which was what Indians believed, but it could also come later in this life (现世报), which was more to Chinese taste. Thus transmigration was downplayed in Chinese Buddhism. It only served as a back up—if one is not judged in this life, he will be in the next. Buddhism was moralized. Moreover, though Buddhist practices such as meditation were embraced as a means to alleviate stress and pain, the view that life itself is nothing but suffering never quite took hold in China. Chinese were not that desperate.

As Buddhist temples spread in China, Confucians were further exacerbated. In addition to the issue of hierarchy, they also found fault with philanthropy practiced by many Buddhists. This is a clash of moral values. Philanthropy was preached by Mahayana Buddhists as a high virtue, but Confucians saw it as undermining state control: if people could get free food no one would be willing to work for the ruler anymore. Monks did not obey rules and were essentially a group outside the Confucian social hierarchy; now if poor peasants could get free food the ruler would lose an important leverage over them as well.

Because of strong Confucian and Daoist opposition—and these two schools were well established in the ruling class—Buddhism was never able to gain the status of a state religion in China, despite patronage from many rulers. Frankly they would very much like to make Buddhism a state religion, for it ends the debate on social justice once and for all by postponing it to the next life. However the tradition was entrenched since the Warring States that legitimacy of a ruling house must be morally justified. After so many different attempts in that effort, including various interpretations of Heaven's Mandate, it had become a central issue. It was impossible to turn Chinese into Indians who would not question their fate.

Be that as it may, Buddhism did spread far and wide, through a kind of religious organization—the Buddhist temple organization—that was hitherto unknown to Chinese. Unlike the Christian church where a single Bible was canonized by a single authority, there was no authority on Buddhism intellectually or administratively. Literally hundreds of Buddhist sutras (texts) were written by early Indian priests. The typical starting point of a temple organization was for a Buddhist scholar, who could be ethnically Indian, West Asian or Chinese, having acquainted himself with the Indian language and studied one or several sutras, to persuade a king of his message, such as to pacify the oppressed by helping them eliminate their earthly desires, accept their fate, and commit to non-violence. Once convinced the king would finance a temple structure and endow it with sizable land and peasant slaves. The said Buddhist scholar became the head priest and chose the official doctrine of his denomination, often one or two sutras. He then recruited monks/disciples, who would become his lifelong servants living in the temple, similar to Confucius and his disciples. In fact Buddhist priests were regarded as teachers—remember the three words teaching, indoctrination and religion are one and the same in Chinese.

As temple organizations grew with time the first generation of foreign born priests were succeeded by a much larger number of second, third and later generations of Chinese monks, and Confucian family values began to take hold. Like any other organization consisted of many people relations between them had to take some form. Buddhism itself says nothing about secular human relations, and to Chinese all such relations were defined by Confucius—father-son, elder brother-younger brother, etc. Thus the head priest in each temple took the role of a father, other lesser priests acted like his younger brothers, and monks like his sons. These relationships were ratified in the Tang Code (legal code for the Tang Dynasty, 618-907 AD), for example a monk committing an offense against the head priest would be treated the same way that a son would against his father.

Benefits of such independent organizations were obvious, such as exemption from taxation and other obligations, and Daoists quickly followed the Buddhist example and built temples of their own. Daoism thus became a religion as well, with priests who observed celibacy, just like Buddhist priests and monks. These two schools of thought have something in common, which is the attempt to escape from burdens of daily life dominated by Confucian doctrine, although they take different approaches. Daoism insinuates skepticism of Confucian morals and the demanding duties that they imply on the individual, as a son, an official and a subject of the ruler. It tells people to instead focus on their own physical wellbeing, enjoy a long healthy life and all the small pleasures therein, which is the whole point of living. If you have to follow Confucian rules to survive then do the bare minimum just to get by, but do not throw your energy into it, because that is not the natural way. Daoist expertise in medicine, in astrology and knowledge about nature in general helped their popularity. For those who are mentally tormented with anxiety or depression, however, there is the Buddhist approach. Once you realize that life is short and meaningless anyway, all the trappings of life that cause anxiety or depression would go away. You shun all earthly pleasures. You desire nothing, not even survival, thus you would not be angry or distressed about anything. You have seen through the futility and stupidity of this world, and retreated to the peace and tranquility of your own heart. An enlightened soul is literally out of this world (出世).

Both schools would fundamentally transform each other. Daoism used to be completely about the material world. Nature and humans are equal parts of this world governed by the same laws, collectively known as Dao. That is why all Chinese thinkers, from Daoists to Confucians to Legalists, all based their theories on natural phenomena. Man is born with a nature; Mencius saw the benevolent side of it, while Xun saw the malignant side of it, but whether good or bad it is a manifestation of Dao, just like iron and wood have their own different qualities. By observation most everyone wants something, delicious food, sex, material comfort, wealth or power. That is taken as human nature, and Daoists have always promoted a life in compliance with nature. Then came Buddhist monks. They live in a temple. They eat only rice and vegetables because they do not believe in killing a life, any life (an animal can be reincarnation of a human in a previous life cycle). They follow strict rules. They pray all day and never party. They swear to celibacy and sobriety. By conventional wisdom their way of life is no fun at all. And yet the enlightened monks are truly content. They crave nothing, certainly not the kind of temptations that motivates the lay person. Some of them have no concern for their own lives, even. They truly see this world including themselves as nothing but dust. Daoists like others were both shocked and awed by this phenomenon which no one thought was possible. The founder of Daoism, Lao, stated that Dao was present in the ancient past, when people were pure, pristine and without desires (for wealth and power). Buddhist monks demonstrated that even in the present world that has decayed and completely lost the Way it is still possible to regain that pure and desireless state of human existence. Thus Daoist would gradually move away from their traditional businesses, such as food recipes, sexual techniques, prognostics/palm reading, sorcery, and retreat to reclusive lives in their temples deep in the mountains, swearing celibacy and sobriety just like the Buddhists. They want to go back to nature, purify their minds and find Dao, but they feel that Buddhists may have found it first.

Before entering China Buddhism was basically a collection of techniques to relieve suffering. It has a psychological theme, which is to believe in fate, the life cycle and the nothingness of the world as well as of life itself. It also has physical methods to help that psychotherapy, which includes slow starvation, meditation, mental concentration, breathing and other yoga techniques. All of these are designed to solve practical problems people may have, particularly the anguish over heightened insecurity. Chinese could use such a therapy but they always want any theory to be ultimately based on truth, which is Dao. Each school including Confucianism may have its own interpretation of Dao but this word means the ultimate truth in the philosophical sense. It is not good enough for a particular worldview or way of life to be effective in relieving pains; it has to be the truth because only truth can grant it moral legitimacy. So Buddhists would gradually incorporate the idea of Dao in their doctrine. Dao lives in everything, in nature, animals and humans alike. The whole Buddhist practice which is aimed at eliminating human desires—used to be seen as natural and part of Dao—is now interpreted as helping practitioners to reach the real natural state: a pure and desireless state of existence, the true state of Dao. An enlightened Buddhist monk is now called a "high monk with Dao" (得道高僧). Buddhism has redefined what is or is not Dao when it comes to human desires and branded itself as the possessor of truth.

While both schools had great impact on Chinese perceptions of life, neither was able to directly challenge Confucian morals and hierarchy that dominated the secular culture, because by nature both schools are escapism that provides no answer for human morality or social order. As a result Buddhist and Daoist priests having grown up in Confucian families subject to Confucian rule of the state inevitably bring these values to their temples, even if they may not realize it themselves. If we just look at the hierarchical inter-personal relationship and power dynamics within a Buddhist temple, a Daoist temple and a large Confucian family, we wouldn't be able to tell the difference. Over time both Buddhist and Daoist priests incorporated Confucian values such as filial loyalty in their doctrines, either to keep hierarchical order in their organizations or to reduce pressure from increasingly powerful Confucian officials serving the unified Tang court, or both. Filial loyalty thus became universal and an undisputed truth in all religions.

By the time Buddhism reached China centuries of Confucian indoctrination had ingrained a moralistic worldview in the Chinese mind. They quickly latched on the one Buddhist moral doctrine of causation (based on karma), i.e. good deeds now portends better luck later, evil will never go unpunished, though judgment may come in the next life. Outside a few monks Chinese never quite accepted the Buddhist view that everything is a void or nothingness, including life itself. Meditation, fasting and other Buddhist practices were adopted by some to relieve stress and anxiety, but the inquisitive Chinese mind would not stop at easing pain. If these techniques did bring enlightenment, Chinese wanted to know why, or what is the Dao of it. Buddhism changed Chinese perception of human nature, which would eventually reshape Chinese morality, as we shall see in the birth of neo-Confucianism. When the same Buddhism was imported to a primitive and pre-moral Japan, however, it had a different kind of impact.

CHAPTER 8

JAPAN: THE ADVENT OF CIVILIZATION

The Japanese archipelago had always been a recipient of immigrants from the Asian continent, some by way of the Korean peninsular, others possibly by way of Taiwan through island hopping, primarily to flee wars and chaos. This process started before there was a Chinese civilization and continued into historical times. Ancient immigrants came from a number of different cultural and ethnic groups, which makes it hard to define the Japanese ethnicity, not to mention the Chinese ethnicity was itself an amalgamation of all sorts of agricultural and nomadic peoples. Immigrants who called these Japanese islands home lived in various small tribes, each with its own lifestyle depending on their location: farming, fishing, or hunting. Among them the wet-rice farming communities proved to be the decisive force in shaping Japanese civilization, simply because they were the most efficient in food production and supported the greatest concentration of people, and that is where we shall focus our attention. The Nara Plain in present day Kyoto region, for example, though minuscule compared to Northern Plains of China, was large enough to nurse hundreds of thousands of people. Civilization would develop from these crowded farming communities in the interior, not the coastal fishing/pirating tribes.

Chinese contact with Japanese tribal chiefs started after the Han Empire founded four prefectures in Korea (later reduced to two), to which other Korean/Japanese tribes were forced to pay tribute. Subsequent Japanese chiefs would send envoys to the Chinese court, via Korea, and ask for recognition or favor, in exchange for homage. What we know about Japan at this stage largely comes from Chinese court records, which have the following passages:

"The land of Wa (Japan) is warm and mild. In winter as in summer the people live on raw vegetables and go about barefooted. They have houses;

father and mother, elder and younger, sleep separately. They smear their bodies with pink and scarlet, just as the Chinese use powder. They serve food on bamboo and wooden trays, helping themselves with their fingers. When a person dies, they prepare a single coffin, without an outer one. They cover the graves with earth to make a mound. When death occurs, mourning is observed for more than ten days, during which period they do not eat meat. The head mourners wail and lament, while friends sing, dance and drink liquor. When the funeral is over, all members of the family go into the water to cleanse themselves in a bath of purification . . ."

"Whenever they undertake an enterprise or a journey and discussion arises, they bake bones and divine in order to tell whether fortune will be good or bad. First they announce the object of divination, using the same manner of speech as in (Chinese) tortoise shell divination; then they examine the cracks made by fire and tell what is to come to pass."

"In their meetings and in their deportment, there is no distinction between father and son or between men and women. They are fond of liquor. In their worship, men of importance simply clap their hands instead of kneeling or bowing. The people live long, some to one hundred and others to eighty or ninety years. Ordinarily, men of importance have four or five wives; the lesser ones, two or three. Women are not loose in morals or jealous. There is no theft, and litigation is infrequent. In case of violations of the law, the light offender loses his wife and children by confiscation; as for the grave offender, the members of his household and also his kinsmen are exterminated. There are class distinctions among the people, and some men are officials of others. Taxes are collected. There are granaries as well as markets in each province, where necessaries are exchanged under the supervision of the Wa officials . . ."

"When the lowly meet men of importance on the road, they stop and withdraw to the roadside. In conveying messages to them or addressing them, they either squat or kneel, with both hands on the ground. This is the way they show respect."

This was written in third century AD by Chinese officials who were already thoroughly Confucian, which explains the attention paid to burials and family hierarchy, or the lack thereof (Chinese burials must have two coffins, one inside another, for extra protection of the corpse). From these we can see a well defined social hierarchy complete with prostration. Other customs cited here and elsewhere are close to pre-Confucian Chinese culture. Wet-rice farming, barefoot, body painting/tattooing and small stature of the Japanese all resemble coastal peoples of southeast China in early Zhou Dynasty (越). There was no difference in body deportment between father and son, and woman could be head of a household just like man. Incest was not considered a sin, in fact it lasted well into recorded Japanese history, in the royal house no less. Baking of animal bones for divination, lack of a Confucian style or otherwise clearly defined hierarchy in the family, honesty and simplicity (no theft and little litigation), crude penal practice that included immolation for minor infractions and draconian collective punishment—enslavement or extermination of the whole clan—for grave crimes, a long period of official mourning (ten days) for the deceased and a clear master-slave style social hierarchy are all reminiscent of pre-Confucian Chinese.

There are also significant differences between the two. Similar to ancient China when one farming tribe conquered another, the two merged, the losing side would become peasant slaves, remain in their rice fields, only to labor for the winning warriors. A few victories later, a situation would arise where a small number of warriors would be in possession of a relatively large number of slaves, laying the foundation for a pyramid society. Slaves were drafted to fight, enlarging the army, and victory begot victory. In China's case this snowball effect did not stop until it reached empire proportions. In Japan's case it was limited by the mountainous terrain, as well as the absence of horse in its early history. Everyone was on foot. Consequently each warrior clan could only control a limited territory. In china the dominant clan lived in walled towns, and peasant communities spread over a large area. The need for walled towns and moats around them was due to chariots and cavalry. Japanese warriors lived among their peasant slaves. In China peasants did not face their masters on a regular basis. They lived by themselves. Rules like the well-field system made it clear that they were all equal in the eyes of the ruling clan. Over time they developed a sense of proper behavior that was shared by all. They knew what equality was—not equality between free men, but equality between slaves. Japanese peasants had to deal with their masters on a daily basis. One warrior was coming, peasants nearby had to retrieve to the side of the road. The sword was visibly hanging over their heads all the time. In such a life they were less concerned with what other peasants would do. Their minds were preoccupied with hierarchical rules and avoiding the wrath of each of their masters. There was a code of conduct since time immemorial for inter-personal relations between peasants and their warrior masters. Chinese peasants did not have that.

This crude code of conduct was not conceptually the same as Chinese *li*. *Li* was originally a set of rules written for and observed by only the ruling elite. It prescribed moderation, politeness and civility. It was obviously a man made vehicle for civilization. Thus Confucius and his disciples found it convenient to edit many of its rules to reflect a strict hierarchical order, and it was no surprise that both its utility and validity came into dispute in the Warring States period. The Japanese code of conduct between warriors and peasants developed well before there was a written language or the ability to conceive abstract ideas. It was mainly bodily expressions of the master-slave hierarchy. Since it developed naturally out of social conditions for a primitive people, it was not seen as a man made devise serving a higher purpose, but rather part of nature, of subconsciousness. No Japanese would ever question its existence. Unlike Chinese, Japanese had a vivid sense of strict hierarchy built in their common sense at the very outset.

In third to fourth century AD advanced military technology—iron swords, helmets, body armor and horses—made its way to Japan, and the snowball effect of tribal warfare reached its conclusion, as the first Japanese kingdom—the Yamato Kingdom—emerged and gradually took hold in the Nara basin, the largest fertile plain in Japan. Yamato culture was in many ways similar to early Shang China. People were grouped into clans defined by blood ties, real or perceived. Each warrior clan worshiped a deity, called kami (神), who was not an omnipotent god but merely a symbol of clan prowess. In the very beginning kami were mostly sacred animals. Later on the most prominent deceased clan chief who had led the clan into victories and conquests in the past was often chosen as the clan kami. If one clan lost a battle to another, people would think that their kami lost to the other kami. This tradition of kami worship continued into the Yamato period. Having achieved hegemony in much of Japan, and with increased direct contact with China in the last half of sixth century, however, the king's scope of vision and cultural awareness greatly expanded. His clan kami now took the form of Sun Goddess, a female deity whose parents created the islands of Japan out of nothing, and thus gave her descendents the exclusive right to rule the entire kingdom. Early Shang kings in China worshiped similar gods, many of whom were deceased kings, who would exclusively bless the king's clan. But later Shang kings abandoned all worship and by Zhou Dynasty the state ideology was completely revamped to the deity of Heaven, who was not supposed to be partial to any clan. Japanese kami worship survived, because the royal house never obtained total dominance over the rest of Japan and the imperial clan deity, the Sun Goddess, was necessary for the crown. Worship of this clan deity was called Shinto, literally kami Dao, or the Way of deity.

Just like Shang China the Yamato king's clan was militarily the most powerful. Other chieftains were granted nobility titles according to the strength of their respective clan. Professional groups like metal workers were also grouped in such a fashion. In short, the clan was the way early Chinese and Japanese organized themselves. In China the overthrow of Shang changed everything. Zhou rulers implemented the well-field system where individual peasant families were directly accountable to the state, breaking up the clan structure. By Confucius' time the clan system totally disappeared. Japan did not have limitless arable land, or the incentive to break up large families, so the clan structure survived. In and around the capital where the Yamato king ruled, for instance, there were several other prominent clans besides the king's. Although their chiefs had blood ties to the king through marriages, they would keep their own clan kami, their own land properties and peasant slaves from which they could recruit soldiers, and therefore retained a certain degree of independence. Moreover, the mountainous terrain in Japan gave remote clans far from the king's capital a natural defense that was not easy to breach under primitive conditions, making it impossible for the king's army to sweep through the entire Japanese archipelago.

Events surrounding the Yamato royal family, as recorded in Japanese historical records compiled much later, suggest a people still quite primitive and judged by then Chinese standards, total savages. Incest was rampant. The royal clan history was full of stories of murder, between brothers, uncles and other relatives in connection with succession and power struggles, and these were often done at a fit of rage, with no pretexts, no plots, no intrigues, and no cover-ups afterwards. If the king had his eye on a girl from an aristocratic family, he would send gifts and ask for her hand; and if rejected, he would kill her entire clan and then still take her in, and later make her queen.

In late sixth century the Chinese Empire was finally reunited. Shortly thereafter the Japanese court started sending envoys to the Tang court, after a long period of interruption due to political chaos in Korea and China. This was the first time Japanese diplomats were able to visit the Tang Empire at its most splendid, and see a well ordered, well developed and very refined culture in a land of immense proportions, a world that wildly exceeded their imaginations. Wide, straight roads and canals linked all major cities and ports; grand scale Buddhist temples and super-sized statues were everywhere; nobles were dressed in silk with exquisite embroidery and traveled in horse carriages with comfort and style; the capital city had a huge population, its streets swarmed with people—merchants, blacksmiths, artisans, courtesans, travelers, bureaucrats, monks, other urbanites—of not just Han Chinese, but many other ethnic groups including Huns, Turks and various other northern nomads; one could find restaurants, tea houses and all kinds of merchandise from food, clothing to shields and swords of superb quality; people enjoyed fashion (many wore hats), literature and music; they were polite, courteous and open-minded; the rich and powerful lived in mansions behind enclosed walls and gates, with large courtyards and gardens, multiple two-story high halls, polished stone steps and roofed corridors that linked all houses; the imperial palace was decorated with paintings and gold-inlaid furniture, its many gates, guards and rituals evinced majesty and solemnity; a complex and effective bureaucracy reached all local communities of the empire, supported by an elaborate revenue system, and a detailed legal code with thousands of articles, provisions and clauses. For visitors from Japan, where there were no such thing as shoes and everyone including the king went barefooted, clothes were just pieces of cloth, houses were small pits with dried grass stretched over wood poles and had no doors, and there were no written language, no music, no paintings, no calendar, no medicine, the Chinese experience must have been overwhelming. It was literally taking someone from the stone-age and putting them in the center of a highly developed civilization. To say they were shocked and awed would be an understatement.

Outflow of Chinese culture to Japan had been a trickle up to this point, delayed and filtered by various tribes and kingdoms in Korea, but with establishment of direct diplomatic relations and sea routes between China and Japan in early seventh century, it became a torrent. The size of Japanese delegations went from dozens to hundreds of people, with the specific goal of learning Chinese language, customs, statecraft, religion, technology, everything. Some stayed years and decades before going back—a few of them later became architects of sweeping reform. Chinese scholars of Confucianism and Buddhism were invited to Japan. Confucian and Buddhist classics arrived by the shipload. Within a few decades, more than a thousand years worth of Chinese and Indian cultural and intellectual development was presented to the Japanese, who were still in a primitive stage of their own cultural development. The question is: how much were they able to absorb?

An administrative system modeled after the Tang Empire was set up in Japan. In reality, however, Japanese were really applying Confucian rules developed and refined over a millennium of changing Chinese realities to a primitive society that culturally and politically resembled pre-Confucian China. The Chinese system was based on the idea that the emperor owned all-under-heaven, which he sent magistrates to govern on his behalf. The Japanese king did not own all of Japan; he was merely the largest of all land and slave owners—he did not even own the entire capital area. What he sought was more land at the expense of other chiefs all over the kingdom, who would usually donate part of their land holdings to him, either to curry favor or to stave off hostility. The king then sent governors and supervisors to manage these imperial properties; often the local chief himself was appointed to the position. As a result, although on paper the Japanese political system looked like a copy of the Chinese empire, with positions from high ministers to local governors carrying similar titles and ranking structure, many of these officials were actually tribal chieftains. Japan was still largely a tribal society, though each tribe was ranked in a vertical hierarchy, as reflected in the nobility title of its chief.

Of the three main intellectual forces of China, namely Confucianism, Buddhism and Daoism, Buddhism was by far the most enthusiastic in proselytizing, Confucianism was indispensable in state building, while Daoism was not part of state doctrine, although by then the three could not be completely separated as basic Confucian tenants and the concept of Dao (synonymous to truth) were baked into Chinese Buddhism. As a result what the Japanese received was a two-in-one mixture of Buddhism and Confucianism. The imperial house accepted the idea that Confucianism and Buddhism were different pieces of the same coherent system, totally oblivious to the history of these schools in China. One Korean king who sent Buddhist classics to Japan in sixth century told the Japanese that the Duke of Zhou and Confucius both knew about Buddhism and agreed with its teachings, but the Duke of Zhou actually predated Buddha by several centuries. It is no wonder that Confucianism and Buddhism were mingled, as is shown by prince Shotoku's seventeen article injunction dated to seventh century:

1. Harmony is to be valued, and contentiousness avoided. All men are inclined to partisanship and few are truly discerning. Hence there are some who disobey their lords and fathers or who maintain feuds with the neighboring villages. But when those above are harmonious and those below are conciliatory and there is concord in the discussion of all matter, the disposition of affairs comes about naturally. Then what is there that cannot be accomplished?

2. Sincerely reverence the Three Treasures. The Buddha, the Law, and the religious orders are the final refuge of all beings and the supreme objects of reverence in all countries . . .
3. When you receive the imperial commands, fail not scrupulously to obey them. The ruler is Heaven, the official is Earth. Heaven overspreads, and Earth upbears . . .
4. The ministers and functionaries should make *li* their leading principle, for the leading principle in governing the people consists in *li*. If the superiors do not behave with *li*, the inferiors are disorderly; if inferiors are wanting in proper behavior, there must necessarily be offenses. Therefore it is that when ruler and official behave with *li*, the distinctions of rank are not confused; when the people behave with *li*, the governance of the state proceeds of itself.
5. Ceasing from gluttony and abandoning covetous desire, deal impartially with the suits which are submitted to you . . .
6. Chastise that which is evil and encourage that which is good. This was the excellent rule of antiquity. Conceal not, therefore, the good qualities of others, and fail not to correct that which is wrong when you see it . . .
7. Let every man have his own charge, and let not the spheres of duty be confused . . .
8. Let the ministers and functionaries attend the court early in the morning, and retire late . . .
9. Trustworthiness is the foundation of right . . .
10. Let us cease from wrath, and refrain from angry looks. Nor let us be resentful when others differ from us. For all men have hearts, and each heart has its own leanings. Their right is our wrong, and our right is their wrong. We are not unquestionably sages, nor are they unquestionably fools. Both of us are simply ordinary men. How can any one lay down a rule by which to distinguish right from wrong? For we are all, one with another, wise and foolish, like a ring which has no end. Therefore, although others give way to anger, let us on the contrary dread our own faults, and though we alone may be in the right, let us follow the multitude and act like them.
11. Give clear appreciation to merit and demerit, and deal out to each its sure reward or punishment . . .
12. Let not the provincial authorities or the Kuni no Miyatsuko levy exaction on the people. In a country there are not two rulers; the people have not two masters. The sovereign is the master of the people of the whole country. The officials to whom he gives charge

are all his servants. How can they, as well as the government, presume to levy taxes on the people?
13. Let all persons entrusted with office attend equally to their functions . . .
14. Ye ministers and functionaries! Be not envious. For if we envy others, they in turn will envy us. The evils of envy know no limit . . .
15. To turn away from that which is private and to set our faces towards that which is public—this is the path of a minister. Now if a man is influenced by private motives, he will assuredly fail to act harmoniously with others. If he fails to act harmoniously with others, he will assuredly sacrifice the public interest to his private feelings. When resentment arises, it interferes with order, and is subversive of law. Therefore in the first clause it was said that superiors and inferiors should agree together. The purport is the same as this.
16. Let the people be employed in forced labor at seasonable times (when it does not interfere with farm work) . . .
17. Matters should not be decided by one person alone . . .

The prince was trying to move one step closer to Chinese civilization by outlining the principles of governance, for the first time in Japanese history. Though clearly a learned man, his understanding of the Chinese system shown in these seventeen articles was skewed by Buddhist ideas. In China Buddhism was never part of the official ideology, therefore irrelevant in state building or social order. Confucianism defined moral values, social hierarchy and political philosophy. When prince Shotoku incorporated so much Buddhist values in this political document, called by some the first Japanese constitution, it became an incoherent set of rules.

Article 10 reflects the Buddhist worldview that since everything in this world is meaningless, so are all views of right and wrong, and it is stupid to fight for what you believe is right, what is important is just to get along—principle is nothing, congeniality is everything. That is blasphemy to Confucianism, the most important part of which is its moral ideology, which is to be guarded by the state with the utmost fervor, against all competing views. All the rules that make the society work, from government organization to legal code to rules of propriety, are derived from this moral core. It is as unchallengeable as self-evident truth, more so than any of its manifestations such as legal codes, more so than even the royal family. Emperors and dynasties come and go, laws and rules can be changed from time to time, but Confucian morality stays. If this can be challenged then the entire political system immediately loses foundation and legitimacy. If every view is as good as the next, and I do not accept the emperor as my ruler, then why should I obey him? If I can spread my idea and convince a significant number, the system would be in danger—Confucianism was specifically devised to prevent that danger.

It is Buddhist temperament, not Buddhist philosophy (transmigration, suffering, karma, etc.), that permeates this document. There is a spirit of consultation, of curtailing one's anger, resentment and envy. Harmony is exalted in article one, before anything else. Even the cornerstone of Confucian values, filial loyalty, is interpreted as a way to achieve harmony. Confucian rules are imported, but not the principles or reasoning behind these rules—an understanding of human nature based on observation and an interpretation of Dao, and moral values congenial to that understanding of nature's laws. Harmony becomes the ultimate objective, the de facto principle behind all these imported and incomprehensible Confucian and Buddhist rules, which is why Japanese call themselves the people of "Great Harmony" (大和). But harmony is a state of human relations, a desirable one of course, not a principle in and of itself. It does not say how disputes ought to be resolved, or how people should live their lives. It is just a hope, a wish, a promise.

Confucianism starts with the assumption that the ruler owns all lives and property in his domain. The nature of social hierarchy, rites and rituals, relationship between ruler and subjects, father and son, superior and inferior, the concepts of public and private, right and wrong, are all dependent on this idea of ownership, without which the entire system falls apart. In China a small fraction of all arable land was temporarily given to officials for them to collect rent as stipend. In Japan each clan chief had his own private estate, and the imperial clan was just like any other clan except that it owned more private estates. This meant that clan chiefs, who often doubled as government officials, played a different role from that of Chinese magistrates. They often collected rents not for the crown but for themselves. An orthodox Confucian ruler would see the main problem of this picture as being that rents collected did not go to the imperial coffer, not the exaction itself, although if done excessively it would also be an issue. Moreover no reason was ever given for tax collection. A Chinese emperor collected rents because he owned everything and that was simply his right. The Japanese royal house never owned the entire kingdom. They were copying Chinese measures without understanding the rationale behind them, or even realizing that there was a rationale at all.

In short this seventeen article injunction has serious philosophical contradictions. On the one hand it admonishes officials to obey their ruler unconditionally (article 3 & 12), on the other it says matters should not be decided by one person alone (article 17). Nothing is proposed in the way of a decision making process or who in what position should have what power. On the one hand there is a clear hierarchy that must be followed, father over son, ruler over minister, superior over inferior. Even the Heaven and Earth analogy is used to justify it (article 3). There is good and evil and one should not fail to correct a wrong when one sees it (article 6). That sounds like a moral principle not to be violated. On the other hand, there is the Buddhist view that there is no right or wrong, people should be allowed to disagree, and we should all curb our anger, greed and envy, and simply get through this life amiably.

The inability to perceive these conflicts is indicative of the state of the Japanese mind. At the time when they had access of a written language, an example of a civilized and prosperous empire to follow, and were contemplating for the first time the formation of a state, they were unable to take an intellectual approach, coming to an understanding on a grand scheme of things first, and then devising rules to implement or uphold values derived from that understanding; instead they merely borrowed some visible elements of the Chinese civilization, and used them to achieve immediate and tangible purposes, such as to gain more power, wealth and order (for the ruler), more peace, harmony and less bloodshed, and the appearance of a more civilized culture. It is not that they took stock of the Chinese civilization as a whole, and then decided which part to adopt or reject, but rather that only the most visible parts of that civilization, such as concrete rules, legal codes, administrative procedures, court customs, rites and rituals, religious practices, and so forth were comprehensible to their limited intellectual capacity. In adherence to these forms they were going to outdo Chinese, without ever attaching any moral significance or reasoning to them.

Starting from the second half of the seventh century, the imperial court had an increasingly firm grip on power, which enabled a wholesale replication of all things Chinese, from a capital city designed and built on the Chinese model, a strong centralized administrative bureaucracy, a detailed legal code that governs every human behavior and human emotions, a finely graded vertical social hierarchy, to court rituals, rites of propriety, music, architecture, costumes and makeup. Some old traditions were abandoned, such as live burials of servants. All of a sudden there was only one correct way to do everything, and it could be found somewhere in the official documents of the court, written in Chinese that none but a few learned scholars could read.

The following four centuries, from eighth to eleventh, would see the gradual adaptation of these Chinese rules by the court. For instance filial loyalty was adopted in the legal code, and filial sons were rewarded by the state. The Japanese approach was straightforward. By default an attempt was made to apply all Chinese rules on the book to any given situation, but if reality prevented it from being carried out, the attempt was abandoned with no prejudice, and people accepted it calmly and moved on. There was never conviction behind these attempts beyond the immediate interests of the parties. Because Japanese imperial power even at its strongest point was not nearly as absolute as that of China, many of these rules ended up being ignored or distorted, resulting in situations that would appall Chinese Confucians, but hardly raised any eyebrows in Japan.

In late seventh and early eighth century, when imperial power was at its height, the new Chinese style laws were implemented in most of Japan (not including the northeast which was still barbarian territory). Traditionally clans fought over land and resources, peasants were dependent on their local clan for work and survival, and the royal house was just the biggest of all clans. Kings were able to impose rent or tribute on many of these clans, particularly the weaker ones, but the basic social structure did not change. Now the society was to be reorganized. All land and peasants were to be registered and put under imperial control, and local chiefs were appointed imperial officials charged with collecting rents for the court. Every peasant man was assigned an equal amount of land, so was every woman (two thirds of a man's share), and every family slave (one third of a man's share), following Chinese practice. Upon his or her death land was returned to the court. For the duration of their tenure, peasants were required to pay a certain amount of rice, cloth and other local produce every year, in addition to unpaid labor. Every fifty households were to provide a soldier. Every official household was to provide a daughter (apparently peasant girls were not good enough for the court) as a servant for the court's pleasure. Officials were assigned different grades of nobility, and given three types of land holdings. One was tax free and intended as a stipend, but had to be returned when the person relinquished his position. The other two were taxable, of which one type could not be sold or inherited, the other could be inherited for anywhere between two and four generations depending on the rank of the person. Land holdings of Shinto shrines and Buddhist temples were private and tax free. These rules are a mixture of Chinese practices and Japanese convention, often at odds with each other in conception. In Zhou Dynasty China land was given by the king to the nobility (princes), which became their private properties, or state-families. Within each state the prince owned everything. By Tang Dynasty the emperor owned everyone and everything under heaven. Land given to high ministers was a form of stipend. Eighth century Japan was culturally at the stage of Shang China, essentially a confederation of tribes, but it copied rules from the highly centralized totalitarian Tang regime. Thus three forms of land holdings coexisted in the Japanese system, ranging from fully owned private property to temporary stipend. It was against Confucianism for an official to have permanent private property. In this confused state of affairs Japanese could not develop a consistent rationale for taxation. The royal house basically taxed whoever and however much they could, decided by their military muscle, which was subject to change from one king to the next.

In the long line of imperial succession there were bound to be some weak rulers, and the high minister could potentially seize power in such cases. What made the imperial system sustainable in China for hundreds of years at a time with remarkable stability was the fact that Chinese believed in the principle behind the rules, namely that the ruler owned everything, and ministers were just his servants. Japanese, however, did not realize that there was such a principle, since it was not in the Tang code or any other official document. Without a principle or rationale the rules then became negotiable between the court and high ministers. Since ninth century ministers who managed to marry their daughters into the royal house started to change or distort many of these rules. Their land holdings previously given as a form of stipend gradually became inheritable private property. One particular clan, the Fujiwara's, was dominant in tenth and eleventh century, to the extent that for many consecutive generations the Fujiwara clan chief was the de facto ruler of Japan. He could kill an emperor and install another almost at will. He completely revamped the imperial bureaucracy so that not only all the important offices were occupied by his servants, but laws were made and handed out from his office, not the emperor's residence. The royal household was totally cut out of the process, effectively put under house arrest much of the time, and always lived in fear. In the end this predicament was broken when the Fujiwara clan was at one of its weakest moments, headed by two brothers who were positively senile. Nevertheless by then a system was entrenched such that all the officials actually worked for the Fujiwara house, not the emperor. The emperor then came up with a trick, called *insei*, or "cloister government", whereby he deliberately retired from the throne, enthroned his underage son, and moved out of the imperial palace, into a Buddhist temple, where he gathered supporters and established another set of bureaucracy to bypass the one in Fujiwara's control, thus wrestled power away from the high minister. This practice was so common that the period from late eleventh to late twelfth century is called the *insei* period. And when the retired emperors gained real power, they joined in the practice of amassing their own private estates throughout the land.

This whole situation would have made any Chinese Confucian cringe. The emperor has to retire into a temple in order to gain real power? Every now and then in Chinese history there would be a high minister taking de facto rule of the empire over the will of the sovereign. But everyone would immediately recognize that the minister in question was committing the most heinous crime possible, and be constantly looking for opportunities to defeat him and return power to its rightful owner. By Confucian teaching they were supposed to defend the rights of the absolute ruler (for he owns everything) against any usurpation. It would weigh on their conscience not having the courage to act. Thus the minister in power could not afford even a moment of vulnerability, and usually by his death at the latest his entire family and those who followed him were exterminated with extreme prejudice. The only forceful change of power sanctioned by Confucianism is when a ruler is deemed cruel and erratic, therefore losing the mandate of Heaven, in which case he not only can, but ought to be replaced. Under this Confucian logic the pressure is high for a usurper or a would-be usurper to either give up the attempt or go all the way: kill the sovereign, start a new dynasty and declare the last one immoral. Half way measures like gaining power at the expense of the ruler without declaring a moral imperative are not sanctioned. This explains the high number of attempts in Chinese history at dynastic change, some of them were successful (a total of more than thirty dynasties in recorded history) but most were not. Moreover, the idea of the royal house amassing private property is simply incomprehensible in China. Everything under heaven is the ruler's private property; it does not make sense for him to set up private estates.

Japanese had no idea of these Confucian principles. Hence the nature of rulership was never clearly defined, and unlike China, hereditariness of the imperial bloodline was justified by Shinto (the legend of Sun Goddess). The royal house would always be the royal house, with or without power. Who controlled what and the nature of ownership were determined by ever changing political reality. Japanese politics was a pure power struggle with no principles or any sense of right or wrong. When the Fujiwara's effectively treated the imperial household like puppets for over a century, it was not only accepted but taken as a norm. When an emperor eventually wrestled power away from the Fujiwara's by going into retirement, he did not purge them as if he was enraged for being wronged for so long, instead he merely pushed them aside from positions of influence and let them be. In such a culture the Fujiwara's had little reason to change dynasty when they could. They could rule comfortably for generations like real hereditary rulers without anyone raising an issue, pointing fingers or plotting their downfall behind their back, and when they finally lost power they were able to withdraw peacefully into the background. Whatever happened was accepted as fair game with no recrimination. Had they attempted a dynastic change, however, they would have offended a long standing Shinto belief and potentially faced opposition. This explains continuity of the Japanese imperial line. In reality the two systems were not at all the same. The Chinese system is based on a set of demanding moral principles (ownership, absolute power, but also mercy, commiseration and kindness) which are impossible to be followed by a single bloodline forever, and which also make it indefensible to separate the ruler—the owner—from real power, thus exacerbating the tension between moral ideals and reality, for absolute power corrupts absolutely. The emperor has to have absolute control, otherwise it is un-Confucian, and he also must be a merciful ruler, otherwise it is still un-Confucian. The Japanese version, on the other hand, is the result of an attempt to directly apply rules of the Chinese system without comprehension of the ideas behind them. Thus it seriously deviated from a prescribed course without detection. Eventually it turned out to be an ad-hoc system of patchworks with no rationale, which can therefore adapt to any situation, take any shape or form, and still be seen as perfectly legitimate. The fact that the royal house was amassing private estates shows that tribal mentality remained intact by five centuries of Confucian style administration.

In addition to tribal heritage, political and social conditions also affected Japanese adaptation of Chinese culture. For a Chinese ruler Confucianism mandated a moral purpose to his ruling, which was to bring civilization to his subjects. Newly conquered barbarians must learn to follow rules of propriety and hierarchy, and change their violent ways. Others already familiar with the rules must internalize them into a conviction, so that they did not need to be enforced under pain of harsh penalties. The scholar-officials were not just tax collectors and law enforcement, more importantly they were indoctrinators sent by the emperor to all corners of the empire to set examples of mercy, concern and devotion to parents and ruler. Chinese culture was actively maintained by the scholar-official class. Such a class never had a chance to fully develop in Japan. For much of the time the emperor was not even the real ruler; sometimes he could not control even his own personal matters, such as whom to marry. The imperial court was often a battleground for different factions. Provincial governors owed their loyalty to the court nobles who appointed them. Their primary concern was to fight for the interest of their faction, and they were no scholars. While the imported legal code contained basic Confucian rules such as servile loyalty, filial loyalty and a vertical hierarchy, little more of Chinese culture reached beyond the capital.

Over time a stark cultural divide emerged between the capital and rest of Japan. Taxes collected all over the country constantly flowed into the capital, sustaining a civil and leisurely lifestyle for the nobility, which evolves around poetry, literature, music, romance, ceremonies (*li*) and Buddhist sermons. Some of the highest ranking nobles began to develop feelings of commiseration. They grew sentimental over loss of friendship and love. They mourned misfortunes and mental torment of those close to them. Although insecurity (even at the highest level) and Buddhist denial of life's moral significance prevented them from articulating these feelings in moral terms, they were moving closer to Chinese moral sensitivity, aided by increasing volumes of Chinese literature from the Tang Empire.

None of their culture survived the arduous transportation outside the capital, over narrow, muddy and winding roads through the mountains. Here there was a much heightened sense of insecurity. Native traditions of private land ownership did not sit well with imported Confucian legal code. Officials having attached themselves to one faction or another were vulnerable to power struggles above them. The farming population were divided into many classes in a vertical hierarchy: those who managed estates for court nobles, those who had rice paddies to their name, those who worked for others but was entitled to a stable share of the yield, those who could be bought and sold, etc., and no one at any position in this hierarchy felt safe, because everything was ultimately subject to power shifts in the capital, far beyond their control. This insecurity eventually led to the rise of the warriors, who chose to take matters in their own hands, and the leisurely culture and budding moral sensitivity died with the power of nobility in the capital.

To an outside visitor of the Japanese capital in these three or four centuries (the Heian Period), Japan may very well look like a mini version of China. Its capital was built on the Chinese model: layout of streets, position of the imperial palace, cordoning of different groups of residents, architecture—everything was a duplicate, only on a smaller scale. Its legal code, from what we can tell, was largely a copy of the Tang Code. Its political structure was similarly fashioned, with power radiating from the center, and each official being granted one of some forty different grades of titles. Court rituals, from customs, body language, to form of address, tone of voice, facial expression, and procedures, were taken from the Book of Rites and followed with such dedication and meticulousness they put the Chinese court to shame. Buddhist temples were everywhere, like in China, and they largely belonged to the same sects found in China, reading the same religious texts translated from Indian to Chinese. Currency was directly imported from China—copper coins. Other technologies, such as iron metallurgy, farming tools towed by oxen, large irrigation systems and other crafts were also learned from the continent, though Japanese quickly managed to produce paper of a higher quality than their teachers. The Japanese written language, which was developed in the ninth century, was essentially a set of pronunciation keys to the Chinese language, a Chinese dialect of sorts, which is why Japanese call their own written language the "fake names" (假名), and Chinese characters "true names" (真名).

Looks can be deceiving. Japanese of seventh to twelfth century AD can be better compared to Shang Chinese in some ways, early Zhou Chinese in other ways. They were pre-moral. They just stepped out of barbarism and abandoned some of the atrocious customs like live human sacrifice. They adopted rules of propriety and hierarchy in the ruling elite. To Zhou Chinese these rules were devised as a practical measure to keep masters from fighting and killing each other over trivial matters, thus stabilizing and solidifying a hereditary ruling class. That was also how they were understood by the Japanese court. Its copying of contemporary Tang Empire can be summed up as: a centralized administrative system complete with governors and magistrates was imported and imposed on a Japanese reality still in the age of tribalism. Tribal chiefs were assigned titles of governor but their mentality did not change. The emperor did not see himself as owner of all Japan but merely the highest ranking chief. Thus the imported political system could not possibly be justified by Japanese conceptions of power and ownership. These new rules would be distorted, some discarded. Even those that were kept intact often did not serve the same purpose as in China.

As Chinese civilization was imported and taken by Japanese as an integrated whole, they were unaware of the history of intellectual conflicts between its two main parts, Confucianism and Buddhism. Their primitive state of social and intellectual development did not afford a full comprehension of morality. As a result Buddhism started as part of the official doctrine at the outset and became a permanent fixture of the Japanese scene, and the Buddhist view that everything in this world of dust including morality is ultimately meaningless was fully absorbed before any other idea. The impact of this view on a pre-moral people can hardly be overestimated. It takes a moral awakening to appreciate the value of life and distain senseless violence, a major intellectual development for savages that all of human ancestors once were, a mental step that can not be replaced by rules enforcing a semblance of civility. The Buddhist worldview played a key role in thwarting such a development in Japan.

Chapter 9

ZEN, EN AND THE SECOND SYNTHESIS: NEO-CONFUCIANISM

Chinese thinking had been stagnant for a millennium since the end of Warring States period in third century BC and canonization of Confucianism as the only official ideology in the subsequent Han Dynasty. No debates were allowed. All deviating views were banned. For the intellectually curious political entrepreneur, Buddhism presented the only available alternative. Since Buddhism does not have a centralized organization like the Roman Church or a single scripture like the Bible, instead there are hundreds of Buddhist texts written by various Indian Buddhists over time, and the meaning of key words can be distorted or lost in translation, it provided a great opportunity for anyone with intellectual ambition to interpret it in new ways. As there was no room to maneuver within the Confucian framework, for a time the most active Chinese thinkers flocked into the fold of Buddhism. With the help of several Tang emperors, the number of Buddhist sects mushroomed, each prescribing a particular way to achieve enlightenment. Some focused on discipline: in addition to the standard no killing, no theft, no sex, no lies, no alcohol and no meat (Chinese Buddhists all became vegetarians by decree of a devout Buddhist king, while earlier they would eat anything they could beg), there was also a set of strict rules much more demanding than can be found in many modern military forces. Some focused on concentration of the mind: how to stand still or sit still for a long time, breathing techniques, how to battle "impure" thoughts, anxiety and other emotions. Some focused on philanthropy, believing that good deeds will wash away sins committed earlier or in previous lives. Some focused on spreading the Buddhist idea, wandering all over the world begging for a living. Some believed that only the very gifted can ever become enlightened. Some believed with enough effort everyone can be

Buddha. One sect believed that just by repeatedly calling the Buddha's name one can reach the "pure land", where the Buddha lives, a world that is peaceful, happy, clean, and without any trace of private interest.

What the Confucianized Chinese mind was most interested in was to what extend human desires could be reduced and how. The debate between a benevolent human nature proposed by Mencius and a malignant one proposed by Xun was never settled. Meanwhile what was previously unimaginable was demonstrated by Buddhist monks, who showed no desires for power, fame, wealth, women, wine, or anything else lay folks spent all their energy chasing after. Confucianism was based on the understanding of human nature that everyone would seek to maximize his own material interest, which is why post-natal training such as filial loyalty is needed to keep that tendency in check. Was human nature misunderstood? Or had Buddhism found a better way to shape human character than Confucian indoctrination? What is the ultimate truth, or Dao, of human nature?

With a new found interest in human nature Chinese intellectual quest turned from the material world to the human heart. The truth, it appeared, is not out there, but in here. By seventh century a new Buddhist sect emerged, carrying this search to its logical conclusion. It made the audacious claim that no religious texts, or sutras, are necessary or important to enlightenment. The various Buddhist activities such as philanthropy, begging and recitation are all missing the point. To be enlightened is to find one's true nature before it was contaminated by corruptions of the world. In order to do that one has to cleanse his mind of everything he has learned in this world, and return to a pristine state of purity, which can not be described in words, but has to be experienced by each individual to know what it is. This true nature of the human being is none other than Buddha, in other words there is a Buddha in every one of us, but we can not find it by learning, reading books, or reason. Yet if someone becomes so enlightened, often through a sudden revelation or turning of the mind (顿悟, pronounced satori in Japanese), he will be overwhelmed with emotions of elation and ecstasy. Enlightenment comes in the form of a sudden glimpse of the truth, often after arduous efforts to liberate the mind from all rational activities. It is hard to achieve, though potentially achievable by everyone, and the best hope is with those who live their lives in a special way professed by the new school, Zen (禅).

Zen was originally a way of meditation that Buddhism adopted from earlier Indian Yoga practices. A typical body position would be to sit on a flat surface, bend both legs inward, put left foot on right thigh, right foot on left thigh, right hand on left foot, and left hand in the palm of right hand. The body is so positioned for the practitioner to relax and sit still for a long time. After settling down, he then attempts to cleanse his mind of all unwanted thoughts. The body may feel various kinds of discomfort, such as hunger, cold, or pain, particularly after maintaining the same position for hours. These "thoughts" need to be blocked; the body must be impervious to physical disturbance. The mind may also wander around, recollecting memories of past and present, arousing emotions of one kind or another. These also need to be extinguished. The mind must concentrate on one thing, which may vary from one Buddhist sect to another, such as the Buddha, the birth-death-rebirth life cycle, the pure land, etc. Breathing techniques are often incorporated in the excise to help concentration. The goal is to follow a similar thought process by which the Buddha found enlightenment under a tree.

What Buddha found after such meditation was the Four Noble Truths, transmigration, and related ideas all recorded in the sutras. For Buddhists in the past the search for truth was done by Buddha and everyone else just needed to follow his teachings. But for the Zen sect even the most sacred teachings in the texts are not absolute truth. Instead truth is not expressible; it is a state of mind that has to be experienced. The whole purpose of meditation, and indeed life itself, is to find that truth which lies deep in our hearts, buried under secular knowledge and emotions acquired after birth. True nature of the human spirit is born with every one of us, only that we have lost touch with it because we have been altered by the man made rules of this world, rules that tell us right and wrong, good and bad. Our actions follow our emotions, our emotions follow our value judgments, and our values are based on false premises—social conventions. In order to find truth, we need to abandon everything we learned in this world, which is exactly what Buddhism preaches, and it is in perfect symphony with Daoism, as it should be, because there can be only one truth. The difference between Daoism and Buddhism, seen in this light, is only in the ways to attain that truth. While Daoists had traditionally looked outside into the natural world, Buddhists looked inside into the human heart. To Indians Buddhism may have been a mental exercise to deliver the individual from otherwise inescapable suffering, to Chinese Zen monks it is an effort to find truth. And if one can become a Buddha by finding enlightenment, as is taught by Great Vehicle Buddhism, then Buddha must live in the heart of every human being, where truth must ultimately reside.

This school of Buddhist thought began as early as the fourth century. Although at the time it was just one of many schools, its simplicity and intellectual superiority would set it apart from all others. Few Buddhist monks could even hope to understand the meaning of the religious texts, or the sutras, which were essentially an arduous attempt by ancient Indians at explaining human psychology. Over time many sects became dogmatic—a natural reaction to something you revere but do not understand. The idea that Buddha lives in our hearts, and to find Buddha is the same as finding true human nature, which is a manifestation of Dao, on the other hand, was easily comprehensible to not just Buddhists but all Chinese.

Once the definition of truth is known, namely the true human nature in one's heart waiting to be discovered, Buddhist texts naturally lose much of their significance, since the purpose of these words are simply to help disciples grasp the truth. What is important then is how to find it through meditation. By seventh century this school of thought finally matured into the Zen sect, which declared that the various religious texts are not only unimportant but really a hindrance to real enlightenment, because they tend to confuse rather than enlighten, distract rather than focus. The whole religious practice is to center on meditation and purity of the mind, and the goal is to achieve a sudden enlightenment that even Zen masters are at a loss of words to describe.

What is called a sudden enlightenment is something akin to the following metal process. When you first enter a Zen monastery as a young man, you bring with you knowledge and emotions of this world. You were brought up with Confucian family values, aspiring to be a high minister. Somewhere along the way you hit a snag. Your plans did not pan out. You may resent your parents for not giving you a good enough education or opportunity. Then you may feel guilty about that resentment. You may have become a monk to escape harsh reality at home, or to learn something profound and acquire wisdom, or to use it as a stepping stone for your secular ambitions. Whatever your circumstance is, as a young man you are emotionally charged. If your goal is to learn Buddhism, you may treat it as if you are learning Confucianism, look for sacred texts equivalent to the five classics to read, and as you flip over the pages you know where you stand in that endeavor, in short you want to see progress everyday. When there is nothing to read and you are told to sit there meditating all day, you get frustrated as months and years pass without seemingly getting any closer. You think about what you might have otherwise done had you not left home. Between your secular thoughts, ambitions, youthful energy and hormones, you find it hard enough just to sit still for long, much less concentrate.

The first thing you need to do is to calm down. You can reflect on your mental activity and always ask yourself: what am I thinking right now? Put yourself in the position of a third party observer. Once you are conscious about your thoughts, you can quantify them. One thought comes into your mind, stays there for a while, and then another thought comes into focus, replacing the former. As you become increasingly aware of your thoughts, you can try to seize the moment when one thought just exited and the next has yet to fully arrive. If you do you will find your mind in a void, a split second when you are not thinking about anything. Another technique to bring about this state of mind is to stare at a wall. Whenever your mind wanders off on something you can bring it back by refocusing your eyes on the wall in front of you. But you are not studying textural details of the wall. The wall is a nothing that helps you focus on the void.

Through months of continuous practice you may be able to stay in this void for longer and longer periods so that you can have a feel in its duration. And it feels great. The secular world is a harsh one to live in. Growing up involves trauma. Living in the society requires such an arduous effort and diligence because every human relationship is regulated even inside the family, and one can not afford to make mistakes. You may resent a younger monk for not showing you enough respect or regret that you did not win favor from your master. You may hate the person who did not pay back your kindness or hate yourself for not paying back favors to others. The emotions that are generated by every triviality of life are endless. Once you are in that void, however, you are free of all these considerations and by comparison you realize that all the emotions you used to have were just a burden. Now you feel as light as a feather, because at this moment you are no longer concerned with rules, morals, and emotions. You realize that for your entire life you have been laboring under the exacting rules of society, for a meaningless purpose on which you staked your emotions, your strong moral conviction and your entire being.

From this point on you will look at the secular world in a completely different light. The position of a high minister, modeled after Confucius' own career, loses its appeal, as does every other career path you have imagined yourself in. In a Confucian society no one is free of serious worries, because everyone is a slave to higher ups. Within every family the father is always a despotic figure who has to be carefully served. The stress that Confucian rules place on each individual is overwhelming. When you have dismissed all of that as man made rules and morals that do not reflect true human nature, you are able to look at the gains and losses that people constantly fight over as utterly meaningless, as if they are playing a silly game that they themselves invented. Not only have you attained a calmness of the mind, but a feeling of elation ensues, and you have never felt so free. When you see other people still fighting over wealth and power, you feel so lucky that you are above the fray and your mind is totally at peace.

With this first step of discarding all your long cherished desires and ambitions, which you previously thought were common sense, you are experiencing a shift of paradigm. You are confronted with the question, what, then, is human nature? You have never asked questions like this because they were meaningless in the past when you were forced to live a life scripted by the official doctrine and shaped by popular sentiments like everyone else. Confucianism has its own answer which is packaged in the rules and shoved down your throat. However, your own meditation experience has cast doubts on your perception of human nature, which so far has explained everything in this world for you. It creates a void in your heart. You have lost compass, directions, a means to make sense of everything including your own existence. Every human activity that used to mean something to you—an act of kindness from a superior which deserves loyalty or an act of disobedience from an inferior which calls for moral condemnation—now loses its meaning. Buddhism does not provide an alternative explanation except by telling you that meaninglessness of the world is part of the truth.

If everything in the world is meaningless, a void, an emptiness, then it naturally follows that your existence is also meaningless. You sit here meditating, and you are hungry. In past stages of Buddhist training you tried to suppress that urge by thinking about something else, by your strong will to control your mind. Now you may look at the situation in a different light, from the position of a third party observer. You face your hunger straight on and challenge it. You think about transience of this world and precariousness of human life in it, like duckweed floating in a river (浮萍), pushed and shoved by currents, not knowing where it is going. The duckweed will be dismembered by forces of nature, ending its short and meaningless life, and so will you. So what is hunger to you? What is pain to you? They are nothing. By giving up and diminishing the meaning of your very existence, you can then look past the common struggles of life, whether they are over wealth, power, or ease of pain, see through the transient and meaningless world before your eyes, and reach a state of calmness, even numbing indifference, that will forever relieve torment, pain and unrest in your heart. By conquering hunger and pain you also gain a sense of achievement, as well as security and confidence in yourself. You will finally feel enlightened, as though you are as pure as a drop of water, free of all emotions and desires, and ready to accept whatever fate is about to bestow on you, with an indifference as if you were watching events unfold on a stranger or grass in a river. You will be able to face danger without fear, for you have overcome the animal instinct of self-preservation. Even a brief glimpse of this "truth" can bring permanent peace and calm to your heart. And this transformation, not just of your worldview, which you changed by breaking free of your physical body and secular rules and put yourself in the position of grass floating in a river, but of your entire being, that you can now face hunger, pain and even death with complete peace of mind, is the essence of sudden enlightenment of Zen.

Each individual case of sudden enlightenment may vary, and it can happen at any time and place, not necessarily during meditation. For illustration purposes I have outlined a more complete version of the mental process. For many Zen believers it may not be so complex. Due to their life experiences some may find it easy to accept the futility and transient nature of human life, particularly those who live in constant war and turmoil, and with little or no practice of meditation directly go to the last step of sudden enlightenment. Regardless of how long you needed in preparing yourself for the transformation, when it happens, it is almost always a sudden event, for the change in you can not be measured in degrees—you are an entirely different being after the transformation. You are born again, or more precisely, you are now a dead man walking. You have identified yourself with that duckweed floating in the river or some other inanimate object and realized the nature of life in this world. You have understood your heart and true human nature, which is that void, emptiness, futility. You have eliminated all your desires, not by other traditional Buddhist practice of suppressing them gradually into insignificance, but by a sudden revelation of truth that all is meaningless. You entered the process a secular being with all the trappings of the world, wanting to succeed in your career, to climb that social hierarchy, to enjoy material wealth, to indulge your senses, to be obeyed by others, and to be loved. By the time you come out the other end you are a different man, and none of these secular concerns that used to dominate your thoughts make any sense any more. By seeing your heart and your true nature, you become an instant Buddha (立地成佛).

The original objective of Buddhist meditation, namely nirvana, which is to deliver the individual from the birth-death-rebirth life cycle, is now replaced by seeing true human nature and achieving that sweeping transformation of body, mind and soul. Here the Chinese tendency to rationalize everything into a grand theory is at work. If the truth is nothingness and emptiness, then instead of trying to mentally escape from life (hoping for the next), they would rather firmly embrace the truth and use it to direct their current lives. Through the precious experience of sudden enlightenment Zen followers have found a spiritual bliss, an offloading of all burdens, an ecstatic elation accompanied with a total liberation of the mind from all concerns. The experience is real and it goes way beyond the original Buddhist purpose of relieving pain. Other Buddhist sects may curry great favors from various kings and courts, but without a total transformation of the mind like this their followers are torn between human instinct to enjoy material life and Buddhist teachings against it. In the end most of them descended into dogmatism, stagnation and decadence. The Zen sect has the rare spiritual and intellectual integrity in their beliefs and actions, for it revealed or induced a human nature that is pure, austere, spiritually and aesthetically compelling.

None of the above discussion about the intellectual and psychological process of the transformation could be stated explicitly by Zen masters, however, in part because Confucian rules could never be challenged outright. It is one thing to say that there is nothing but emptiness in this world, which few understand its meaning, but suicidal to say that Confucian values are meaningless, even though that is exactly what emptiness implies. Add to this the difficulty in explaining human psychology, the Zen sect adopted an enigmatic way of oral teaching, called *koan*, and acquired an aura of mysticism.

A monk asks the master, "Master, I am still a novice, show me the way to enlightenment!" The master says, "Have you finished your breakfast?" "I have." "Then go wash your bowl!"

A flag is flapping in the wind. One monk observes, "The flag is moving." Another monk argues, "No, the wind is moving." The master says, "Wrong, your heart is moving."

Dialogs between master and disciple like these, or *koan*, are recorded, collected and passed on, following a Chinese tradition started by the disciples of Confucius. These conversations are all illogical to the rational mind, but they are the best attempt by the masters to express the inexpressible, and the illogical nature of that experience is part of the message. The masters would not hesitate to impart their worldview, that the world is nothingness, human body is emptiness, but these do not make any more sense to the average folk who have already adopted a materialist view of everything without realizing it. What modern psychology calls a schema, the very basic framework of views and values passed on from generation to generation in every culture, which is subconscious to most individuals, has to be identified and washed out, leaving a clean slate of mind, in order to achieve enlightenment. Neither the truth nor the key to enlightenment is in these *koan*; they are only an auxiliary tool to first convey the hidden message unstated for fear of political repercussions that everything you learned in this world should be discarded, and then show you what an enlightened view of the world sounds like. However, since the Zen sect does not use any religious texts for scripture, these *koan* become the only reading material for the monks, and many of them try to approach the matter as if they are studying Confucian classics, which would lead to a smack over the top of their heads by their master and a great deal of bewilderment in their minds. Because of these *koan* Western scholars tend to identify Zen with mysticism, which is a mistake. There is one other Buddhist sect that is closely associated with mysticism, called the mystic sect (密宗), of which Tibetan Buddhism is now the most prominent representative.

Private interest (human desire) is denounced one way or another in all pyramid cultures. In China the well-field system forced peasants into a situation where their private interest was against that of the "public", which really meant the ruler, but felt like the community since the community was held collectively responsible by the ruler. Xun and other Confucian scholars condemned born human nature, when they saw ministers who put their private interest before that of the ruler. In reality scholar-officials had no private interest independent of the ruler, as everything was owned by him in theory. In India people were told by Buddhist monks to eliminate all human desires, because these are the source of human suffering. Of course that did not stop the Brahmins from enjoying a lavish life. What was pleasure to them—food, sex, etc.—was the source of lamentation and suffering for the masses. Regardless of specific social customs, the nature of all pyramid cultures is the same: the masses are slaves, and social values reflect the will of the few masters. A good slave must not have any private interest at heart. Better yet, they should not even have human desires that are born with every animal.

It is not a surprise that Buddhism was supported by many Chinese emperors, over the objection of Confucians and Daoists. A Buddhist would never rebel under any circumstance. The same can not be said about Confucians. In the counter-evolution process, theories had been proposed on how to indoctrinate the masses, to inculcate a servile character, to foster voluntary obedience to hierarchy, to force self-curtailment of human desires, and so on, for the interest of the ruler. These in the form of Confucianism had been implemented. They became law, and over time culture. But Chinese never thought that a total annihilation of the self, of all human desires, was possible. Buddhism opened their eyes, as well as new possibilities for more servile theories.

Since the reunification of China in late sixth century a system of national examinations was put in place to select officials by the imperial court (科举). These would be held at county, provincial and national levels, where participants—adult males of any age or family background—were tested on their knowledge of the canonized Confucian classics. Top performers were given official posts. At first only a small number of officials were appointed in this manner, but over the following centuries it would gradually become the predominant way for the selection of officials.

Traditionally officers were recommended by high ministers, who often took advantage of this prerogative to insert their own relatives and cronies and build private networks within the ruling class. In such a system the prime minister (宰相) was typically a powerful figure because through his faction he controlled key posts of finance and military affairs. He could sometimes disobey the ruler without fear of persecution. The national exam system was introduced largely to take away the prerogative of official recommendation from high ministers and dismantle their private networks, thus concentrating all power in the hands of the emperor.

This measure accelerated the counter-evolution process. Officials selected this way often had a humble birth and owed their loyalty entirely to the crown. By Song Dynasty (960-1279 AD) these exam overachievers were even put in charge of military forces, ranking above professional officers, a practice which minimized chances of treachery by capable generals. The new breed of scholar-officials lacked the intellectual purview of their predecessors, for they were selected not on their own thoughts but on mastering old textbooks, whose confines they were not allowed to breach. Thus they found themselves in positions of high power and privilege quite undeservingly: they were not original thinkers, they had no experience in managing the economy, finances, agricultural production, military affairs or anything else, and they would be in charge of statecraft and rank higher than experienced generals, all by virtue of their ability to recite a few ancient books. Ridden with guilt and trying to justify their unbelievable fortune, they felt deeply in debt to the emperor, grew passionately concerned about his interest and emotionally committed their lives to his service and his empire. "Worry before all-under-heaven and enjoy life after all-under-heaven" (先天下之忧而忧，后天下之乐而乐) and "When in high positions worry about the people, when exiled worry about the emperor" (居庙堂

之高则忧其民，处江湖之远则忧其君), these lines of poetry that made it into everyday Chinese language were indicative of the typical mentality of scholar-officials at the time.

Of course just worrying about the empire was not quite enough. The strong guilt worked its way into the Confucian ideology and the idea of *en* (恩, pronounced *on* in Japanese). The word *en* was first used by Mencius, where it meant a favor, usually a big and potentially life saving one, bestowed by a superior to an inferior. A king who practices mercy by reducing rent is bestowing *en* on his subjects, for example. To Mencius *en* was an act of benevolence, and it did not imply an obligation for repayment on the part of the beneficiary. Scholar-officials of Song Dynasty, however, strongly felt that they needed to repay their emperor's *en*, namely giving them power and wealth for nothing, only that they did not possess any ability either on the battlefield or elsewhere to do so. The guilt and consequent anxiety led them to the conclusion that they would never be able to pay back the *en* of their ruler no matter what they did or how hard they tried.

That sense of guilt was further heightened by political reality at the time. The Chinese Empire was under mortal threat from northern nomads. Why an empire the size of China could not defend itself against primitive nomadic hordes deserves some attention here. Internal cohesion was not an issue. The scholar-official class was by and large loyal and motivated to serve their emperor. The masses were for the most part content with their lot; mercy as a principle was expected and generally observed; officials functioned like Confucian parents to their subjects, stern and domineering but not cold hearted. Although putting bookworms in charge of military affairs certainly did not help matters and in a few specific battles proved to be disastrous, that was not always the case; there were indeed capable generals. Besides, with the shear size of Chinese army, the abundance of resources, even the worst strategists and tactical commanders should have been able to just bulldoze any potential enemy.

The real weakness of China's defense, which has manifested itself repeatedly in history against small and primitive tribes to the north, is lack of motivation from the military (not a professional force but hastily recruited from the peasantry in times of war) and its generals. There have been too many cases where a triumphant general who had just smashed foreign invaders was promptly executed on phony charges upon returning to the capital, because he represented a threat to the throne. Legitimacy for a Chinese ruler comes from Heaven's Mandate, which in reality means whoever controls the military. A well liked general with a strong army loyal to himself could potentially topple and replace the emperor. Consequently a capable Chinese general must also be a skillful and obsequious politician just to survive, unless he has unspeakable personal ambitions. After winning a war he must immediately give all credit to the emperor while claiming none of his own, and ask for retirement from military post. Doing all that may not even be enough to save his life, if his brilliant campaigns earned him a high reputation. The same is true for a capable minister who initiated successful economic reforms. Thus the best and brightest would often adopt the Daoist approach: to hide their talent, pretend to be mediocre or even stupid, and shun great responsibilities. The underlying issue is the master-slave nature of ruler-minister relationship. Confucianism made sure that the ruler owned all-under-heaven, which means no one else is a real stakeholder. When everyone is a slave of the emperor, what is their motivation to fight for his sake? Material interest does help somewhat, but an army of mercenaries can only do so much, particularly when its top generals stand to gain little in victory. A slave army tends to disintegrate at the first sign of defeat, real or perceived. Coercion can force many onto the battlefield, but the first thing they do is to look for excuses to desert.

It was a great challenge to motivate slaves—including generals who knew that winning was not necessarily a blessing—to fight for their emperor. If the entire empire belonged to one person, why would anyone else risk his life for it, in both defeat and victory? Legalism (total coercion) was a proven methodology in third century BC, but it only worked for an amoral people. When mercy as a value was expected by the masses, the ruler could no longer enact harsh rules that would, for example, execute deserters. Confucianism emphasized indoctrination, with coercion as an auxiliary tool. Naturally Confucian scholars searched for a rationale by which the masses would voluntarily devote themselves to their ruler, and the concept of *en* was tailored for that purpose.

Just like their forbears they looked inside the family for inspiration, since the empire was seen as the emperor's enlarged family, and ruler-minister relation was equated with the father-son relation by ancient saints. Why a subject must devote himself to the emperor would be equivalent to why a son must devote himself to his father. The necessity of filial loyalty was explained by Confucius as that the filially loyal are not likely to rebel, rationalized by Mencius as dictated by mercy to helpless seniors. After centuries of indoctrination sons were indeed submissive in character, averse to rebellion, and felt obligated to serve their parents. But that was no longer enough. They needed to go one step further, to harbor such a fierce devotion that they wouldn't hesitate to give their lives. Sons must feel that they owe their lives to parents.

Confucianized legal code made that feeling not only possible but pervasive. Under the law fathers could literally kill sons at whim. Just as saving a life is an act of *en*, not taking a life when one can is also an act of *en*. Thus by default parents have *en* over their children, by giving birth to them, by feeding them, by keeping them alive, by not killing them. When life and death are concerned, *en* is no longer just a favor, but a divine favor, and children carry an *original debt* from birth. This is not a monetary debt that one can repay with materials or labor, but a divine debt that one must repay with life. As givers of life parents become living deities to their children. Similarly the emperor becomes a living deity to his "children subjects". Though ancestor and ruler worship had been there for a long time, the old worship was taken by Confucius and Xun as a way to instill fear and obedience. Neither of those two saints really believed in the divinity of ancestors or the ruler. The new interpretation of *en*—divine favor/original debt—changes father-son and ruler-minister relations in a subtle but profound way. Parents and ruler as objects of worship now become sacred, not just masters to be feared and obeyed. You first owe *en* to your parents, who gave birth to you. Then you owe it to your ruler, who provides peace and order for you. These debts born and carried with you can never be repaid even one ten-thousandth whatever you do. But in trying to repay your debts, in devoting your entire being to your creditors you become a moral being. Parents and ruler are now by default divine and benevolent, because you are alive. Filial loyalty (孝) becomes filial piety. Servile loyalty (忠) becomes pious loyalty. Both are no longer just duty the faithful discharging of which fulfills obligations. They become a lifelong devotion for which there is no true fulfillment short of sacrificing your life.

Only unlimited obligations defined by this *en* logic can adequately describe feelings of the scholar-officials, who were burdened with debt and guilt. However, obligation alone is not enough for the average individual to plunge to death. He must also overcome fear and the instinct for self preservation. Previous Chinese understanding of human nature included self preservation as a given, and the principle of *ren* (mercy) allowed deserters to get away with little or no punishment. Zen Buddhism opened Chinese eyes to a new possibility that human beings can voluntarily enter into a mental state where they do not care about their own lives anymore.

Confucian scholars had always tried to discredit Buddhism, but there was one thing hard for them to deny, that Buddhism had truly changed the lives of many of its followers in a spiritual way that Confucian moral teachings had never been able to. Since Confucius' own time, the virtue of selflessness had always been exalted but never thought to be fully achievable. Confucius wrote about the ancient world, long before the dynasties, where everyone lived in peace and harmony because they were all selfless. That world may have existed only in his imagination, the virtue of selflessness which was developed out of the well-field system and ultimately from the fact that the ruler owned all-under-heaven, had been imposed on inferiors by Confucian doctrine in the form of selfless serving of one's parents, and had been the official goal that every good person should strive for. Reality on the other hand pointed to the opposite: everyone was motivated by self-interest, regardless of what they were professing. Confucian scholars had been calling on officials to curb their greed, to no avail. Many moralizing scholar-officials could hardly discipline themselves. The entire Chinese society, from Confucians who studied for office and power, to Daoists who looked for elixir of life, to the low classes who sought better food on the table or a profit in the market, had all been consumed with the passion to enjoy this material life to the best of one's ability.

Against this back drop came the Buddhists, particularly the enlightened ones. They had no such desire. They were fully content with a simple and impoverished material life. They were happier in shabby clothes than officials in lush silk or velvet. Despite their perceived dreadful conditions they were concerned about others. Some went about helping people. Some gave food. Others taught, trying to share their enlightenment. In the face of threat and imminent danger, only Buddhists, particularly Zen monks, were able to remain calm and undaunted. Their bodies were not made of steel. They were just as easily cut down by a sword as everyone else, but in their utter indifference to both temptation and threat many lay people saw a kind of selflessness and courage that was at the same time unfathomable and breathtaking. From the Buddhist perspective none of this is morally motivated. Selflessness is a result of enlightenment, of grasping true knowledge of human nature and essence of all existence. Buddhism does not consider the unenlightened immoral. Their tolerance only added to their spectacle. To lay Chinese these Buddhists were highly moral beings in comparison to whom Confucians looked increasingly pale if not hypocritical. Neo-Confucian scholar-officials wanted to serve their emperor with the same kind of selflessness and total disregard of their own lives exemplified by enlightened Zen monks. In order to reach that state of mind they borrowed extensively from Zen philosophy and practice, and incorporated it into Confucianism.

They first adopted the Zen distinction between human nature and human emotions, and that the purpose of life is to find human nature hidden deep inside us, behind all emotions. Zen preaches the elimination of human emotions because they are a hindrance to enlightenment. Confucians are not willing to go that far but now start to cast a negative moral judgment on uncontrolled outbursts of emotions, seven of which are identified: happiness, anger, sorrow, fear, love, hate, and desires. To Buddhism human nature is nothingness, a void. Confucians proposed that it is the five virtues: *ren* (mercy), *yi* (propriety), *li* (rules and temperament of propriety and hierarchy), *zhi* (wisdom) and *xin* (keeping promises). These five virtues have always been exalted, but it does not make sense to call them human nature when most people find it hard to live up to all of them. So there are said to be three grades of human nature: the moral ones with these five virtues have the highest grade, the immoral ones have the lowest grade, and the rest the middle grade.

This may explain the existence of good and evil, but it leaves more questions unanswered. How can human nature be graded? Is the grade innate or acquired? It rekindles the ancient debate over benevolence or malignance of human nature between Mencius and Xun, only to add more complexity to it. Zen on the other hand has a simple message that is so much more appealing: there is one human nature, Buddha is in every one of us, we just need to look inside and find it. The Confucian human nature, namely the five virtues, is not hard to find, everybody understands it. It is just impossible to follow, and worse, you may be born with a low moral grade. Here Confucian scholars are faced with the problem to explain morality with Zen ideas of human nature and emotions, which are taken as a fact of life with no moral significance.

In the next development Confucian thinkers assert that human nature is pure virtue and all vices come from out of control human emotions. This means everyone has the possibility to be virtuous. The ancient saints like Confucius were born with the same human nature and human emotions, the only difference between them and the average folk is that they were able to control their emotions so that these do not interfere with human nature. When they were happy, angry or sorrowful they expressed it in such a way that their emotions become a manifestation of their true moral nature. The average folk exhibits resentment to his father on his face. That would be letting his emotion go unchecked, which in turn obscures his true human nature. Unlike the sages most people let their emotions run according to their desires, they indulge in their own emotions, are confused by them, which is why they do not know their own true nature. To be a moral being is to restore one's true human nature. This is essentially the same as Zen teaching to find one's nature in one's heart, except that it is interpreted in a moral sense.

But how to restore one's true human nature? Zen preaches meditation—calm down, eliminate all thoughts, concentrate, try to feel what inanimate objects feel, and intuitively sense the truth. From Zen practices Confucian thinkers realized that one has to have a calm mind so as to concentrate, and true devotion so as to persevere in the lifelong effort to forever better oneself morally, just like many Zen followers persevere in their lifelong effort to find enlightenment. To that end a hitherto obscure passage of the Book of Rites, the Great Learning (大学), and an equally ancient and neglected book, the Constant Middle (中庸), were dusted off and studied with new found enthusiasm. The main thesis of Great Learning is that for a ruler to rule according to Dao, he must first study material objects (格物), learn their cause and effect, gain knowledge of nature (致知), and then be truthful in application of that knowledge. The Constant Middle teaches that human nature is given by Heaven's mandate, and to follow human nature is to follow Dao; because Dao is omnipresent, we should act the same way whether we are in front of others or alone; a gentleman should be particularly careful when being alone (慎独), so as to stay true to Dao when no one is watching. These two doctrines are now combined to form the Confucian simulation of Zen meditation. One should study ancient classics not to gain an official post, but to become a moral person. The process of learning is a process of self-cultivation, which is in and of itself inspiring and spiritually rewarding.

With these two books Confucian thinkers claim that Buddhist ideas and practices have been part of Confucian teachings all along, just that no one so far has paid any attention to them. These texts were written at a time when Dao was thought to reside in the universe, and only by carefully observing the natural world can one attain its secret ways, which can then be applied to human societies. Now with Zen influence Confucian thinkers start to look inside human heart for the ultimate truth, so they unify Dao with the concept *li2* (理, a different word from but pronounced the same as *li*礼, hence the 2).

Li2 was originally used for the nature of things as opposed to their outward appearance. Iron is harder and more heat conductive than wood. These qualities are manifestations of the true nature or principle—*li2*—which is thought to reside within each piece of iron or wood. Philosophically Dao and *li2* are the same concept: Dao is the collection of *macro* rules that govern the universe and movements of everything, while *li2* is the collection of *micro* rules that determines the nature inside everything. There is only one sun in the sky, thus there should be only one ruler on earth. This is a direct application of Dao to human society. The atoms, molecules and their structure in a piece of iron is its *li2*, which makes iron iron with all its qualities. Human nature which resides inside the human body is the human *li2*. Upon seeing a dreadful death we all feel sad, why? Mencius told us, it is because we share a common human nature, or *li2*, which is the basis for moral values.

Since there can be only one ultimate truth, Dao and *li2*—the truth out there and the truth in here—are now seen as one and the same. This truth lives in all of us, making up the virtuous part of our human nature. In order to explain immorality the above mentioned dichotomy between human nature and human emotions evolved into the human nature of Dao/*li2* (天理之性) and the human nature of Qi (gas) (气质之性). The human nature of Dao is the part of human nature that is a manifestation of Dao, and it is pure virtue. Although there is only one truth, when it is reflected in each one of us, it takes a different form, just like there is only one moon, but when we look at it in different bodies of water, such as ponds, lakes and rivers, we see slightly different images. This explains that we do not all have the same disposition, but there is nevertheless truth in each one of us, which Buddhists may call Buddha, but Confucians call Dao.

Qi (gas) has been used for a long time for things that can neither be seen nor touched. Yin and Yang, for example, are believed to be two kinds of gas. Now a theory is advanced that all things including the human body are made of condensed gas. So the other part of human nature, the part that controls our desires and emotions, is called the nature of gas, because desires and emotions are thought to be a direct function of the physical body. Even now Asians are still using the term "nature of gas" (气质) to mean a person's temperament. In Chinese gas has since been associated with one particular emotion: anger. To be angry is to be gassy (生气).

Thus every human has two kinds of nature: a heavenly nature that is a reflection of truth (Dao or *li2*) and is pure virtue, and a gas nature that is associated with our desires and emotions, which tends to confuse us and prevent us from seeing the truth. In keeping with long standing Confucian tradition of cultivating human character, the first nature is deemed innate, the second acquired, and everyone can become a virtuous sage by eliminating human desires which are acquired. Up until this point, the only Confucian sage who has openly declared that humans are born with a benevolent nature and all evils are acquired after birth, was Mencius. The book of Mencius which has been largely ignored now gains prominence. Following the example of Buddhism, where every sect traces its lineage all the way back to Buddha himself, however tenuous some of these links are, the new Confucians come up with a Confucian lineage of canonized saints, starting with ancient kings Yao and Shun, to Shang Dynasty founder Tang, Zhou founder Wu, the Duke of Zhou, Confucius and Mencius. Thus Confucius and Mencius who were previously regarded as great teachers but still human, are now saints of moral perfection. The previously canonized five classics—the Book of Odes, the Book of History, the Book of Rites, the Book of Change and the Spring and Autumn—are now supplemented by four other classics: the Analects (quotations from Confucius), the Book of Mencius, the Great Learning and the Constant Middle, which are to be used in national exams.

As with previous versions of Confucianism, perceived philosophical coherence is necessary but not the core message. It is necessary to say there is only one sun in the sky to ground your theory in Dao, but the real message is that there should be only one ruler in a state and one master in a family. The same is true with the new theory of Dao, *li2*, its manifestation in human nature that leads to virtue, and human emotions that cause trouble. The goal is to define morality as total voluntary devotion to the ruler, and to provide a means to turn the masses into moral beings. The key idea in the real message is *en* that one owed to his ruler and to his parents.

Ambitious young men have always studied Confucian classics assiduously, trying to understand and remember every word in order to do well in national examinations. But their motivation has largely been power and wealth. Neo-Confucianism on the other hand is not a few books or knowledge to be used in political governance, it is also a belief. When you sit there reading, do not think about how you will do in the exams or a life of privilege afterwards, but think about how you can better serve your parents, try standing in the shoes of your father who has to work hard to provide food for the family, his sacrifice to his undeserving children, his love and condescension to the worthless you, and how you could never repay his *en*. If you are moved by his small acts of kindness which you have previously taken for granted, and you have strengthened your resolve to faithfully serve him for the rest of his life, even to the point of giving up your own life, you have made the first major step in self-cultivation. From there you can try standing in the shoes of the emperor, think about the endless problems that he has to face, from floods, droughts, famines, to quarrelsome and worthless court officials, each with his own self-interest in mind. Think about the love of the ruler and his undeserving subjects. If you start to hate those officials for not devoting themselves to the ruler, and are moved by every act of mercy by the ruler, and think that a high minister who is sentenced to death for uttering a wrong word that offended the ruler as being more than deserving his punishment, you have made another major step in self-cultivation: you now have the ability to transpose yourself, a slave, to the position of your master. From there you contemplate how human desires have driven so many officials and common folks into greed, corruption and disservice to their parents and their ruler, and come to realize that human desires are the source of all evil, and wage an epic battle against them. You cut down your expenditures, stay away from all temptations, and try to live a simple life. You give up all your hobbies and any other distracting activities, and concentrate on how you can better serve your parents and your ruler. You are concerned about unrest in the empire and skirmishes with barbarians. You are worried that the military ranks are incompetent and your country may not be able to resist foreign invasion. You become restless at the slightest hint of trouble, and you can not wait to throw yourself into the service of your master, not for any material gain or recognition, but for the satisfaction of having made yourself useful and hopefully worthy of his divine love, to relieve that burden of *en* on your shoulders. Now you are a cultivated and moral man.

Neo-Confucianism also mended the long standing Confucian-Mencian rift in a way. Confucius exemplified a servile and cautious character while Mencius preached fearless independence. Scholar-officials have been torn between the two opposite role models. They crave the dignity of Mencius ("power and force can not bend him"). If someone exhibits such a character, it puts pressure on others to follow, and sycophancy to shame. However, such independence is dangerous. One never knows how a superior or an emperor will react. Reality forces most to adopt Confucius' approach, albeit reluctantly. Neo-Confucianism advises the ruler that as long as his servants are loyal at heart, their objections to specific policies and dignity in character should be allowed. It is unwise for the ruler to turn everyone into fawning sycophants, who are usually useless on matters of importance. A capable person must be afforded dignity to serve voluntarily and effectively. If the ruler shows enough tolerance and care, then his loyal servants will be grateful and dedicated. Scholar-officials will do their part indoctrinating the populace with the *en* logic, instilling a sense of debt and guilt, because of which everyone will be eager to serve. If rulers and superiors all buy into this mechanism, dignity (face) will be preserved as well.

Confucius explained filial loyalty as inductive to an obedient character, thus making it easier for the ruler to rule. Mencius explained it as a virtue, thus saving seniors from helpless misery and making for a more civilized society. Neo-Confucians see filial piety as the most important part of self-cultivation, in the making of a moral person, such that if at home he will be a filial son, if serving in high position he will be a loyal and diligent officer, if demoted to the countryside he will be a loving person to his neighbors and still concerned about the welfare of all-under-heaven, wherever he goes and whatever predicament he finds himself in, whether in power and privilege or in abject poverty and adversity, he will never have a concern for himself, and always devote his energy to his parents, his ruler, and all-under-heaven (the ruler's flock). Now filial piety and pious loyalty are truly one and the same, and there is no real distinction between a moral person and a capable minister. To help the ruler manage his empire one does not need any special knowledge, whether it is about the economy or military affairs, because the purpose of the whole empire, and indeed of human existence, is to strive for that moral perfection, which is not as previously understood acting in full compliance with rules of propriety, but an inspiration, a spiritual fulfillment unrelated to any rules.

Confucian principles like "one ruler in the land" is no longer justified by simplistic observations of Dao, such as "one sun in the sky", but by the new understanding of rules of universe as well as human nature. With this new logic and inspiration values such as filial piety are perfectly wedded to Confucian politics in a dignified manner, rather than the ancient "servile character less prone to rebellion" argument. Self-cultivation leads to a moral person, who is devout, upright and pious (not timid and fearful), then a harmonious family (for he serves his parents with inspiration), then order in the state (for he serves his ruler with reckless abandon), and finally peace under heaven (修身齐家治国平天下).

With all the metaphysics concerning Dao, *li2*, two kinds of human nature and so forth, neo-Confucianism managed to push servility to a new level that it does not even look like servility. Cultural dynamics of the counter-evolution process dictate that new theories would always serve the ruler better than previous ones, which usually means that the masses would be indoctrinated to increasing degrees of servility. Remolding the human character has always been the main purpose of Confucianism. Inspired by Zen monks, who showed that human desires can indeed be eliminated, neo-Confucians are no longer satisfied with regulating human desires, they utterly condemn human desires as categorically immoral. For the masses, obedience is no longer sufficient. After all, obedient slaves do not make a brave army. A sense of indebtedness is now the main message of state ideology. One can and must strive to pay his debt, but as long as he remains alive, he is always a debtor. Every kindness shown by parents and ruler adds to his debt. The motivation to serve is to relieve the burden of indebtedness. Self-preservation is no longer a valid excuse to avoid that obligation. Neo-Confucianism raised ethical standards for the slaves to superhuman levels.

With canonization of neo-Confucianism, Buddhism is under increasing threat of persecution. Buddhists have always been outsiders to the Confucian society and its hierarchical structure, therefore deemed useless to the ruler in direct material terms; their only redeeming value has been the promotion of selflessness. Now that neo-Confucianism has absorbed the same teaching in its curriculum and used it in direct service to the ruler, Buddhism has lost much of its value. Over time a series of imperial decrees to ban Buddhism resulted in burning of most temples and mass slaughter of monks, at least those who refused to return to secular life. Most sects died. Very few including Zen have survived till this day, albeit in a much diminished capacity. By Ming Dynasty neo-Confucianism had basically driven Buddhism off the center stage of Chinese cultural and political life.

Long before that, however, all Buddhist sects were forced to teach Confucian values just to survive. The Confucian idea of *en* both to parents and to the emperor was incorporated into Buddhist doctrine. In addition to these two kinds of *en*, Buddhism added the *en* of all lives (your life depends on others' good will, therefore everyone has *en* to you) and the *en* of the three treasures of Buddhism: the Buddha, the Buddhist Law and the monk. Most Buddhist priests would teach these four kinds of *en*. So we not only have infusion of Buddhism into Confucianism, but vice versa. Buddhism was thus transformed under political pressure from a religion that advocated an escape from the secular world, including its social mores and customs, to a supplement of the state ideology. By twenty first century the two have grown so intertwined with each other that from listening to present day Buddhist sermons it is often hard to tell what is being preached more, Buddhism or Confucianism. Most Buddhists from the Confucian world today regard filial piety as a Buddhist value, or more precisely, a universal value that transcends religion.

Zen spirit may have been heart felt for some neo-Confucians, but once adopted as the state ideology the kind of total selfless devotion becomes required of the official class, who in turn passes on a much raised standard of moral compliance to the masses at large. The great synthesizer who gave birth to neo-Confucianism, Zhu Xi (朱熹, often rendered as Chu Hsi), for example, was also a stern county governor who apparently sought to eliminate much of the human desires of his poor subjects. The first victim of his new doctrine, once adopted by the imperial court, was women, because they are the object of men's desires.

In ancient times Chinese women were equal with men, many of them were heads of their own households. With the advent of Confucianism they suffered the first major blow, because Confucius said that "only women and low lives are hard to deal with" (唯女子与小人难养也). The Yin-Yang theory formally defined their status as inferior to men. But still divorce was allowed and divorced women could remarry without prejudice. Virginity was not an issue. With neo-Confucianism they are about to suffer a second major blow. The husband-wife relation in addition to the hierarchy previously defined now has a moral dimension. A wife's highest virtue is to stay submissive and loyal to her husband, thus she can no longer divorce him. He on the other hand can still divorce her if she committed one of seven crimes laid out in the legal code, including disrespect for his parents. A woman divorced by her husband thus becomes an evil person who would bring shame to her parents. Even a widow can not remarry because she has to transfer her loyalty to her son, the successor of her deceased husband. As a result the wife's position in the family is now not just inferior but a slave to the husband, since a divorce would essentially end her livelihood. She is to obey her father before marriage, obey her husband after marriage, and obey her eldest son after the death of her husband. Zhu Xi orders women in his jurisdiction to wear scarves, much like the kind worn by some Muslims today, whereby her face is concealed, leaving just enough opening for her eyes. This is to prevent them from stoking men's desires. He also orders them to wear shoes with wooden soles, so that they make noise when walking. This is to prevent them from running away.

Rules for men are also tightened, although with men there is always that last excuse: filial piety. A man can easily remarry with perfectly moral excuses, for example to have male heir to the family line, which is considered a major filial duty, or to better serve his parents. Men can not have casual conversations with their house maids and other female servants any more, especially joking and laughing, which is considered flirting—now a sin. Every family must have only one ruling patriarch. This rule forces large families to be run like small nuclear families, with a clear hierarchy. After the death of the senior patriarch, his adult sons have no choice but to establish the elder brother/younger brother hierarchy, even if the brothers do not feel like dominating each other. The eldest brother in this case will not only have power over his own children, but over younger brothers, their children and all grand children. The standing of each wife or concubine depends not only on favor from her own husband among his many female consorts, but also the standing of the husband within the large family, which can easily grow to three or even four generations and fifty members strong. This large family structure continued until early twentieth century.

Neo-Confucianism was unable to save the Song Dynasty, or subsequent dynasties from foreign invasion, for the simple reason that however well argued, a slave's interest will never completely overlap that of his master. Guilt resulted from not paying a divine debt can push the masses to great lengths in terms of sacrificing their time, money and labor, but when their lives are on the line, human instinct of self-preservation still trumps other ethical codes. Zen enlightenment is not easily acquired. It needs extensive training that can not be applied to the masses—they can not all become monks. As long as mercy is observed, deserters have to be forgiven if they do it in droves, because a ruler who orders the execution of thousands of his subjects at the same time, for whatever reason, will be deemed cruel and unfit to rule. However, when the same *en* logic, the same piety and the same guilt were introduced to an amoral culture like Japan, it worked beyond the dreams of founders of neo-Confucianism.

CHAPTER 10

CONFUCIAN CHILD REARING AND FORMATION OF THE CONFUCIAN MIND (1)

As we continue with our Confucian story, I feel this is a good place to introduce Confucian child rearing practices. Many later events and social phenomena can not be fully understood without a grasp on the Confucian character, which owes its formation to the experience of the tender years of an individual, in the context of the family. The two core Confucian values—filial piety and pious loyalty—are not just philosophical ideas; they prescribe a psychological profile that must be trained against born human instincts. In that objective all Confucian cultures agree, Chinese, Japanese, or Korean.

Even without state enforcement of values like filial piety, mentalities of a slave parent and a free parent are dramatically different to begin with. No free man in his right mind wants his son to grow up to be a servile character. In the Western world such a person would be at a disadvantage when it comes to competition with other adults. The stronger man, in both body and will, is more capable of defending his property, his family, and his aging parents. A timid character tends to cut a pathetic figure, pushed around, used and abused, or at best ignored. In a pyramid society the fortunes are reversed. Free competition is banned. Every peasant gets the same lot. Being a self-reliant, assertive or independent person does not gain anything materially; it only means trouble with authority. The individual does not need to protect his family; the state takes care of that. The way to get ahead is to follow orders, study hard and/or curry favor from higher ups. Thus for parents the preferred kind of children are the ones who are docile, timorous, and would remain unconditionally loyal to them throughout their lives.

The key word here is unconditional. By human instinct of reciprocity every parent knows that if he treats his children with love and compassion, they are likely to pay back in kind when they grow up. But such an equation does not always work. Even a loving parent has to discipline his children from time to time. He may think he is doing something good for the child, but the child may not agree. The role of parents implies power and authority, which is naturally resented as the child grows. In the span of eighteen years a million things can go wrong, many of which are out of parents' control. In the end there is no guarantee that their love will be returned in kind. Due to previously discussed circumstances of a pyramid culture, Confucian parents want a more assured way to secure their children's lifetime obedience and devotion, as well as love, instead of leaving their own retirement to chances. From the ruler's perspective the same pusillanimous character is preferred of his subjects, making them easy to control. Pious loyalty (忠) to ruler and filial piety (孝) to parents are psychologically one and the same. Thus ruler and parents conspired to subjugate generation after generation of children.

Some parents, despite their own interest, may not want their children to serve them. Their love can be so great that they are willing to give their own lives just so their children are happy. But these parents face an external pressure from the state to rear their children the Confucian way regardless. Qualification for any office and any job starts with filial piety. Scholar officials of all levels preach it as the only moral way. Outstanding filial sons are rewarded with office. On the reverse side, there are severe penalties for violations. According to the legal code, for example, a grown son can not leave his parents and start his own separate household, or else he may be executed by the state. Since the totalitarian regime controls every aspect of everyone's life, a child reared any other way simply would not be able to survive even if his parents approve of his independence.

With such a contrast between reward and punishment, the official doctrine exalting its virtue, and a natural desire of most parents to keep their children as permanent possessions, filial obedience and parental worship become a requirement. The choice is only in sincerity and degree, in other words how real and how strong the devotion is. When parents meet in towns and villages, the conversation typically goes: "I envy you. You have so many sons and all of them are so obedient. You must have an enjoyable life." Or, "Your son is a scholar official, an outstanding figure, and he still kowtows to you and fulfills his filial duty, how did you educate him? I want to learn something from you." Peer pressure alone forces many parents who might otherwise take a more laissez faire approach to compete with others on how much they control their children, because if your son does not follow your every order like a well trained dog, neighbors will see you as an incompetent man not capable of establishing order in your own home, they are not likely to show you any respect—if your own children do not respect you, why should we? Your honor and reputation suffers. In Confucian jargon this is called "losing face", and it is not a trivial matter; it concerns one's standing in the community. As a result of the competition, most Asians in their early years are bombarded repeatedly with tirades like "Look at that Chen kid. He does all the household chores. He rubs his parents' feet and massages their backs. He never asks for anything. He never thinks about himself. He is so mature and selfless. Why can't you be like him, you useless thing?!"

The desired character of a son, as well as the nature of parent-children relationship has been discussed in detail in Confucian classics, but there are no manuals on how to train them. In Confucius' own language, different pupils must be taught differently, according to their specific propensities, so that they all end up with the same kind of character. In other words a parent must look for his own ways, sometimes several different ways, if he has several very different children.

As a general practice, for the first few years of a child's life, he is pampered to the best of parents' ability. Western parents tend to ignore a baby's cry if they know it is just for attention, because they do not feel obligated to grant attention whenever requested. For Asian parents that would be tantamount to ignoring one's most valuable possession. In this period the mother attempts to build an exclusive emotional bond with the baby. The message is not only "I will always take care of you", but more importantly "In the whole world, *only* I will take care of you".

In a traditional family the mother is an inferior figure, much like a servant to the father. A son's emotional tie to her thus becomes one of the only things she can leverage to enhance her own position in the family. The average husband would look down on a sonless wife, but he must pay some respect to the mother of his precious boy, especially when the boy could not live without the mother. Owing to this dynamic the mother must jealously guard emotional dependence of the baby, making sure it does not divert from her. Pampering is in part to fill the baby's world: whenever he opens his eyes, he sees his mother and no one else. If there is a wet nurse she is usually banished from the family right after weaning, not to be seen again.

In some households the father likes to spend time with the baby. The mother of course can not compete directly with the man for time, so her pampering carries another message: I will do things for you that your father will not do, I am the one who cares about you the most. The baby's every call is answered and every need satisfied. He experiences nothing but total devotion from a loving and gentle servant in his mother. He always gets his way. He is never punished or disciplined. He can order her to do his bidding by a simple cry. In his little world and little mind, he is a despot.

Asian kids at this early stage are typically unruly. The duration of this stage varies greatly from family to family. It can be as short as a year or two, or as long as several years. It ends with a parent's (usually the father) first show of disapproval. Perhaps he is not happy the toddler cries too much, or the five year old behaves badly and embarrasses him in front of guests. He decides it is time the kid learned some rules. He starts by pulling down his face, reprimanding the child and ordering him to behave. Having never seen anything like this the child is a little shocked, but he does not obey—it is not in his habit. The irritated father then raises his voice and violently grabs him. The child is scared and starts to cry, looking for his mother for help, who quietly withdraws from the scene if she happens to be there. The child is still thinking that by crying he will get his way since that has always worked in the past, but what await him are yelling, threats and perhaps a good spanking.

To some two or three year olds this would be a traumatic experience, because it comes without warning, without explanation, and without the child understanding why or what is actually happening. He does not know what his father is going to do to him. His world has been a fairy tale with himself at the center of the universe. All of a sudden he feels helpless and as his incessant cry at the top of his lungs goes unanswered, desperation sets in. His mother can no longer protect him. His father who may have been distant but nevertheless kind has suddenly turned into a monster. His sense of safety is completely shattered. His entire world tumbles down. Physical pain if any is negligent in comparison, the loss of all sense of the familiar world plunges the young and underdeveloped mind into total darkness. Not only has he tasted fear for the first time in his life, he can not get out of it afterwards, for his tormentor is always around reminding him of his insecurity.

To others perception of a mortal threat may sink in more gradually. The kid gets a warning the first time, a severe dress down the next, threats the next, and if all that fails, finally the beating. Some of them, the smart ones, quickly perceive the power relationship and cave in without reaching the final showdown. Regardless of how it happens, the child now lives in fear, and that is exactly what Asian parents want.

Western parents try to distinguish between discipline and love. Since very early the baby is taught discipline. The hand is taken out of the mouth, feeding and sleeping schedules enforced, toys taken away, etc. When the child starts to talk, rules are given and explained. But none of this is done in a malicious manner, seen from the child's position. The message from parents is: I want you to behave, I explain why you must behave, I am not happy and may punish you if you misbehave, but under no circumstances, even when I am extremely upset with your behavior, will I forsake my love for you. It is critical for the child to feel safe as he goes through the process of learning the rules. This education is aimed at teaching values so that when the child grows up he knows how to make good decisions independently.

That is not the objective of Confucian child rearing. In fact it is the exact opposite. Asian parents do not want their children to be independent, ever. Discipline is less about inculcating good manners, more about establishing the Confucian father-son hierarchy, a master-slave relationship. Parents demand obedience from their children. They routinely threaten their young with abandonment at any sign of disobedience. The message is that my love for you is predicated on the condition that you obey me.

At a very early age the Asian kid learns that he is not safe at all, even in his mother's arms. The mother rarely beats her children, but she would readily threaten them with abandonment—"I will leave you outside to starve, to freeze", "I don't want you anymore", "I don't like you anymore", etc.—whenever they upset her. One common practice is to deliberately leave the kid outside in an unfamiliar area, with the mother hiding nearby, watching. Sooner or later the kid realizes his mother is gone. He wonders around, calling mommy. No answer. He is anxious. He searches frantically, left and right, back and forth, his calls increase in volume and frequency. As time passes he grows desperate. Tears start to drop, his calls turn into sobbing. At this point the mother shows herself, like a savior. She warmly embraces her child, wiping his tears, kissing his cheeks, "mommy is here, and don't you worry". Timing of the rescue is important. Too early the kid may not appreciate it all that much. Too late the kid may reach a point beyond despair, a state of emotional death, in which he does not care about anything anymore, either because he has toughened his nerve by having survived desperation and become somewhat immune to threats, or because he has lost all hope and become suicidal. Either way it is counter-productive, so the mother tends to err on the safe side: spring out of hiding as soon as he starts to cry.

"Skills" like this are not written in the Confucian classics. They arise from generations of practice, are passed by word of mouth, and eventually become widely adopted. Not all parents play this particular trick. Fathers generally prefer beating. In some families the mother gets the first try and if she fails then the father comes in with his heavy handed approach. Sometimes it takes repeated beating, in increasing severity, for the message to get across. But all parents do something to achieve the same purpose, whether it is the mother implying without me you can not survive or the father insinuating I can take your life any time I choose to. Such experience not only exacerbates the child's insecurity, but makes a strong impression on his mind so that he is always acutely aware of it, even when he is away from home having a good time. The rescue if successfully done carries the emotional game one step further. The mother figure who comes to the rescue at a moment of desperation is not only a human who feeds and clothes the child, but a god like figure with all the love and care. Here is a person with power of life and death over you, yet she loves you. That means she has *en* (divine favor) to you, and you owe *en* (original debt) to her. She is your *en* person (恩人). So far she may have been a mixed image in the child's mind, as sometimes he hated her. But an experience like this leaves an indelible imprint on the brain that overwrites previous feelings and preempts future ones, because for the first time it establishes a new kind of relationship. The mother has been someone the child intuitively turn to for food and comfort, which as he grows he realizes he can get from other sources as well. However, having tasted fear and desperation, the same kiss and hug by his mother now have a whole new meaning. In other words the child feels extremely vulnerable and develops a strong emotional need and sensibility that Western children typically do not have. The child becomes emotionally dependent on his mother. The same reprimand hurts more than before, because every word threatens to tear apart that emotional bond in his eyes. It is like God telling you in person he does not love you any more for a Christian. At the same time every word of encouragement becomes all the more heart warming, like a divine blessing.

After this first step the child is generally obedient. He fears his father and abandonment by his mother. At the same time, he is still a child not able to fully control himself or his emotions. Every now and then he may be upset with his parents and it shows in his facial and body expressions. He may want something his parents would not buy for him, or he is made to do more household chores than he is willing. He understands that he must obey, but he is disgruntled.

If this situation is not rectified soon there will be noticeable changes in the child. He does not feel like playing the games that he used to enjoy. He loses all initiative. He becomes withdrawn, afraid to do anything that he is not instructed to do, and disinterested in all activities. He daydreams a lot, and in his dreams he tries to escape from reality. The emotional tie between him and his mother starts to weaken, as it becomes increasingly apparent to him that his father is the master of the house, his mother can not really protect him from the father, and sometimes he wonders subconsciously if his mother really wants to protect him or merely takes advantage of his perilous state. He says less and less to them except answering questions. He avoids all eye contact. He hangs his head low in their presence.

The growing emotional detachment alarms parents, to whom possession of their child includes possession of his love. Confucius specifically stressed this point, that diligently fulfilling one's duty to parents by itself is not filial loyalty; one has to do so willingly. What parents can not tolerate is the resentment in the child's heart as he carries out their orders. They know over time that could develop into hatred, and that means disharmony under the same roof. Every Asian parent intuitively understands the seriousness of the problem.

There are two ways to approach a sulky child: to placate or to intimidate. Usually mother would try the first and father the second. Often both approaches are undertaken simultaneously. Having been through devastating scares the child is already frail emotionally, so he is ready to give in to any demand. But the message may not be immediately clear to him. Parents may say, look at that Chen kid in the neighborhood who did this and that for his parents, while the child is thinking, I did the same just yesterday, so why are you mad at me? The problem is not that he did not do a good job, but he did it grudgingly, and that can be a difficult message to get through to a four year old.

At this age his brain is still developing through interaction with material surroundings, by which he learns how things work in the natural world. At the same time he is forced to try desperately to figure out the rules by which his parents judge him, in order to avoid their punishment, physical and emotional. It may take some time, depending on the individual, to realize that it is often the facial expression and body language that provokes the ire of parents. In addition to a countenance of resentment when it is not expected, failing to show joy or excitement when it is due, such as when given a present, failing to exhibit sorrow or anguish when it is called for, such as when a parent is sick or in pain, and any other expression that counters what parents feel at any given occasion, are all sources of their displeasure and wrath.

After this revelation the child is afraid to ever show his true emotions again, because he is not at all sure he always has the "correct" feelings expected by his parents. Of course he can not say what he thinks and how he feels either, for the same reason. In routine situations such as those mentioned above, he learns how he is supposed to think and look, and talk or act his part. In less familiar surroundings such as when adult strangers are present, he becomes shy, withdrawn and taciturn. It is not that he fears adult strangers, but he is apprehensive of how his parents might react to his interaction with other adults. If he is rude he might embarrass his parents. If he is friendly he might hurt their feelings even more: you have hardly ever been so genuinely happy with us, and we feed you, you traitor!

By now the child has completed the second step of Confucian training. He acquires many of the characteristics recognizable in Asian adults. These include a largely emotionless face, a body and four limbs that are reluctant to move one way or another for fear of misinterpretation or any negative interpretation by parents and others, a quiet and timorous demeanor around strangers and superiors, and a high degree of sensitivity and concern as to what others in the room or relevant in any situation are thinking. This is also the time when the parent-child ownership hierarchy takes form in his mind. He understands he is completely at the mercy of his parents, and he has to be extremely careful not to hurt their feelings.

In such a relationship there is no such thing as what the child deserves, or a guaranteed set of services for him, such as food, clothing, shelter and safety. He depends on them, yet he can not count on them. It is made abundantly clear to him that all these services are conditional, and that he deserves nothing, instead it is the parent's mercy that keeps him alive. This presents a problem: how does he approach his parents when he needs help or wants a favor?

A Western child can talk to his parents openly about what his entitlements are, including allowances, and what his responsibilities are, including housework, as well as what is fair and why. It is generally understood what a child needs is provided unconditionally, as long as parents are able, and what he wants is subject to negotiations and rules, which once agreed upon are binding to all sides. A child who broke the rules must apologize and explain, so does a parent. In the Confucian parent-child relationship nothing is granted unconditionally to the child, therefore no distinction is made between needs and wants; hierarchy is sacred, therefore negotiations are impossible and rules if any are only made for the child. Parents can abuse one child while at the same time spoil another, which is a common practice.

The child can not complain or get angry at mistreatment. He can try but that would only worsen his predicament. For whatever he desires, whether it is food or an expensive toy, he has to beg. "Can I have that please?" (with an ingratiating smile). If that does not work, the kid climbs into his mother's lap, shaking her gently back and forth, pouting and humming. This is not the same as sulking, which implies animosity. This is one example of a distinct Confucian phenomenon, called amae (撒娇). It carries three messages: A. I am not happy. B. Yet, I do not resent you. Instead, I still love you as I recognize I am totally dependent on you. C. Given my loyalty and obedience (乖), could you grant my wishes?

Amae is an art of begging and toadyism. Unless the demand is outrageous it usually works. It is also far more effective than sobbing and pleading, which essentially plays on mercy. Amae reaffirms hierarchy and loyalty in a way that is appropriate for children, who do not yet understand formal rituals like prostration. It is also an expression that can not be easily faked: a sulky child angry with his parents would not do that. Moreover, it helps maintain a strong emotional bond. In order to keep playing this trick, the child has to be on friendly terms with parents, any resentment in his heart would prevent him from carrying out the whole act. So from the parents' perspective, it provides a monitor and a tool to keep track of the child's filial mind: how loyal he is, how submissive he is, and how willing he is. During the process of such an act the parent can also do something extra to further test the child, such as by faking a rejection. If the child becomes upset and leaves in disgust, he is dangerously independent and the training has a long way to go. If he keeps pleading until he breaks down in the mother's arms but does not try to get away, it means his perpetual fear of abandonment far outweighs any immediate displeasure, and he is totally dependent and loyal.

The vast majority of Asian kids complete these two major steps of Confucian psychological training before school age, most of them well before that age. As years pass the child spends less time with his mother and more with the father, who is usually much harder to please. He has to perform in school, or learn a trade, and hopefully bring honor to the family. At some point he is not allowed to beg for favors anymore, even in the toadying way he is used to, even with the mother. He must search for new ways to win their approval. His first attempt is to follow every instruction to the best of his ability, striving to learn every skill as fast as he can and practice as hard as he can. But sooner or later he realizes that these are not enough. It is not like there is a fixed target—they simply raise the bar if he happens to be a hard working genius. The key to pleasing them, as it finally dawns on him, is to show his unwavering love and loyalty to them, that he is constantly thinking about their well being, that he is always ready to sacrifice himself for their sake, that he is mindlessly devoted to them, body and soul, particularly in the face of mistreatment. All the skills that he learns are supposed to serve that purpose.

But human nature does not make it easy for us to love someone who constantly hurt us, physically or emotionally. Though the Asian child has had some training in that regard earlier, new demands and harsher punishment by the father presents a second round of tests and training. The child is likely never really close to the father to begin with, and his affection is naturally not with this tormentor. On the other hand, if he does not show affection to him, he is bound to suffer more pain, particularly when there is more than one child in the family competing for favor. Thus the child finds himself fighting his natural instinct of associating hurt with resentment and anger, which is a hard struggle since merely controlling himself by subduing negative feelings is not enough, but he has to take the second step to completely wipe out all negative feelings towards his father, and the third step to develop a strong love for him.

The child needs help in this struggle to make sense of it all. He needs a rationale. And so at the earliest convenience his parents will indoctrinate him with the concept of *en*. Applied to the parent-child relation, it essentially means that a child can not survive without his parents, therefore he owes his life, and *en* (original debt), to parents, a debt he can never repay. Parents often remind children of their *en* (divine favor), when they feed them and clothe them, and threatens to withdraw that favor from time to time. In the dynastic era the *en* logic was a self-fulfilling prophecy: by enforcing a legal code that made helpless children slaves to their own parents and declaring it the highest virtue, the state ensured that it became a self-evident fact. Over time fathers developed a sense of moral righteousness in treating their children as slaves, just as a Westerner feels righteous in disposing his private property anyway he wants.

However self-serving this logic sounds, it is eagerly accepted by the child. He is already desperate. He wants to survive and the only way to do so is to please his parents by demonstrating total devotion to them, and the only way he can bring himself to that is to have an explanation that the fact he is treated like a slave is entirely within their rights and is the natural order of things, the Dao as it were. The idea of *en* puts everything in perspective.

His parents own him logically, because they feed him. They can kill him or dispose of him as they please, and that would be perfectly reasonable. For them to *not* do that, but instead feed him and clothe him, is therefore a tremendous show of grace and an act of *en*, which the child can never repay even by serving them for life, but that is the least he can do. Seen in this light, any physical or verbal abuse can not be interpreted as punishment, for if parents really wanted to punish him they could have abandoned him. These actions therefore can be taken as disciplinary education meant for the child's own good. In fact they are often interpreted as tests for the sincerity of the child's devotion to his parents, which any worthy human being should be able to pass. I may be called a useless animal numerous times, which I might have taken offence at first, but come to think of it, maybe I am useless, after all, I have not made any money for my parents. Every verbal abuse seems trivial, now that I have positioned myself as a slave; it no longer registers as an insult (打是亲, 骂是爱). Every physical abuse seems reasonable, for I am forever in debt just by being born, and no matter how hard I strive I can never pay back my parents' *en* to me.

With this revelation the child's mind is finally at ease. Everything makes sense now. He thinks he deserves all the abuse from his parents. He is grateful to them for his life. When he finally understands that all the scolding and beating are the just result of him not fulfilling his end of the bargain by being a dedicated servant, these formerly painful episodes no longer induce resentment. Moreover, any show of mercy and affection on the part of the parents is taken with extra gratitude and engenders an intense feeling of warmth in a heart aching for love. The emotional bond that was under severe strain is not only restored but strengthened with the whole new enlightenment.

This is also the context within which the child learns the Confucian idea of love, which embodies the full content of parent-child relation, complete with ownership. Love from a superior means condescension. Physical abuse by a superior, even savage beating, is also an act of love, because it shows concern, as opposed to disengagement. From the inferior love means total devotion. When parents are masters who have arbitrary power over but no obligation to their children, their every act of kindness out of human instinct is seen as an act of divine grace. In this sense the term filial piety is accurate. For the child, even physical punishment becomes meaningful, if no less painful. By enduring all pain his life acquires meaning: to strive for the prototype of a filial son, who when tortured even by mistake, stoically endures the ordeal without uttering a word of explanation, and from that mistreatment grows all the more resolved in his conviction to serve his parents, as if it were a religious awakening by which he gains a spiritual satisfaction for being a worthy child and therefore a worthy human being. Suffering itself acquires a spiritual as well as an aesthetic value.

Worshiping parents who live with you all the time is not the same as worshiping a supernatural deity. God does not give concrete everyday instructions, such as to massage his back, nor are his feelings known. What the child has to obey is not a set of written rules, but arbitrary demands that change according to circumstances and mood of his parents. The key to pleasing them is to understand and anticipate what they want in any given situation, preferably before they issue any orders. The father sits down in the living room. The child knows by habit he may want some tea, so he goes to the kitchen, fetch the tea set and lay it on the table. The mother complains about her back, which is an obvious signal that functions like an order. On New Year's Eve many kids in the neighborhood get presents. But this father wants to forego presents, perhaps because he did not do so well last year and is tight on budget. Yet he does not explain. Confucian parents never explain their decisions candidly to children, for it would undermine their authority. The child (five years or older) jealously looks at other kids with wonderful new toys, but he must suppress the urge to ask for anything, which he knows would annoy his parents. Moreover, he senses that they are watching his reactions, so he finds a way to show that he is happy, that he does not mind, that he appreciates whatever he has. Maybe the child can recite many Confucian classics. Neighbors tell his father with envy "how lucky you are to have such a smart kid!" The child knows that his father is flattered but does not like to see any pride from the kid, for pride undermines authority—a proud child tends to gain confidence and become emotionally less dependent on parents. So he adopts a modest posture, shy, reserved and submissive, which pleases his father who likes to intimate to others that this kid is brilliant, but more importantly *his*.

As the child grows up he acquires a skill to discern his parents' motives which are always unspoken. This not only requires experience but active thinking. He must constantly try to stand in their shoes, think about what he would have liked if he were the father or the mother with children to order around, and present suggestions. Such a practice of transposition helps the child to stay in tune with his parents. It is also psychologically tempting. The child is unable to bear his real world existence, which is fearful, precarious and humiliating. He enjoys daydreaming that he is the master of the house. A Western child under the circumstance would dream about take revenge on his father, but early experiences left too deep a scar on the mind of the Asian child to go down that road. He might attempt it in his dreams but it quickly invokes a paralyzing fear and turns him back. Over time this repeated character substitution confuses his sense of identity. The self becomes a convoluted idea that is both the slave and the master. When the father is upset, say from some business dealings outside, the child becomes upset as well. He does not know the reason why his father is upset, but that in and of itself induces a true feeling in him. The next day his father lightens up, and he immediately follows that mood.

Now the child has completed the third and final step of Confucian training. The first step instills fear and perpetual insecurity. The second step turns him inward and subservient. After the third step the child suffers from a particular form of permanent Stockholm Syndrome. He not only falls in love with his tormentor, now cast as his savior, but emotionally identifies with him. Coercion in a perceived inescapable confinement induces Stockholm Syndrome, while the *en* logic rationalizes and solidifies it. The child is now mentally full grown as an Asian (懂事), even if he may only be a few years old. He understands the full psychological meaning of hierarchy. With this preparation at home they are easy to govern, because the state can be both the oppressor and the object of worship at the same time.

Behind these steps there is a simple push and pull mechanism that is repeatedly applied by the tormentor. He first pushes you to desperation, by threats, by inflicting pain, and by letting you realize that there is no way out, ever. This heightens your awareness that your life is and will always be in his hands. Thus his animosity is doubly threatening. This push is called the threat (威) method. When you are desperate, he then pulls you back with acts of kindness, showing his gentle side, doing you some favors (*en*). This gives you hope, that his love and kindness are obtainable, so long as you can please him, which sets you off on a search for ways to do so. This pull is called the *en* (恩) method. A skillful master uses both (恩威并施) to train a subject into a willing slave. The mechanism is not only used by parents, but by military commanders on their troops, by teachers/masters on their pupils/apprentices, by officials on their clerks, by rulers on their ministers and common subjects, by any superior on his inferiors.

This lengthy and painful process establishes for the child the Confucian parent-child relationship, which will serve as a model for any future inter-personal relations, and it significantly shortens the learning curve for him when in adulthood he inevitably encounters superiors, such as teachers (of literary or of any other trades), village elders, state officials, and if he is lucky enough to climb high on the social hierarchy, the top ruler himself. In each of these encounters he perceives that his superior holds the power of life and death over him, just as his parents did earlier. So he quickly gets into the familiar emotional state he has had with his parents. He acts submissively. Whenever he is mistreated and resentment begins to germ, he tells himself that this is his *en* man, that he owes his life to him, an *en* he can not ever repay, and he tries to put himself in the shoes of this superior, from where he realizes it was really an act of mercy, by which he is then moved. He develops an emotional bond with the boss. Every act of concern, including verbal and physical abuse, only serves to strength that bond.

One day he will be a superior to someone, if no other adults then at least his own children. It is finally his chance to enjoy the dominant side of the Confucian parent-child relationship. This in many ways is a dream come true. Having served others all his life, and being thoroughly humiliated in the process, he is left with deep psychological scars. He is full of latent hatred and anger, which he takes out on his inferiors. On paper or in his words, he is educating the young, training an apprentice, or teaching a subordinate, but what goes on in his mind is a combination of releasing long accumulated anger and the pleasure of seeing other people suffer what he once suffered and continue to suffer at the hands of his own superior. As he moved higher in social hierarchy, there are fewer people above him, more below him, and he plays the inferior role less, the superior role more frequently. But wherever he sits in that pyramid structure, there are always superiors and inferiors. What binds the layers together is the Confucian parent-child relationship.

This relationship stretches the meaning of love, a word I have occasionally used in the context for lack of better alternatives. Parents do care about their child, who is their most valued possession. They feed him, clothe him, invest in his education, and hope that one day he will climb high in the social hierarchy. Yet at any point of his life if the child becomes independent or shows any sign of not wanting to serve his parents, they immediately turn against him with the utmost fury, righteous indignation, and malice: if we can't have you, we want to destroy you. Is this love? The child's emotional attachment and devotion to the parents are very real. Many would not hesitate to give up all their possessions, even their lives, for the parents. But considering this emotional state is brought about by a long term coercive training program, where the child is inflicted with tremendous pain and psychological torture, which left permanent and devastating damages to his psyche, can it be called love? Maybe not to a Westerner. But to Asians, this is love.

In his formative years the child also observes the material world, and learns cause and effect, reason. But when it comes to inter-personal relations, his mind is fully occupied by the emotional turmoil of Confucian training, which is inherently coercive. However, this is not called coercion, for coercion is a negative concept, and Confucian training is the right thing to do. While a Western child learns about fairness and justice, and more importantly, calling a spade a spade, the Asian child is given a tortured logic that does not make sense by objective reason. If you ask any Asian adult why filial piety, he will give you the standard answer: the *en* logic. But this is not the result of objective reasoning. What happens is that after the brutal process the mind learns a trick: to close parts of it to reason, the parts related to social relations, because in the distant childhood past trying to reason filial piety led to doubts and resistance which in turn caused unbearable pain. That memory of early childhood may have faded into obscurity, but the scars it left behind are clearly palpable. The mind subconsciously knows that there are certain forbidden areas reason can not touch. Realization of the existence of a superior-inferior relationship in any situation would quickly trigger this reaction. Over time the individual learns that everything concerning social relations—family or state—follows the same fixed pattern, and belongs in that untouchable realm. The only category of knowledge left open for reason is that about materials and the natural world, such as numbers and objects. The brain is thus bifurcated into a realm of absolute rules beyond reason and a realm of normal development concerning mainly with the material world. The rules and psyche that were originally forced into the brain are fully digested and accepted, to the extent that the individual does not even realize that these were forced on them in the first place.

Beyond the question of whether this kind of possessive relationship can be called love, there is a more profound issue: are the actions of an individual in such a perpetual inferior position out of free will? Is someone suffering from Stockholm Syndrome acting out of his free will? One is tempted to say no. But it is not that simple. In an earlier stage the inferior may constantly sense coercion. He acts out of fear. But when pushed further he took the step of emotionally identifying with his tormentor. Then the fear disappears or becomes latent, imperceptible on a conscious level. A son can be ingenious in finding ways to please his father, as can students, peasants, clerks, merchants, officials, and ministers to their respective superiors. Their actions are voluntary, not prescribed and not always for material rewards. If we say yes, it is free will, then we are basically saying that coercion leads to resentment, but further coercion that forbids resentment leads to freedom.

We face this issue over and over again in Confucian conceptions of courage, honor, devotion, love, patriotism, etc. Do Japanese kamikaze fighters act out of their free will? Are they brave? The apparent answer is yes. But they are all trained in a program similar to Confucian child rearing process outlined here. In the first step of training they are all coerced. They all become fearful of superiors, now taking the position of parents. In the next step they are pushed further. They are not allowed to harbor resentment. They have to find a way to persuade themselves of the *en* logic. They have to go through the mental process of transposing themselves to the position of their superiors. They have to act like fierce fighters and make the acts convincing, in which process they turn themselves into real fighters, fearless of enemy, but fearful of superiors (more on that later).

Confucian child rearing is a form of coercive persuasion. It is more thorough going than the previously discussed form of using ambivalent language that implies threat. Here the threat is materialized, amplified and often repeated in blatant fashion, applied to helpless children before they acquire the language skill or brain capacity to articulate it, in order to maximize the push effect. Once pushed to desperation any act of mercy will be keenly felt, making for a powerful pull. This is in Asian eyes the process of education, indoctrination, and civilization, similar to domesticating animals.

CHAPTER 11

ZEN, EN AND THE BIRTH OF JAPANESE CIVILIZATION: BUSHIDO

In the five centuries between the seventh and the twelfth, Japan had a political system that on paper looked Chinese, with a centralized administrative structure and a replica of the same legal code, but was operated by people with a tribal mentality, where each clan tried to maximize its land and slave holdings, with the imperial clan simply being the most prominent if not always the most powerful of all. One of the most glaring dilemmas in this scenario concerns land ownership. In China it was understood that the emperor owned everything under heaven. High ranking officials were given land temporarily as a stipend in the form of rent collected therein. Continued "ownership" of such land depended on continued service in royal court down the generations. Only in very rare cases, such as close relatives of the emperor, was permanent land ownership possible. Consequently the Chinese legal code had no clause protecting private land ownership.

Japanese never had the idea that the emperor owned everything under heaven. When Chinese style taxation rules were introduced they were not given any justification, instead they merely reflected military muscle of the imperial court in seventh and eighth centuries. Since ninth and tenth centuries powerful ministers like the Fujiwara's and prominent Buddhist temple chiefs were able to bargain better deals for themselves at the expense of the emperor, who was often a puppet. They obtained first tax-exemption then legal independence for their land holdings, which imperial agents were barred from entering. In other words they owned their mini independent states. Meanwhile rich farmers with smaller estates adopted the practice of naming their rice paddies after themselves, thus becoming "named masters" (名主, *myoshu*), in an attempt to permanently keep private land property.

The need to name rice paddies after oneself stemmed from the contradiction between a culture that traditionally accepted private land ownership and an imported legal code that did not give it any recognition. A name might help solidify claim to a particular piece of arable land, but it did not define the nature of that claim. Named masters were still subject to Chinese style taxation and unpaid labor laid on them by governors and magistrates of the court, which were often exacting. Some of the local gentry were compelled to donate their estates to a powerful minister or priest in the capital, in exchange for tax exemption status.

The resulting situation was one of confused land ownership. A rice paddy may be named after a farmer, who controlled the peasants plowing it and claimed a share of the yield, but at the same time owned by a court noble hundreds of miles away in the capital, who also claimed a share of the yield. The partition of their shares was decided by their relative power. For centuries court nobles took the lion's share and were the rich oligarchs in Japan, while the local gentry who managed the estates that bore their names were at the mercy of these nobles, who controlled taxation, judgment over disputes and enforcement of the penal code through court appointed provincial governors. If one had no backer in the court, his status as an estate manager or land owner would immediately become vulnerable. Under the circumstance the best that local gentry could do was to arm themselves and their trusted servants with swords, armor and horses, making it harder to dislodge them from their entrenched positions (naming rice paddies was obviously not enough to secure ownership). Thus small bands of warriors (武士団, *bushidan*) were formed in many communities. Now a noble trying to bully a disobedient estate manager would have to think twice, for if not careful the situation could turn violent quickly.

Such a measure would not have worked in China but it did in Japan. Though the imperial court could in theory summon an army from anywhere in Japan, its mountainous terrain made mobilization costly, therefore such a measure was reserved only for the direst occasions where there was a real crisis of national proportions. Local disputes over land were resolved between concerned parties. Authority from higher ranks was still considerable, but fearless local fighters were often able to keep their share better than others. Of course nobles in the capital could also hire armed agents, which they did. But that did not change the power dynamic: brute force was now a factor and here to stay. Meanwhile some nobles in the capital left for the provinces, either of their free will or by demotion. A few of them seized opportunities of the time and established themselves as powerful estate owners with sizable warrior battalions, thus becoming warlords.

An ostensible Confucian system where there was supposed to be no power centers outside the imperial court, and the vast majority of the land was to be evenly distributed among the peasantry, gradually gave way to a system of many interest groups, comprised of powerful court ministers and their cronies, large religious institutions, various local officials and land controllers who found their niche in the system either by association with court nobility or by clan based military prowess. The peasants who were supposed to be controlled by magistrates directly appointed by and loyal to the crown, were instead dependent on these interest groups, which often took the form of clans, on whose land they worked. The native and ancient Japanese political structure made a comeback by weakening the adopted system from within. This process took place quietly and met with no outrage, even when an insurrection broke out and large scale military action was called for by the court.

The way military was supposed to be organized, according to the Chinese code adopted earlier, was for peasant families to provide foot soldiers and equipment (i.e. every fifty families supply one soldier), local magistrates to provide mounted officers, all of them to gather at the call of the emperor, who would appoint a general to lead the troops. Since land was gradually gobbled up by court nobles and local gentry, peasants were fully controlled by and thus only loyal to their immediate masters. In the first large scale insurrection that happened in tenth century the prescribed mechanism did not work. What came to the emperor's rescue was not a peasant army directly at the disposal of the court, but powerful warlords with their private armies. This was a clear sign that the imported system was breaking down and would have raised red flags for any Chinese Confucian, but the Japanese emperor apparently saw nothing wrong with it, as he awarded the meritorious warlord the fifth rank—the highest rank allowed for military officers by the imported code.

Regardless of rank the top warlords gradually replaced court nobles of old as the real rulers of Japan, and they ushered in a new culture to the capital. To these warriors who grew up in the provinces, reality was often brutal, following a simple and straightforward logic. They hardly ever had the luxury to choose between different courses of action, separating the proper from the improper. Though they preferred material comfort and convenient services in the capital, their mental callousness born out of rough experiences prevented them from fully appreciating the humanitarian side of a refined culture. Their approach was practical, effective and often cruel.

From the tenth century onward small scaled armed conflicts never ceased in the provinces. Some spilled over into the capital. The imperial residence was burnt on average once every six years by armed rebels. Even in times of tranquility the danger of bloodshed was never far from the surface. The old system was showing signs of crack. Law and order was on the decline. Everyone including retired emperors needed the protection of armed servants—the samurai.

Back then a warrior could be from any family origin, estate managers, small land owners, peasants, homeless wanderers—rich patrons would hire any man able and willing to fight, and warlords themselves were armed and trained as well. The word *bushi* (warrior) denotes their profession regardless of rank. A warlord was also a *bushi*. The word samurai specifically refers to a servant who happened to be a man of sword, as opposed to other types of servants. They were not just guards. They were warriors who had to be always ready for battle, which could come with or without notice. A small land owner might hire several samurai as permanent family servants. He might swear loyalty to a large land owner, who could in turn swear allegiance to a major warlord. Bands of warriors were organized in such a hierarchy. Buddhist temples had no choice but to train professional warrior monks, whose job was to protect temple property.

By late twelfth century there was a new political development. After a few large scale wars between the most powerful warlords in the name of protecting the crown and putting down rebellions, where the imperial court often played important political roles siding with one faction or another, a warlord from eastern Japan finally emerged as the big winner, and established hegemony throughout much of Japan. Unlike his predecessors who were content with a privileged life in the capital (present day Kyoto area), he chose to stay with his powerbase in the east (close to present day Tokyo area), and rule the country from there.

What prompted this change had a lot to do with the newly imported idea of *en* (恩, pronounced *on* in Japanese). Though a band of warriors had always been a hierarchical organization, *en* changed its nature just like it did to Chinese father-son and ruler-minister relations. Earlier relationship between a warlord in the capital and his warriors in the provinces was one of calculated mutual interest. The warlord needed his followers to solidify his position in court, and the warriors needed him against encroachment from other court nobles, governors and other factions. Each land owner and his tiny group of warriors lived on his own land. Only by membership in this loosely associated larger organization did them find security, for private land ownership was not legally recognized. This relationship was more like an informal contract, which the warlord in the capital tended to breach over time, and individual warriors had no recourse. With the introduction of *en* a landowner who provided a job for his warrior servants (samurai) became their *en* man (恩人), just like a father is the *en* man of his children. The entire *en* logic—such an *en* can never be repaid even one ten thousandth—kicks in, and the samurai became loyal and devoted slaves of their master. Through wars and conquering this relationship was solidified among the ranks. A warlord would give parts of newly conquered land to his generals, which constituted his *en* (divine favor) to them, in exchange for their pious loyalty (忠). The generals would repeat a similar process down the rank and file. Lower ranks did not get land but a fixed stipend. Thus we have a vertical hierarchy where each man was the *en* man of his inferiors, therefore their master, and at the same time a slave of his superior.

Such an organization is structurally and emotionally far stronger than one based entirely on mutual interest. Warriors are required to be always willing and ready to sacrifice their own lives for their *en* man unconditionally, which is more than any rational calculating man can accept. It is to replace one's father with one's warlord and treat him as an object of pious worship. Such an emotionally charged relationship can hardly be managed remotely. A warlord must play the role of a father. He must take concern in private matters of his inferiors—their marriage, their children, their family disputes—and make decisions to settle these things, just like a father would do for his grown sons. It is through these constant interactions that a warlord refreshes his *en* to the followers, and reinforces their sense of debt and resolve to serve. If a warlord moves away for an extended period, any memory of his *en* will fade and be replaced by whoever is in charge locally, the closest father figure.

Thus the new triumphant warlord in twelfth century chose to stay with his warriors, and adopted the title shogun, short for "Barbarian Conquering Generalissimo" (征夷大将軍). This title was usually granted to a general in a remote area, facing barbarians or other potential uprising, where the emperor's administrative bureaucracy could not reach, for him to have total power—including the power to kill without asking for permission from the court first—in that region. Earlier Japanese courts used it for expeditions into the northeast barbarian territory, and took it back from the general as soon as the intended military action was completed, following Chinese tradition. But now the title was used in a creative way: it granted the shogun unlimited power over much of Japan—not remote territory—for perpetuity. He then started governing Japan from his bakufu (幕府), or "tent government", a term used earlier by Chinese generals to refer to their military command centers set up on battlefield.

A Chinese general under the same circumstances—having gained military hegemony—would have simply demolished the old dynasty and started a new one, Confucian—or more precisely Mencian—principles did allow such an action, when the reigning emperor was deemed immoral and unfit to rule. That principle, which was part of the Confucian moral system, was not in the legal code, which contained only rules governing the subjects. It was apparently unknown to Japanese. Misuse of the title shogun was yet another gross violation of Confucianism, but it was also telling of the Japanese mind. Human beings like predictability, for it gives us a sense of security, while constant change tends to frustrate and frighten us. It was largely this desire for certainty that drove early humans to investigate nature and human society, trying to find out the rules or the Way of all things, as soon as the human intellect awakens. For Chinese that search led to Confucianism with which they felt they knew everything that they needed to know, as it provided a rationale for everything in this world. For Japanese, Confucian reasoning might have evaded their comprehension, but at least they had had a centralized system complete with worship of the imperial lineage and legal codes that ensured a semblance of peace for five centuries. To abandon that system by dethroning the imperial house would be stepping into uncharted waters, or total intellectual darkness. It was not that they truly believed in the divinity of the imperial line, or else the Fujiwara's would not have dared imprison much less kill a reigning emperor. It was exactly because they understood very little of the reasoning behind the adopted Confucian system that they wanted to hold on to as much of the forms and tokens of it as possible, so as to keep in touch with something familiar, and gain a limited sense of security in what must have seemed to them a mysterious and unreliable world.

Establishment of the shogun government (bakufu) did not end disputes over land ownership. It merely added a second administration to the already confusing layers of authority. The shogun rewarded some of his warriors by substituting them for earlier estate managers. A conflict of interest ensued. The warriors owed their positions to the shogun, but in theory they were managing estates for some court noble in the capital. As the warrior class gained more power relative to the old nobility, they began to keep a larger part of the rent to themselves, sending an ever shrinking portion to the capital, even though the court nobles were still on paper owners of these estates. In the four centuries from late twelfth to late sixteenth, the warrior class as a whole from shogun down to the lowest samurai would gradually take wealth away from the imperial court and nobility in the capital. By late fourteenth century estate-revenue for the warrior class exceeded that of the nobility for the first time; by late sixteenth century even urban commercial activities were under warrior control, many nobles in the capital were reduced to poverty, even the royal house was not faring much better. Through this process land ownership was never clearly defined, but who could claim what portion of the harvest was clearly understood as decided by military power.

Two attempted Mongol invasions of Japan in late thirteenth century shortly before and after their conquering of the Chinese Empire were both defeated by kamikaze, or "divine wind", a typhoon like weather condition that decimated the Mongol fleets. Japanese archeologists have recently found out that the Mongols used inland freshwater ships that were not at all sea worthy for their campaign; they were lucky enough just to reach Japan. Nevertheless, the legend of kamikaze was born, giving credence to the invincibility of Japanese, a divinely blessed people. Blessed indeed they were. Had there not been a sea between Japan and the mainland, they would have stood no chance against Mongol cavalry.

The large scale mobilization to fight Mongols weakened the shogun government and eventually brought about its downfall in early fourteenth century, to be replaced by a short lived imperial rule and then another shogun. By now central command was debilitated, and powerful warlords divided the country into many semi-independent states. About a century later the shogun government buckled and Japan entered its own version of Warring States period, which just like the Chinese version was not a precipitous change at a particular moment in time but a gradual decline of order and escalation of widespread skirmishes and wars.

A comparison between Chinese Warring States (481-221 BC) and Japanese Warring States (1467-1573 AD) can shed some light on both cultures. In both cases a long standing previous order collapsed, not due to violent uprisings fueled by a strong sense of injustice, or a foreign invasion, but by accumulative erosion from within and gradual diminishing of central control. The previous order was imposed on a primitive and amoral people with no justification given or sought; in its duration people tasted peace and stability maintained by inherited rules which they did not fully understand (Confucius did not fully understand the design by Duke of Zhou centuries earlier). When that system finally succumbed to changing realities people were ill equipped to analyze what exactly went wrong and what to do about it. Some of them had nostalgic memories of the past. Others embraced new found opportunities amidst declining order. It was the demise of the old order that set the stage for ingenuities of the people, as the Warring States period in both cases gave birth to their respective civilizations.

If we look closer conditions were quite different between the two. Chinese warring states—Zhou states—started as state-families of their lords; they were as old as the Zhou Empire itself, always independent of each other, thus their legitimacy was never an issue. When Zhou imperial power perished, it was simply an overlord fading away, which did not fundamentally change balance of power between states. Within each state peace and order was largely maintained. Origins of Japanese warring states were far more dubious. Most of them were pockets of land, gifts of *en* from a succession of shoguns to family members and high ranking warriors, a practice that certainly could not be found in the imported legal code, by which legitimacy of the shogun government itself was never really settled. The fact that each of these shogun regimes failed to last a decent period without internal strife did not help, nor did a wave of usurpation where high ranking samurai in the family service of the lords took over their respective states (下克上).

In short the Japanese states had little legitimacy save brute force, which only added to the already heightened sense of insecurity in an era of chaos. For a Chinese minister to topple his king, he would have to accumulate power, wealth and reputation for decades, then find a once in a lifetime opportunity, devise a careful plan including a thoughtful cover up, to finally succeed. In the much smaller and unstable Japanese states with shifting borders the ruling elite were warriors struggling for survival and recognition, rather than nobles used to a leisurely lifestyle and court intrigues. They never parted with their swords. Danger was always just around the corner. All it took to topple a warlord was a close up opportunity and one good swing.

In a Chinese state that was typically a hundred times larger than a Japanese one, the focus was *macro* management. War was a distant danger, rarely an immediate threat; kings had ample time to entertain sweeping reforms, even the most successful of which took years if not decades to fruition. Political and moral philosophies, statecraft, and diplomatic maneuvering were issues of the day. War was an extension of foreign policy and not taken lightly. It was about strategy, planning, battles between not just powerful personalities—kings and generals—but also social, political and military ideas. When diplomacy failed, treaties torn, promises broken, compromise rejected, all other alternatives exhausted, and they finally came, wars were epic battles of immense proportions where hundreds of thousands could perish in one setting and fate of the empire could turn on the outcome.

Japanese idea of war was quite different. Land was limited and there was nothing a warlord could do domestically to increase income. To get rich he had to raid other states' crops, horses, and kill their warriors. In addition to state military forces numerous hordes of nomadic warrior bandits were roaming around the country constantly looking for opportunities. These homeless bandits usually raided for profit and run, but if a weak state presented itself they would not mind taking over either. In much of Japan there was no order whatsoever. The pressure was high on a lord to lead his samurai into battle frequently, for only by conquering other states could he have land to reward his warriors and revenue to recruit more, and sitting still content with his own minuscule territory was tantamount to suicide. Wars were much smaller in scale than in China, but far more frequent, prevalent and unpredictable. Thus in a Japanese state the focus was *micro* management of a small professional military force. To establish himself a lord had to first fight rivals on his own turf, which often included his own family members. A brother killing another was not at all uncommon. He then must find a way to guarantee loyalty of his professional warriors, when every one of them could be secretly planning to take his life and place. The Japanese condition was far more violent and ruthless on a personal level.

Drastic conditions call for radical measures. A lord must set in stone a master-slave relationship with his samurai. It is not enough that such a relationship is acknowledged, but it must be taken to heart by all samurai. They must see him as their *en* man, and feel that they owe him what they can never repay. In other words they have to accept the *en* logic. Since the *en* relationship is a very personal one that can not be remotely managed, warlords wanted to gather their samurai in their castle towns. For centuries warriors stayed close to their own rice paddies scattered around the landscape, even after they swore loyalty to a warlord. By mid sixteenth century they were forced to move in with their lord, and start the process of psychological conditioning, similar to Confucian family training.

When a samurai first settles in the residential compound of his lord, he may have some sense of pride in his independence and self-worth. After all, as a warrior he has been a strong man on his own turf. He realizes that the lord is his boss and he can not afford to offend him in any way, but his pride keeps him from acting like an abject slave. He may ask questions as to why he is ordered to do this and that, and is usually rebuked, for his lord does not like to be questioned. He may then become a reluctant subordinate. He is a little soft in answering orders, a little heavy-footed in going into action, and a little disgruntled in his facial expression or body language. His lord can not tolerate any of that. The samurai is subjected to a beating and a threat. This is to be his wakeup call, if he continues his reluctant ways next time it will be his head.

This is enough to scare anyone who wants to live on because the threat is palpable. If the samurai is of a passive nature, fear now dominates his mind and blocks out all preconceived thoughts, leaving only the part necessary for survival. From now on he will blindly follow all orders without even thinking about them, because it was the thinking that caused doubts, slowed his action and brought him to the brink of death. In other words he forces his mind into a state of cognitive freeze. The human instinct of self-preservation is transformed to the instinct to follow orders. Initially following orders is to stay alive, but for many the brain loses that part of its capacity over time due to inactivity, and even an order of suicide is taken without question.

From a more assertive samurai the initial reaction is not only fear but also anger. Yet he knows he can not show any displeasure with his lord. He is tormented inside. He can not resolve the mental conflict between the adrenaline urge to take revenge at his emotional enemy, the lord, and his inability to even utter a word. To make matters worse, the humiliation continues, as he still has to kneel, prostrate and take orders from the same lord. His immediate solution is to release all his energy in physical activities, in training or in battle. He takes it out on his enemy in battle or inanimate targets in practice, sometimes innocent peasants as well. By the end of the day he wants to be so tired that there is no more energy to even think, sparing him further torment. This mental state may last a while. Though he can get through the day, he knows there is something in his heart that is acutely painful, something he dares not touch, and he desperately looks for a way out. Mentally he is pushed to the brink.

The opportunity comes when his hard work in battles is rewarded by his lord, typically in the form of a promotion. The lord now has a benevolent side to him (the pull), softening his image. The samurai then faces a touch choice. If he continues to hold a grudge secretly, he would have to be an actor—and a pretty good one—indefinitely. On the other hand, if he chooses to accept the lord as his *en* man, which he can now justify to himself with the promotion and privileges that come with it, then all his mental sufferings are gone, and he can be an honest man again. It is hard for a bystander to accept the logic that a little reward is enough to turn a man into a loyal slave, but the man is willing after the hard push. By embracing the lord as his master, he can finally settle all the anger caused by humiliations suffered at the lord's hand: it is simply unwarranted and stupid. In fact had the lord not disciplined him in the first place, he would not have had the energy and made the career progress, now he tells himself. The lord is a divine figure and even his harsh treatment is a blessing in disguise. Now the samurai is transformed and enlightened. He retains his assertiveness and confidence, in the way intended by Chinese founders of neo-Confucianism.

Regardless of their personality traits in the end all samurai become obedient slaves. But that state of mind can not maintain itself just by momentum alone. It has to be refreshed and reinforced constantly. Samurai are ordered to prostrate whenever and wherever in presence of their lord, and speak loudly when addressing him. When swearing loyalty, they must shout with all their strength, red faced with veins bulging on their necks, so that everyone can hear and see, making it psychologically harder for them to go back on their words: when one has so publicly and forcefully professed his loyalty, the sense of integrity and shame will present an insurmountable barrier for most to renege.

To prevent the few good actors from slipping through the cracks, the lord constantly abuses his samurai, verbally and physically, to see if they snap. Calling a samurai a useless fool is a good start, followed by a good kick to the side, and see if he quickly returns to the prostration position in spite of pain. Sometimes cruel punishments are deliberately meted out over trivial offenses, and reactions are observed. If one is feigning loyalty he would harbor animosity towards his lord. Repeated humiliations at the hands of his emotional enemy will eventually push him over the edge. Only the piously loyal, who worship their lord as their *en* man, who think that they owe their lives to him, will consider whatever he does to them including taking their lives as not only justified, but an act of divine concern, a form of love. These extreme measures will surely weed out the imposters, because they far exceed human tolerance without internalizing the *en* logic.

These training techniques were of course not invented by someone in a morning. They were the result of centuries of trial and error in cutthroat reality for survival, in which the *en* logic first developed in China found its most literal interpretation. A warlord (called a *daimyo* or "big name") could kill any one of his samurai at will, a power that he practically flaunted every day by humiliating them with verbal and body languages. Unlike the Chinese ruler's ownership of his subjects, which was remote, vague and softened by moral ideals of *ren* (mercy), a *daimyo*'s ownership of his samurai and peasants was direct, in-your-face, and immediate. A samurai who offended his lord was ordered to commit suicide. A peasant who failed to withdraw to the side of the road and kneel when a samurai passed by was promptly beheaded without even a word of explanation. The budding sentiment of mercy among court nobility in the capital died with their wealth and prominence. Out in samurai country, life had always been harsh and straightforward. Mercy was not a valid argument for a samurai's life: his lord could not afford it.

There were other more egalitarian forms of relationship among warriors in the early stages of nationwide chaos. In some places there were no lord or a lord was driven away, and the local gentry who armed themselves would form a band on more or less equal basis and mutual interest—to defend the community and their exclusive control of its peasantry. But in the long run these other types of organization proved no match to the *en* based master-slave structure. The idea of equality is ill-defined in Confucianism which by then Japanese had adopted in their family training. While individuals in casual relations can certainly go by human instincts of reciprocity, and maintain a rudimentary system of equality, close knit organizations having to make decisions on important matters concerning life and death can not function without a rich culture that defines code of conduct and mentality for each member. The *en*-based organizations had the richest cultural support from Confucian family values and training, which provides in detail not just how members in different positions should act, but how they should feel. Every samurai intuitively understood that relation, they only had to substitute their lord for parents, pious loyalty for filial piety. In political domain *en* logic fit Japanese reality much better than it did in China. The punishment and favors of a Japanese warlord were much more direct and keenly felt than those from a remote Chinese emperor.

Warlords and samurai found themselves in a perpetual state of violence, which typically came in the form of small scale but deadly skirmishes. In the early stages of the Warring States period, when warlords everywhere were trying to consolidate their power bases, fighting happened in such a frequency and unpredictability that most of it was not major planned actions by a state, but lethal brawls between small factions. In each locale warriors were fighting to the death to decide who would be the lord. Once a winner emerged every local samurai became his family slave. They then set out on battles against neighboring villages and states. The entire country was at war, but it was not a clearly defined civil war of a few sides, it was just a state of chaos from which no one, warriors or peasants, was spared. At such time a man had basically two choices: to be a peasant or a warrior. A peasant could avoid fighting, but he would be lower than the samurai in hierarchy, which meant he could be arbitrarily killed by a samurai. It was a reality where no one could find safety whatever their choice.

One might wonder what happened to the imported Chinese civilization. The fact is the previous centuries only looked like Chinese style rule by copying its practices, but without an understanding of its reasoning failed to capture its moral essence. Warriors took Confucian family hierarchy to heart, but not the moral idea of *ren*—mercy, commiseration. The Confucian hierarchy prescribes absolute obedience on the part of the inferior, but also mercy on the part of the superior. The latter part was totally lost on Japanese. For a long time local officials fought each other for control of peasants and a share of their harvest. There was no cultural norm or moral justification as to who should own what. It all depended on power—backing of court nobility early on and military muscle in later periods. Buddhist indoctrination that everything in this world of dust is of fleeting nature and meaningless added to the perception that there is no good or evil—one must simply take what he can get or accept his fate. If one warrior cut down another and laid claim to his rice paddies, for example, it did not at all stir any widespread outrage or any righteous indignation in the community. Instead acts of aggression were taken as a natural way of life, survival of the fittest. The orderly society installed by the imperial court earlier was merely understood as the imperial clan imposing its will on the masses and nothing more. The subsequent semi-orderly society controlled by the shogun was taken similarly: a new power clan imposing its ways in the same manner as the old. Now that both clans were falling by the way side, it was time for anyone with a sword to stake his claim. A similar mentality may have existed in pre-historical Japan, but back then the land was sparsely populated, people had no horses and only stone-age weapons, and waging constant war was not practical. After centuries of Chinese style centralized rule and order population ballooned, competition for land intensified, the nature of social hierarchy became more exploitive and oppressive, and anger among warrior ranks exploded, not in the moral sense that oppression was wrong and there needed to be a more fair system, but a more primitive sense that they were squeezed and looked down upon, and they deserved a higher position in the same hierarchy, which they intended to get by force. What emerged then in many communities throughout the land was a cannibalistic environment of unmediated violence.

The Japanese condition is not to be confused with that of feudal Europe, where it generally took some justification to start a war: in the name of a king, a duchy, the Church, an ethnic group, to reclaim their land that they had historically held, to restore their tradition and glory, etc. Under normal circumstances a European lord could not simply attack a neighbor just to grab his land and possessions without a pretext. There was a sense of right and wrong in the society, largely based on the Greco-Roman idea of justice, which kept relative peace most of the time. As a result violence was not frequent. When a knight fought, it was to defend a peaceful and privileged way of life, something he looked forward to as soon as he finished fighting. Japanese on the other hand did not need any pretext to start a war. One lord would attack the next as soon as an opportunity availed itself. When a lord died and his heir was underage or appeared to be incompetent, his family servants would start killing each other over his property. War was less a result of strategic planning to permanently enhance the wealth and power of a state, more a necessity of survival in the jungle. Warlords for the most part did not plan way ahead in the game of domination; it was largely pointless—anyone, even the most powerful warlords, could be cut down the next day without warning, either on battlefield by enemies, or at home by usurpers and conspirators. They did not have the choice to opt for peace, either, for if one were to flinch from a military challenge, regardless of how or why it was waged, he would merely show weakness, invite more enemies and alienate potential allies. There was no sense whatsoever that one side was justified and the other was not; the entire country was an amalgamation of hundreds of turf wars going on all at the same time; moral justification was not attempted or even conceived.

Another reason for the incessant fighting can be explained by the difference between a samurai and a European knight. A knight was a free man. Owing to Greco-Roman tradition a free man could not be arbitrarily punished much less killed by his lord, he would first have to be convicted of a crime by a court, judged by his peers or by nobles. He could also move freely and engage in any business that he chose to. These rights gave the knight a great deal of leverage when dealing with his lord, in fact he was treated as an equal in the legal sense. His obligation to his lord was essentially an item of a contract between two equals, from which he could withdraw. Knights sometimes refused to fight for their lords when they deemed the cause unjust, as did barons sometimes reject their kings. The knight's life was decent and worth defending, which was the whole point of his obligation. The samurai on the other hand was a fully owned slave of his lord the *daimyo*, who could arbitrarily order his death or any other punishment. His obligation was not just to defend his master's interest, but to do anything and everything his master ordered him to do, including suicide attacks, selling his own sister to prostitution, killing a friend, or whatever else was deemed necessary for the lord's purpose.

He could not engage in duels of his own choosing, in fact dueling was banned between warriors of the same lord, because he did not want to see two valuable slaves killing each other. A samurai had no way out but to fight to the last breath whenever and wherever his lord ordered him to. Even though "face" (shame) was of utmost importance, and insult was taken seriously, it was routine for a lord to insult his samurai, while the same derogatory comments if uttered by a fellow samurai of equal or lower rank would enrage him.

No one naturally liked being a slave, and the samurai was no exception. His desire was natural for anyone in his position: to get out of the short end of the master-slave relation by climbing the social hierarchy. He could do it by helping his master win wars and conquer enemy territory, whereby he might be rewarded with some land, and become a master in his own right. With his own rice paddies he would have a steady income, peasant slaves, and the opportunity to arm his own family servants, fight wars on his own initiative, and become a *daimyo*—big name—himself. The predicament of a petty warlord was similar. He might have a piece of farmland to support a small clan, but his foothold in the age of violence was by no means secure. The only way to enhance his security was to conquer, expand and turn himself into a dominant force. War was the only means of upward social mobility and personal security, and there was no moral obstacle to its waging for the sole purpose of material gain. The two conditions—an amoral culture and a master-slave hierarchy, which reinforced each other—made for a unique situation in world history, where fighting was not to defend or obtain a way of life; for Japanese warriors, it *was* life.

In the harsh Japanese condition the Confucian social hierarchy adopted a more naked and cruel form, where master-slave relations were applied between virtually all grades, even where it was not warranted by orthodox Confucianism. The relationship between elder and younger brothers, for instance, was not supposed to be a master-slave relation, but predicament of the proverbial warrior family changed its nature. In order to keep a warrior clan from weakening due to division of property between brothers, a practice became prevalent where the eldest son would inherit all and his younger brothers nothing, which made the latter family servants of the former at the death of the father, just like other samurai in the clan. To prepare younger sons to accept this eventuality, they were trained as they grew up to be absolutely obedient to their eldest brother as well as to their parents. Thus even within a nuclear family there were three levels of ownership type hierarchy. Among all the samurai serving one lord there were many more levels of hierarchy, all of which took a severe form, as in a person of a slightly higher rank could arbitrarily abuse a person of a slightly lower rank. Without the moderating value of mercy Japanese social hierarchy was not just about privilege, status and wealth, it was about survival. A lord could arbitrarily kill any of his samurai, a high ranking samurai could kill his own warrior servants, and any samurai could kill any peasant with impunity. Because of this awesome power of a superior over an inferior, the meaning of a warrior's rank was far more basic than honor, ego or material benefits, it was literally his life.

To understand the cruelty of the Japanese condition, we can look at the practice of *hara-kiri* (disembowelment), a ritual suicide, often ordered by a lord for one of his samurai. Here is an Englishman's eye witness account of one of these rituals in the nineteenth century:

" . . . Bowing once more, the condemned allowed his upper garments to slip down to his girdle, and remained naked to the waist. Carefully, according to custom, he tucked his sleeves under his knees to prevent himself from falling backward; for a noble Japanese gentleman should die falling forwards. Deliberately, with a steady hand, he took the dirk that lay before him; he looked at it wistfully, almost affectionately; for a moment he seemed to collect his thoughts for a last time, and then stabbing himself deeply below the waist on the left hand side, he drew the dirk slowly across to the right side, and, turning it in the wound, gave a slight cut upwards. Through this sickeningly painful operation he never moved a muscle of his face. When he drew out the dirk, he leaned forward and stretched out his neck; an expression of pain for the first time crossed his face, but he uttered no sound. At that moment, the *kaishaku* (the helper at the ritual), who, still crouching at his side, had been keenly watching his every movement, sprang to his feet, poised his sword for a second in the air; there was a flash, a heavy, ugly thud, a crashing fall; with one blow the head had been severed from the body."

Once a samurai is ordered to commit *hara-kiri* he has no way to dodge death. Suicide is an honorable way to die; it basically says that the condemned made a mistake which his master can not forgive, but he is still recognized as a samurai and his family will be taken care of after his death. If he resists he will be beheaded, in which case he will be seen as unworthy of a warrior's name and his family will suffer the shame. To be able to go through such a gruesome procedure, however, one needs a lifetime of training, of growing accustomed to abuses, numb to physical pain. Spiritual/psychological preparation is indispensable in that effort.

Predicament of the samurai strongly resonates with Buddhism's worldview. Warlords frequently abused their samurai both verbally and physically, showing them no mercy at all. The samurai was ordered around, scolded, insulted, beaten and made to commit suicide, without even a shred of leniency being detectable in this bare bones master-slave relation. No prisoners were taken in battles, because one who surrendered was considered a traitor to his master, and therefore not worthy of the samurai's name. He would be branded a coward and immediately executed by the opposing side, for no lord wanted to take in a spineless traitor. To go into battle one must be prepared to die. To stay at home one must also be always prepared to die, not just from enemy attacks but from the sword of his own master as well. In the world of the samurai everything changed quickly and unpredictably. Death was common and discomfortingly abrupt. Life was cheap, short and meaningless. If he was to cherish life and try to find its meaning he would not be able to bear the perpetual threat and subsequent anxiety. He would tremble every time he talked to his master and fumble with words. He would shake at the sight of an enemy. He would suffer a nervous breakdown and not be able to perform his duty. The only way to find peace in his heart in a life of constant change, gory mutilations and sudden death, was to diminish the value of life and be psychologically prepared to die at any moment. Zen Buddhism came just in time to validate his view of life and give him a permanent peace of mind.

If Zen was inspiration for Chinese neo-Confucian thinkers, it was the air that the samurai breathed every minute of his life. For Chinese monks who try to gain the Zen perspective on life, a lot has to be done in terms of cleansing one's mind of all the trappings of this world and emotions generated from it, to see one's true human nature, as it were. For the samurai this comes naturally. His mind is not sophisticated enough to contemplate moral judgments in the first place, it is rather demanding just to survive and keep his place in the social hierarchy. His life is even less predictable than duckweed floating in a river. It is more like a chrysanthemum which after a short lived blossoming quickly falls to the ground. The world hardly mourns its death. It knows that. But before the end of its short and irrational life, it struggles to stay clean, to blossom, to be as splendid as it can be, and to savor that brief moment of brilliance, of pure bravery, of defiance of the circumstances imposed on it by fate, in a hope to capture the essence and leave traces of this otherwise meaningless journey. So does a samurai. For his entire life he suffers, he endures, he perseveres, and when his time comes, he wants to go out with a bang. Whether ordered to commit suicide or embark on suicidal missions, it is when he senses the end is coming that he shines the brightest, for this is the only moment he can truly be himself. Suicide is not merely a demonstration of loyalty, obedience and bravery; it is the ultimate expression of his essence. Thus taking the easy and quick way out, like slicing one's throat, will not suffice. Only when death involves excruciating pain and the samurai defies it by steadfastly holding back wince and moaning, does he feel that he transcends the mundane of this world, and obtain glory and significance for his entire existence. It is the blossoming of the chrysanthemum, the brightest moment of its life, when it gives all it has, before dropping to the snow covered ground, ending its transient existence in a surrounding befitting its meaning: pure, clean, austere, and breathtaking in its shear resolution.

In the world of Japanese—samurai and peasant alike—the Buddhist worldview proved a self-fulfilling prophesy: that this world and everything in it including human life are utterly meaningless. Because Buddhism was adopted at the very outset of Japanese civilization, it provided amoral explanations to death and human sufferings which otherwise would have evoked deeply felt human emotions like sympathy (*ren*). Everything including death and suffering is part of the life cycle; it is predetermined; it has to do with the previous and the next life; it is fate; it is nature's way, the Dao; we struggle enough just to stay alive, why indulge in morose sentimentality?

This view was developed by Indians who already had a moral sense to reduce the extent of mental torment. If one can not make sense of sufferings of this world, why not look away from it? If one can not physically escape from this world, why not mentally? Indian Buddhism is all about relieving pain, which is seen as a result of human desires. Chinese Zen masters took it in a different direction: in a search for the ultimate truth, the Dao. By looking inside one's own heart and concentrate on meditation, one may find true human nature: a desireless, emotionless and selfless being at peace with the world. It became a quest and a path to true knowledge. Japanese warriors drew solace from the Zen spirit that all things material are but an illusion, and the way to enlightenment is to transcend them all, most importantly life itself. It is this spiritual revelation that proved decisive on battlefields. Those who see life as nothing are always prepared to take it, others' or their own, while the less enlightened have too much on their mind to be ruthless and efficient fighters. Thus Buddhism underwent a dramatic transformation on its northeastward journey. It started as a psychotherapy in India to relieve pain, during the Chinese Zen development the birth-death-rebirth life cycle faded into obscurity, after the samurai adopted it, even the idea of Buddha lost significance. What survived these transformations are the Buddhist view of human life—its meaninglessness—and the psychological implication that fate should be accepted as it is.

Some may question how Buddhism, the religion widely known for advocating peace, can be associated with the samurai, the world's most extreme fighting machine. In its philosophy of escaping suffering by way of self-denial, Buddhism does engender a temperament of peaceful withdrawal in the face of potential confrontation. In fact Buddhism teaches that no life should be taken, because even an ant might have been a human in previous life cycles. In India, Tibet and elsewhere in South and Southeast Asia, where Buddhism/Hinduism (Hinduism carries a similar psychological message) is a state religion, this temperament is strongly encouraged for obvious political reasons. To Asian Buddhists peace means one should refrain from potentially violent protest and passively accept his condition, interpret suffering in this life as fate, instead of what is unjustly imposed on him. It is not a principle or a conscious conviction of an independent and active individual in full possession of his born capabilities, both mental and physical, but rather a manifestation of his passivity and timidity, a survival tactic of slaves. If one's master wants him to be peaceful, as is the case for South Asians, he certainly will be; if the master wants him to fight, as is the case for the samurai, he accepts that as fate too. From the ShaoLin monks in China who invented martial arts to the Ikko monks in Japan who fought warlords, Buddhist temples were routinely engaged in armed conflicts as well as political struggles. Peace can not be a principle all by itself, the history of Japan—the people of "great harmony" (大和)—bears that out, for the question remains: peace under what terms? It is a wish, a feeling, a temperament. In fact the intellectual view of Buddhism is carried to its logical conclusion by the samurai. If life is meaningless anyway, what is wrong with taking it? The enlightened can see the loss of a life as nothing more than the withering of a chrysanthemum, a quintessential Buddhist view that gives him a peace of mind in an otherwise nonsensical world of incessant violence.

What helped the Japanese transformation of Buddhism was the cannibalistic environment of a primitive and amoral culture. Violence was for certain not started by Buddhism. But Buddhist influence did help escalating it by removing the innate human instinct to cherish life and revulsion to gore. By the same token Zen also helped to shape the samurai character, whose fearlessness in battle has less to do with courage but more with utter callousness, the inability to perceive any value in life, others' or his own. Years of exposure to harsh discipline and violence added physical numbness to mental insensitivity, and an awesome fighter unlike any other in the world was born.

A samurai is trained either at home or in a Zen monastery, usually starting at about seven to ten years of age. In both cases the curriculum is the same. It involves archery, horse riding and swordsmanship. These are not to be taken as mere military skills; they are all part and parcel of the Zen spirit. Archery is not about techniques of how to position the bow, draw the arrow, shoot it many times and perfect a skill. You are told instead to draw the arrow and hold it for as long as you can without shooting it. In short order your arm gets sore. The scientific explanation may be that your muscle is stressed or fatigued. The Zen explanation is that you are still thinking about your arm when you need to concentrate on the bow and arrow, as if they were parts of your body, feel their tiny movements, find their tendencies, get intimate with them, until you are able to predict and control their every move, until you know them like the back of your hand. You have to become one with your equipment. When you are holding it, or rather when you are with your weapon, you are not to think about anything else, but to calm down, breathe slowly, and concentrate, just like meditation. The same is true with your sword. By staring at its blade and feeling its sharp edges, you hope to get a glimpse of your own heart, which must be as pure as a drop of water, cold as a block of ice, austere like a mountain cliff, and utterly without emotions like iron. To be a samurai you can not be sentimental. You can not be melancholy, depressed or anguished over the loss of your friends or relatives. These emotions come from veneration of life, which you need to get out of your system. Only when you see the meaninglessness of life can you cut off human heads with the kind of ease and surgical precision as if you were cutting inanimate objects, and face the imminent prospect of your own demise with indifference. The training is less about physical skills and more about psychological conditioning.

To that end the samurai is taught to live a simple life, both materially and intellectually. He is to endure harsh physical punishment and get used to it, at the hands of his father or a Zen master. Physical discipline has at least three purposes. First, it forces absolute obedience to rules and superiors. When an order is issued, actions must follow immediately without thinking, no excuses are accepted. Second, it highlights the irrationality of the rules. The trainee is not supposed to ask questions about why the rules are what they are. Some rules do not make any sense, but that is just the way life is, and you are supposed to observe these rules with no less fervor. Everything handed down from authority is to be believed literally without reason and without reservation. Third, pain is often deliberately inflicted on the body, not as a punishment for mistakes, but to test the will and enlightenment of the individual. Necessities of life such as food, clothing and shelter are kept at a minimum. Trainees are not just to learn skills, which come as a distant second in objectives, but to adopt a way of life, to build their character, to be a warrior, obedient, stoic, fearless, emotionless and resolute.

Zen spirit also worked its way into Japanese art, flower arrangement and tea ceremony. Traditionally Chinese like a big bunch of flowers with various colors and shapes all represented, particularly bright colors, to symbolize richness, warmth and vitality of life. Zen sees the true nature of life as simple, pure and emotionless, like a single leaf of duckweed in clear water. Japanese flower arrangement reflects this view. A single white or purple flower at the end of a long stem surrounded by a few green leaves is the typical style. Its cold colors, solitude and tranquility are all in line with the samurai spirit. To Chinese tea is akin to its modern counterparts smoke or coffee, it refreshes so that one can stay up late at night, or be more alert, alive and thoughtful in a conversation. Tea is part of fleshly desires and drinkers are usually connoisseurs of different kinds of tea leaves, production techniques, taste, quality, etc. They like to show off their fancy tea sets, meticulously embroidered cups, pots, and plates, different sets for different tea: red, green, ruminated, non-ruminated, as well as their knowledge, water temperature, whether to put the lid on to keep flavor in the cup or let it out in the room, whether the first or the second pot is the best. To the samurai none of these matters. Drinking tea is a ritual. In the tea room there is usually a hanging scroll of a few large Chinese characters in calligraphy. There is also a simple flower arrangement and incense. A small tea table and a plain looking tea set. The room is otherwise undecorated. Each person must follow strict dress codes and body language according to their rank. For the one serving tea and the ones drinking it, hands and feet must be in correct form. Tea leaves are grounded into powders so they won't stick to lips. Everything has to be precise. Voices must be low, conversation must be patient. This is no place for a lively debate or frivolous jokes. One wrong move or faux pas would ruin the whole party.

In Japanese tea ceremony Zen and Confucian *li* (礼, pronounced *rei* in Japanese) have come to full marriage. Spartan decoration and complex rituals help the warrior concentrate on the here and now. The atmosphere induces tranquility and cleanses the mind, much like Zen meditation. However the objective is different from that of Chinese Zen masters. To

Chinese Zen monks, human nature lives inside one's heart and outside the material world. To find enlightenment is to first abolish human desires, and second escape from social hierarchy, in other words to achieve spiritual freedom. Japanese warriors see human nature as not only simple and selfless, but also social and hierarchical. What the samurai concentrates on is not intellectual freedom in the privacy of his heart, but his duty as dictated by his social station. Instead of emancipating his mind he freezes it. The samurai needs to get into the mental state of seeing himself as a walking dead man and stay there, so as to be battle ready at all times. Vigorous physical training gets his mind to that state, but for the rest of the day he must vigilantly guard against "impure" thoughts. Tea ceremony and its spirit if taken to heart and applied at meals and other times of leisure will keep the mind from asking any questions. The born human capacity for cognition is consciously and strenuously suppressed, so that the individual will act in reflex, without hesitation or regard to his own life, according to Confucian hierarchical rules.

Now we have the key elements of bushido (武士道), or Way of the Warrior, which is a code of conduct for the samurai that came to define Japanese culture. The objective of this code is to turn every warrior into a devoted slave of his master. Justification of that master-slave relation is provided by the neo-Confucian logic of *en* (恩), and further solidified by Japanese reality that the samurai truly owes his life and livelihood to his lord. Even when that logic is accepted it is still not easy for a man to overcome his born instinct of self-preservation and readily plunge to death for his master. An adrenaline rush caused by a pep talk and some shouting right before battle might help in the short term, but the samurai must be in that state of mind all the time. Here Zen comes in. Adrenaline rush circumvents the issue of death by temporarily disabling the individual's cognition. Zen teaches the samurai to look at death in deliberate contemplation and accept it. He is told to always think of himself as already dead. He is to cut off heads periodically to stay close to death. Dying of old age is not the samurai way. He dies either in battle or by committing ritual suicide. Either way he dies at the sword. He is to always anticipate that eventuality and prepare for it, by regularly subjecting himself to physical pain, sometimes self-inflicted, so that when the moment finally comes, he can keep his good name and avoid shame. With all these training the human instinct of self-preservation and self-interest will not entirely go away. Given a chance they will come back. So the life of the samurai is a constant battle. He needs to stay vigilant. He internalizes the Zen spirit and lets it permeate his everyday routine.

From the moment he gets up in the morning to the time he goes to sleep at night, he carefully controls his every move and does not let his mind wander. Thinking about fairness or why the world is the way it is brings questions to the mind and hesitation in action, which will prove disastrous. A samurai does not think about these or much else. He springs into action upon hearing an order, as a matter of reflex.

This code was developed by high ranking samurai with pious loyalty at heart, just like neo-Confucianism was developed by high ranking scholar-officials with the same motivation. Although many of its elements were there in the Warring States period, it was not articulated until the Tokugawa era, where a stable shogun regime ruled Japan for two and a half centuries (1600-1868). In war time the samurai's trivial mistakes were still forgivable, in peace his value declined and strict adherence to exacting rules was mandatory. Both neo-Confucianism and bushido were important milestones in the counter evolution process, as the entire population were pushed further into slavery with increasingly demanding ethical codes of devotion forced on them. In terms of severity bushido is unmatched in other pyramid cultures. The ethical code literally requires slaves to give their lives for their masters and Japanese warriors actually followed it to the letter.

Chapter 12

JAPANESE CONFUCIANISM

In the year 1600, the last major battle of the Warring States period was fought, in which warlords were divided into two opposing camps, one of them led by lord Tokugawa. At the end of the day his faction won what was the largest battle in several centuries of continuous civil war, where each side boasted about one hundred thousand troops. A new shogun emerged, more powerful than previous ones, and peace was to stay under this shogun government for a long time (1600-1868).

One is tempted to call this a unification or reunification of Japan, since from this moment on there was a shogun government that issued laws and administered various affairs throughout the land. Civil war was over for good. Yet we should not confuse this with unification of China in third century BC after its own Warring States period. There the Qin State conquered all other states one by one, without any outside help or alliance. The Qin army smashed all adversaries or drove them to far away barbarian territories. The Qin ruler was in total control of the entire empire. Tokugawa on the other hand was merely the most powerful of hundreds of warlords. He had under his direct command perhaps thirty thousand warriors, by far the largest of all armies, but without allies he could not maintain hegemony by himself. The Warring States period might be over, but the states—the *han* (藩)—remained.

By virtue of the victory Tokugawa confiscated much land from lords of the losing side, and rewarded his family members and other lords of the winning side. He reorganized the states geographically in such a manner that they formed three circles around the seat of his government—Edo (present day Tokyo). The inner most circle were domains belonging to his family members. The intermediate circle consisted of domains belonging to those lords who allied with him in the deciding battle, therefore proven their loyalty. The outer domains were previous enemies and the least trusted. This was the same political/geological setup of Xia and Shang Dynasty China, if we recall, dominated by a defensive mentality.

By then there had been several shogun governments, neither of which lasted very long. The main reason is that in previous times the *en* logic had yet to be fully absorbed by Japanese warriors. In fact the first warlord to achieve hegemony status in sixteenth century, Oda Nobunaga, was also the first one to force all his samurai to move in his castle town. Without this silent but significant cultural transformation, previous alliances were not nearly as solid. With it, the mental and emotional state of every samurai was visible in his daily actions, in his body language and demeanor, making it almost impossible for internal rebellions to materialize. New rules that forbade the peasantry from possessing any weapons further reduced risks to authority. All that Tokugawa needed to worry now was to keep the lords (*daimyo*) in check.

He devised some clever measures. Every lord was to have a permanent residence in the capital (Edo), where he must stay every other half year. During the time a lord was not in the capital his wife and his heir must stay there as hostage. Lords were prohibited from marrying into each other's family without the shogun's permission, to prevent unwanted alliances. They were not allowed to build strong fortifications in their own domains, taking a page from Confucius' own playbook (he advised the duke to destroy the walled towns belonging to the three barons). Lords were also required to supply free labor for the shogun's construction projects. These measures weakened the lords financially and politically, paving the way for a long reign by the Tokugawa house.

However, to maintain lasting power the new shogun must look beyond experiences of previous warrior regimes, and turn a military force into an administrative apparatus. Laws from past shogun governments did not help, because they were concerned primarily with one thing: land property disputes. That was no longer an issue now lords all established themselves as owners of their respective states. The new shogun government needed a system that tells everyone what is the right (proper) thing to do in all situations, so as to reduce the samurai's tendency to resolve everything by the sword, and bring about an orderly culture.

Seventeenth century Japanese cultural and political reality was in some ways similar to early Zhou Dynasty of China, when *li* was first authored by the Duke of Zhou as a code of conduct for the ruling class, therefore this elaborate system of rules naturally fit the needs of the shogun government. *Li* was known to the imperial court for centuries but largely unknown to warriors. Now interpreted by the crude warrior class, however, most of its egalitarian meanings were downplayed or ignored, such as moderation, yielding, remaining aloof above contentions, and an overall civilized temperament with an aversion to violence. On the other hand, its hierarchical aspect was heightened far beyond Chinese practices. All elements of mercy and emotions surrounding human suffering seemed to the samurai pointless and unmanly. In China evolution of *li* went in the direction of its moral significance (*ren*/mercy); eventually most of the original rules were lost, the rest modified to suit ever increasing moral sensibilities. In Japan largely due to the ascension of the warrior class *li* became a rigid code of hierarchy completely devoid of mercy.

In the adoption by amoral Japan the asymmetry of Confucian ethics is clearly demonstrated. It prescribes detailed, concrete rules when it comes to behavior of the inferior towards the superior, but only vague, abstract moral ideals when it comes to behavior of the superior towards the inferior. What Japanese learned from Chinese, since they could not comprehend abstract moral ideals, were then only the rules that govern the conduct of the inferior. Pious loyalty (忠, pronounced *chu* in Japanese), for example, is supposed to be conditional, predicated upon *ren* (仁, pronounced *jin* in Japanese) on the part of the superior. Since mercy can not be quantified and regulated, the way it worked in China was that forgiveness took its place and was usually expected. When a low ranking officer or clerk botched a job either by lack of effort or ability, he could expect forgiveness by citing his health problems, his family obligations or even his incompetence, and his superior would be compelled to grant leniency by the principle of *ren*. A high ranking officer who strictly enforced harsh rules would earn ill repute, even if he did not violate any written code, and become vulnerable to his political enemies. Because Japanese warlords never had absolute power over the entire empire, and competition for dominance was a permanent fixture of the political scene, none of them was in a secure enough position to grant leniency as a matter of policy to his subjects, which would be seen as a sign of weakness and encouragement for disobedience. We have to remember that in China this moral principle developed only after thousands of years of secure despotic ruling, when the ruler had the confidence to grant mercy without fearing rebellion. Japanese warlords did not have that luxury, nor did their subjects expect any mercy. Stripped of all the mediating virtues, Confucian rules thus became rigid, harsh and brutal. When a man received an order to do something, he was required to accomplish the job, even if circumstances made it impossible. No excuses were accepted. In fact even an attempt at an excuse was seen as a violation of pious loyalty.

One seventeenth century edict reads: "Dress materials must not be used indiscriminately. White twill may be worn only by those above the status of chief minister, white wadded silk only by those above the rank of high official. Purple kimono, and garments with purple lining, of glossed silk, or of crestless wadded silk must not be worn indiscriminately. It is contrary to traditional practice to permit retainers and warriors of various domains to wear garments of twill, brocades or embroideries. These practices must be prohibited by law." It also states: "Those who are allowed to ride palanquins (a litter typically carried by two men) are restricted to dignitaries of the Tokugawa clan, lords of domains, lords of castles, sons of retainers receiving over 10,000 *koku*, sons of *daimyo*, heirs of lords of castles and of those with the status of chamberlain and above. Those above the age of fifty, and invalids under the care of doctors and practitioners of the art of yin-yang are exempt from this prohibition. Others are prohibited from enjoying privileges reserved for those of higher rank. However, those with special permission are exempt. Each *daimyo* may exercise the right to permit certain people to ride palanquins within its domain. Court nobles, heads of monasteries and temples, and monks are exempted from this regulation."

In China rules of hierarchy only applied in inter-personal dealings. If we are both officials and you rank higher than me, then I kneel or kowtow to you when we meet in formal settings, which are rare. When it comes to quality of dress and other material indulgence, one can do whatever one can afford to. Even the average peasant girl rides on the largest palanquin (carried by eight men) on her wedding day. It is one thing to differentiate the style of dresses—for instance, a particular suit in a particular color is designed just for a certain rank—but Japanese took it further to limit the material of which clothing is made to higher ranks. There were numerous rules regulating what each class should consume. Peasants, for instance, were forbidden from buying logs, tobacco, wine, tea, or eat rice as mainstay of their diet, they were supposed to submit all the rice they grew and feed on coarse cereals like pigs. Since time immemorial Japanese culture had always been harsh, partly because there was no physical separation between masters and slaves. Centuries of war pushed cruelty to new highs.

Though Confucius interpreted *li* as primarily an instrument of hierarchy, he could not have possibly foreseen conditions of the samurai, which made it acutely felt. Let us compare what hierarchy means in Chinese and Japanese contexts. Of the five Confucian relations—father-son, ruler-minister, husband-wife, elder brother-younger brother and between friends—the father-son relation is the most severe. The father fully owns his son as a slave for life and can do what he wants with him; the son has no escape and is supposed to serve his father no matter what. The ruler-minister relation though modeled after father-son is less severe because in the era of Confucius and Mencius the minister could simply quit and sever that relation. After unification of China imperial power grew over time, so that eventually a minister usually could not quit over a disagreement with the emperor, but he could still retire for private reasons, such as to take better care of his own parents. In addition, the ruler is supposed to treat his ministers with courtesy and not interfere in their private lives. The Chinese *shi* class—the *wen-shi* (文士), or scholar officials—have always had a strong sense of self-worth. Confucian ideology which made it possible to rule such an immense empire was their creation, and it is not a set of rigid rules, but a living organism that needs to be maintained and sometimes reformed or reinterpreted by these scholars. They are priests, judges, and shepherds of the masses, adult supervisors and care takers of all-under-heaven, often on behalf of an ignorant ruler. Though they are forced to submit to imperial rule, which often favors the servile, the heart and soul of this class always gravitate towards the dignified, and despises the spineless, due to a strong Mencian influence. This is reflected in their lifestyle. They live in separate residences. They rarely visit homes of direct superiors or inferiors, preferring to have a private space. They generally say little and remain reserved in office and only show their true personalities in private with family and friends. Though in theory a superior has awesome power over his subordinates, it is tempered by the Mencian moral principle of mercy. As a result his power rarely manifests in the form of harsh punishment, instead he prefers to use it as an unstated threat. Thus rank usually means a social position that is somewhat removed from or at least softened in daily life. Though everyone is still keenly aware of it, because it defines his social station, it is not intimately felt on a daily basis.

The Japanese *shi* class—the *bu-shi* (武士), or warriors—are less subtle. Their culture was formed in centuries of incessant violence. They operate by the values and emotional bounding of an *en* based relationship, where the lord is the *en* man, to whom his samurai owe their lives and pledge pious loyalty. To maintain that bounding they all live together or in close proximity of one another. The lord is intimately involved in the lives of his high ranking samurai, arranging their marriages, settling their family disputes, playing the role of a Confucian father, stern but also caring, above all controlling. This group live like a large family; and no secrets can possibly be held from each other. Each high ranking samurai then play the *en* man or father figure to his own family servants—lower ranking samurai under his command. The pattern can go down multiple layers in a pyramid. What binds this large group of warriors together, sometimes numbering tens of thousands for the largest state, is the *en* based master-slave relationship between each pair of layers.

Nowhere in Confucian classics does it say that the father-son relation applies between officials of different ranks. In China it rarely does. But the samurai are organized in a pyramid family structure, from the lord—the grandfather—on down to sons, grandsons, etc., so the most severe of all relationships is applied between the ranks. If a Chinese officer is abused by his superior, he can appeal to a higher authority or ask for a transfer, or simply quit. A samurai has no such recourses because he is treated like a son by his superior. Since they grow up in an amoral culture where blood and gore are not just common scenes but necessary courses in their training even after the Warring States period, the father-son relation loses its only mediating factor—mercy. The standard way a lord shows his displeasure with one of his samurai is by ordering him to commit suicide, by way of disembowelment (*hara-kiri*). A high ranking samurai can do the same to lower ranks in his family service. Even if it is discovered later that the judgment was a mistake, based on a rumor or misunderstanding, there is nothing wrong with it. A samurai is supposed to show his pious loyalty by willingly die for his master, that is the core of bushido—the Dao or Way of warriors.

In this environment one's ranking is acutely felt every minute of every day. A samurai not only prostrates for his superior, he is often scolded or beaten and always under the threat of being ordered to die, because no justification is ever needed for that to happen. Simply by virtue of ranking higher one can order his subordinates die. No charges are filed with any court, no process is due, no mercy is called for, just a word can mean a life. This is what hierarchy means in the Japanese context.

Given the nature of this hierarchy every samurai desperately craves to climb the ladder. In times of war he can take enemy heads for credit, but in times of peace how does he compete with others for the lord's favor? The answer is typical for counter-evolution processes: on who is more piously loyal, which in the Japanese context often means who is more reckless with his own life in serving the lord. The lord gives me a job that usually takes three days, I swear I will do it in one, and if I fail, I am ready to cut myself open. This kind of tactics may be risky but the gamble may also pay off, in the form of a promotion. Less dramatic approaches are employed by most, such as strictly following the ever increasing volume of rules adopted from *li*, and working hard and selflessly. By living a diligent life without a fault one will eventually get promoted when the older generation retires at the age of seventy. Committing no fault in one's entire life is a tall order, particularly given the stringent code one has to observe, sometimes requiring death.

Because of fierce competition, particularly among lower ranking samurai who rarely get a chance to see their lord, one can not afford even a slightly tarnished reputation. A rumor like "that guy Yoshiro is a coward" or "that Aki screwed his assignment" is all it takes to ruin one's career. A samurai has to defend his name like defending his life. Because higher ranks do not personally know him but hold all power over him, his name *is* his life. Even his close friends have to be careful making certain jokes about him, since there is no privacy between them. Sometimes a samurai is so enraged by a derogatory comment he would charge the offender to a duel, though duels are prohibited under death penalty, just to scare away any future slant against him.

The relationship between shogun and lords was not father-son, though the shogun tried to force a similar hierarchy on them. Lords had to be treated carefully as potential enemies. Measures taken by the Tokugawa house were aimed at freezing political reality on the ground, and they were quite effective. Although the shogun still ruled in the name of the emperor like before, he had unprecedented power. Previous centuries had seen a tug of war between imperial courts and shogun governments, with land ownership in a state of confusion. Now the warriors had taken total control. The emperor was put under virtual house arrest, his revenue cut to such a level that he could not afford to host a significant ceremony. For the first time the military government of the shogun was in a position to make laws that applied to entire Japan. Land ownership was resolved, and now there was growing commercial activity as well. Merchandise like muskets introduced by Portuguese tradesmen played a major role in the final years of civil wars. To deal with an increasingly complex national economy, foreign trade, Christianity, in addition to the need to hold on to power for as long as possible, Japan again looked to China for something to copy. The Tokugawa's commissioned the study and spread of Confucianism and followed the earlier Chinese practice of making them into law. For the first time in Japan Confucian schools were founded everywhere, Chinese classics became widely available, and it was said that by eighteenth century someone in every Japanese household could recite the Analects (citations from Confucius).

This was actually the second importation of Confucianism. Back in the heyday of the imperial court one millennium before, these classics were already read, albeit by a select few. As we have discussed earlier, moral principles of Confucianism were not absorbed, only its form was copied, often without understanding the purpose behind it. Back then the mentality was one of curious imitation, of fascination with a far more advanced civilization that seemed so sophisticated, organized and majestic. That image was shattered first by the Mongol annihilation of China in thirteenth century, when divine wind saved Japan from the same fate; then by the Sino-Japanese war in late sixteenth century, waged in Korea, in which both sides basically fought to a tie, despite the fact that the Japanese invasion force was hated by the Koreans, while the Chinese force that came at the request of the Koreans had local support; moreover, the Ming Dynasty (1379-1644 AD) in China crumbled not long after the Tokugawa house came to power in Japan (1600), this time defeated by the Manchurians, an obscure coalition of tribes in northeast China, as if Chinese were going out of their way to demonstrate incompetence.

So this time around Chinese learning was not seen as imitating a higher culture with a sense of reverence, but taken for its utilitarian values. Confucian theories, particularly the neo-Confucian theory that became state ideology of China, were objectively examined with no holds barred. As they studied Confucianism Japanese scholars also wanted to find an answer as to why the Chinese civilization declined, first losing to Mongols then to Manchurians, and they tended to blame it all on neo-Confucianism, because its rise at the end of the Song Dynasty roughly corresponded with the start of a decline in Chinese military competence. They obviously did not know that neo-Confucianism was an unsuccessful attempt to resurrect an already corrupt and cynical culture. Nor did they realize that the *en* logic fully adopted by Japan was originally part of neo-Confucian thought, only that it was not clearly articulated in the canonized texts.

When for the first time serious Japanese scholars studied Confucianism, they could not agree with its reasoning process. As we know all Confucian theories lay claim to Dao, to nature's ways, as the foundation of human morals. In Confucius' time it was "no two suns in the sky; nor two kings in a state; nor two masters in a family". By neo-Confucian era it was replaced by this "heavenly principle", that manifests itself in human nature and regulates all things in heaven and on earth, hence the same morals govern the person, the family, the empire and everything else. Laying claim to cosmic truth was essential to Confucianism, because Chinese statecraft was a two pronged approach of indoctrination and penal code, with emphasis on the first to reduce the need of the second. In the dynastic era China did not have a professional army, and a typical county with thousands of residents had only a few police, both of which testify to the effectiveness of Confucian indoctrination. Of course Confucian reasoning in practice is always coercive persuasion: it sounds true to the ignorant peasantry, but is not open for debate. As soon as neo-Confucianism was decreed as official doctrine every part of this elaborate theory immediately became sacred. Questioning its merits was criminal. Banning debates helped maintaining authority of the official doctrine, which in turn helped indoctrination.

Japanese governance was purely by brute force. The number of samurai in each state was comparable to the number of peasants. Since samurai were obedient slaves too, a lord could implement whatever rules he liked without the need of indoctrination. From their experience Japanese were keenly aware that power was decided by brute force, settled in a compromise, and it had nothing to do with heavenly ways. The Confucian historical view that a good ruler will prosper and an immoral ruler will end up ruining his dynasty clearly does not apply to Japan: there had never been a ruler with total control of entire Japan, and on battlefields there was no place for morals. Because of unchallengeable imperial power Chinese tended to be thinkers or dreamers: there was nothing they could do to share political power. Japanese had always been doers. A sharpened sword and a band of fearless fighters could decide one's own fate. Therefore the entire notion that social order is somehow controlled by an invisible force of nature or moral principle was completely nonsensical to them.

What they found most objectionable was neo-Confucian morality, which says that human desires are immoral. Buddhism preaches that human desires are the root cause of pain; neo-Confucians borrowed the idea and turned it into a moral doctrine in order to achieve a state of selfless devotion to parents and emperor. For a Chinese official to get in that state of mind, he had to voluntarily deprive himself of life's pleasures. The samurai on the other hand had reached the mental state of total devotion to his master with reckless abandon of his own life, but not by choice. He was forced into it through years of harsh training, both physically and mentally, and it did not involve curtailing food, sex or drinking.

Japanese Confucian scholars, now largely cut off from China save for the books, also due to their amoral culture, was unable to perceive the Chinese context in which there were moral choices, or the real intent of neo-Confucianism, that being a state of mind Japanese had achieved without condemning human desires. The entire neo-Confucian metaphysics and moral indoctrination was pointless to Japanese, thus discarded wholesale. It was not uncommon for a high ranking warrior to take his trusted samurai to "pleasure quarters" of a city and have a good time. In fact that was an important way to bound. Even normally reticent men tend to open up after getting drunk in the arms of women. By sharing this otherwise intimate experience master and servants become truly transparent to each other.

Aside from neo-Confucian morality which is an unrealistically high bar for all but a few, even the basic Confucian moral value, *ren*, was unfit for Japan. Holding wives and heirs of lords hostage would be against *ren*. Collective criminal penalty for the crime of one would be against *ren*. For superiors to arbitrarily sentence subordinates to death would be against *ren*. To deprive everyone's privacy would be against *ren*. For samurai to kill members of lower classes with impunity would be against *ren*. The nature of Japanese social hierarchy was against *ren*. And the practice of disembowelment was, to Chinese at least, shockingly cruel.

All of these were reality in Tokugawa Japan. And there was certainly no sense that any of the above was wrong. As rules of *li* continued to be propagated down the warrior ranks at the directive of the shogun government, the samurai as a class all gradually adopted the same set of etiquette, complete with prescribed body language, facial expression, modes of address, and attention to every detail. Yet underneath that civilized veneer a primitive mentality remained, motivated by the very basic survival instinct. A Chinese would have a hard time understanding how a person could entertain his guest in such a polite, civilized and considerate manner, but moments later at the order of his superior cut off the head of the very guest he just warmly received, without even a trace of mental struggle or agony. But to Japanese everything was about following orders, hence there was no difference between homicide and drinking tea, as long as both were commanded by the master. These same rules were supposed to cultivate civility which includes aversion to violence, but to Japanese they were just rituals, and civility meant when a head is cut off it must be done cleanly and emotionlessly, not that human life must be cherished.

Coming from an amoral world there was a genuine difficulty for Japanese to comprehend the concept of morality, for on matters of any importance they never had a choice. The following comments on *ren* (mercy) from a leading Japanese Confucian scholar, Ogyu Sorai, reflect this deficiency:

"The (Chinese) government prohibits violence but used military law to execute people. Can this be called *ren*? But it all stems from the need to maintain peace in the land."

"Confucians of later ages speak of *ren* and explain the principles of sincerity and commiseration. But even if they possess the spirit of sincerity and commiseration, if they fail to bring peace to the people, they are not *ren*; however much compassion they have, it will all turn out to be wasted *ren*, the *ren* of a woman."

The phrase "*ren* of a woman" is a Chinese idiom that means in some rare cases overly concerned with mercy can be disastrous, thus one should cut corners. It is not a denial of mercy but a caution against its over application, because women tend to have too soft a heart for situations that call for immediate and resolute measures. Here Sorai applies the idiom categorically and unconditionally. To him *ren* is an ethical code, a political strategy, such as low taxes and lenient rules, hence it should be judged solely by the result of its implementation. If it can not bring peace it is no good.

To Chinese *ren* is a moral principle. A benevolent person who tries to help others may end up hurting them unexpectedly, but that does not diminish his goodness. A benevolent ruler may be concerned about his subjects and implement lenient rules, unfortunately some bad guys take advantage of it and create chaos, but that does not detract from his kindness. The lessons learned from these failures are to do better next time, perhaps plugging some legal holes to prevent abuse. The *ren* principle stands independent of results. It is about conscience and motive. Ethical codes can easily change with circumstances but a moral value like *ren* once internalized stays. For example, one of the Confucian ethical codes says man and woman should not have any body contact unless they are married to each other. One student asked Mencius, what if a woman is drowning and the only man nearby is a stranger? Mencius said of course save the woman. To Chinese ethical code (*li*) and legal code—the two gradually merged into one—are necessary to ensure peace and order, but they should not violate the moral principle of mercy, otherwise it would be savage peace and barbarian order. They tasted it under the fifteen year rule of Qin Empire, and they could not stand it. Peace and order without mercy is unacceptable. An ethical code should be a manifestation of *ren*. A moral person does not need to remember any of the rules to know what the right thing is to do, and rules should not be rigidly interpreted to punish moral people.

Japanese never had a moral principle. Their culture was close to that of Qin. To them all Confucian values are ethical codes intended to bring concrete results—peace and order. Though they adopted the Chinese term morality (道徳), their understanding of it is a personal code of conduct, as opposed to the legal code, which is a public code of conduct. Morality becomes "private morality", and it has nothing to do with governance or public law. To Chinese morality is the ultimate principle, it governs the person (修身), the family (齐家), the state (治国), and all-under-heaven (平天下). To Japanese morality is private, thus irrelevant to laws of the land.

Looking at it from an Asian perspective, Chinese are idealistic. They first define a moral principle, then seek to transform human nature to conform with it, starting from child rearing, the goal is to achieve an ideal state where everyone is moral and no laws or punishment are necessary. Japanese are practical. They do not believe in any abstract ideas, but start from concrete steps to make peace and order, which for them is harder to obtain than for most other cultures on earth. They judge people not by how good they sound or how lofty their ideals are, but by what they actually do to help others, to make the lives of others better. They do not care much about motives, they only care about results.

This practical approach is a result of the extreme condition of the samurai. After vigorous training many samurai have reached a mental state where they do not think much but simply act on command. Other than following orders their mind is occupied with rice, wine and women. In such a life it is hard to say what his motive is in doing everything he does. His only purpose is to serve his lord, and that "motive" is forced on him by years of training. He has no choice. Willingly or unwillingly his life is fully controlled by his master. For higher ranks who do initiate actions, such as the lords, motive does not matter much either. The shogun knew full well that the lords would have his head if given half a chance. Who would not if you hold his wife and son hostage? But hatred does not get one anywhere in this world ruled by brute force. The winner enslaves the loser, that's the way it is. Japanese are used to this amoral world where one does what is ordered or takes what he can get; motive is made irrelevant by lack of choices.

Since its first synthesis in first century BC, Confucianism has always been Legalist practices guided by Confucian principles. Because Japanese rejected these moral principles what they copied from Confucianism was then purely Legalism, or the pragmatic side of Confucianism. Granted the body of Chinese legal code by then had a large dose of *li* in it, in other words it was no longer the Qin code. But without principles the legal code itself however decided by whoever had the power to do so, became absolute, in need of no justification, and taking precedence over all other concerns; that is the philosophy of Legalism.

There is no better story to illustrate this point than the culturally rich and emotionally charged tale of Forty Seven Ronin, a true event at the beginning of eighteenth century, the national epic of Japan known to every Japanese. For simplicity I omit all the names here. Lord A was in charge of interior decoration at a ceremonial event where the shogun was to attend.

Unfamiliar with *li* he did not know how to arrange floor mats, or how to dress himself, depending on the version of the story, so he consulted Lord B. B was a corrupt person and expected bribes. A being an upright person did not bring him any gifts. The upset B then gave A incorrect information. Consequently A was embarrassed publicly at the event, and became furious at B. Not able to contain his temper, he drew his sword in shogun's court and wounded B.

This was a violation of rules and shogun ordered A to commit *hara-kiri*, or ritual suicide by disembowelment, which he did. His domain was confiscated as well. With his death the hundreds of samurai in lord A's family service all instantly became *ronin*—masterless samurai (thus no longer officially samurai). Forty seven of these *ronin* decided to take revenge against Lord B, though they knew they would not have shogun's permission and they would have to die for the transgression.

Publicly the forty seven scattered and pretended there was to be no revenge. Privately each was preparing for it. One needed money so he sold his wife into prostitution. Another wanted to kill a woman because she knew about the plan. Another killed his father-in-law who tried to dissuade him. Another sent his sister to serve as concubine for Lord B, placing a spy in the enemy's bedroom. The woman knew she would have to commit suicide as well after the revenge, for she had violated her master's trust. The leader of the pack pretended to be a drunken womanizer, to throw off suspicion. Eventually they succeeded, and by law they all had to commit *hara-kiri*, and they gladly embraced their fate, in a glorious fashion, having done what to them and to everyone else their duty as samurai—to give their lives to their lord even after his death.

Stories of loyal servants (忠臣) that exalt the virtue of pious loyalty are the mainstay of official propaganda throughout history in all Confucian cultures. Japanese history produced many more such tales beyond the Forty Seven *Ronin*, while China has Guan Yu (关羽) and Yue Fei (岳飞) among hundreds of similar minded historical figures—the "heroes" of Confucian culture. Though the main didactic message of all these legends is the same, their details reflect a major difference between these two cultures. For Chinese the loyal servant having done everything right naturally deserves credit, not punishment. Whoever kills the hero is consequently the bad guy and condemned. If the emperor ordered the hero's death, then history books must be revised, since the emperor—the Son of Heaven—can not be the bad guy. Consequently we have bogus historical records that read: "an insidious high minister through court intrigues brought down our loyal general."

Japanese are far more straightforward, in large part due to their lack of such moral concern. There is simply nothing wrong for a master to kill his servants, even if they are loyal. Because the actions of the Forty Seven *Ronin* generated widespread sympathy, there was a serious debate among Confucian scholars about whether they should have been punished in such a way for their violation of shogun's law. By the bushido code they did nothing wrong, in fact avenging the master's death is a good way to show pious loyalty. The problem is that now there is an overlord, the shogun, to whom they must pledge pious loyalty as well, which implies following all shogun's laws. It is a case of having multiple masters and their interests are in conflict. What is a slave to do in such a case?

If Chinese Confucians are faced with such a scenario, they would be compelled to find a solution, a righteous course of action, such as which obligation takes precedence, by following which the subject should not be at fault. The logic goes, if one performs a moral act, then the state should not punish him for it, much less by death, otherwise the state would be immoral. To Japanese Confucians it is about following two conflicting ethical codes at the same time, one is shogun's law, which as legal code for entire Japan must have authority to ensure peace and order, the other is loyalty to one's lord, which is similar to filial piety, a personal code of conduct. The Forty Seven *Ronin* did the right (appropriate) thing by following samurai ethics, and the state did the right (appropriate) thing by ordering their suicide. Both their actions and their execution were correct. A prominent Confucian scholar (Hayashi Kazan) wrote:

"If we consider this matter in accordance with the spirit of the (Confucian) classics, we are forced to conclude that on the basis of their motives, it was proper for them to sleep on rush mats, use their swords as pillows, and take revenge upon their sworn enemy, who could not be permitted to remain under the same sky as theirs. It violated the way of the samurai to cling to life and endure shame. But from the standpoint of the law, those who behave as opponents of the law must be executed. Although they acted to fulfill the wishes of their deal lord, they broke the law of the land. In this respect, their behavior was wanton and disobedient. Hence it became necessary to arrest and execute them, and to make them an example to the nation and to future generations. In this way we can uphold and clarify the law of the land. The two (considerations) may seem to differ but in fact they can co-exist and do not contradict one another. At the top of society there must be a *benevolent* prince and *wise* officials who clarify the law and issue decrees. Below, there must be loyal subjects and righteous samurai who find free play to their feelings, fulfill their wishes, and willingly accept punishment for the sake of the law. How could they have any regrets as a result?"

In other words some scenarios require a samurai to die, and that is perfectly fine. It is clear from this that Japanese did not understand what Confucianism defines as a benevolent prince or wise officials. Chinese would have called the shogun's law callous, his advisors wicked, and most everyone involved in the episode barbarous. Since Japanese rejected the Mencian principle of *ren* (mercy, benevolence), they looked to Confucius' own writings for an alternative definition. As we know Confucius defined *ren* as a psychological state depicting the kind of character with a steadfast adherence to *li* (hierarchical rules) over natural human desires to the contrary. Japanese scholars took *ren* to mean simply adherence to official rules, voluntary or involuntary they did not care. The Confucian *ren* unlike the Mencian *ren* requires no mercy from the superior, which is why Japanese Confucians were able to claim their reality was in accordance with Confucian principles. After all, Confucius' main goal was peace under a hierarchical order. But even Confucius would have objected to the execution of these loyal samurai—in his view legal code should be taken with flexibility, for it is to serve a principle: rewarding the obedient, punishing the rebellious. The Japanese view by most of the prominent Confucian scholars at the time, when they thought they were following Confucianism, was clearly Legalism.

What made contradictory rules and a seemingly incoherent system stand was that life was deemed of little value. Rules can never be broken but life can always be sacrificed. If certain situations offer no way out under the rules but to end one's life, so be it. It worked in Japan because it reflected the Japanese view on life, heavily influenced by Buddhism. Another unstated difficulty faced by Japanese Confucian scholars trying to apply Confucian doctrines to Japanese conditions was that political reality of Japan did not lend itself to any high-minded principle, since the shogun government lacked absolute power to enforce it. Unlike the emperor, the shogun was not ordained by the Sun Goddess or any other deity. If measured by virtue, other lords may well be more qualified to rule than he. Without divine sanction or moral justification, his rule was purely based on military muscle, and that much was obvious. But there was never guarantee that military dominance of one house would last long. The shogun was happy just to keep his position. People's individual conduct as long as not threatening his rule was not his concern. Japanese Confucians working for shogun's government or sympathetic to the status quo were mainly focused on finding a justification for this ad hoc unorthodox political system.

The first question is why the shogun and not anyone else should rule. The real answer is that he beat others with his sword. But one can not find that in Confucian doctrine. So the answer becomes: the shogun is the only one able to bring peace and order, without him the civil war will continue indefinitely. The next question is, why these but not other laws. Since shogun's laws treat human life with contempt, they can not possibly find support from canonized Confucian texts, old or new. Japanese Confucians argue that laws are decided by events, or political reality, and customs. If it takes holding warlords' family members hostage to maintain peace and order, then that law is justified. The shogun has no luxury to devise laws as he wishes, for purposes of moral or aesthetic satisfaction. It is hard enough just to find a way in line with custom to keep peace.

Since peace is so hard to come by under the Japanese condition, everything remotely helpful can be justified in its name. The Tokugawa house sent out spies to every state, to see what each lord was up to, if they were building defense fortifications, making swords in large quantity, smuggling muskets, recruiting warriors, etc. The shogun would be glad to find the lords all indulging in alcohol or carnal lust. The lords on the other hand wanted to stay alert. If one's military strength diminished, by lack of bushido training, discipline or in general loss of focus, his domain could be target for bandits or internal peasant uprisings. If a lord could not keep order in his own domain, he would be in real trouble and might lose his lordship. In short, security consumed all energy of the government, national and local.

With this mindset it is not surprising that peace and order becomes *the* principle in lieu of other principles. As to peace under what kind of order, that is decided by power balance on the ground, which is out of anyone's control and influenced by invisible forces, tradition, personalities, luck. To Chinese Confucianism is a grand design to be sold to and implemented by an absolute ruler; to Japanese it is a collection of rules parts of which are to be borrowed to patch up an existing power sharing reality, to give it doctrinal support and make peace last. Thus Japanese Confucianism is not a coherent system uniting morality, family values, statecraft and worldview in one package, but broken into unrelated pieces that play a role in each of these categories. This is exactly the same pragmatic and amoral approach taken by the founder of Legalism, HanFei.

Politically it is reduced to a single principle: peace and order justifies everything. When there are no other competing values, this is equivalent to might equals right, for the ruling elite can use peace and order to excuse everything they do to the subjects. On an individual level Confucianism defines a strict hierarchy for Japanese, which is solidified with state sanction. As we have discussed before, Japanese interpretation of hierarchy is merciless, but it is in keeping with the peace and order or might equals right principle. The shogun might be harsh in dealing with the lords, but that was nothing compared to how lords treated their own subjects.

In any state under the lord there were his family servants—the samurai—who played the role of Chinese scholar-officials: helping the master to rule. Under the samurai class there were three lower classes: peasants, workers/artisans, and merchants. In the Warring States period demarcation between samurai and lower classes was not rigid on an individual level. A peasant boy brave enough to risk his own life could make it into the warrior class, as chances of fighting for his master abounded and demand for good fighters was limitless. In that sense the era of violence and chaos also saw a high degree of social mobility and individual ingenuity. In the orderly Tokugawa era that mobility was much more limited. Peasants were not allowed to possess any weapon, each registered to a particular village from which they could not escape, and had no chance to ever become a samurai. Moreover, the law granted any samurai the right to kill any member of a lower class on the spot if proper "respect" was not shown, which was to be judged by the samurai. This gave the samurai arbitrary power to kill an inferior.

Consequently a peasant must adopt a body language in presence of a samurai that basically says I am a slave you are a master. Kneel, prostrate, quick to answer inquiries, quick to act on orders, one could not afford to cause any displeasure for the master, or else his life might end right there and then. Rules like this were both a reflection of the predominant view that life is worthless and an enforcer of that view. By this stage of economic development Japanese had grown out of the primitive conditions of stone-age humans who would naturally harbor such a view, but unlike most other civilizations it persisted. If prior to the Warring States period that culture was still in flux, by now it was highly codified and solidified by a rich literature. This mentality was not only expressed but extolled by officially sanctioned samurai ethics. If someone happened to cherish life and felt that taking a life so easily was wrong, all literature and popular culture would tell him that he was wrong instead, and he must quickly change his mind. One who complained about existing order was usually ostracized if not terminated in the name of peace and order.

As discussed earlier there are three keys in making Legalism work, aside from the precondition of an amoral culture. The first is to block all escape routes. Every member of society has to be ranked in the same hierarchy, or else it loses some of its coercive power. The second key is transparency of promotion and demotion rules. This is to take the subjects in one uniform direction so as to easily harvest their energy. The third key is collective liability. All three were met in Tokugawa Japan. Its political system and bushido code ensured the first two, and collective criminal liability was written into law. Families of commoners were grouped into tens and fives. The group was responsible as a unit for paying rent, carrying out orders and following all rules. If one of its members was convicted of a crime the entire group was punished. This was similar to Qin practice in third century BC. Since then collective punishment beyond the family had been abolished in China due to growing moral awareness, which implies that everyone is responsible for his own action, and punishment is due only for the immoral. Japanese like Qin Chinese did not have such a moral sense. The samurai class was subject to an elaborate code, they were judged on an individual basis only because each was known to his superior. Peasants were managed by samurai, who rarely set foot in the fields and did not care to know who was who. Collective punishment was obviously more efficient and economic. As a result most Japanese peasants did not have individual names in the Tokugawa era, they were simply known as belonging to a certain group in a certain village (like Chinese of early Zhou Dynasty), while most Chinese peasants by then had full names and a genealogy dating back generations. Here is a small sample of collective liability laws of Tokugawa Japan:

"(1) If there should be living among you any men formerly in military service who have taken up the life of a peasant since the seventh month of last year, with the end of the campaign in the Mutsu region, you are hereby authorized to take them under surveillance and expel them. If persons of this type are kept concealed in any place, the entire town or village shall be brought to justice for this evasion of the law."

"(2) If any peasant abandons his fields, either to pursue trade or to become a tradesman or laborer for hire, not only should he be punished but the entire village should be brought to justice with him. Anyone who is not employed either in military service or in cultivating land shall likewise be investigated by the local authorities and expelled. If local officials fail to take action in such cases, they shall be stripped of their posts for negligence. In cases involving concealment of peasants who have turned to trade, the entire village or town shall be held responsible for the offense."

Collective liability laws have a tremendous impact on the state of mind. If the law says that I will be ostracized, mutilated or executed for crimes committed by any of my neighbors, then I have to know what they are up to all the time. It is not good enough to report suspicious behavior, for if a crime takes place it is too late for me. First I have to get intimate with these families. I have to know the temperament and everyday routine of each individual, so that I can determine A. if a certain behavior is normal for a particular person and B. if not how bad it is. But even if I know everyone in the group like my own family, and exactly what they are thinking, I still may not feel safe just playing the role of an observer. I have to prevent crimes. I must have some control over their actions, especially teenagers and young adults. I want to limit their chances of engaging with strangers in any way. I want to see them following their routines everyday with predictability. And above all I want them to be of a timid character not bold enough to move a finger without permission.

My neighbors want the same from me. So we watch and control each other. However, it is part of human nature to desire some privacy. No one is perfect, and there are always some "impure" thoughts in our mind that we do not want others to know. In the Confucian context it could be secretly held resentment against one's parents or the ruler, which if known to the community would be like harboring heresy or irreverence against God or the Church in medieval Europe. But unlike irreverence to God resentment against one's secular masters and often oppressors—parents and lords—is quite common. Mutual spying means there is no one I can treat as a confidant, a soul mate, to whom I can speak my mind unencumbered by any concerns. On the other hand, humans are social animals. We are capable of abstract thoughts and perceptive of subtle feelings, and we invented language to express them. It is painful for us to constantly suppress ourselves. Thus in a community under the law of collective criminal punishment, everyone becomes everyone else's tormentor.

This has several effects. In order to alleviate mental stress one tries to internalize the rules as much as possible. If the law says I must "respect"—to have filial piety for—my parents, then I must convince myself that is the only correct thing to do. Otherwise I would have to conceal my true feelings for the rest of my life. But as much as we try, we can not possibly consent to all the rules. A samurai can kill any one of us for no reason, that I can take as a fact of life but I can not help pitying myself and others in my peasant class. In order to not only live with it but show no bitterness, I have to blunt my sensibility and practice a blank facial expression, so that under most circumstances I no longer feel any strong emotions one way or another, and in rare cases that I do, no one can tell.

All these painstaking transformations of myself forced on me by the circumstances take their toll. I am no longer a person tolerant and generous in spirit. When I see a youngster making a mistake, which I used to make when I was young, I would have been philosophically inclined to forgive him, for I know it is quite understandable, but psychologically I can not bring myself to do it, not after the ordeal I have been through for making similar mistakes. The anger that I have accumulated over the years as I grew up is now vented over the younger generation. I know how hard it is to keep everyone in a lockstep. I have already adopted the logic that the community comes before the individual because that is the only way I can justify the brutal oppression that we exert on each other. The youngster may have made a trivial mistake, but he violated the unwritten code of the community, he scorned our suffering, he hurt our feelings. He must be taught a lesson, which is not really about the specific thing that he did, but about obeying rules as a form of respect for the community. There is a hatred for anyone who violates even the most trivial rules. I call this Collective Liability Syndrome.

Under such conditions the distain for private interest goes to extreme. While Chinese neo-Confucians see private interest as the bad part of human nature which one must constantly battle through self-cultivation in order to become a moral man, Japanese see it as a public matter. By law peasants are supposed to submit almost all of their rice and live on lesser grains, but some of them find ways to put away a certain amount and conceal it from authorities. If exposed the entire group will be punished. This is just one of many examples where even the most basic private interest, which in China would have been entirely reasonable, is directly endangering the community. To Japanese private interest is not just a matter of personal ethics, but of public concern, directly related to peace and order, the ultimate principle. Just as peace and order is unchallengeable, private interest becomes absolutely wrong.

Collective liability and the spirit of public overriding private was espoused by Confucian scholars and applied to the samurai class as well. Here is Sorai's comment on the Forty Seven *Ronin* incident:

"*Yi* (义, pronounced *gi* in Japanese) is the way to uphold one's personal integrity. Law is the standard of measurement for the entire society. *Li* (礼, pronounced *rei* in Japanese) is used to control the heart, while *yi* is used to control events. The fact that the forty-six samurai avenged the wrong done their lord shows that they possessed the sense of honor of the samurai. They followed the path of integrity. Their action was righteous. But this aspect of the situation concerns only them and is a private matter. The fact is that they came to regard (Lord B) as their enemy when their lord was punished for improper behavior in the Palace. And without sanction from the government, they conspired to create this public disturbance. An action of this kind is prohibited by law. If the forty-six samurai are judged guilty and, in accordance with the principle of *li* fitting to a samurai, are permitted to commit *hara-kiri*, . . . the loyal conduct of the forty-six samurai will be properly honored. This policy will best serve the public interest. If private considerations are allowed to undermine public considerations, it will be impossible to uphold the law of the land."

Here the shogun's business is public, while a lord's business is private. But within each state, the lord's business is public, and a samurai's business is private. Within a community of ten or five households, the community is public, and each family is private. So public and private are relative terms in Japan, unlike in China, where the emperor's business is public and all else is private. The two Chinese words public (公) and private (私) acquired a distinct sense in Japan. The shogun is public, while the powerless emperor is private. Later on during the Meiji restoration when the imperial house overthrows the shogun government, the emperor becomes public, and the shogun is simply called military (武). In other words, in the Japanese mind, public and private are really hierarchical terms, and public is always higher than private. The shogun admonishes the lords that they should devote themselves to public interest, which is the shogun's interest. A lord warns his samurai that they should sacrifice themselves for public interest, which is the lord's interest. They use the same words—public vs. private—and they mean the same thing: pious loyalty. This model is copied by the entire society, and everyone accepts that the collective is higher than the individual. A collective can be a business organization, owned by a single person, but its employees are still taught that each individual must sacrifice for collective/public interest, since the hierarchy between these two words is carved in stone.

The word *yi* has taken different paths in China and Japan, quite representative of the two cultures. Back in Confucius' time *yi* meant propriety. A person was called *yi* if his behavior was appropriate according to *li*—rules of propriety/hierarchy. By Mencius' time the word acquired a moral sense of *ren*—mercy, commiseration, benevolence—because what was appropriate included the value of *ren*. Since then the word has lost its original meaning, become a moral value unrelated to any specific rules, and almost exclusively applicable to non hierarchical situations. A person is called *yi* if he is genuinely concerned about the welfare of others, if he possesses the quality to generously help strangers without seeking any reward, by giving away his money, his time, his energy, by risking his life to save another, to punish evil doers or to correct an injustice. Japanese did not absorb this moral sense of *yi* at all. Instead they took its original meaning—appropriate according to hierarchical rules—and further developed it into a set of duties that one must fulfill. Those duties mandated by the state, or public, such as filial piety and pious loyalty, were called *gimu* (义务). Failing a *gimu* was punishable by death. Other duties concerning personal relations, such as *en* based private relations between master and apprentice, were called *giri* (义理). These were unwritten rules the failing of which would affect one's credibility and social standing, depending on the seriousness of the violation. In Japan *yi* has become purely tangible rules, while in China an abstract moral value.

Just as the public/private complex worked its way from lower classes into samurai culture, the *en* based hierarchy as well as the nihilist view on life of the samurai class metastasized in the entire society, under the invisible leverage of counter evolutionary force, by which values and practices beneficial to the ruling elite are always selected. Between parents and children, teacher and students, master artisan and apprentice, business owner and employees, the *en* based ownership hierarchy became standard. Since the samurai competed among themselves on who was more reckless with his own life, many members of lower classes saw it as a sign of nobility. Merchants began to swear to their credit worthiness on their own lives, artisans liked to wage their heads on the quality of their products, and the favorite declaration of love was a double suicide. Harsh rules prepared the Japanese mind for these extremes, but the ultimate act was for the individuals to shine, to gain recognition in a culture that flaunts its distain for life.

Both Chinese and Japanese conceptions of the idea of public were strictly speaking the private interest of the ruler, but because there was only one ruler in China, whose interest was interpreted by orthodox Confucians as the protector of a civilization rather than his personal material gain, the Chinese conception was closer to its modern sense. The emperor was the empire. Neo-Confucian scholar officials approached their jobs in the spirit of transforming human nature and building a moral society. No quarrel was too small a matter for their attention, because morality reflected in these everyday trifles was of utmost concern. As a result Chinese society was largely free of violence with limited law enforcement. The Japanese idea of public was much closer to personal interest of the shogun and the lords. They did not want to spend time and resources to settle personal disputes between commoners. If one merchant savagely beat up another, it was not a public concern and samurai administrators often ignored such cases. The shogun's government was strictly a clan enterprise and provided no services to the populace. As a result Japanese felt even less secure. Not only did commoners have no protection against the sword of a samurai, the state did not help them to fend off local thugs either. So the life of the average commoner was in the hands of multiple layers of superiors, from the shogun to the lord to street toughs, none of whom had any claim to legitimacy other than brute force. While the average Chinese would feel terribly wronged and outraged if physically violated by anyone for no good reason, Japanese saw it as just a fact of life. The amoral culture reinforces itself.

The Japanese condition has an element of decentralized power, not by design but by inability to implement the Chinese system due to geological restraints. The Confucian value of pious loyalty was fully absorbed and vigorously enforced. In other words decentralization of power is *against* the principles intrinsic to the adopted Confucian ideals and Japanese intensions. In contrast decentralization of power in feudal Europe was *because of* its values. The Magna Carta stated that kings could not confiscate land from nobility, among other rights granted to barons. This was compatible to local beliefs because the Greco-Roman idea of justice was based on the inviolability of private property, which was inherited by Europeans. The consistency between their values and their legal practice made it possible later to extend the same rights to lower classes. Japanese on the other hand regret decentralization of power. It run against their Confucian beliefs and was blamed for violence and chaos. This paved the road to a rather different kind of modernization process.

CHAPTER 13
TOTAL HYPOCRISY

The unification of China in 221 BC and the subsequent Han Dynasty (206 BC-220 AD) was the pivotal point in the evolution of Chinese civilization. Before this four and a half century span there were many possibilities for the morally and intellectually awakening and ethnically diverse peoples in the Chinese domain, as different schools debated their worldviews. After this transforming period Confucianism would be in the veins of every individual, not only as a moral and political doctrine, but more importantly as a psychological profile. The empire would break into pieces under foreign invasion, but the state of a broken empire is perceived as against the cosmic order, the Dao. In the mind of every Chinese the empire is an enlarged family. The family stays together because of filial loyalty/piety and the psyche derived from it, and so must the empire, or all-under-heaven. The cosmic order is easily understandable to even the most ignorant, since it is found in every family. Confucian family training once popularized solidifies the culture to the point that it is impervious to any philosophical challenge.

From that point on Chinese history entered a never ending cycle, as one dynasty replaced another, without moving the culture in any new direction. Quite the contrary, any new intellectual development would have to further ossify basic tenants of Confucianism, neo-Confucianism being a good example. Intellectual atrophy dulls the spirit. The masses grew more and more servile, timid, and content. Laws became strict and all encompassing. The ruling apparatus had its tentacles in every obscure corner of life. Civil society no longer existed. The same family model captured all members in all situations. By Ming Dynasty (1379-1644 AD) the administrative system was so well developed that no loopholes could be found by any potential usurper, and totalitarian imperial rule was super stable.

Maintenance of that system fell on the shoulders of the scholar-official class. Depending on the dynasty they were generally ranked in seven to nine major grades. First and second grade officials were high ministers who gathered at imperial court regularly. Third and fourth grade were provincial governors and inspectors. Fifth and sixth grade were usually military generals. Seventh grade were county chiefs. Confucianism does not endorse separation of powers, in fact a Confucian official—called "parent official"—is supposed to be mentor, judge and police all in one. Therefore county chiefs and provincial governors were practically despots in their domains.

A Chinese county is as large as a Japanese state. A county chief has sweeping powers over his subjects (called "children subjects"), just like a Japanese warlord (*daimyo*), but unlike a *daimyo* he does not own his county in theory. He merely manages it for the emperor. A manager having sweeping powers over someone else's property is usually a recipe for disaster. To compound matters there is no good way to effectively supervise local officials in the immense Chinese empire. Japan does not have this problem. A lord has thousands of samurai working under his nose, all cramped in tiny spaces. There is no way any samurai could overtax a peasant behind the back of his lord. For one thing, the lord can personally tour around all rice paddies in his domain and get to the bottom of every discrepancy. For another, samurai watch each other every day. No one can hide a new kimono or a better diet from everyone else.

A Chinese county chief rules by himself. He has a few clerks and a few police officers in his command (compare this to thousands of samurai in the tightly controlled Japanese state). There is no other authority in the county. He is supposed to collect taxes and send them all to the provincial governor, who should send them to the capital. He is also to settle disputes among his subjects according to legal codes, Confucian principles, and fairness. He must maintain peace and order in his county, be a propaganda machine for the emperor, uphold and exemplify Confucian values, and extinguish unrest at the budding stage. His responsibility is great, his power is virtually limitless, and the only check on him is his own moral conscience, with which he has to battle a variety of temptations and forces.

Suppose I am a county chief. The imperial tax rate on farm products is a lenient 20%, following the prudent advice of good hearted scholar ministers in court. I know if I collect just that much, peasants will be happy and thank heaven for their benevolent ruler. But my family members want better food and clothing, which my meager stipend, also decided by the same honorable ministers in the same spirit of less government and low

The Confucian Mind

taxes, can not provide them. My relatives near and far, upon hearing the news of my ascension to officialdom, are all eager to share in my glory and benefits. They come to my home, some of them from far away across county lines. They bow, kneel, and kowtow to me, complain about their wicked local official, cry their misery, and beg for financial help. What do I do? Say I can't spare anything for them? They are going to hate me for the rest of their lives and it is against Confucian principle to have disharmony in one's family. On top of that my clerks and police ask for a bonus. I know they all have families and their stipend is even less than mine. Dragging their feet in compiling reports and apprehending criminals will wreak havoc in my administration, not to mention playing tricks with numbers and spreading rumors could ruin my career.

Just when I am struggling to balance duty required for an officer with Confucian humanistic concerns of the family, a shrewd clerk suggests that I can levy a small fee on the local population. We can always build a new bridge, a new road, a dam, etc, and in its name we can collect in advance. Would another 10% kill the peasants? They are doing fine. So I start to search for a morally acceptable explanation for my own conscience. I studied hard since childhood, I passed the competitive national exams to get this position, I use what I learned in practice to cultivate a moral culture so that the population can be ruled with minimum force, everyday I read so many files and judge so many cases until my head hurts, I alone am responsible for peace and order of tens of thousands of subjects in my jurisdiction, I work hard and my job is so important, do I not deserve some compensation? I do have mercy for my people, but by the same token my merciful heart can not bear the tears of my family and relatives, or the hardship of my subordinates.

A decision is made to charge an extra fee for a new road. I set aside part of the proceeds for that purpose, still feeling uneasy to divide it all up among relatives and coworkers. Some peasants complain. But they have nothing to say when I really start building this road. They have no right to inspect my accounting books. The rules favor me. Everything goes smoothly. My family and relatives are happy, so are my colleagues, for now.

Come next year the same problem reappears, because our stipends remain the same. Having tasted meat it is hard to go back to cabbages. So the 10% fee becomes permanent. After all, the road is not finished yet. Five years later it becomes obvious to everyone that the funds have been misappropriated. Some peasants file a complaint with my superior, the provincial governor. I know if he sends in an inspection team I am finished. But come to think of it, he has a family too. He faces the same kind of pressure and lives on a similarly inadequate salary. So I prepare a generous "gift" for him. I may have to go into debt for this gift, but there is nothing else I can do. I present it to him and say that this is a gift from the people of my county, who want to repay his *en* to them, by giving them peace and prosperity. He may ask me why some of them are complaining, I reply that it is all a misunderstanding. He is relieved to hear that, accepts the gift, and tells me that he trusts me to handle my own affairs.

The case is officially sent back to my jurisdiction. I might punish these trouble makers or release them with a warning, depending on my mood. But more importantly there is a new spending item in my spreadsheets: the governor will expect a similar gift next year. My family and friends all congratulate me, as this is a great opportunity to advance my career, having established a private connection with the governor through the back door. Regardless of how I feel about it once I am in this boat I have to keep peddling. New fees are added, now with implicit sanction from the governor. If peasants resort to violence, they are put down swiftly, in the name of squashing rebellion, a high Confucian virtue. The provincial governor might even recommend my promotion for defending the emperor's interest.

Peasants are doomed. A 20% imperial tax gradually balloons to a 60% real tax or higher. But they have no recourse. Confucianism says the ruling elite should be merciful, but the imperial house follows the principle mainly for the purpose of preempting unrest. As long as large scale unrest does not break out, the court can proclaim evidence of merciful rule, particularly when it does not know what is really happening in rural areas. On the other hand, Confucianism condemns all rebellion, all levels of government are well justified to use force against any disobedience.

Inevitably the practice of embezzlement and other abuse of power quickly spread in both scope and degree. A county or provincial chief has powers far beyond taxation, which include enforcement of penal code. They often target merchants for extortion. If there happens to be a domestic dispute in a rich merchant's household, say between different wives and sons, and one of them brings the case to court, it is a golden opportunity. With this pretext the merchant is jailed and subjected to torture. He can stop the torture by paying a handsome fee. Regardless of the merits of the case it can be settled anywhere between long prison terms and not guilty, all depending on how much the defendant is willing to pay. At the end of the trial he is usually penniless. In some places whenever there is a reported theft, the county chief arrests members of rich families in the surrounding area first, in connection to the crime. They then have to buy their way out of jail one by one. Because a county or provincial chief is prosecutor, judge, jury, sheriff, teacher, parent all in one, he can accuse and convict any powerless person of any crime. Confucianism demands that he treat his subjects like his own children, which in the minds of the framers would entail a loving relationship. But Confucian scholars failed to recognize that a parent-son relationship is "loving" only because the son is a fully owned slave of the parents. He can not have his own wealth; everything he owns belongs to his father; he has to live under the same roof, constantly serving his parents' every need. None of these is true between an official and his subjects. A county chief might think: if I am the father of my people, why can I not take all their money? Why can I not beat them at will? After all, a father has such rights. With sweeping power given to them, officials do function like Confucian parents in character: abusive, controlling, and self-serving.

Rich merchants with on power backing are just waiting to be robbed. That is also true in Japan but Japanese do not need any legal pretext. The shogun once confiscated all property of a wealthy merchant, simply because he "lived a lavish lifestyle". Samurai often "borrow" money from tradesmen which both sides know will never be returned. Neither culture protects private property, so merchants have to buy protection from the ruling class. In China this is somewhat easier than in Japan, because there is no rigid line separating the classes. A merchant can marry his daughter to an officer. He can have his son study hard and become an officer through national exams. In the end the wealthiest merchants and the official class become one and the same, though on an individual level one can experience dramatic ups and downs. Say a merchant is the father-in-law of a provincial governor. With that powerful backing he can monopolize important trades like salt and iron in his province, becoming as wealthy as a king. If for some reason the governor loses his favor with the emperor and is demoted, the merchant is immediately on shaky ground. A new governor can easily throw him in jail and confiscate his property on trumped up charges. Wealth moves to a new clan of cronies.

Over time corruption and abuse of power becomes an unofficial culture of the officialdom. On paper both salaries of officials and imperial tax on commoners are admirably low. In reality salary is an insignificant portion of an official's real income and imperial tax is but a fraction of real tax. Lower ranking officers from county chiefs on down who are directly involved in tax collection would exact whatever they can from the peasantry. Though severe torture and death penalty are rarely used, due to the principle of mercy (*ren*), anything else from blackmail to thinly veiled robbery is fair game, and the government becomes essentially a giant mafia organization. Higher ranking officers take regular "donations" from lower ranking ones, on fixed occasions such as Chinese New Year and personal visits. If these gifts are not forthcoming repercussions are often immediate. The "offending" officer can be dismissed or jailed on fabricated charges. Thus the entire scholar-official class becomes a web of parasites sucking blood from the powerless masses, who have been turned into such docile sheep by Confucian upbringing it is almost stupid not to take advantage of them.

An experienced ruler of course knows all about this culture, but there is not much he can do. There are already laws on the book barring such abuses. The problem is that the scholar-official class is supposed to prosecute itself. The emperor sometimes sends inspectors to the provinces with the specific aim of clamping down on excessive exploitation. These inspectors usually end up as part of that parasite web, if they are not in it already. It is very hard to punish any officer on corruption charges even if a particular prosecutor wants to, in no small part because the entire officialdom is tied in that same web.

Suppose I am an upright inspector bent on fighting evils of the world, and I have reports that a certain county chief is levying unwarranted fees on his people, so I travel to this place to investigate. Gathering evidence is usually not a problem, I can catch his agents red-handed. When I prepare to make charges against him, however, problems begin to fall in my lap one after another. First the county chief sends in a bribe through one of my relatives, who he apparently has bought. Now he becomes a friend of the family. If I were to turn him down it would be a slap in the face of my relative, who may have some influence in the circle of my father's family or my mother's family, neither of whom I can afford to upset. If for some reason I am stone-hearted and able to clear this hurdle, the offender convinces his superior, the governor who relies on him for a regular source of his own income, to meet me and have a friendly chat. When I am fully prepared to refute all the defenses the governor might conjure up on behalf of the county chief, such as he is a good man who makes occasional mistakes and so forth, the governor does not even mention the offender or the case. Instead he fondly relays the close friendship he shares with high ministers and other influential figures, precious gifts like jade pieces and paintings that they exchanged between them, how these are items of art worthy of our ancient civilization, how they enrich our lives beyond the material realm. Then he turns and asks me if I think any of this is possible with his salary. I suddenly realize that as a good officer my life is so poor not just materially but culturally as well. If every officer is like me then the only people who can afford art would be merchants, and that is against the right order of things, for merchants are by Confucian definition unprincipled profit seeking low lives, art in their hands will be vulgarized and demoralized. The governor continues our amicable conversation by recalling memories of national exams, years of diligent study, nerve racking intensity in the examination room and anxiety over results afterwards, something all scholar-officials can relate to.

I have to admit he is human, reasonable and friendly. I also understand that my case could potentially expose him, if the county chief decides to provide an excuse for his transgressions, in the form of "these are the names of my superiors who demanded a contribution from me". I am apprehensive of that prospect. What if high ministers are involved? I will be in way over my head. Besides, unless I am totally blind I have to see the big picture. Who am I to fight an ensconced system that permeates the entire empire? Am I to single-handedly resurrect a decadent culture? The emperor did not give me that much authority. I am really cracking my head against granite. On the flip side, against this mountain of forces what power does the plaintiff (peasants) have? Nothing. If I dismiss the case there is nothing they can do. The extreme power imbalance in the pyramid structure proves a much more potent force than moral teachings.

The emperor faces a similar predicament as many officials. He may want to rule according to Confucian doctrine, with moderation, benevolence and care, but his multiple wives and their relatives have other ideas. The emperor once enthroned is secure in his place, but fate of his female consorts is totally dependent on his favor. If a woman happens to have his intimate interest for the moment, she must take full advantage of it *now*, before she is inevitably replaced by others sooner or later. So she uses pillow talk to install her family members in prominent positions and these guys are in there for one purpose: to amass as much wealth as quickly as they can. In the end rulers have to recognize such an unofficial culture. Some of them take it one step further by openly selling official posts. If a poor scholar just qualified through exams for a certain position, he has to pay the emperor a lofty sum to take it, plunging him into debt at the outset of his career, which he will have to clear by collecting from his subjects somehow.

Given the enormous profitability of official posts, they are fiercely contested. There are two ways to get a low ranking but powerful position (like a county chief) to start off one's career: recommendation by higher ranks and national exams. In theory recommendation is supposed to be based on one's virtue and ability. When it comes to virtue, most every

Chinese has filial piety and pious loyalty at heart. If *ren* (mercy) is defined as great reluctance to take a human life, most people qualify too. Ability for the scholar-official class has been equated with virtue by Confucianism, because their job is essentially to bring about a moral society, by teaching, by example, by their principled rule. Most Chinese are virtuous by Confucian standards. Even an officer who takes bribes can not be called immoral because he has not violated any Confucian principle. There is no commandment that says "thou shalt not embezzle". One may argue that such an officer undermines the emperor's interest, but the emperor is the ultimate judge of that, and if he consents to it, however implicitly, that absolves the guilt. Thus recommendations become a way to install one's own cronies in the system, to expand one's influence, and to enlarge his share of the pie. It can also be sold outright to the highest bidder.

Even the seemingly fair exam system is rigged. Participants are usually asked to write an article on the topic given, such as how officials should be selected. Judges often leak exam topics to their own students and contributors, and since there are no standard answers to these questions, they can pick winners that suit their taste. Passing the exams is only the first step for the office seeker, by which he gets a degree and certain privileges that come with it, such as tax exemption for life. For real power he has to wait, since there are more degree holders than jobs. Those higher ranks charged with official assignment are sitting in their homes waiting for generous gifts. Setting foot in officialdom is only the beginning; there are numerous chances of promotion in years to come, which is purely based on recommendations. Here the stakes are higher and rules are non-existent.

Since there is a need for bribes everywhere, and the society accepts it as part of the unwritten code, a culture of bribery develops. One can not do it in a straightforward way by presenting money and asking for help. There are so many potential bribers the officer can pick and choose. The size of the payola is obviously a consideration, but more so is risk. Though the entire officialdom is doing it, it is nevertheless illegal. Though chances of getting caught is low even if they do it out in the open in broad daylight, but the ones with clear evidence left behind are obviously at more risk. Every now and then a ruler wants to mollify increasing public outrage, or a new fame seeking inspector is eager to add some merit to his resume, and the least skilled embezzlers are sacrificed to redeem the scholar-official class. In order to forestall that fate officers take some precautionary measures. Bribes are accepted only from trusted individuals, only on legitimate occasions, such as birthdays and holidays, and no paper trail. The briber has to first break a private path to the officer, by way of mutual friends, relatives, etc, so that he comes with some reference. Obviously the possibility of a sting operation must be preempted, though such things are extremely rare. More commonly the briber must not be the type who brags about his connections. Tight lips are essential. When the bribe is delivered, it is usually hidden in the box of a more tasteful gift, such as calligraphy.

Chinese ingenuity is fully reflected in this endeavor, so much so that bribery becomes an art. In addition to the form its arguments have improved as well. It is always presented by the familiar face of a friend or relative. The briber is always a virtuous person. In fact his sole purpose in obtaining office is to better serve his parents, who like most other parents have longed for honors of the family line. For ten generations the family lived in poverty, spent all their limited resources on education, hoping that one day, one of their sons will have the glory of serving the emperor. Now one of them finally passed the exams, and the fate of the family is in your hands, can you deny the aspirations of such loyal citizens? It is almost inhuman to reject a bribe.

Just as the corrupt culture can bring enormous profit to high ministers, it can also put them in difficult and potentially dangerous positions. Some bribes come from the emperor's personal servants (eunuchs), some from his concubines, some from his relatives, none of them a high minister can afford to offend. When there are not enough to satisfy them all, a minister must choose between them, and that is always a dangerous game. Chinese like Japanese take their positions in the hierarchical world seriously. If you give it to someone else but not me, that means you sneer at me. Such insult is not easily forgotten or forgiven (only the ruler/lord/father—true owners of their subjects/children—can do so without arousing such intense animosity). When it becomes a hopeless impasse between these rival factions, high ministers often resort to an escape route: promotion on the bases of seniority.

There are obvious advantages to this approach. One's age and years of service can be quantified in numbers, harder to dispute than abstract ideas like virtue or ability. Older officials are teachers and mentors of younger ones; their higher position fits the Confucian teacher-pupil hierarchy and is easily accepted by the younger generation. Everyone eventually grows old, so the young always have a chance and do not feel left out. It gives a sense of regularity and predictability, and releases some of the anxiety surrounding one's career. Officials promoted in such a way are less likely to form parties and factions, because they do not owe their positions to particular individuals—*en* men—as much. Once established the system is hard to break, because those who are approaching seniority have waited long and they demand their reward. Finally it provides relative fairness, compared to arbitrary decisions by corrupt officials, and relieves some of the burden on high ministers having to deal with those close to the imperial family.

Seniority temporarily settles the question of who get to exploit the masses, but not whether or how they will be exploited. As long as they remain obedient slaves, their fate is sealed. Occasional self-restriction on the part of the ruler and the official class does not change the dynamics of power and profit. As officials grow greedier by the day, the size of officialdom expands through nepotism, the burden on tax paying peasants, artisans and small merchants inevitably increases, eventually to the point where they can hardly survive. As Chinese history progresses down the centuries, one finds that creativity of the people diminishes with time. Apart from Confucian intolerance which prevented the development of science, the political and economic reality stalled the invention of everyday practical technology. Suppose I am an artisan and I make farm tools. I intend to sell these to peasants in the hope that they will enhance productivity. But regardless of how much peasants produce, they are always left with just barely enough to feed their families. Higher yields only benefit the official class. As a result peasants have little motivation to grow more. In fact many of them try to escape from their assigned lot (the same in Japan), and become bandits, pirates or wanderers. The situation is similar in other trades. There is no demand for new technology, and energy is better spent to study Confucian classics, to grease the palms of judges, to get in the official class, and to join in the officially sanctioned robbery.

This power dynamic eventually leads to massive starvation and unrest, such as in case of a severe drought or flood, since there is no mechanism to limit official exploitation. Though indoctrinated into believing that rebellion is morally wrong, desperate people can find security and solace in numbers. If there is large scale unrest, it can be taken as a sign that the royal house has forfeited Heaven's Mandate. Once it comes to that point, it is the beginning of the end of a dynasty. The emperor has to spend more on his military to put down the insurgency, which means he has to levy even higher taxes, which pushes more peasants into the insurgency.

Thus no dynasty could help but fall into a vicious cycle that repeats over and over again in Chinese history. The first few rulers of a dynasty, fresh from the memory of the downfall of the last one, always manage to address some public concern and allay some major grievances. They understand their success in overthrowing a mighty empire depended on widespread corruption and malcontent. As new rulers they still keep discipline and a modest lifestyle. Taxes tend to be low and officials from the previous regime are executed in hordes. People are happy and the empire experiences a period of growth and prosperity. Generations later, their distant offspring who are brought up in security, and accustomed to docile acceptance by the masses to their abuses, are unable to perceive any danger. They never meet peasants. They do not know what their life is like, or how real taxes on them increased to prohibitive levels over time. They are educated with the same Confucian historical view which says that only an immoral ruler would lose Heaven's Mandate. The last emperors of a dynasty are not necessarily worse in character compared to their predecessors. When the empire crumbles they often fail to understand why or even believe it is happening.

Confucianism gives absolute power to the ruler on the one hand, requires him to regulate himself with moral cultivation on the other, and the result is not as Confucian theorists thought it would be. Morality proves no match to human desires combined with unlimited power over obedient slaves. So great is such a force that it is the Asian equivalent of the invisible lever of free market in the West. Corruption in the Chinese sense is not an individual behavior. It is a fixed character of Chinese culture. It is not limited to officials either. Secretaries, clerks, family servants, anyone who is a state employee or close to officials, thus with some power in his hands, even as small as that of a messenger, takes full advantage of his position and turns it into cash. Peasants may be oppressed, but if they ever have an opportunity to seize power, they may turn into the same kind of oppressors that they hated so much. While the average person endures tyranny throughout his life, he often daydreams about two things: one is to be an emperor some day, or at least a county chief, the other is the sudden appearance of a good officer—a true parent officer—who cares about him and addresses his grievances.

It is amazing under such overwhelming odds there are still a few virtuous officers in Chinese history. Not surprisingly they are worshipped as deities by helpless commoners. They are true believers of benevolent rule in the world and moral self-cultivation. Being contempt of the corruptive culture they invariably live in poverty. They are ridiculed by other officials. They reject requests from friends and relatives, and are consequently shunned by them. They live in total isolation. They are so lonely in their resolute pursuit of virtue against the whole world that they sometimes develop paranoia. Their very existence against all odds testifies to the power of neo-Confucian devotion, while their fame, scarcity and personal misery testify to the impracticality of the same moral principles that require absolute obedience on the one hand and absolute virtue on the other. The more servile the masses are, the more difficult it is for an officer not to abuse his power. However, for these few gentlemen, it is exactly because the temptations are so strong, indulgence is so easy and safe, and the one-man crusade against the immoral world is so hopeless, that they acquire spiritual fulfillment and a deeper sense of satisfaction. Just as death is the ultimate redeemer for a samurai's otherwise meaningless existence, a life of voluntary poverty in a position that guarantees wealth is the only way a neo-Confucian scholar-official can stay true to his belief.

For the vast majority life is about material wellbeing and indulgence of the senses. Since neo-Confucianism encompasses all subjects of what we would call natural and social sciences, and it is unchallengeable, there is nothing left in the intellectual or spiritual realm that Chinese can safely engage in. Even poetry, the most loved traditional literary form that virtually every learned man from sixth to twelfth centuries enjoyed as the favorite pastime, by fourteenth century had lost its appeal because too many officers were prosecuted for what they wrote. The Chinese language is imprecise which makes it less than perfect for reasoning. But that is also its beauty. Its vagueness and richness in emotional sensitivity are perfect for poems. A good poem is short but carries multiple meanings with each line. Nuance in the feelings conveyed can only be fully grasped by highly cultivated literary minds. In comparison puns and witticism in English seem so obvious and pedestrian. Unfortunately this ambiguity makes it easy to incriminate the author. In the fierce battle for power, many fine poets fell victim to what was called "language crimes" (文字狱). Thus Chinese classical poetry withered under persecution.

With few things to do Chinese devote much of their pent up energy to food. Confucius was a known connoisseur of food, which means this indulgence is safe from any possible moral condemnation. If one sees food as simply a source of energy and nutrition, his main concern would be what to eat. That is not the Chinese focus. They want to get maximum pleasure from food, in taste, in smell, and in looks too. It is not what but how. Gnawing at a big chunk of meat smacks of savagery, though it is occasionally appreciated as a symbol of masculinity in the lower classes. A formal dish has to be made of small pieces of various material, all cut in similar shapes, and fully cooked until the flavor of seasoning penetrate every piece. No time or effort is spared in preparation. Soy sauce, for instance, takes months to make, so do many other kinds of pickled, preserved, soaked, dried, hung, buried, fermented foods. The source material is only limited by availability. Virtually everything that moves is eaten. It is not because Chinese are so short of food that they have to eat everything, as the exotic dishes are mostly reserved for the rich, but with a fully developed brain otherwise largely unoccupied, food becomes an obsession, one of the very few conversation triggers, where one can safely explore, debate, assert one's preferences. For Chinese rich and poor meals are the highlights of the day. In absence of visiting friends a traditional man likes to eat alone, before his wife and children have a chance at the table. In slow chewing the individual attempts to regain his consciousness, or find his essence, when during other parts of the day he feels like a zombie driven by unpleasant but powerful forces. I eat, therefore I am.

Man's primary pleasure used to be woman, not food. But state adoption of neo-Confucianism led to prohibition of all vices, including that ancient profession, prostitution. Every woman was required by the new doctrine to follow one man for life. Widows could not remarry. They had to stay loyal to their dead husbands, even if it meant they would starve to death. Women were not to work outside home, in order to avoid contact with other men, including eye contact. Arab muslin women had to cover their bodies; Chinese women could not leave home, all for the same possessive mentality of men. Now that neo-Confucianism officially defined women as slaves to men, the effort to imprison them in their own homes acquired a moral righteousness. Their feet were bound since childhood to hinder their movements. By adulthood they were deformed. Modern revisionist historians ashamed of the episode spin it as a voluntary sacrifice for beauty, which can not be further from the truth. There may be beauty in natural small feet, in the eyes of some, but none whatsoever in deformed feet where toes grow underneath the sole. Women with natural feet could not find husbands not because every man loved such a ghastly sight, but because such women were deemed morally loose and those who married them were subject to public ridicule and condemnation.

One of the problems with many pyramid cultures, and this is certainly not limited to China, is that everything that is seen as moral is enforced by law. For example, licentious behavior is immoral. As such, it is banned by law and violators are severely punished. The law may be there, but there are always people bold enough to defy it, sometimes they think they can get away with it, sometimes they just can not control themselves. When the ruler decrees such a law, however, he aims not at curtailing but at stopping licentious behavior, period, for even sporadic violations upsets a heavenly moral order, the cosmic ways, on which legitimacy of power is based. Absent of human rights there is no limit as to how far he can go to eradicate such behavior. He knows that however harsh the punishment, when young men and women meet freely, there is always a chance they will make a mistake. Hence his next law is to forbid unrelated men and women from meeting each other. If they have to work in the open or go to the market, where they inevitably meet, then they are forbidden from touching each other, not even shaking hands. But that is not enough; they still get to know each other through conversations and flirtations. The next law says they can not talk to each other. But that is still not enough. A man can fall head over heels for a woman just by looking at her. A strict dress code is enforced. Their movements are confined. They are made possessions of their fathers (before marriage) or their husbands (after marriage), and the law makes it easy for them to be accused of infidelity, very often a rumor is enough to end a woman's life.

Chinese and Arabs have both been down this road, and the above pattern of progression of moral codes does not just apply to women but to all members of the society. With the advent of Buddhism and the possibility that human desires can be totally denied, the moral bar is pushed up to a stratosphere far beyond the reach of mere mortals, leaving Chinese with no option but to cheat. If they can not have geisha girls or pleasure quarters like Japanese, if they can not touch or see any women outside home, they'll have multiple wives and sleep with their maids. If their salaries are not enough for a decent life, they'll get it whatever way they can, by hook or by crook. If all other desires are frustrated, they'll indulge in food. The official doctrine says that they should have no desires of their own, but devote their entire beings to parents and ruler. They can not escape their parents, but the emperor is far away. Whatever they do their actions are a subconscious effort to avoid service to the emperor, and to enrich themselves at his expense.

This is after all the emperor's domain. Everyone else, officials and commoners alike, are but servants and temporary dwellers at his mercy. Confucianism gives the scholar-official class a secured place in the social hierarchy but no real stake or security for any individual. If the ruler often shows utter indifference by delegating the most important jobs to uneducated and ignorant eunuchs who have hardly ever stepped out of the imperial palace their entire lives, what is a scholar official to think? A Chinese emperor is far more secure than a Japanese shogun or warlord, as there are no potential challengers in his domain. He can waste his entire life in dissipation and negligence and the empire will go on as usual. The primary objective of Confucius—to have long lasting peace and order in the empire—has been achieved. The neo-Confucian objective—to have a moral society—takes time, one can console oneself. It has to await a virtuous ruler, who seems to be slow in coming but is always possible in the future.

The problem is in the mean time reality and moral ideals are 180 degrees apart, and there is no way to address the issue without risking one's neck. Thus generation after generation of scholars are brought up idealists, only to have their perception of the world smashed at the beginning of their career in the real world, but with no courage to openly challenge this culture of hypocrisy. Worse yet they force their own children to learn the same doctrine that they do not believe themselves, because it is the only way to climb the social hierarchy.

True observations and insights into the mechanism of this world are carried not in official documents, but in folklore, which often has the flavor of Daoism. As we recall Daoism has been a form of escapism to official doctrine since its creation, by this stage it has permeated the entire society. Back in the Warring States period Confucians and Legalists were political activists, while Daoists were cynical bystanders and non-cooperators. Now Confucian scholars are in positions of authority, but the state ideology is so carved in stone and "language crimes" so widely and loosely applied, they no longer have the freedom to debate and advance the theory the way their predecessors could. It is one thing to argue your own theory which you have put a lot of thought in, quite another to have someone else's interpretation of Confucianism shoved down your throat. The neo-Confucian theory was formulated in Song Dynasty when the Chinese empire was under imminent threat from northern invasion. Now after a century of Mongol rule it is hard to argue that every emperor, even a barbarous Mongol, is worthy of Heaven's Mandate and devotion of his subjects. The scholar-official class begins to take a closer look at their ruler, what they often find is a human being not worthy of their service, let alone worship. Naturally they turn away from statecraft, thoroughly disgusted with political theories. A small number of them, the diehard moralists, continue the pursuit of individual inner virtue along the lines of Buddhist meditation, giving birth to the Study of the Heart (心学), which declares that action and knowledge (morals) must be consistent, in essence a protest against the hypocritical culture. But most of them remain incurable cynics, just like Daoists. This pervasive mentality, needless to say, fuels the corruptive culture and is in turn reinforced by it.

For all the versions of Confucianism and political changes in the past, basic principles of Daoism still apply. A physically weak peasant is less likely to be recruited in the army or construction projects, yet he gets the same land from the state. An obliging individual with no strong wills is less likely to be the target of hostility. A county chief may be an absolute ruler in his domain, but he has to put up ingratiating smiles to inspectors and agents of his superiors, and always be highly flexible in his business dealings with various characters, for who knows one of them might become his superior one day. A strong willed person even in a high position will never win any friend or likely have a desirable ending. This world is decided by human relations, not high minded principles as advertised.

The Chinese political system is a combination of Confucian indoctrination and Legalist coercion. It is not Legalism because the emphasis is on indoctrination. As we recall there are three key elements to the success of Legalist rule: no escape routes, open rules, and collective liability. All three conditions are met in Japan. None of the three is present in China. Neo-Confucians developed the *en* logic to inspire slaves to fight for their master. Again this was successfully adopted by Japanese and utterly failed in China. The *en* based relationship is an emotionally charged one, but its emotional intensity relies on a close knit family type of environment. A Japanese warlord lives close to his samurai and plays the role of a father figure. Their emotional ties are nurtured in everyday interactions. A Chinese emperor is supposed to play the same role to his scholar officials, but he lives an isolated life in the Forbidden City. Most officials have not a single chance to ever see him. Although officially the word *en* is used by officials in all formal interactions with the emperor, he is such a remote figure that they can not perceive much if any human emotion coming from his decrees, read by eunuchs in high pitched voices. The emperor for his part does not feel that the hundreds of thousands of nameless and faceless officials are all his family members. He grows up among his father's multiple concubines, maids and eunuchs, and these are the only people he knows and trusts. He treats officials as mere tools, and they in turn derelict their duty. Lack of an emotional tie dooms this relationship. The *en* logic works fine for Chinese within each family, but not for the ruler.

One is tempted to say that cynicism is a necessary result of lack of real stakes. But the samurai owns nothing either. If he slacks off on his job, he is usually ordered to cut himself open. Thus for slave societies we can not draw that conclusion. Not having a stake gives the slave a reason, or a natural propensity, for cynicism. But for that mentality to materialize into a culture, the slave must at least have the limited freedom to be a cynic. A moral culture where a life is generally spared except for the most egregious crimes, in the spirit of mercy, gives the slave enough opening to be his irresponsible self. An amoral culture allows no such shenanigans, as it can exert a far tighter control over every member of its population, by means that are deemed cruel for a moral culture.

In this cynical culture few are willing to risk their lives for the ruler. The Chinese empire, with its initial expansion largely accomplished by an amoral Qin State in third century BC, has seen declining military prowess ever since. Meanwhile, its consumer culture having absorbed much of the energy of its people is very advanced. Fine cuisine, clothing, furniture, decorations, and other conveniences far surpassed those of other cultures for much of history. Militarily feeble China is conquered over and over again by northern nomads, such as Mongols in thirteenth century and Manchurians in seventeenth, but the conquerors tempted by the comforts of this corrupt culture all choose to make China their home, thus adding their original territory—Mongolia and Manchuria—to Chinese domain. The more times China is conquered, the larger it becomes. Moreover, after centuries of ruling these former barbarians become thoroughly Chinese, losing their own cultural heritage completely. Apparently Chinese people are vulnerable but Chinese culture is invincible. Though neo-Confucianism failed to save the Song Dynasty, it is vindicated in a different way, at least in the minds of Chinese: that it is universal truth. Whoever becomes the ruler, whatever his ethnicity, customs, language, he abandons all of them and embraces Chinese neo-Confucian culture. Thus Confucianism, which used to be judged as a political theory by its impact on the fortunes of a ruling house who implemented it, is now beyond such assessment and becomes self evident as a superior cultural form. By tradition the scholar-official class ought to be ashamed of themselves, or even commit suicide, if the dynasty they serve crumbles before foreign invasion. Now they are much less concerned. Confucianism does not say China has to be ruled by Chinese. Mongols and Manchurians ruled according to Confucian principles, just like Chinese rulers would, so what's the difference?

As such when the empire is under external threat, the average person could not have cared less. Peasants are drafted into the army but they intend to desert at the earliest convenience. Officers are calculating how and how much they can siphon off military funds and get away with it. They need that money to bribe court officials, so the latter will report great victories to the emperor, even though his army suffered embarrassing defeats on battlefield. This practice may sound ludicrous but is commonly employed by generals, whose predicament leaves them little choice. Very often they are given a ragtag army to fight a formidable foe. A defeated general can not escape punishment, from demotion to decapitation, depending on the emperor's mood. In rare cases when they have personally trained competent forces, by the only means possible in a Confucian culture, namely a close nit *en* based family type relationship between the general and his lieutenants, the troops are loyal to him, not the emperor. The ruler fears such a force, and as soon as the invasion is defeated or perhaps even sooner, he would find a way to get rid of the general. So what is a general to do? He reports victory of a battle but not the war (regardless of reality), which certainly pleases the heart of his majesty, and see what happens next. Upon hearing a victory the emperor may promote him to take charge of other armies, which gives him more room to maneuver. With a few more "victories" he can report heavy casualties, complain about inadequate force, foods, equipment, funds, etc. His strategy is to stall and buy time. Wars last years and decades, the emperor continues to throw money and men the general's way. Court officials for their part do not want to be bearers of bad news either, for there is no telling what the ruler will do in a bad mood. These officials are not directly responsible for military defeat, but a frustrated emperor can easily take it out on them. By the time the enemy finally reaches the gate of the Forbidden City, our general is home free: the emperor is no longer in a position to punish him. He can surrender to the new ruler and retire on favorable terms.

It is often hard to tell whether a Chinese general is fighting a foreign invasion or collaborating with the enemy. He may have every desire to fight and win, but his actions are often in the opposite direction. He may not consciously recognize it, or be willing to admit it, but the fact is that his emperor is always a bigger threat to him than any foreign enemy. Reporting defeat, regardless of the circumstances, will be at the very minimum the end of his political career, and that is if he is lucky. Confucianism requires each individual to give his life to the emperor, and there is no better place to do so on battlefield. But the ruler also must show mercy. So as a common practice he forgives the defeated foot soldiers (the peasants), but not the officers, who are supposed to conform to a higher standard. Japanese operate under the same Confucian code but their military culture is honest because A. cheating is impossible and B. death is nothing to the samurai, let alone other lesser punishments.

Now we have a brief sketch of the traditional Chinese society. Everyone professes pious loyalty to the emperor. The scholar-official class, who are teachers, mentors, priests, judges and parent officers of the herd, are supposed to eliminate their own human desires, or at least try, to be worthy of the emperor's *en* to them. But in their minds the first priority is their own lives, the second and the third are their physical and financial wellbeing. Imperial service which is supposed to be their life's calling has become a gravy train. By enforcing an unrealistically high moral standard, neo-Confucianism not only failed to raise morality of the population but completely destroyed honesty and integrity.

Loss of honesty accompanied implementation and evolution of Confucianism as a state ideology. Confucianism whether in Confucius', Mencius' or Xun's articulation is an indoctrination tool. All three thinkers made it clear that the ultimate objective is to turn everyone into a good person, however that is defined. When everyone is good, peace and order naturally follow. Its utilitarian value and methodology inevitably undermines the integrity of its reasoning, because the theory is judged by whether it is effective. In the minds of ancient thinkers what is effective must be true. Over the centuries doctrines like Heaven's Mandate were cynically manipulated by so many rulers—many of whom were clearly unsavory characters—that the educated and historically knowledgeable person could not help but realize that nature of the game is coercive persuasion, whatever its claim to Dao or cosmic order. Moreover, after reading the classics anyone with half a brain can see that the saints—Confucius and Mencius—were liars themselves, except lying for a "good" cause was not considered a problem. Consciously or subconsciously the scholar-official class imitated character traits and demeanor of these two saints, and dishonesty, often rationalized as a consideration for other people's feelings (truth hurts), a sign of civility, of refinement, was exalted, while straightforwardness was shunned as crude insensitivity and deemed detrimental to peace and order. Even though Xun's articulation of Confucianism was by far the best reasoned, it was not inducted into the list of canonized texts, because it was so candid it shattered the benevolent façade of a Confucian regime.

Superhuman neo-Confucian moral standards exacerbated the already hypocritical culture. The single most significant difference between Western and pyramid moralities is the self-worth of an individual. In the West the individual has an undeniable intrinsic value that is more basic than other values. Pyramid societies unfortunately did not develop a free man class, and the value of the individual/slave is often defined in his service to someone or something else, parents, ruler, religion, empire, etc. In absence of such service the individual has no value in and of himself. While self-sacrifice and altruism is treasured across all cultures East and West, in the West it is voluntary, since the individual is fully justified not to practice it, while in the East it is required. The individual is not allowed, at least in theory, to have any human desires at all, thanks to Zen Buddhists who showed that such a state of existence is indeed possible.

This presents a dilemma. It is against human nature to give up born desires for self preservation, without which no one could have survived. Unless one is forced he is bound to find excuses to avoid such moral obligations. To escape risk in imperial service one has to say that he has an aging mother at home who needs his intimate attention. To enjoy sex one has to claim that it is strictly for reproduction, to continue the family line, to fulfill a filial duty. While virtually every official takes bribes, in formal settings they all profess selfless devotion. One can not overtly assert any private interest at all. If a friend or acquaintance makes a request of any kind, I can not just politely turn it down by saying, sorry that is too much trouble and I don't want to do it, because I, like everyone else, am supposed to be selfless. Thus I have to make a promise to every request from everyone I know, and find excuses to break it later. If I serve in the imperial court, I not only have to know what to say according to neo-Confucian doctrine, but train my body language and facial expression to reflect that I truly believe what I say, and instantly present an emotion dictated by the circumstances. For example, the emperor expects teary eyes, a trembling body and a voice choked with sobs when he hands out a favor, an *en*. There are numerous similar situations between parents and children, teachers and pupils, masters and apprentices, superiors and inferiors, and everyone is constantly watched and judged. Who is more filial or more loyal is a never ending competition between siblings and inferiors. Regardless of how one feels in his heart, he at least has to act the part to survive. Chinese are categorized as either good or bad, and everything is either right or wrong, with no middle ground, since allowing a middle ground defeats the purpose of indoctrination. They are faced with two difficult choices: either to conform to a moral standard that is humanly impossible; or be condemned as immoral and ostracized by society. The pressure to fake is rather high.

Two thousand years of Confucian rule has turned lying and acting into must-have skills for Chinese, particularly for the scholar-official class. Peasants are not entirely immune to this culture, but chances for them to lie or act outside the family are lower. As a result peasants are generally more honest than educated urbanites. Chinese reality is such that an honest person who does not lie and can not act is either ignorant or foolish, and that becomes part of common sense. Basic trust between strangers, sometimes even friends, is totally lost. Credibility is a thing of the distant past. No one expects anyone to mean what he says, and a hidden agenda is always assumed. Outside hierarchical relations Chinese will be surprised if their words are taken seriously.

CHAPTER 14
MEIJI RESTORATION AND REFORM

An inconsistency lasted throughout the Tokugawa era, between the imported Confucian/Legalist administrative system and an unorthodox political reality: the emperor, the only legitimate ruler of the land according to the imported ideology, had no real power. If the Japanese emperor was suspected of trying to take back power from the shogun, Japanese would say "the emperor is plotting rebellion" (谋反). To Chinese this is a contradiction of terms. Plotting rebellion is the most serious crime in Confucian lexicon, but it is absurd for the emperor, the supposed owner of all-under-heaven, to be the perpetrator.

That inconsistency was about to be resolved through an avalanche of events triggered by an uninvited guest. In 1853 a few American warships forced their way into Japanese waters, demanding opening up of the self locked country for trade. A political crisis ensued in the shogun government, as the shogun, short for "barbarian subjugating generalissimo", was unable to subjugate this American barbarian. Eager to spread responsibility for failure in a way they were never willing to share power, the shogun sought approval from the long neglected imperial court on trade treaties with America. That was an unprecedented move for the Tokugawa house. They did not consult the emperor when they decided to lock up the country, following China's example, two and a half centuries before. The emperor was utterly unprepared for such responsibility. Having been out of power for centuries, the imperial house was just a slightly more glamorized private residence. It had no military force under its command and no bureaucracy at its disposal. The emperor took a keen interest in current affairs but was not willing or able to make a decision one way or another. For one thing he was not even sure what kind of political game the shogun was playing.

Nevertheless, weakening of the shogun's political standing was quickly perceived and exploited by some states, especially a few "outer states" formerly excluded from the shogun's court. Since even the shogun now upheld the emperor as the ultimate authority, it was an opening that any state could, with the emperor's tacit approval, engage Western enemies, bypassing the shogun government altogether. While the emperor was unwilling to openly endorse any actions by these states, for fear of antagonizing the shogun, they began to agitate under the slogan of "revere the emperor, repel the barbarians" (尊王攘夷), the very slogan founders of neo-Confucianism in Song Dynasty China used to galvanize devotion in the face of imminent northern invasion.

The willingness to sacrifice one's life for the sake of his master was shared by most samurai, especially lower ranking samurai who longed for a chance to prove their worth. But pious loyalty was directed at their lords, not the emperor. The slogan was promulgated by those lords who were either frustrated with the shogun's inability to protect the land, or keen to exploit the situation and break the shogun's control over them, given that the shogun's policy was peace and compromise with Western powers and to keep the status quo, in violation of his duty as dictated by his title. It was a perfect excuse to act independently.

In the name of protecting the emperor two of these states at the southwest corner of Japan—Choshu and Satsuma—waged independent wars against Western fleets, breaking the shogun's long standing laws that prohibited unauthorized military action. They of course were beaten badly by modern warships, but the action was endorsed by the samurai class as a whole and in so doing they shook loose of the shogun's control. Shortly after losing the battle, they began trading with these same Western powers that had just defeated them, buying advanced weapons, training new military forces, sending their clansmen overseas to study Western technology, all done without approval of the shogun government. Within a decade or so these two states had modern armies equipped with nineteenth century Western weaponry, as well as modern military training. The power balance had silently shifted.

It was not that the shogun was closed to Western technology. In fact he sent many of his own men to the West. It was a case of political competition, long frozen by a rigid system, beginning to thaw with its weakening, and a few blocks at the edge shaking completely free. During this process that lasted over a decade, the political center of Japan shifted from shogun's court to the emperor's court, largely because the latter had been empty, thus free of vested interests, and open for political entrepreneurship. The shogun's court in comparison developed symptoms reminiscent of China: officials feeling secure and comfortable in their positions and a hedonistic lifestyle tended to be conservative, for they had the most to lose in any potential changes. There was no lack of proposals for reform on shogun's desk, but any reform would involve major financial commitment, as well as shuffling of personnel, hence resistance was significant and pace inevitably slow. In the end the more light footed newly semi-independent states won the race to adopt modern military technology.

I call these states semi-independent because they could not stand all alone. As soon as they run afoul of the shogun they needed support from the imperial court. It is un-Confucian to be independent. It is un-Japanese to violate laws. Any state that violated shogun's law must either replace the shogun or seek approval from the emperor. Thus the capital city of Kyoto became a fierce battling ground, where states and the shogun all stationed troops fighting for the right to "protect" the emperor. Assassinations were so common they became routine and an accepted part of the political scene. The emperor became an official seal of legitimacy that all power brokers wanted to have in their possession.

In this time of destabilized political environment, any ambitious lord not resigned to fate had to fight for the future of his own domain. The bushido code, pious loyalty, resoluteness in the face of death, all of that though present in most samurai was not enough to defeat cannons and steam ships. A lord needed someone who could quickly adapt to the times, had no xenophobia, and could learn new skills from the enemy. A number of young and lower ranking samurai rose to the occasion. They brought in Western technology and ideas, and became movers and shakers of this turbulent era. By 1868 the joined forces of Choshu and Satsuma states defeated shogun's forces, ending 260 years of Tokugawa reign. The new emperor Meiji, still a teenager, became nominal ruler of Japan. Prior to this point Japan had never been a unified empire in the Confucian sense. Spread of Confucianism in the Tokugawa era gave learned samurai a vision of absolute imperial power, for the first time in Japanese history. Guided by their pious loyalty and Confucian training, they helped the imperial house reclaim all the land of Japan formerly held by lords, found an imperial army, and force the lords into retirement.

This was another case exemplary of the counter-evolution process. As values of servility like pious loyalty are the cultural core, individuals pushing for any social change have to raise that banner for legitimacy. Low ranking samurai abhorred the Tokugawa system. They were born into a station deemed privileged by peasants, but still at constant mortal danger from higher ranks, and there was no easy way out. In trying to abolish that system, however, they could not directly rebel against their lords, for that would have been against pious loyalty. Instead they had to claim pious loyalty to the emperor, in the name of the emperor deprive the lords of their power, and persuade the emperor to issue a decree ending hereditary classes. Those samurai who opposed such a measure, and considered it an insult to be ranked as equals with peasants, in turn could only argue that they were really more loyal to the emperor than the young upstarts advising the court, whom they accused of being self-serving. This explains why there were numerous assassination attempts at high ministers, but not one against the emperor. As the emperor grew up and started to put his weight behind the reformers all dissent quickly vanished for lack of a legitimate argument. In the end low ranking samurai got what they wanted, but were at the same time fully committed to pious loyalty to the crown. In the past political power was fragmented, with each lord owning his state. Now the emperor owned everything, and the Japanese political system became true to its Confucian doctrine for the first time. The term *banzai* (万岁, ten thousand years) which was used by Chinese exclusively for the emperor finally found its way to Japan. As a long neglected religion Shinto was reestablished nationally, and the emperor as its new object of worship claimed a divine status. In the old days Shinto was a clan totem worship of the Sun Goddess (founder of the imperial blood line), not a living emperor. Now it was a Confucianized religion, with pious loyalty as its main doctrine. Once the pyramid is there, there is only one way the culture can develop of its own accord: towards more concentration of power and more devotion to the state by the masses.

The Yakusuni Shrine set up in 1885 by the imperial house is symbolic of the Meiji reform. Worshiping loyal servants (忠臣) is a Confucian tradition encouraged and propagated by all ruling regimes. Raising these servants to divine status helped inculcate the masses with an aspiration to selflessly serve the master. It is the highest honor to die for one's owner. In China only a few high ranking officials were deified in such a manner (关公庙, 岳王庙), because the average foot soldier—peasants temporarily recruited for a war effort—were at the bottom of the pyramid and deemed not worthy of worship. With a military tradition Japanese samurai—professional warriors close to the top of the pyramid—who died for the emperor were all inducted in the Yakusuni Shrine as gods. Imperial soldiers of the Meiji era had the same mentality of the old samurai: to die for their master and then be worshiped as gods, except that the master was now the emperor, not a warlord.

Despite further Confucianization Meiji Japanese by and large felt quite liberated, as they were indeed freed from the sword of superiors. The emperor, after all, was a remote figure, much more benign than a samurai or daimyo who could kill people at will. The Meiji reform was in essence moving from a barbarous but highly disciplined system governed by warlords to a more humane framework, allowing more choices, under a centralized imperial regime. Arbitrary beheadings and ritual suicide were abolished as official forms of punishment, which meant indoctrination had to take a more prominent role, so as to achieve a high degree of mental conformity, or in Japanese, "a nation of one mind". Here is a quote from one of the influential thinkers at the time, Aizawa Seishisai:

"The means by which a sovereign protects his empire, preserves peace and order, and keeps the land from unrest is not the holding of the world in a tight grip or the keeping of people in fearful subjection. His only sure reliance is that the people should be of one mind, that they should cherish their sovereign, and that they should be unable to bear being separated from him."

This is the gist of Confucianism, indoctrination first and foremost, physical coercion as an auxiliary tool in a two pronged approach to statecraft. After two and a half centuries of learning, Japanese scholars finally grasped its essence, and only in the new era, where the shogun was gone as a savage ruler, were they able to air this Confucian principle. To Chinese it had been common sense for two millennia, except they had grown cynical, but to Japanese this was a major improvement in their human condition. Ironically Meiji thinkers saw it as part of "Westernization" or liberalization.

When Meiji thinkers came into contact with Western ideas such as freedom, they had no way of comprehending its meaning in the Western context. When they traveled to the West, they could see that the average Western citizen could do a lot of things that were previously prohibited in Japan, such as freely seeking jobs. Of course Westerners were free from arbitrary killings by superiors as well. What also impressed Japanese was that with so much freedom Westerners were still willing to serve their state. That, in Japanese understanding, was "a nation of one mind". The British all had one mind, so did Germans. To Confucians this is a logical conclusion. Without coercion why should slaves serve their master? Indoctrination. Asians—Japanese and Chinese alike—can not fathom a state of human existence that is not a slave.

Meiji Japanese felt they were free. By the new rules superiors could no longer arbitrarily kill inferiors. There were no longer restrictions on career choices based on birth and class. They thought they were Westernizing, not knowing Chinese had always enjoyed such "freedom" and taken it for granted. Every Japanese man was still a servant to the emperor and to his parents, and must be a loyal one ready to give his life at any moment, but how he wanted to serve, in what profession, in what capacity, was now of his own choosing. Human relations were still hierarchical, but each individual now had a chance to advance his station. This was Japanese freedom, which they call "public freedom", as opposed to "personal freedom". A samurai used to be able to kill a peasant at whim; that was his personal freedom. Because of it peasants were slaves to the samurai class. Therefore "personal freedom" is bad. New laws prohibited such actions, which meant the society now had "public freedom". In order to promote "public freedom", then, the superior must suppress his "personal freedom", abandon his independence, in other words sacrifice his freedom for the community. This is the same intellectual trap that plagues all Asian ethical systems. Because the individual has no value in and of himself (core cultural values inherited from antiquity define the individual as a slave), the Western idea of freedom if truly understood can not possibly be interpreted in a positive light. After such a twist the Japanese sense of freedom is the exact opposite of the American sense. Though everyone felt that it was a progress that more people had more security in the Meiji era, the Confucian tradition that depicts everything private as bad—including "personal freedom"—and everything public (imperial) as good confused their understanding of this imported idea, and turned it into the same old private/public conflict. In 1992 when a Japanese exchange student was killed in Louisiana in an accidental shooting (he was mistaken as an intruder to a private residence), Japanese interpretation of the event was that American freedom—personal freedom—is bad, because it allows an individual to kill another. Only when no one has any personal freedom beyond those prescribed by the government (such as to choose a career), can there be public freedom.

From the standpoint of an amoral culture this is also a logical conclusion. If you beat a Chinese man, he will hate you, because he thinks he is wronged. You have just created an enemy. If you beat a Japanese man, he will obey you, because he thinks you are naturally his superior. You have just created a loyal servant. Having never had any real choice but to face a brutal reality, Japanese have the tendency to dominate others in a cruel fashion for fear of being dominated the same way, if not put under strict control. Thus coming from the Tokugawa culture that institutionalized such dominance, the Meiji regime had to promulgate detailed rules governing personal conduct. Not only that, a standard mode of behavior had to be trained since childhood.

When everyone was trained to have the same mind, and their conduct all followed scripted rituals of propriety (*li*), it was indeed a peaceful and pleasant society far superior to previous barbarism. When the imperial decree came that they were free to pursue their own career regardless of birth, and everyone had equal opportunity to promotion, it is hard to overstate their gratitude, the indebtedness they felt towards the emperor, their *en* man. They were truly united in their zeal and unwavering dedication to serve the sovereign. The feeling was universal and genuine. This consensus made it unnecessary, at least in the short term, to resort to harsh measures. "Freedom" had brought about conformity, as strange as that sounds.

In theory Japanese had rights too. These rights, as defined in the Meiji Constitution, were conditional, in essence privileges granted by the emperor to his loyal servants. Here are a few examples:

Article XIX: Japanese subjects shall all equally be eligible for civil and military appointments, and any other public offices, subject only to the conditions prescribed by Laws and Ordinances.

Article XXII: Subject to the limitations imposed by law, Japanese subjects shall enjoy full liberty in regard to residence and change of abode.

Article XXIII: No Japanese subject shall be arrested, detained, tried or punished, except according to law.

Article XXV: Except in the cases provided for in the law, the house of no Japanese subject shall be entered or searched without his permission.

Article XXVI: Except in cases provided for in the law, the secrecy of the letters of Japanese subjects shall not be violated.

Article XXVII: The rights of property of Japanese subjects shall not be violated. Such measures, however, as may be rendered necessary in the interests of the public welfare shall be taken in accordance with the provisions of the law.

Notice that every right is subject to "law". What is law? It is imperial edicts, rescripts, and government regulations. This reflects the Legalist view that law is absolute, no matter for what purpose it is devised, but most certainly for peace and order, and everything else, such as freedom and rights, is bestowed on the subjects as an *en*, a divine favor from the ruler, which is conditional upon and to be repaid with pious loyalty. One may own his house, as private property is protected under this constitution. But if he happens to harbor "dangerous thoughts"—ideas that undermine the harmonious *en* based emotional tie between ruler and subjects, or that undermine national conformity (one nation, one mind)—then his property can and should be confiscated, all his other rights including the right to a trial are forfeited, because he violated the "law".

Nevertheless, having these "rights" published was a major progress. At least superiors could no longer behead their inferiors. There is also a psychological difference between Japanese and Western views on rights. As undeserving recipients of divine favor, Japanese were moved by the benevolence of their emperor (granting them all these rights/privileges they never even heard of before), and resolved to give their lives for him. The individual sees no value in and of himself; he feels guilty just to think about his own interest; his entire worth is defined by his service to the emperor, and he intends to enhance his worth; it is the psyche of a grateful slave to his master. The rights are not meant to be enjoyed by the individual in a care free fashion. A good person should voluntarily give up his rights instead, or at least feel guilty every time he invokes them, for he has not made enough contribution to the sovereign and does not deserve his kindness. A Westerner on the other hand feels that he is the ultimate value in and of himself, "man is the measure of all things", and his constitutional rights reaffirm his sense of supreme confidence, as a master of his own domain.

The very idea of rights contradicts Confucian virtue, which is designed for the slave. A slave's virtue is his pious loyalty and filial piety. Individual rights are a matter of private interest, thus immoral or unethical by Confucian definition, since a good slave must not have any such interest. Consequently there were debates over what should be taught in Japanese schools. The emperor favored traditional Confucian values, while some progressive thinkers pushed for Western ideas like freedom and democracy. In the end these thinkers could not agree among themselves as to what these Western terms really mean, and their liberal movement disintegrated. The organization, control and curriculum of the education system went through a few changes during the period, but in the end Japanese schools became a place where Confucian ethics was taught alongside Western science and technology.

When faced with a Western concept like democracy, there are typically two different approaches leading to two different interpretations in Asia. One focuses on the institutional side of things, political elections, three branches of government, constitutional rule, and the like. This is the approach taken by Westerners, who are by default free. The other approach focuses on the fact that Asians are by default slaves. Japanese samurai, for example, were keenly aware that they had been slaves to their lords (daimyos), while Western officers who served in the name of their king were not slaves of superior commanders. For the samurai or the peasant, the pressing issue of liberation was not institutional democracy, but getting out from under the sword of their superiors. Thus the term democracy when translated into Japanese/Chinese (民主) literally means "people being masters". Samurai and peasants alike wanted to be their own masters, and this interpretation became the mainstream.

By abolishing the Tokugawa system Japanese thought they had democracy, when in fact the Meiji political regime was similar to the Chinese dynastic system that lasted two thousand years. The emperor was sacred and pious loyalty was due ultimately to him, which by Confucian definition meant every one of his subjects was his slave. However, there are several cultural differences between the two countries in late nineteenth century. Chinese indoctrination centered on moral ideals. Scholar-officials had arbitrary power over peasants, but few would resort to torture or killing, because of the moral barrier of mercy. Japanese indoctrination centered on rules. Mercy was not a concern as officers routinely drove subordinates and themselves harshly, in discharging an imperial duty. In domestic settings they were forbidden from killing subordinates by rules, but in situations where these rules no longer apply, such as when they later faced conquered peoples of China and Southeast Asia, arbitrary killings and torture of captives were rampant, often done for fun. The amoral side of Japanese culture was not easily discernable to the Western eye, as one of the unwritten rules in Japanese training was to treat Westerners as superiors in general. To superiors Japanese would come across as polite, trust worthy and pleasantly disciplined.

Aside from different mechanisms to ensure a civilized society, Japanese in the Meiji era had only recently stepped out of savagery and gratefully enjoyed their new found freedom, while Chinese had long grown disillusioned to the imperial apparatus. One of the marked differences between Meiji society and a traditional Confucian one is the active participation by the entire population in all activities of the state. Imperial Confucianism sees the masses as passive slaves. It encourages a servile character that tends to hold back, to remain silent, to show little emotion in public, and to take no initiative. Neo-Confucianism and its sibling bushido made it possible for the *shi* class of both cultures to adopt a more assertive posture, provided that the intension was loyal. The bulk of populace however remained reserved and taciturn. Meiji reformers wanted every Japanese to assume the samurai character, reserved in the private sphere but dashingly brave and vocal in service to the state. They were inspired by what they saw in the West, where the average citizen was a much more active participant in state affairs. They thought that was an effective way for the state to harvest the energy of its citizenry. The state was likened to a machine, a citizen a screw in it. The Western machine worked so well because every citizen played a part. The problem with Confucianism, they concluded, was that the majority of citizens were excluded from the state machine, and herded like sheep. They needed to start contributing. Thus for Japanese participation in industry, commerce and other activities is not an exercise of free will, but fulfilling a duty to the state. Peasants were dragged from their homes and fields into factories and mines, and were forced to work in sub-human conditions. That was done not to generate profit for capitalists, but to enrich the state. It was their duty to become a useful screw for the state machine.

With new found freedom and opportunities the educated were zealous believers of Confucian imperialism, as they became managers of these sweat shops, as well as scientists, engineers, doctors, teachers. They were not cynically exploiting the illiterate poor, for they shared the mission of "enrich the country and strengthen its military" (a modern reiteration of pious loyalty), and were willing to give up their own interest if necessary. As they built roads, railways, electricity, steamships, modern cities, changing the entire landscape every year, the newly educated class—from a variety of family backgrounds—were the first generation of Japanese to be truly optimistic, forward looking, and enthusiastic. They were a kind of character who under most circumstances remained reserved, but in the context of a state organized activity, whether in school, in workplace or in military, quickly sprung into an assertive mode. Their optimism was partly based on new found security. Superiors now needed valid reasons to punish inferiors, and if so only according to rules. Dissent and disobedience was sometimes allowed if the inferior had the right intension, for in the end every high ranking officer had to be judged by his contribution as well, and in those years, one's effort would quickly yield visible results.

In that spirit the ruling elite combined Confucian ethics and tactics developed in centuries of samurai training in school curriculums. Strict discipline was introduced at an early age, so were shouting, quick to follow orders without thinking or hesitation, energy and enthusiasm in carrying out orders, and selfless devotion. National education was so high a priority to Meiji government that virtually no effort was spared in its implementation. By early twentieth century some ninety percent of Japanese children were enrolled in schools, surpassing even the West. Schools played a critical role in shaping the uniform Japanese character.

In this nationwide optimistic rush to industrialization, where the educated class, now the ruling elite, was enjoying unprecedented possibilities, a constitution was hardly needed. After all, the idea of a constitution as it developed in the West was an expression of public will, an instrument for enlightened people to assert their rights, and to put checks on their government's power. The vast majority of Japanese, including educated ones, had no such desire. In fact, having been through centuries of harsh military style rule, the new and much more benevolent absolute monarchy was the best thing that ever happened to them. A constitution was only needed to prove to the West that Japan was now a civilized country, so that the unequal treaties signed under the cannons of Western warships could be repealed.

The Meiji constitution on paper followed conventions of many Western constitutions, except that every right stipulated therein was subject to "law", which would be Japanese customary law. That law includes the bushido code, which is largely unwritten but understood by everyone. The tricky part is that bushido embodies the principle of sacrificing for one's master, like a faithful dog. It is virtue of a loyal slave. It solidifies the master-slave relation by giving it flesh, in the form of an *en* based emotional tie. In its nature it is diametrically opposed to the very idea of human rights.

Of course none of this is apparent from the text of the constitution, at least not to outsiders ignorant of Confucian culture and psyche. Japanese understanding of this document is that everyone is supposed to behave like a samurai, piously loyal to the emperor, always ready to give his or her own life, and having such a "correct" mentality, they qualify for new freedoms/rights/privileges, such as free choice of career regardless of birth, by the grace of their benevolent and divine ruler. But just because the constitution has these articles, does not mean the average Japanese can enjoy these rights. It depends on the particular item. On the matter of career choice, no one is shy of taking the opportunity, because choosing a profession is choosing the best way to serve the emperor according to one's unique talent, it is honorable. On the entitlement to a trial when accused, it is an entirely different story. It is against the bushido code, the principle of pious loyalty, to challenge accusations made by the state. The government works for the emperor, whom one is supposed to serve. A samurai is supposed to die when ordered to, without questioning that order, even if it is a misjudgment by his lord. One can urge caution and patience, on the part of the master/government, in finding out the facts of the case, or mercy (in China) in handing out punishment, but in the Confucian framework one can not posit the right for a subject, by nature a slave, to a fair trial, or to anything else. Therefore, articles of this nature, with even the slightest hint of disobedience, are rarely evoked by the average defendant. Unless one is a famous person who has proved his loyalty with past merits, citing the constitution for protection would usually add disloyalty to one's offenses and make things worse.

Just as the rights declared in this constitution are understood by Japanese in a dramatically different way than the text would suggest to Westerners, so is the role of the emperor.

Article III: The person of the Emperor is sacred and inviolable.

The German advisor who participated in the draft of this constitution explained this article as follows:

"This article defines the sovereign rights of the Monarch with regard to His person. It rests upon the notion of the divine nature and origin of the supreme power which is testified by the Christian as well as by every other religious belief and is only denied by philosophical freethinkers. It is an express rule of the Christian faith that submission is due to the supreme power because it is instituted by God himself. The Emperor holds His power from Heaven through the medium of His glorious ancestors, but not from any human authorization or concession; consequently He cannot be held responsible to His subjects, but to Heaven alone."

In an effort to gain legitimacy in the Western eye, here Heaven is presented as the Confucian equivalent of the Christian God. God and Heaven are not the same kind of idea. One can say we are all created equal by God. God can be cited to advance the idea of equality. But Heaven is not a humanized deity. It created no one, and is never concerned with equality or justice for an individual. God had his messages written in the Bible, which has a story of breaking away from slavery in search of freedom, so that any European king ruling in the name of God could not rule against the principles carried therein. Heaven has no written message; it has been used by Confucians as an excuse for absolute rule, such as "no two suns in the sky (heaven), nor two rulers in a land". Christianity by its doctrine and by its independent church organization does place a meaningful restraint on a secular ruler. Heaven has no church and no doctrine. It is merely a puppet in the hands of rulers. Confucian classics do not enjoy the status of the Holy Bible (they can be canonized or de-canonized by any emperor), because those who wrote them were thinkers, not prophets of Heaven (Confucius, Mencius and others never claimed any association to Heaven, only a ruler could claim such association).

From a legal point of view, if we see the purpose of a constitution as reaffirming native traditions, then the only right thing to do would be to assert tradition as the highest principle. And if we further ignore the difference between cultures and belief systems, then we can have "equivalent" constitutions for all nations in the world by simply replacing the word God with Heaven, Allah, Buddha, or what have you. But if we are to keep our intellectual integrity, we have to ask the question: what if the native tradition is against all the human rights declared in the same document? Why do we have a constitution in such a case?

For Emperor Meiji and his faithful servants the answer was simple: to get Western approval. To that end a diet was introduced, as well as political parties. When all was said and done, the Meiji political system at least looked somewhat modern and Western. And it worked. Western powers eventually revised their unequal treaties with Japan. It is hard to blame anyone for being thoroughly impressed by Japanese achievement: within just three decades, Japan transformed itself from a backward agricultural society to one of the leading industrial powers of the world, something that took Western European countries centuries. There was a lot of abuse no doubt, but the dedication and stoicism of the entire nation was nothing short of breathtaking.

Industrial revolution in the West followed the enlightenment movement and rise of individual freedom, thus Westerners often associate Meiji reforms with the same spirit. This view was reinforced by educated Japanese who truly felt they were far freer than their predecessors. But as we just discussed, Western concepts like freedom have no counterpart in Confucian societies, and the Meiji system meant something dramatically different to Japanese than it would suggest to outsiders.

Take political parties. In the West it is a way for free citizens to have their views, their will and their values represented in the political process. In Japan the citizen is not supposed to have his own view or value or will. Meiji Japan is supposed to be of one mind, which is to serve the state, and vigorous indoctrination in schools turns that into a reality. But seeing that political parties energized Westerners in their active participation of all enterprises, Meiji reformers concluded that passive obedience was no longer enough, Japanese must assert themselves aggressively in service of the emperor and the state. Political parties became a venue for them to put forth their own proposals, just like in the old days samurai would compete on who was more loyal to the lord by putting forth daring plans.

In theory the public, having achieved a single mind/objective, would organize themselves around different proposals/approaches on how to best serve the crown. But an education/indoctrination system aimed at conformity does not breed active thinkers. Thus the parties from the outset represented factions within the ruling elite rather than the public, who remained obedient followers excluded from the political process. Moreover, as Confucian inter-personal relationships defined the inner workings of any organization, each party/faction took the same form of an *en* based family style hierarchy reminiscent of the lord-samurai relationship. Party members were not loyal to an idea, but to a man.

Even parties organized in such a fashion did not have much power, for the diet was just one of many organs serving the emperor, who only trusted his close assistants in the administrative branch. Because the competition was about who could best serve the emperor, to enlarge his domain, to bring bounty to his coffer and glory to his name, the culture quickly became aggressively imperialistic. While administrative officials diligently worked to industrialize and strengthen the nation from within, the diet was typically beating the drums of foreign expansion into Korea and Manchuria, accusing the administration of dragging its feet, of not doing enough for the crown. This was not a case where the educated class inevitably embraced nationalism for survival of their culture, since Western powers never really occupied Japan or intended to do so. Nor was it a case where the crown consciously embarked on a global expansion plan (that came much later) in order to divert domestic problems and tensions. It was a case of lack of alternative and legitimate arguments. Just like in old times a samurai could not be faulted for recklessly plunging into battle for his lord, even without the latter's specific order, when a few diehard militants among the new generation of Japanese men—all educated in the bushido spirit regardless of birth—shouted out foreign expansion in the name of the emperor, no one could raise any counter argument without sounding cowardly or disloyal, instead everyone felt pressured to sing the same tune, even louder than the next. Quickly militancy became the chorus of the entire nation. Bushido, the core of Japanese civilization, is after all a militant culture. All Confucian and Buddhist values are tailored to its need, whatever argument against it is inevitably unethical to the Japanese ear.

We have discussed the process of counter-evolution in slave societies, where over time the independent-minded are replaced by the servile, and the servile replaced by the more servile, because of competition between slaves for favor of the ruler. In moral cultures such as China this process has its limit. The ruler can exploit his subjects, draft them in wars, but he can not force them to give their lives for him. In training camps officers can not beat soldiers as a matter of standard training just to toughen them (punishment can be accepted only when someone did something wrong), or else they are likely to mutiny. When they desert en masse on the battlefield, there is nothing the ruler can do, as he has to show mercy. The moral principle of *ren* serves as the limit of what can and can not be tolerated by Chinese.

Without such a moral principle, Japanese are able to go much further in their servility. Competition in serving the emperor exists in China too. But just because a few fanatics are willing to risk their own lives, does not mean the rest of the official class are pressured to follow their acts. Just saying invading a certain country helps the emperor's interest is an undisputable rallying call to arouse Japanese devotion, but not so for Chinese. Unless the Chinese emperor himself has made the decision, proposals for such foreign expeditions can be refuted. A scholar official could calmly assert that the ruler should strive for the wellbeing of his subjects, instead of ordering them to die for his material gains. The average person could claim that staying alive to serve his sick parents is a higher priority than serving his emperor. These Mencian arguments did not survive the journey to Japan. Here it is mandatory to be willing to die when ordered. Bushido itself is a form of military fanaticism. As a result, even though military zealots are a small minority in any culture, in Japan they and they alone occupy the high ethical ground, and the rest are easily shamed into following their call.

In such a culture where the citizenry are not just loyal, but slavishly, piously, and zealously loyal, the emperor of course holds awesome powers. Such power usually corrupts, as we have seen in the Chinese case. But the unique history of the Japanese imperial house saved its modern emperors from falling into the same trap. Since almost as early as Japanese became literate and started recording history, the emperor had been more of a symbol than a real ruler. A prime minister, the real ruler, could easily dethrone the reigning emperor and install a kid much more controllable. Such practice became routine and the whole bureaucracy was built around the prime minister, to the point that an ambitious emperor had to retire and set up an independent government outside the imperial compound to bypass all the officials, who were loyal to the crown in name but to the real ruler in reality. In later centuries Japan was dominated by warriors, but the shoguns treated the emperor in a similar way previous prime ministers did, only more restrictive and humiliating: the emperor was often put under permanent house arrest as a hostage.

As a result Japanese history and literature lacked a template of absolute imperial power and procedure that Emperor Meiji and his successors could follow. He was in a new era and an unprecedented position. People in such a situation tend to be cautious, which he was. Abuse of power by Chinese rulers did not become a pattern overnight. The earliest rulers were more down to earth and open minded, but as power became secure, they grew more indulgent of slavish services, less tolerant of dissent, arbitrary and irresponsible in their decisions. Each generation would add to the size of bureaucracy, insulation of the ruler from reality, and more abuse to recorded history. Centuries later the culture became such that a loyal officer could be working diligently for the empire, but just because he failed to bribe someone close to the ruler, such as a eunuch, he could be easily demoted or jailed on phony charges. A meritorious military general could be executed exactly because he successfully defeated the enemy. If previous rulers did all that and suffered no consequence, it would only embolden successors to more ghastly acts. No Japanese ruler, emperor or shogun alike, was ever so secure in their power, that they had not even a shred of apprehension in their hearts when making important decisions, hence the corrupt culture did not have a chance to develop in Japan.

Instead of reckless abuse of power as a form of self-indulgence Japanese history is filled with warrior stories, in which the samurai plays the role of a faithful servant and the lord is also a warrior who embodies the same spirit of stoicism, self-control and a simple material life. Though the lord owns his samurai as slaves, and has the awesome power of ordering their suicide, he uses it judiciously for practical reasons. The punishment is cruel, but it is only invoked when the violation concerns discipline, diligence or loyalty, in other words matters directly related to military prowess. If a lord favors toadying and cowardly characters for the convenience and flattery that they bring to him and his family, or if he lashes out on his samurai for personal reasons unrelated to the bushido code, he will sap the strength of his troops and is not likely to last long in the fierce military competition with other lords. At the very top level Japanese rulers never developed that sense of total security and were always ready to reach a compromise with domestic foes.

In keeping with that tradition Japanese emperors from Meiji onward took a quiet role behind the scenes, leaving all state operations in the hands of administrative officials. Their trust in the loyalty of all their subjects was not abstract: the culture was such that loyalty to the crown was manifested in everyday life. When politicians debated in the diet, argued behind closed doors, it was always about what course of action best served the emperor. When an engineer worked in any industry, he was not trying to make a profit for a private employer. What motivated him was the idea that he was actively serving the emperor, which his father a generation earlier did not have the honor or opportunity to do. He considered all his hard work and sacrifice a privilege. Of course he would like to rise further in the social hierarchy, which he had a good chance, but being an engineer was like being a samurai of old, it enhanced his position in the family. For young adults gratitude towards the regime and acknowledgement of the emperor's *en* is due more to their rise in social hierarchy, particularly among family and neighbors, than to any material gain. In the old days a twenty or thirty year old had to obey parents and elderly members of the community. Imagine how the same person would feel if all of a sudden in his life circle elders could no longer order him around and his words carried more weight. Just as Legalist reform in the Qin State of fourth century BC China had unleashed the energy of the youth by separating them from their families, and propelled Qin's meteoric rise to hegemony, the same mechanism was working in Meiji Japan.

In order to present Japan as a civilized society similar to the West or at least quickly moving in that direction, which the Japanese intellectual elite truly believed, history and culture was reinterpreted along Western lines. The Tokugawa period and the centuries before were called feudal, and Meiji Japan a modern capitalist society. The samurai was equated with European knights, bushido likened to chivalry, Shinto compared to Christianity, *yi* (propriety) translated to justice, and ideas with fundamental importance in Japanese culture that can not be even remotely associated with anything Western, such as *en* (恩), were conspicuously missing from this presentation.

If we set out looking for similarities between Tokugawa Japan and feudal Europe, in a way that a bookworm scholar would do, we can find plenty. Politics, economics, production, labor, religion, folklore, on an abstract level, all human civilizations have something in common. And if we are to compare Tokugawa Japan with various periods in Western history, the medieval feudal period does come the closest. But such comparison obscures the fundamental difference between East and West. Western civilization since its budding in classical Greece has always been dominated by free men. Asia had become pyramid societies before recorded history, in which one was a master of his inferior and a slave to his superior at the same time. At the bottom of the pyramid sit the vast majority of the population who dominated Eastern cultures since the very beginning, by their predicament, their struggles, and their psychology. Confucius was such a slave trying to obtain office by selling his obsequious ideas.

Without knowing this distinction one can not understand the relationship between Confucian parents and children, or between lord and samurai, the *en* logic, the emotional pull of such a relation. We may compare economic statistics, means of production, political institutions, and find Japan to be on par with Western Europe in a lot of ways, but once we get into the mind of Japanese, which none Westerner has been able to do so far, for no fault of their own (lack of Confucian psychological torture in their upbringing and permanent Stockholm Syndrome), all the similarities become superficial.

This is not to say that Meiji thinkers went about their intellectual pursuit in a cynical manner. Just like earlier Japanese failed to grasp the moral aspect of Confucianism, which to Chinese is its backbone, Meiji intellectuals had no clue of the nature of Western civilization which they devoted their whole lives trying to imitate. And for both Chinese and Japanese, as well as other Asians, understanding the Western mind is as big a challenge as it is the other way around. It is relatively easy to observe actions and habits, and try to copy them, but analyzing the mental process is a completely different matter.

The Meiji regime promulgated detailed rules to emulate Western patterns of behavior, how to greet people, how to salute, how to behave in various public occasions as well as at home. These were the new *li*—rules of propriety—to partially replace Confucian ones. Outdoors and in many other cases a deep bow was substituted for prostration. Inferiors were taught to raise their chin and stick out their chest in front of superiors, instead of recoil in fear, which was a natural posture adopted by peasants trying to avoid the vengeful sword of samurai. In a few decades as the school system worked over an entire generation, Japanese behavior quickly caught up with Western standards. They were polite, courteous, and understandable in body language to Westerners.

But these imported customs did not reflect the underlying mentality. Prostration may be reduced, but the individual still felt like a slave to his employer, simply because that was the only way he knew how to feel as defined by four out of five Confucian relations, and he certainly could not treat his boss as a friend. Though a superior could no longer behead subordinates any more, he could still ruin their career or livelihood. The average individual still saw his boss as a Confucian father figure, an *en* man, to whom he must stay blindly obedient. Thus behind the façade of Western style courtesy, the strict hierarchical social order did not change at all.

Regardless of such contradictions, which only an amoral culture can sustain on a long term basis, the comparison with Western history and concepts done in the Meiji period remained in the written language, in Chinese characters, which laid a faulty framework and deprived subsequent Asian thinkers of an objective foundation to their cultural studies. The English word slave was translated to *dorei* (奴隷), which in China and Japan meant the kind of domestic servants who could be bought and sold. But the word means something different in the West, as the opposite of free man, which never existed in the Confucian context. Most Asian peasants were not *dorei*, they had their own lot assigned by the state, and in general they were not bought or sold, so they were called "free farmers". Following Western practice the vast majority of Asians were called free people. That view persists today. People do not even think it as an opinion; it is part of the language and therefore the truth. That prevents a good understanding of Confucian culture for all subsequent researchers, Asian or Western. Western scholars need to learn the Japanese/Chinese language in order to study Japan/China, and in the process of that learning they unknowingly absorbed these mistranslations and misleading ideas, upon which a coherent social theory could not possibly be built.

Intellectual confusion involving imported Western terms did not stop indoctrination efforts. Confucians are not great at objective reasoning but they know intuitively that pious loyalty does not come with natural birth; it has to be cultivated in coercive training, and maintained in part by having the subjects believe that this is the Dao, nature's Way of things. Once they realize that Westerners do not believe in this Dao, it will be much harder to control their minds. In order to allay this fear but also meet the urgent need for new technology, a slogan was advanced by Meiji reformers that read: Japanese soul, Western skills (和魂洋才). The new Japanese was to remain piously loyal to his emperor, but equipped with Western technological know-how.

In a moral culture this would be difficult to achieve. Historically Western science could not have blossomed without religious reform that started with the protestant movement. The immediate political reason was that the Church monopolized all intellectual inquiry, and it saw some of the new theories as blasphemous. But power of the Church ultimately rested with moral conviction of the populace. Many people agreed with the Church that it was wrong to think the earth revolves around the sun because it is not in the Bible and not in line with the man centered theology (God created man in his own image), therefore not God's Way. It took an intellectual revolution just to bring about the possibility that scientific research may not violate moral order, in the argument that we do not really know God's Way/design, so let us find out. The difficulty is rooted in the fear that any intellectual endeavor could have potential moral consequences, because morality in the end is an intellectual construct, a set of ideas. Chinese run into the same kind of roadblocks in the nineteenth century. Dao is Heaven's Way, upon which morality is based. If one is to discover that heaven/sky (the two are one and the same word in Chinese) is nothing but air, nitrogen and oxygen, then who is the emperor? The son of molecules? Neo-Confucianism as a moral theory based on cosmic order can not withstand modern science, as we shall see in the difficulty China faced in attempting modernization.

An amoral culture like Japan does not have this problem. The Japanese idea of ethics is just a set of concrete rules, and a particular psyche acquired after being subjected to these rules throughout one's life, which they call "Japanese soul". Chinese needed a moral conviction to have peace and order, because the immense empire was managed by the lettered scholar-official class, who would not be able to control the peasantry if the latter lost faith in the doctrine. Japan had been a highly militarized empire for centuries. There were swords and harsh punishment around every corner. The culture was dominated by a military code. Voluntary moral conviction was not a must for peace and order, and in any case non-existent. Thus whatever science teaches has no bearing on social order. Modern Japanese schools carried on a resemblance of samurai training, making sure that rules alone, with little or no justification given, have enough authority to maintain peace and order.

Chapter 15

CONFUCIAN CHILD REARING AND FORMATION OF THE CONFUCIAN MIND (2)

Japanese child rearing practices have a lot in common with Chinese practices at home. However, since its establishment in the Meiji era the public school system played an important role in forming the Japanese character. The Meiji government put a high priority on education/indoctrination. The guiding principle of this education was "Japanese soul and Western skills". Western skills referred to natural science and technology. Japanese soul referred to the bushido spirit, the samurai psyche and ethics. The objective was to train every Japanese child, including sons and daughters of peasants, into a modern servant of the state, with the zeal and devotion of a samurai, and skills of a Western engineer.

This objective was not the result of arbitrary designation. Unlike Chinese society which relied on indoctrination as the primary instrument of stability, Japanese society had always been tightly controlled militarily by a high concentration of samurai—warrior servants. The problem with the Chinese model was hypocrisy: what was preached—commiseration—was often violated in reality to varying degrees. Japan had no such problem. Rules were harsh but transparent. You fail to observe etiquettes of hierarchy, such as kneeling before a superior, you are executed on the spot. No questions asked, no excuses given, not even mock trials. The culture was honest, straightforward, and brutal.

For people of such a culture the loss of tight control was not an option as long term policy. They were used to navigating a narrow pathway of life restricted in all directions by numerous rules, written and unwritten, the violation of which was sure to bring dire consequences. To Japanese "thinking" did not mean judging between viable options and making choices based on one's self-interest or moral conviction, but recalling all relevant rules in a given situation and figuring out a way, most likely the only way, to avoid violating any. Sometimes there was simply no way to satisfy all the rules (e.g. the Forty Seven Ronin), and the subject who found himself in such a dilemma was required to commit suicide by the implicit ethical code, even though he did nothing wrong. In the harsh vertical society one's limiting parameters were decided entirely by his rank: the higher he ranked, the less people he had to serve, the more people who had to serve him. If most rules were removed and individuals were given as much choices as Westerners had, then the Japanese tendency was to try to dominate others by violence. There was no widely accepted moral principle that would prevent the entire nation from breaking up into violent gangs and killing each other, just like the Warring States period of sixteenth century.

Moving from a society where one's life is literally owned by his superior to more civility where superiors are no longer allowed to arbitrarily kill inferiors, absolute obedience is absolutely necessary to establish discipline and maintain social order. Thus the first thing students learn is absolute obedience to authority. Obedience is a Confucian virtue. The difference between Japanese and Chinese approaches is the absence versus presence of *ren* (mercy). Traditional Chinese teachers would use physical punishments only sparingly, and usually not on small children. They are careful not to hit the face. Mercy forces the teacher to stop as soon as the kid begins to cry or displays any sign of serious pain. Verbal abuse and foul language are seen as unbecoming of a teacher/mentor, for the same reason they are unacceptable for a Western priest.

None of these considerations exist for the Japanese teacher. Japanese think morality is a sign of weakness, which is understandable given their history. In the Confucian world morality means *ren* (mercy). As a Japanese warrior if you have mercy on your enemy or your subordinates, you will be killed by them sooner or later. From their observation of Western peoples, they conclude that the West is amoral just like Japan. Only "backward" peoples like Chinese and Koreans are moral: they cry at the slightest pain or mistreatment; they shrink from the sight of blood; they are feeble and useless. The "advanced" peoples of the West and Japan are tough. They are resilient in adverse conditions, natural or man made, and ruthless in battle. They cut off human heads with ease and indifference. "Advanced" peoples are merciless.

With this view in mind Japanese teachers approach disciplinary actions believing this is part of the modernization/Westernization process. Discipline means obedience here, to rules and to authority figures. Students must bow and salute to teachers and the principal, and these are made into everyday routine. Teachers can freely beat students, the most common form of which is face slapping. Face slapping is preferred not for the pain it inflicts, but for the humiliation. Coming from the authority figure who has the prerogative to define your character (in report cards and in your official profile that will follow you for the rest of your life), hitting other parts of the body can be interpreted as punishment for mistakes, but hitting the face carries the extra meaning of downgrading your value as a human being. It is saying "you are bad" instead of "what you did was bad". Teachers never apologize to students after hitting them even if it turns out to have been based on an erroneous judgment. The key to training absolute obedience is to not explain why the rules are the way they are or how the teacher makes his decisions (so as not to establish another authority such as a principle based on which one could reason), and to rigidly enforce the often unreasonable rules.

Rules and authority figures constitute the hard, constant and omnipresent set of parameters within which students operate, and against which they can not rebel, or even harbor such intensions. However, human beings are born free; it is natural to resist control by others. We have seen psychological manipulation to help explain away oppression, such as the creation of Buddhism (you are miserable not because of the injustice done to you by your oppressor, but because in your previous life you committed a sin, therefore you should accept your fate as you have no one to blame), but that is for the adult population. Japanese culture goes one step further by building some of these concepts in the language, which when taught to children help shape their minds growing up.

Students learn to use different modes of speech when addressing different people, such as teachers, parents, and classmates. A mode of speech is not just about politeness, such as between "would you please give me that?", "can I have that?" and "give me that." Two Westerners can use all three of these expressions between each other under different circumstances. In Japanese if you are my superior, then something like the first option is the only correct form when I address you, all other options are not just impolite, but grammatical errors. To address a superior one must use "the language of respect" (敬语), a mode of speech comprised of choice of vocabulary alternatives and verb forms. English can not quite capture its essence, but asking a favor from a superior implies the idea of *en*, and consequent indebtedness, while doing the same to inferiors does not carry such connotation. The mode of speech is not in the subtlety or tone of voice but the words themselves that leaves no doubt whatsoever the relative position of the two in conversation. Japanese language goes far beyond Chinese in its clarity and unashamed display of the hierarchical position of each individual. For example, Chinese has two words for "you", one for superiors and one for equals and inferiors, while Japanese has no less than five, addressing different kinds of hierarchy as well as closeness and male/female distinction.

Language shapes mindset by controlling what can and can not be expressed. If a student fails to use proper "respect language" before a superior, he is not said to be naughty, lack of etiquette or refinement, as if he made a minor mistake, but told that he has not yet learned Japanese, or to be a Japanese, to be human, which is a far more serious condemnation. To survive one must learn the language, and that in the Japanese case involves obtaining a hierarchical view of the world. From home and school the kid learns the self as a position in a web of familiar faces: parents, teachers, siblings, classmates. Self has no independent meaning, but is defined by relations to various individuals in this circle. The most prominent relation, often learned the hard way, is of course the one with superiors (parents and teachers). This relation of absolute obedience is an integral part of the idea of self. In other words without hierarchy one would not even know who or what he is.

Though in theory the Chinese kid are defined by the same hierarchy, in practice the value of *ren* (mercy) allows him some choices of action by which he can develop a sense of his self as distinct from others. When hit by a superior, the Chinese kid is usually allowed to cry, and the cry often arouses a sense of mercy from the superior. In this give and take different kids conduct themselves differently. Some are mentally strong and remain defiant, some hold out longer than others, some cave in at the earliest convenience. Adult behavior varies too. Some raise their hands at the slightest annoyance but stop quickly. Some rarely use violence but every time they do they mean business. Physical abuse is a game of many variables through which children learn to use their wits to adjust to each parent, and in the process learn more about themselves. It can sometimes be preempted or negotiated away by acts of submission and/or endearment. Because of *ren* (mercy), suffering is a serious matter and can be used (or feigned) to one's advantage.

For the Japanese kid in school, however, physical punishment is certain to follow any action that irritates superiors. Crying does not help. Suffering is ignored. He has no choice but to comply to orders immediately. Teachers understand they are to train youngsters into tough soldiers, modern samurai with bushido spirit, not cry babies. Of course a teacher can make mistakes. He may hit the wrong kid or do it for the wrong reason. But no apology is ever offered (superiors do not apologize to inferiors). The message to the kid is that the superior-inferior hierarchy is absolute: it needs no justification, and is not mitigated by any consideration. The rigid, unconditional, age based hierarchy is built into the child's mind, in which there is no place for the independent self. The value of the self compared to authority or the group is zero. A Chinese kid primarily thinks of himself in terms of his academic performance and character traits, a good or mediocre student, a serious or laidback type. A Japanese kid primarily thinks of himself as for example a second grader, which defines his position in the hierarchy: inferior to older third and fourth graders but superior to younger first graders.

Within the same grade, same class, a deliberate effort is made to reduce differences and enhance conformity. Here the age old tradition of collective liability is introduced to the education system. From the regime's perspective, collective liability—punishing the entire group for the mistake or crime of any member—is a simple management strategy that proved its effectiveness over time. It also brings about conformity and cohesion through mutual surveillance. It is one of the few defining principles of Japanese civilization.

This training is done in many ways and on many occasions repeatedly, throughout a child's school years. Here is a typical scenario. A teacher instructs his class to finish a certain task individually. When time is up, everyone has finished except a naughty boy, who is just fooling around. The teacher says that we need to get to the next activity, but we have to move on together, and since this one kid has not finished, we all have to wait for him. While the class watches the boy fumble with his assignment, the teacher never criticizes him, instead he applies increasing pressure on the whole class as time passes by. We need to move on, or we will have to go home late, or postpone next activity, or lose to the next class in competition. Everyone feels the pressure, but they do not know what to do. Stress builds up. They begin to hate the boy who is holding up the class.

Such hatred often turns into violence after school, where a group would attack one, for no other reason than the victim is "different". That could mean anything, from a unique dress, a hairdo, an accent, to an attitude. Anything that makes a kid stand out from his class is hated because everyone is judged by the performance of his group, and an odd one out even in a seemingly harmless way tends to disrupt the group spirit by distraction. Each class is usually divided into several groups, the formation of which would typically last a semester. As students are made to take turns to be group leaders, and many activities are performed by these groups rather than individually, everyone knows first hand how hard it is to get the group organized and accomplish a certain objective. Everyone hates the non-conformer who fails to follow orders or is slow to follow actions of the unit. As each group is judged regularly on how well they clean classroom floors, corridors, bathroom, and how well they perform various academic assignments (even math problems are assigned to groups instead of individuals), the pressure is internalized and everyone treats his group, not his own self, as the only thing that matters. The few members who are slow to adopt this mentality will find it hard to survive under fierce peer pressure, as failing to perform in group activity hurts the interest of other members of the group. By second or third grade it becomes subconscious: at every call from teachers or school authorities the class or the school would quickly spring into action, like a well trained army, everyone knows his role and proceeds efficiently and yet seemingly casually, since it has been practiced a thousand times and everyone is mentally in sync.

By now the framework of Japanese culture is laid in the child's mind: he has adopted a distinct psyche compared to all other peoples of the world. Although in Chinese schools the same principle—the collective is more important than the individual—is also taught, but each student is still judged by his individual academic performance and behavior. Though the Chinese class is organized following the Japanese model, there are far less group activities and more to the point, collective liability is simply not acceptable to Chinese. If the group fails a task but some of its members did their best and did well for their part, the teacher is reluctant to fail the whole group indiscriminately. Individual choice and accountability are essential to a moral culture, which prevents Chinese from developing the Japanese psyche even as they try to imitate Japanese education system and practices.

When the "different" kid is constantly bashed, it sends a psychological chill to everyone else, including the ones who participated in the beating. Everyone is born slightly different from others in one way or another. If these minor differences are allowed to develop freely as we grow up, there will be a diversity of adult personalities. As the Japanese kid grows up, however, the threat of violence forces him to hide his individuality, and behave in a "standard" way, down to every detail. This painful effort takes its toll over time, as no one is naturally born to act like a robot. By the time they get to high school, most Japanese teenagers have lost most of their heartfelt emotions. To any given situation Japanese would not react with spontaneous emotion, in fact they often do not even have an emotion, instead they ask themselves: should I laugh, cry, feel bad, or what should I feel at this moment? What are the applicable rules here? What kind of facial expression and/or body language is appropriate for me here and now? The fear to let out one's true feelings and risk behaving in a non-standard way has over time forced them to be numb, to become emotionless except a latent and growing hatred to everything, to the world that they live in. Forcing themselves into conformity has made them bitter and intolerant (Collective Liability Syndrome) underneath a highly trained civil veneer.

An environment where self-interest is denied and group interest is enforced goes against human instinct. We are born with the animal instinct to care for ourselves before anything else. A child's instinct is to wander around, pursue his curiosity, daydream, be distracted by various objects, and satisfy bodily needs whenever he feels like it. When even these basic desires are regulated by the omnipresent group interest (Should I take a leak now? Would it hurt my group's effort? Would I be hated by team members?), a subconscious resentment is inevitable. Human desire grows with age, and so the effort to enforce conformity has to step up, arousing further resentment. Yet Japanese can not find expression for their anger, since everything is done for the collective, for the country, and that is the ultimate Confucian value (pious loyalty). So they bury it inside. Only occasionally do we get a glimpse of that latent volcano. If someone misbehaves, such as littering, in most other countries people would shake their heads, but forgive him, or ignore him, after all, it is a minor infraction and we all make mistakes. But Japanese would sharply scold or even beat the perpetrator, displaying a kind of rage that would have you think that a serious crime was committed against them. This is a violent release of accumulated resentment. If I have sacrificed my whole life, subjected myself to harsh rules, denied myself numerous liberties, all for the interest of the country, then your damaging even a negligible part of it is a direct challenge to the meaning of my entire existence.

An objective observer can look at collective liability with a critical eye, but its reasoning—that the ultimate objective is for the good of the country—can also be used to limit the scope of authority, if not its severity. A superior can order anything from an inferior, including suicide, but it has to be for the country. A corporate boss of a public company can physically abuse his employees, have them work 12 hours a day, seven days a week, but it is also done in the name of the country. The same boss can not treat subordinates as private servants, have them run errands for him or his family, or help him steal from corporate accounts, like many Chinese bosses do. Because rules are harsh, the psychological need for their justification is strong. It fuels the intensity of everyone watching everyone else. Thus superiors can not escape responsibility. If there is a major railroad accident, for example, the Minister of Transportation is obliged to resign, regardless of whose fault it was, because the entire transportation system is seem as a combat unit organized like a Confucian family with the minister as its head, failure of the unit means failure of everyone in it, particularly the head. In other words, collective liability may unduly spread blame to the innocent, but it does not exempt anyone from accountability. In absence of this mechanism, and given that a pyramid society will find it inherently impossible to build a fair justice system like that in the West, many other cultures including Chinese have a hard time holding higher ups accountable for anything. If one ignores the cruelty every individual is subjected to, which Japanese certainly do as they are used to it, one may find some fairness in Japanese culture. Perception of fairness is critical to the success of a culture, for it preempts cynicism. Though Japanese and Chinese both profess the same ideal—pious loyalty (忠) to the state—Japanese are true believers, while Chinese are cynics.

Collective liability and absolute hierarchy set the internal logic for the mind, giving birth to a unique Japanese value system and worldview. To firmly establish these two traditions, and to turn the populace from passive to active servants, a third ingredient is indispensable: merciless treatment, along with the *en* logic and push/pull mechanism.

Suppose I am a teenager who just entered a navy academy in 1930s Japan, reluctantly. I really wanted to become a politician and eliminate corruption in government, but my parents can not afford college tuition. My reluctance naturally shows in various ways to a careful observer, such as my doubts about the government's decision to invade the continent. My supervisor (my parent official) sends a fourth grader—a senior student always ranks higher than a junior—to punch the lights out of me, telling me that I have disrespected the navy, ordering me to wake up from my dreams and be a good soldier (the supervisor does not do this dirty work himself in order to keep a benevolent parent image). Now I am angry. I would have accepted a slap on the face and a reprimand, but I do not feel I deserve this. At the same time I know from past experiences from school and home that I can not let my resentment to superiors show, for it would lead to further more serious punishment. If I am a timid character, then my fear will quickly extinguish my anger and I will immediately turn passive, with a body language that exhibits total submission, try my best to fall in line, avoid standing out in any way. If I am a more assertive character, then my anger can not go away as easily. I need an outlet to this enormous internal energy (the urge to revenge) that can be interpreted as something other than an act of defiance. So I train harder than everyone else. I shout louder, thrust my bayonet deeper into the straw-man, wrestle all my opponents to the ground in judo, run extra miles, and clean all the toilets. As my anger gradually fades together with that extra energy in the following weeks, I also realize that I must succumb to authority and can not afford to remain resentful at heart. On the other hand, my character and my reputation as a brave man prevent me from acknowledging fear. I solve this dilemma by pretending that my extra effort of late reflects a change of my heart, as if I was convinced, rather than forced, by authorities, saving my face/honor. Then to keep this logic/explanation persuasive to others, I have to convert myself into a true believer of what I am insinuating. I will take bold initiatives, risk my life even, to show that I have always been brave, except that now I understand and enthusiastically agree with the war. In this process my thought often follows my actions. In order to prove my case, which is unstated but I know everyone is watching, I feel obligated to exemplify my valiance, commit to any challenge before even thinking so as not to give the impression of hesitation. I may die in the process. If I do not, surviving my own recklessness would convince me that I am truly brave. Then I am really a changed man. I can face death without blinking. But at the same time, I still do not have the courage to challenge authorities. The whole process was started because of my fear for punishment and death. Now I no longer fear death or physical punishment, but in my heart there is a deep psychological scar that I dare not touch, for doing so would reopen old wounds that reveal, to myself, what a shameful coward I really am.

When my effort earns me credit, my supervisor gives me the emotional pull. He presents my diploma, my uniform, my sword, salutes me, and tells me I am now in solemn service of the country. What an honor. My peers respect me. I am given positions of responsibility. My rank rises with my credits. I become a respected (high ranking) member of society. Yes I used to hate my supervisor, but who is to say that he is not my *en* man, who turned my life around, gave me all my success?

Pervasiveness of such training yields a high degree of conformity. Japanese are polite, obedient to superiors, observant to all kinds of rules written and unwritten, almost down to the last person. Visitors to Japan are compelled to believe from what they see that this is a civilized people, even more so than Westerners. For most Japanese forced habits are nevertheless real habits. Violation of hierarchy or rules is not so much unthinkable as simply not contemplated. Underneath the veneer, however, the Japanese soul has not developed any sense of evil. In their fantasy often expressed in cartoons and pornography, or in rare situations where the individual is completely free to act on his own accord, the same person who has always been polite and civil can exhibit true savagery.

The occupation of China (1937-1945) provided a few opportunities for its manifestation. Objection to Japanese by Chinese civilians (not the government) had nothing to do with the war itself, or the fact that Japanese were ruling over them. Chinese peasants did not care who ruled the empire, the Mongols, the Manchurians, or the Japanese, as long as the regime was merciful. Indeed many Chinese welcomed Japanese takeover in northern China, because at first Japanese soldiers were far more disciplined than the looting Chinese warlords. However, as war intensified and discipline relaxed in the imperial army, many Japanese soldiers began to torture and immolate civilians for fun. It was not so much that they executed people out of the slightest hint of suspicion, but the ease and joy with which they cut off limbs, poked holes in people's bodies, raped and sadistically killed women, bayoneted babies, that demonstrated a kind of human being Chinese never thought existed. Shocked beyond belief, they found the Chinese language utterly incompetent to express their feelings.

Back in Japan relatives of these Japanese soldiers could not believe the allegations. Their sons? The polite, obedient, law abiding, filial, loyal, model citizens, committing unspeakable crimes against humanity? The image in their minds of the typical Japanese soldier was a brave young man who would overcome any difficulty, persevere through any hardship, and give up his life if necessary, for the emperor. Reality was and still is that many are fully capable of both. Model behavior in a controlled environment is not indicative of one's true character. Most Japanese do not ever have a chance in their lifetime to act out of choice, thus their forced habits are taken as true character, and for all practical purposes they are how they act. A person who has always been obedient will predictably remain so for the rest of his life, under the same social conditions. He may at the same time be full of hatred. He is too cowardly to fight for his rights against the real oppressors (his superiors), so he takes it out on his inferiors, such as his wife and children, restaurant waiters and other low ranking people of the service industry, or in his dreams/fantasy. Japanese TV shows and cartoons openly indulge in the venting of unexplained anger. The service industry emphasizes servility, to kneel, to bow, to absorb abuses from customers, out of necessity. Harsh training hardens the Japanese heart. Cruelty metastasizes under the façade of highly conformed civility.

CHAPTER 16
REVOLUTION

The Qing Dynasty (清, 1644-1911) continued long standing Chinese cultural trends, but with a twist: it was ruled by foreigners who at first did not want to adopt Chinese culture. The Manchurians were a nomadic people who had somehow acquired great organizational skills, perhaps from their neighbors to the west—descendents of the successful Mongols centuries before. Their conquering of China however was largely due to domestic strife in the Chinese Empire caused by ever deepening corruption. Our analysis of the typical Chinese general whose interest really lies with the invader rather than his emperor applies here famously. The Manchurians knew that Chinese culture was thoroughly corrupt, which made it possible for them to bring an empire fifty times their own size to its knees, and highly corruptive, which explains why the mighty Mongols, having conquered much of earth, quickly degenerated into a bunch of effete dandies after ruling China for just one century.

They tried to force their culture on Chinese to preempt a cultural annihilation by Chinese. Manchurian dress (a sheath with a slit skirt) became standard. All men were forced to adopt the Manchurian hairstyle—shaved forehead and a long braid on the back. This was not an easy change. To Chinese hair is given by parents, thus sacred and can not be removed. Thousands lost their heads refusing to shave. In the end, female foot binding and other Chinese customs stubbornly remained. The Manchurians then tried to separate themselves from Chinese. They were prohibited from inter-marrying. Their females were prohibited from foot binding. They had a separate and much more lenient penal code just for themselves. They maintained their nomadic organizational structures, at least nominally, even though they now lived in cities and traveled in palanquins instead of riding horses on the steppes. With these and other measures they hoped to stave off some of that corruptive Chinese influence and retain their more disciplined and vigorous lifestyle.

They had no idea what they were up against. Once in the position to rule, they realized that Confucianism as a political ideology was indispensable. One can perhaps rule a small kingdom with pure military might, but no military force is by itself sufficient for an empire of two hundred million. It takes full cooperation from the populace, hence a strong doctrine that pacifies them. Neo-Confucianism was inevitably reaffirmed as state ideology, which meant the ruling class, the Manchurians themselves, had to be neo-Confucians as well. It would not have worked if Manchurians preached one thing to Chinese and practiced something contradictory themselves. To Chinese this was a matter of morality based on cosmic orders, to which no one under heaven was immune. You are either moral or immoral, there is no middle ground, and the public has the obligation to overthrow an immoral ruler. Confucianism is race blind, but its principles are inviolable. It was alright that the Manchurians dressed differently, carried themselves differently and did not speak Chinese at first; they could learn to adapt. But had they flouted filial piety, they would not have lasted long.

Once Confucian practices were adopted, Manchurian traditions began to crumble. Their original organizational structure reflected an egalitarian spirit. On the steppes tribes were far away from each other. Though there was a king of a confederacy of tribes, he was still essentially a tribal leader, a first among equals. Large military campaigns and important decisions had to be coordinated between these leaders, each having his own interest that had to be reckoned with. At first this tradition was kept after conquering China as the emperor consulted with other chiefs regularly. But soon the emperor realized, perhaps through education by Chinese ministers, that this was a violation of Confucian hierarchy, a distortion of ruler-minister relationship, and that the Chinese idea of emperor was dramatically different from a nomadic king.

The emperor then began to separate himself from the other chiefs, making all decisions in secret, without consulting them. With the help of Chinese ministers, his heir was brought up to be the sole ruler to whom all else must kowtow. Childhood pleasures, friendship and honesty that are characteristic of nomadic kids who grow up together on horsebacks were replaced by rituals of hierarchy (*li*), regulation of emotions and learning of Confucian classics. These imperial children grew up with an acute sense of hierarchy that made friendship or camaraderie between them impossible. Within two generations descendents of other former chiefs lost all power, and the emperor shed the last vestiges of his nomadic past. He gained awe inspiring majesty, but permanently lost all friends, who were turning from equals to slaves. The counter-evolution process works fast when a pyramid culture is already firmly in place.

By eighteenth century there was no real cultural distinction between Manchurians and ethnic Han Chinese, though legally and politically they were two distinct groups, one above the other. A Manchurized Chinese dialect, the Mandarin, spoken by residents of the capital city Beijing, became the official tongue. By then Manchurians had long lost their horseback skills with bows and arrows, and were now expertly versed in fine cuisine, womanizing and other pleasures. They also adopted the cynical Daoist outlook: no work, no belief, all pleasure.

Had there not been an invasion of the West, the Chinese historic cycle would have continued to eternity. Every dynasty would get a few hundred years, until at last it is corrupt to the point that a slight push would topple it. The new dynasty starts with discipline and some degree of fairness, only to see that quickly erode and fall helplessly into the same vicious cycle. Chinese culture itself, invented and refined for the purpose of controlling the populace, has no answer for its own decay.

The arrival of foreign traders did not present any problem at first. Chinese rulers traditionally viewed foreigners with condescension. These are hapless barbarians ignorant of our heavenly ways, but treated with kindness and generosity hopefully they will see the Way, adopt our culture, and become a model vassal state, like Korea. "Go tell your king that I appreciate his obedience, and I have mercy on his people. If they desire silk and tea from China, I'll let you buy these things here and ship them home." For the emperor there is no such thing as trade between nations, for that implies equality between nations, but the Son of Heaven is the master of all humanity, there can be no equal to his throne. Whatever foreign or domestic traders are allowed to do is an *en*, a divine favor from him, provided that they observe the Confucian order, and the ruler seeks no profit, nor is he interested in such trifle matters. Portuguese merchants and Jesuits of seventeenth and eighteenth centuries were quite compliant, and were thus tolerated by the court. The Jesuits for example allowed their followers to observe filial piety, which essentially places parents where God is supposed to be, rendering the latter a mere symbol, one among many other deities Chinese paid tribute to (the money god, the food god, etc.). Chinese Catholicism became just another form of Buddhism, Daoism, or something like that. In addition to their amenity, what also made Portuguese presence tolerable was the limited size of their trade volume and influence.

By nineteen century China saw an influx of new comers, British, French, Americans, Germans, Russians and others. The British and French were among them the most active traders who encountered the most problems. The key here is to understand that the emperor wants acknowledgment that you are his slave, that your king is his vassal. This does not have to be put on paper to have any legal power; servile body language and rituals (*li*) are good enough. Nothing pleases the heart of his majesty more than for someone of a different race coming from afar just to pledge loyalty and obedience to him, the Heavenly ruler. After that he is in a mood to be generous and business is easy. The emperor does not care about balance sheets at all, and huge profits can be made. The British, however, had a hard time, because their knees were too hard to bend. Having established a global empire they were too proud to acknowledge inferiority, and instead approached it in a business manner. "My king sends his best wishes to your majesty." "We wish to have friendly relations." "Shall we appoint ambassadors to each other and set up formal communication channels." "Let's negotiate ground rules to facilitate trade." None of these means anything to the emperor. The British representative failed his mission the moment he refused to kowtow. Perhaps his dignity prevented him from putting his knees, hands and forehead on the ground several steps below the emperor's feet. This English gentleman later complained about being dragged out of the court in an uncivilized manner. The fact is, he was lucky to still have his head on his shoulders—that was a divine favor.

Without imperial sanction foreign merchants were vulnerable to the abuse and exploitation by local officials. Though bribes can grease the wheel somewhat, it does not change one's position in the social hierarchy. Besides, it adds to the cost. And so business continued rather uncomfortably for them. By 1840 a trade dispute arose over the importation of opium, most of which was grown in British occupied India. Opium had long been used as an anesthetic but by then it turned into a popular recreational drug. To Chinese this was a godsend. For centuries they had been trying to find every way leading to maximum pleasure, but none of the thousands of dishes they came up with had quite the same hallucinational effect that was so addicting. Smoking opium was not just a fashion, but a symbol of happiness, what life was really about.

The Qing government repeatedly banned the sale and use of opium to save itself from financial ruin (that's how widespread opium smoking was in China), to no avail. With the help of corrupt Chinese officials it was smuggled in large quantities. A hardnosed scholar was appointed provincial governor of GuangDong, where most foreign goods came ashore. He immediately confiscated and burned large amounts of opium. Meanwhile an English sailor killed a Chinese civilian in a brawl. Sensing an imperial displeasure at foreign traders, the provincial governor demanded the perpetrator be handed over for capital punishment. This episode made clear social position of foreign traders. In the Confucian world it is usually not a capital crime for a superior to kill an inferior. Had the perpetrator been a ranking official, he would have been able to simply pay a nominal compensation to the victim's family and have the matter dismissed, without an apology (an apology upsets the hierarchy). But it is always a capital crime for an inferior to kill a superior. Circumstances of a homicide case which are critical in Western justice in determining guilt are only relevant here when the two sides are of equal social rank. Fearing that the sailor would be tortured and skinned by a lynch mob, the British side refused, insisting a trial according to their law. The Chinese side then resorted to force, and a handful Englishmen barely escaped with their lives. Then of course came the gunboats, which bombed the Qing government into signing a treaty allowing unfettered trade in a few ports and extraterritoriality (foreigners govern themselves according to their own laws on Chinese soil). Americans and French demanded and were granted similar arrangements shortly thereafter.

This so called Opium War had a lot to do with the opium trade, no doubt, but escalation of the conflict reflected a cultural rift between East and West. It was the coming to a head of a contention between the Chinese side that demanded the British to submit to Confucian hierarchical order, and the British side that stubbornly rejected it. Mistreatment of many British subjects in China, including high ranking Royal British representatives and negotiators, by Western standards, helped sway opinion in the British parliament for the war, even among members who were otherwise opposed to the opium trade. Conclusion of the short war however did not resolve the contention, but exacerbated it, since the British did not overthrow the Qing Dynasty, which would have sorted out the hierarchy issue once and for all. Signing a concession was something entirely new to a Chinese ruler in more ways than one. In the Confucian scheme there is only one absolute ruler with Heaven's Mandate to rule. All-under-heaven are his slaves. There is no room for power sharing. In case of a coup or a peasant uprising the new comer has to claim that the previous ruler forfeited Heaven's Mandate, thus must be replaced, by another absolute ruler. No one can claim that the ruler has too much power, and must share it with others. That would be utterly unConfucian. The master-slave relationship between ruler and subjects is absolute. If two factions fight, they have to fight to the very end until one side capitulates, or they will have to divide the land into two geographical domains and rule their separate empires. There is no way that two rulers can coexist in one domain, just as there can be no two masters in one household, or two suns in the sky.

Given that the ruler is absolute, he never signs any treaty with rules binding on himself. He must wield arbitrary power. The same is true for a father within the confines of his family. Anything contrary to this would be blasphemy. For an emperor to submit to a set of written rules, as if these rules are a higher authority than him, is blasphemous. Therefore the treaty with foreign powers presented a theological impasse for Chinese: if the emperor is the legitimate Son of Heaven, why is he subjecting himself to such humiliation? (the Son of Heaven ought to be master of everyone, including foreigners); if he is not legitimate, then why is he still emperor? It also trapped the officials in an impossible situation: how are they supposed to deal with foreigners? Treating them as superiors would violate pious loyalty to the emperor, since foreigners are not his agents. Treating them as inferiors would cause more trouble. Treating them as equal? But equal to which rank? As a result officials who were supposed to be in charge of foreign trade refused to see foreign representatives, further antagonizing Western powers.

Westerners were obviously unaware of this Confucian crisis of unprecedented proportions, or the anguish of the emperor and the official class. To the West a treaty was an agreement between two equals. They did not realize that the Confucian emperor is supposed to have no equal. While the "strange" Chinese behavior must have struck them as unreasonable and uncivilized, their own "strange" behavior must also have puzzled Chinese, as the British sovereign from thousands of miles away apparently was not intent on overthrowing the Qing Dynasty. Why would they stop at some trivial business deal, some pathetic monetary interest, if they could take the entire empire? There was only one possible conclusion in the Confucian mind: despite their victory the British were still somehow afraid of China, perhaps of its immense size and the sheer scale of its potential military forces.

Seen in this light Westerners became insidious characters not brave enough for a full scale confrontation but cunning enough to exact some concessions through clever maneuvering. The emperor felt wronged by lowly despicable characters, as did many scholar-officials. Westerners may think themselves civilized, and some of their behavior did lend support to that claim in the Chinese eye, but as soon as Chinese learned that Westerners can call their own parents by name, a blasphemy by Confucian doctrine, there was no longer any doubt that these were indeed barbarians. It was doubly wrong for non-Confucian barbarians, who ought to rank lower than Chinese because they were immoral, to be given a privileged position in a moral society. In short the existence of Western military and political power in the middle of a still standing imperial regime presented multiple insoluble problems to Confucianism, as in neither hierarchical nor moral terms did they fit anywhere in the Confucian scheme.

The most straightforward way to solve the theological impasse was to drive Western powers out of China, back to their barbarian land. The ruler however was apprehensive of possible consequences if such an attempt failed. After all, there were many Western powers represented in China, the idea of fighting them all was daunting. He was in a situation where he wanted to do something that he dared not do or even say. The official class, keen to detect their superior's intensions, took the cue. They whipped up xenophobic sentiments among their subjects, who then started harassing foreigners, threatening Chinese who worked for them, throwing blocks in their business process, even ambushing a priest or two. The treaties previously signed were effectively annulled by street mobs and local officials, and Chinese perceived nothing wrong with it, since they were fighting a "devil".

The incident of a French Catholic priest is quite illustrative of the difference between Chinese and Western legal traditions. Based on the treaty signed after the Opium War, a Western priest can legally preach only in a few designated coastal cities, if he wanders into the interior, local Chinese officials have the right to arrest him, but must send him to a Western embassy for arbitration. This rule means extraterritoriality, the idea that Westerners can only be convicted and sentenced by Western authority according to Western law, designed to protect them from Chinese judgment. Perhaps emboldened by the rule, a French priest ventured far into Chinese territory and founded a church community. He disallowed ancestor worship, and allegedly had an illicit relationship with a widow, both of which were capital crimes to Chinese. Ancestor worship is sacred because of filial piety—if parents are divine, then their parents and grandparents must also be divine. By neo-Confucian ethics a widow belongs to her deceased husband forever, therefore can not be touched by any other man. Chinese judgment of a crime is based on how much it violates Confucian morals, so these actions that hardly qualify as crimes in the West are far more serious than, say, a superior killing an inferior, or even a dozen of them. Public outrage over these blasphemous acts prompted the local official to execute the French priest.

The West was shocked. Extraterritoriality was designed to prevent the exact incident, and the Qing government signed it, how could they treat law with such contempt? To Chinese all laws must be subject to moral sanction. Had the priest just ventured into unwelcome territory but done nothing, then it would have been appropriate to send him back. But since he committed acts of serious immorality, he could no longer be let go unpunished, not to mention the treaty itself was deemed immoral, violating it was almost heroic. In other words, in the Chinese mind, all rules are conditional, even if the conditions are unwritten (every Chinese knows them so they are presumed). To Japanese rules decided by brute force are the final word, and there is no "why" beyond that, but to Chinese they are not. In the end the treaty that seemed to be airtight and ensuring smooth sailing for Westerners in China was rendered useless. To the West this was underhanded and dishonest. To Chinese it was fully justified. By 1856 the French and the British had enough. This time their troops marched all the way into the capital, and ransacked the imperial summer palace, perhaps to vent their frustration.

To make matters worse for the regime, a large scale peasant uprising broke out that nearly ended the Qing Dynasty. These rebels claimed to be Christians, obviously trying to bring Western powers to their side. But they might have gone too far. The top leader declared that he was the younger brother of Jesus Christ, another son of God, which hardly appealed to his intended audience. In his mind he was probably still thinking about being the Son of Heaven. For political convenience the Heaven deity and the Christian God were merged into one. Since Jesus Christ was a historical figure, he had to be a different son. He was careful to be the younger, not the elder, brother of Jesus, taking a lower ranking position which he judged would have pleased Christian sensibilities.

After years of struggle the Qing government finally managed to put down this insurgency, just barely. But the second defeat at the hands of British and French was far more devastating than the first one. By the new treaty Western troops were stationed permanently within striking distance of the imperial residence, a thinly veiled threat that any more shenanigans would put the Forbidden City in jeopardy. The West had lost all confidence that Chinese could keep any promise at all, signed into law or sworn before God/Heaven. Western presence was no longer just about trade in a remote southern province, it directly threatened the regime and consequently became a most pressing issue that needed a solution, however impossible it seemed.

This reality further squeezed the scholar-official class who were already in a quandary. They were still shaking in their boots from the prosecution of "language crimes", where a single word that could be interpreted as disloyal, regardless of the author's intensions, would send him to the death roll. Although by now the ruling house had relaxed the intensity of such prosecution, in a hope to gather more ideas for dealing with the Western devil, there was no telling where one would cross an invisible redline. High ministers pressed to make proposals to the throne usually opened up with something like this: "Your lowly servant deserve to die ten thousand times for saying this, but I think it might help if we . . .", speaking slowly and hesitantly, word by word, constantly checking reactions of the emperor, prepared to stop anywhere in the middle of a sentence at the earliest sign of trouble. An orthodox Confucian minister in the room may argue: "That is against tradition, a blasphemy!" The emperor may agree: "That is quite out of line. Well, since you are only trying to help, I'll forgive you this time. Get the hell out of here!" By then the proponent was wetting his pants, pounding his head on the floor, and thanking the ruler for not taking his life. Fat chance he was going to come up with a daring plan next time.

The imperial house understood that China needed a navy and modern Western weaponry to stand its own ground, as did the Japanese ruling elite. But the moral Chinese culture presented two major obstacles that did not exist for the amoral Japanese culture. To Japanese war is about survival. If I lose to your superior technology, I want to get it from you, by direct learning if possible, by begging or stealing if necessary, so that I can survive in later conflicts, against you or others. To Chinese it is about who is right. If I am moral and you are immoral, then I despise you however powerful you are. When you defeat me I feel wronged by an evil force, it only adds to my hatred. How can I learn from someone I despise and hate? The Qing government spent a great deal of money buying modern warships, cannons, rifles, etc., reluctantly. But their officials refused to even talk to Westerner devils. Weapons procurement was charged to lowly clerks and deemed a dirty job that just had to be done. However, hardware alone does not make a military force; one also needs knowledge to run it. In addition, China must make steel, build railways, steam ships, in a word industrialize, in order to be strong and independent. All these involve modern science. Someone had to learn it.

Here the moral culture throws in a second obstacle. As we recall neo-Confucianism has its own philosophy, with a heavenly principle that manifests itself in the human heart as well as in all materials. Iron has the quality of iron which is different from wood, because the heavenly principle participates in them in different ways. Compared with the medieval Christian Church argument that the sun revolves around the earth, which is just one specific claim that did not stop scientific advances in other areas, the neo-Confucian ideology is vague but all-encompassing, hence far more restrictive. The very existence of subjects like physics, chemistry and biology is a blasphemy because these theories attempt to explain the world in a way other than the heavenly principle, by which every phenomenon has been explained, often with the help of yin-yang, gas, the five elements and other ancient ideas, and the explanation has become part and parcel of neo-Confucianism. To study physics, one has to assume that neo-Confucianism does not explain everything, which casts shadows on its legitimacy. Is it manifestation of the true Dao? Or is Western science the true Dao (nature's Way)? If the latter is true, then the entire neo-Confucian structure crumbles down, its moral principles devoid of a firm foundation. Japanese only absorbed the hierarchical (hence psychological) part of neo-Confucianism, rejecting its moral doctrine. Their social hierarchy stands as a matter of fact, independent of moral sanction. People fight for supremacy and if I win, I am the master and you are the slave, quite straightforward, in need of no further rationalization. The entire nation was under military control. For example, Japanese just like Chinese can not call their parents by name. To Chinese this has moral significance. Westerners who violate it are seen as immoral beings or barbarians. To Japanese it is merely a rule. Once defeated by the West, they acknowledge Western superiority, and are eager to learn Western technology, but still do not call their parents by name, because the rule (Japanese soul) is still there. They never saw Westerners as immoral or even perceived the idea of evil. Another example. Japanese like Indians traditionally did not eat beef. In both cases the taboo probably had something to do with scarcity of cattle in ancient times. With a moral culture Indians had to work it into religion, turning cows into deities, so that people are afraid of divine displeasure by offending holy cows. Once accepted as a moral value it will not be changed by abundance of cattle. To Japanese it was again just another rule enforced by the sword. In the Meiji period the ban was lifted and they gladly expanded their diet.

The Chinese system could not survive without a moral doctrine accepted by the masses. The challenge was how one could accept Western science as a valid way to explain the material world, while at the same time maintain Confucian morals. That problem was never resolved by the Qing regime. A prominent scholar-official advanced the theory of "Chinese learning as the foundation; Western learning as a utility" (中学为体, 西学为用), which was approved by the court. This on paper is the same as the Japanese version of "Japanese soul and Western skills" (和魂洋才), but they mean different things to the two different peoples. A "Japanese soul" is an ethical and psychological idea, manifested by the *en* based emotional tie between lord and samurai, in the bushido code, but not a philosophical or moral one. It is solidified by training, incorporated in schools, work places and the military. The individual has no choice whatsoever. Japanese can not argue "this emperor is immoral, we must overthrow him", or "the social hierarchy is immoral, let's abolish it". These things are there by virtue of brute force and accepted as a matter of fact. Japanese soul and Western skills can coexist in the same body because they are independent from each other.

Suppose some Chinese students studied modern science and wrote books on it, explaining the human anatomy, how gravity works, why gunpowder (an ancient Chinese invention) explodes, etc, they would run into serious trouble, because their books undermined intellectual authority of the scholar-official class. Confucian scholars would argue that these youngsters are spreading heresy and confusing the public, rendering Confucian indoctrination ineffective. Remember the widely believed story that Confucius executed a rival teacher because, as the saint put it, "he was spreading heresy and very convincing at it." To rule with minimum force the prestige and moral/intellectual authority of the ruling elite is critical, and any potential challenge has to be extinguished at the budding stage. Once it develops into a nationwide debate it is all over for the regime. Thus Chinese students unlike their Japanese counterparts were not interested in learning Western science—if anything it was a curse. "Chinese learning as the foundation" means national exams remained, and only Confucian classics could get them into the official class. Western science did not help one's career. Who cares about something that only has a limited utilitarian value and if not handled carefully could bring one's downfall?

Hence the new theory sounded brilliant but in reality only papered over the problem. Chinese learning remained much the same. Western learning was a non starter. A few provinces build showcase projects like railroads and steel factories, with the help of Western experts. But the ruling Manchurians did not really care about industrialization, or even understand what it is, they just wanted to feel safer from foreign encroachment. After a few decades of tangling with the West, they realized these capitalists were not after their throne, but profit. A sense of complacency returned, and many of the showcase projects remained just that. Meanwhile, corruption continued unabated. Military generals embezzled funds for ammunition, and splendid warships fresh from Western shipyards became gambling and pot smoking joints for Chinese sailors. The whole scene was eerily familiar.

When in 1895 the Japanese fleet with less tonnage and less firepower but far better trained seamen annihilated the Chinese fleet in a single battle, Chinese were finally shaken, for this time they were defeated by a Confucian state that just a few decades earlier were in a similar situation as China. Taiwan was ceded permanently to Japan, along with 10,000 tons of silver, more than twice the annual revenue of the Qing government, a huge indemnity that was to burden the average Chinese for years to come.

Pressure mounted on the Manchurian regime. According to common understanding, a dynasty is close to its end when there are visible signs of divine displeasure. In such cases Chinese say its Qi (gas/breath) is running out. Repeated defeats to various foreign powers, first Western then an Asian neighbor traditionally seen as a less civilized state, was interpreted by many as ominous signs. The ruling house flirted with political reform but the Empress quickly put it down when it threatened her power. Prominent reformers were exiled to Japan, where the Chinese diaspora including students sent by the government to study Japan were forming political parties, agitating for one kind of social reform or another, from the modest to the extreme. Domestically pressure continued to build as financial burden exacted a toll on social harmony. The regime desperately searched for a way to let off some steam from the pressure cooker, and an opportunity came in the form of the Boxer Movement, which had something to do with Christian missionaries.

Westerners tend to see Buddhism as the main religion in Asia, because it has temples and the appearance of a religion. But the real belief is Confucianism, which has a far greater impact on Asian minds than Buddhism and Daoism (or Shinto in Japan) combined. Buddhism and Daoism/Shinto do not even touch on ethics/morality. If their priests happen to preach values, they are invariably Confucian values, which are at odds with Christian values. Starting from the obvious, one of the Ten Commandments says thou shalt not bear false witness, but Confucius said a son should lie for his father (子为父隐). In the Confucian world one must lie for but not to his superior, and it is no sin for superiors to lie to inferiors, in other words it all depends on hierarchy. In such a culture should a missionary preach honesty or dishonesty? Or is it conditional honesty depending on hierarchical relation of the concerned? Moreover, submission to God precludes all secular masters, including emperors and parents. The Christian spirit is one of summoning internal strength, with the spiritual help of the almighty, to resist oppression. That is diametrically against the Confucian spirit, which is to submit to oppression and love the oppressor.

Confucian scholars sensed that this new religion undermines filial piety and pious loyalty. Through their long history Confucians successfully forced these doctrines into Buddhism and Daoism, but they were under no illusions that they could do the same to Christianity, not when the latter was backed up by gunboats. So they did their best to demonize Christianity, which admittedly was not that hard a thing to do given that Westerners do not observe filial piety (they call their parents by name!). Though there was no imperial decree to the effect, the society was hostile to Christians. On the other hand, the relatively few Chinese converts enjoyed protection by their churches, on law suits and civil disputes. Local officials always yielded to the demands of Western priests, for they knew they could ill afford offending any Westerner. In other words the high social position of Westerners rubbed off on Chinese Christian converts, effectively raising their relative ranking against other countrymen. Seeing this, many others undoubtedly thought about conversion, but strong social pressure, lack of moral justification and family reasons prevented them from taking that risky step.

This created extra anxiety. The Confucian hierarchy had been stable for centuries. There were certain recognized ways to climb it, such as through national exams or cronyism. Everyone got used to the mechanism and accepted it as fair or at least tolerable. Now foreigners budged in and commanded a higher rank than virtually any Chinese, that caused some disgruntlement but still manageable: they were outsiders who did not mingle with Chinese anyway. But when Chinese were promoted simply by virtue of joining the church, it threatened to upset the whole hierarchy and the established sense of fairness. The fact that outcasts in society—widows who lived a wretched existence because no man dared touch or help them, ex criminals shunned by the upright, lowliest slaves who escaped from captivity—could join the church because they had nothing to lose anyway, but mainstream population were taught that as moral beings they must resist this foreign evil, further exacerbated their stress. Whenever an official made a judgment against a non-believer in favor of a Christian, he would privately sympathize with the loser and redirect his anger at the church: "I want to help you but there is nothing I can do. Even the emperor has to yield to them."

Western disruption of the Confucian order, largely unnoticed by Westerners themselves, generated a rare situation where pious loyalty, righteous indignation and an easy opportunity all came together. The piously loyal were hurt when their emperor was humiliated by foreign devils, their sense of order and fairness was destroyed by the same perpetrators through the instrument of Christian missionaries, and there were no easier targets than armless priests and church goers. The Boxer Movement started when a large number of peasants lost their livelihood due to a severe drought, not unlike many other peasant uprisings. But instead of denouncing the ruler in an outright rebellion, they cleverly professed loyalty to the throne and hatred for foreigners, picking on a softer target. The Empress seized the opportunity, gave official approval to the Boxer Movement, and declared war on all eleven foreign powers simultaneously who had presence in China. It was a suicidal move for China from the perspective of any objective observer, but the Empress was a shrewd politician. Though the ragtag army of Boxers quickly disintegrated when faced with machine guns, as anyone could anticipate, domestic malcontent was successfully diverted to foreign powers, securing for the Empress a natural death in peace. She remained the unchallenged absolute ruler through turbulent decades, disastrous decisions, and irresponsible governance that by Confucian standards would qualify her as one of the worst rulers of all time, until the last day of her long life.

The Boxer Movement deserves attention because it is a common phenomenon when and where Western powers are involved with a pyramid society. It demonstrates the dynamics of ruler-subject relationship. The ruler (or regime) wants something done but in this case he is unable to issue direct orders because it concerns foreign powers that are beyond his control. He may want to invade another country, but can not declare his intensions for diplomatic reasons. Or he may want to vanquish a foreign enemy from his empire, but weary of consequences of open hostilities. He intimates this frustration to his top aids and through whom, his subjects at large. To the subjects the ruler is a divine figure from on high, one who usually displays a stern veneer and demands solemn reverence. They yearn for his love and can not get close to him. He feels like God of the Old Testament. Now in a time of crisis he shows his vulnerable side. He lets you share his feelings, his anguish. It is an incredible honor and thrill for the subjects, and an act of *en* (divine favor), by the ruler, to let you get so close to him, to feel his divine love, and his humanity. He feels like the human Jesus Christ. If there ever is a time when repaying his *en* is urgently called for, it is now. The subjects voluntarily take up arms against his foe, whether they know anything about this foreign enemy or not, with the kind of zeal that easily convinces outsiders of genuine hatred. During the struggle the ruler may even disavow their actions under foreign pressure, but that only serves to stir up even stronger desires to protect him and love him. The subjects know that he must be moved by their pious loyalty, and that satisfaction alone is enough for many of them to willingly sacrifice themselves. I call this the Boxer Syndrome.

The Islamic terrorism currently raging in parts of the world is a variation of Boxer Syndrome. The key to understand it is that in any pyramid society, with or without political elections, anger constantly builds up. No one likes to be whipped by their parents, clerics, officials, warlords, etc. But they can not find legitimate expression of their resentment within their language, which reflects core cultural values that enforces such hierarchy. The weight of the culture suppresses their feelings and turns resentment into pious loyalty—the only way one can psychologically accept abuse is to acknowledge the abuser as divine, as their owner, and his actions as somehow for their own good. This psychological mechanism can keep things under control for the most part, but it does not eliminate anger, especially among the youth, who have yet to totally accept their low ranking positions in the pyramid. A foreign enemy that ventures into this picture serves two purposes. One, it provides a convenient target over which to vent anger and frustration. Two, it allows the ruling elite, as well as all kinds of domestic patriarchs—the real cause of that anger in the first place—to portray themselves in a less domineering, even slightly pathetic light, standing next to Western powers. They are now seen as helpless, their actions fully understandable. They are to be sympathized rather than resented. Now for the youth everything falls into line. They do not have to combat core cultural values, which they can not win anyway. They can harbor as much resentment as possible, only redirected at foreigners, which provides an outlet for their energy. Moreover, in exercising revenge, they are fulfilling core cultural values, becoming heroes of pious loyalty to their ruler/state/religion. It is a good but not perfect solution to a perpetual problem in the modern era, since once the movement gathers strength it could potentially turn back at the domestic hierarchy.

The only pyramid culture that has found a way to fully control this vengeful energy, either harvest it in disciplined industrial work on production lines, or to direct it at any target of the ruler's choosing, such as a foreign enemy, in short, turning the problem into an asset, is Japan. But it has a lot to do with the amoral nature of Japanese tradition, which can not be easily imitated by other moral cultures.

After 1895 thousands of young and ambitious Chinese went to Japan in search of an answer. The obvious question weighing on everyone's mind was if Japan could modernize so quickly why not China. They brought back with them various theories. Some thought China should adopt a Japanese style constitution, which would declare divinity of the ruling house, thus securing them from possible dynastic changes, affording them the confidence to leave governance in the hands of a cabinet, in other words separating ownership and management of the empire. Such a system worked well in Japan. The Cabinet had full administrative power and responsibility. The emperor was removed from active governance and beyond blame. If implemented in China it could conceivably solve the problem that plagued the Qing court, where decisions were made by an empress who was shrewd and cunning in internal political struggles but utterly incompetent in state affairs.

However, political traditions of the two cultures are significantly different. Japanese imperial house was powerless for much of its history, and the Meiji period was the first time the emperor had totalitarian control over Japan (no more warlords or private armies), similar to Han Dynasty China. Add to that the fact that the imperial blood line had never been interrupted since ancient times, thus lending support to its divinity, the Meiji emperor could safely delegate administrative powers to his officials without fearing being dethroned. Legalist tradition helped the emperor stay behind the scenes, clear of political struggles and routine operations of the government, when different factions were constantly jostling for position. Since the emperor is sacred with or without real power, it is preferable for him to be seen as an amicable but somewhat helpless figure, which would stir up strong feelings of devotion from his subjects (Boxer Syndrome).

China had two millennia of absolute secular rule, solidified ideologically by imperial Confucianism and neo-Confucianism, according to which dynastic change is allowed. The system concentrates all power in one person and yet allows Heaven's judgment on him. As a result the emperor is inclined to act arbitrarily, thus is prone to gross mismanagement, but at the same time can not afford to relinquish tight control of state affairs, for fear of being overthrown. If the emperor delegates military affairs to a general, for instance, then there is nothing in Chinese culture that could stop the general from declaring the emperor unfit to rule and replacing him. Therefore the ruler must always maintain active control of every major state function to stay in power. As long as foreign enemies (such as Western powers) are not interested in taking his place, the ruler would rather concede to them land, treasure and everything else than to fight them, or else he could be weakened and become vulnerable to a domestic rival. When the culture dictates that all the important functions remain firmly in imperial control, a constitutional government is impossible.

Meiji Japan was not really a constitutional state anyway. Save the emperor's caution there was no institutional restraint on his power. The Meiji constitution was meant to unite a fragmented Japanese society under a single banner, in other words to concentrate all power in the hands of one. But Chinese thinkers at the time did not carefully study Japanese history. They saw Japanese ministers and officials had more freedom in making decisions for the country, unlike Chinese officials who could not do anything without direct imperial order, and they credited it to the constitution. After all, a constitution in theory is supposed to provide a check on the sovereign's power; it is also the most visible difference between the two political systems.

Bowing to public pressure the Manchurian ruling house finally promised a constitution, but steadfastly blocked its implementation, although they tried other reforms based on the Japanese model. National exams were abolished (a 1,300 year old tradition); schools began to teach Western science in addition to Confucian classics; women were allowed to attend school; a police force was set up (though it was hard to get high ranking officials to obey traffic rules since right of way had always been decided by rank); a new professional army was founded and trained by Western officers; industrial plants domestic or foreign owned mushroomed and modern products began to replace traditional ones. Most importantly, a great number of modern words and ideas coined by Japanese (in Chinese characters) were imported, allowing Chinese scholars to translate Western philosophical works. Thirteen centuries earlier there was a cultural flood from China to Japan, this time Japan returned the favor. It is not an exaggeration to say modern Chinese see the West through a Japanese lens.

These measures were intended to stave off the push for a constitution, but they broke a long standing rigid system. In a matter of a few years things changed rapidly in major cities as people tried to adjust to new rules and practices. For centuries Chinese were mired in a culture where everything inherited from ancestors was deemed sacred and untouchable. Now many changes were sanctioned by the court and for the first time it was not a crime to talk about change. Western ideas though not fully understood opened up the Chinese mind. The immediate consequence was a sharp decline in social ethics, just as many traditional scholars warned would happen when national exams were abolished. Pious loyalty needs a strong regime to sustain its vitality, just like filial piety depends on a domineering father. For the push and pull mechanism to work, the push must be powerful, the pull must be gentle, the subject must have no way to escape, and the master must believe in it himself. A regime that is too weak to threaten its subjects and wavering in its doctrine does not engender strong pious loyalty. The regime began to lose hearts and minds of its subjects.

Western science can not replace moral education. When people no longer knew what to believe anymore, chaos ensued. Coastal and southern provinces became semi-independent by allying themselves with Western powers and business interests. They had joint venture banks, import/export monopolies, privately trained armies funded by their own revenue which they increasingly kept for themselves. Imperial orders were routinely ignored. Western powers freely expanded territories under their control in the south and along the coast, while the Japanese continued their land grab in Manchuria, after they beat the Russians in the 1905 Russo-Japanese war. The empire was literally falling apart right in front of everyone's eyes. Meanwhile abolition of national exams plugged the career path of the younger generation of scholar-official class. Their training gave them a sense of responsibility for all-under-heaven, but reality prompted each of them to find his own way to save the empire.

The revolution theory had always been the main alternative to the constitutional reform theory, though it was much less popular in the beginning among Chinese students and scholars living in Japan. For a well trained Confucian who sees morality as total submission to authority, it is psychologically hard to even entertain the idea of revolution. The word was new to Chinese, again, one of those coined by Japanese. It literally means to kill, to take life. Thus most Chinese naturally took it to mean an uprising, an insurgency, a rebellion, and its intended aim to be dynastic change, which was a familiar idea. The leader of this cause—medical doctor Sun Yet-Sen (孙中山)—lived in British controlled Hong Kong and often traveled to the United States. Inspired by American history and its political system, his idea of revolution was not the traditional dynastic change but to redesign the Chinese system, without an emperor, in the form of a constitutional republic, complete with people's representatives and elections.

These Western ideas were unintelligible to Chinese. Moreover, centuries of Confucian indoctrination turned them pious loyalists. Most Chinese would not even rebel when facing certain death. The few brave ones who would were ridden with guilt. It was like for a medieval Christian to openly denounce God. The only thing that could redeem the rebels was for them to successfully topple the old regime, in which case they could claim Heaven's Mandate on their side, regaining legitimacy. For political convenience Sun tapped nationalism, another Western idea, for the rallying call, as in "deport the Manchurians and restore China".

There was no such thing as nationalism in prior Chinese history. Chinese was a cultural not ethnic idea. The scholar-official class secretly hoped for a dynastic change because the Manchurian ruling regime was unable to protect Chinese civilization, not because they hated the Manchurians as an ethnic group. The newly imported poorly understood nationalism provided a cover for their otherwise blasphemous intentions, though it did not by itself stir up any strong emotions. Soon provincial governors in the south declared independence under the banner of Sun's revolution and the top general of the imperial army refused to fight for the ruling house. In 1911 the Qing Dynasty was brought to a relatively peaceful end in a political coup. This created another unprecedented scenario in Chinese history. A dynasty was destroyed not by a conquering military force, but by a popular consensus. Sun was the spiritual leader of this revolution, but he had no army under his control.

By now China's path since its encounter with the West went the opposite direction of Japan. It demonstrates that both peoples decided whatever they were doing before was wrong. Japan had long been a fragmented society ruled by warlords, and it became a centralized empire. China had long been an absolute monarchy, and after decades of struggle it finally broke two thousand years of imperial control (soon to descend into warlordism). Sun was elected president of what was to be an American style democracy, only to be quickly replaced by the top military general. Sun then tried to limit his power by setting up Western like institutions, such as a national congress, with some success. No one had full control of the country, every power broker depended on Western powers for finance and weaponry, and so they all had to pay at least lip service to the idea of the "democratic" revolution. In a decade or so the two thousand year old imperial system, along with the title emperor, was widely condemned as immoral and a symbol of the "feudal" past.

But Chinese had no idea how to govern themselves without an emperor, and China soon fell into the hands of warlords. Though another warring states period was not what the revolutionaries envisioned, they had a hard time trying to forge a new kind of polity based on alien ideas. American political practices and democratic institutions sounded good but to the average Chinese they did not mean anything. People were used to being slaves of one master or another. If the emperor was no longer there, someone, either nationally or locally, had to take the place of the master, to whom the subject pledged pious loyalty, and in whom a social hierarchy was anchored. Warlords played that role in their respective provinces. The national president was not a ruler by design, therefore not a master of the warlords in concept. Thus Confucian hierarchy could not be established between the president, the congress and the warlords. Without such a hierarchy people did not know how to deal with each other. Naturally real power rested with whoever had guns and the national government was reduced to a façade.

Even the façade was torn to pieces over and over. Sun realized after failed attempts to build an American style democracy that he needed an army to unify the country first by defeating the warlords, then it would take years to educate Chinese of democratic values, and only after that could there possibly be constitutional rule. This was called the three stage transformation of China by his Nationalist Party: military (totalitarian) rule, tutelage (authoritarian) rule and finally constitutional (democratic) rule.

This situation was culturally similar to present day Iraq, if we can imagine it without American troops. Though the demise of a previous totalitarian regime makes constitutional democracy politically possible, the masses have been culturally conditioned to accept absolute authority, without which they do not know what to do. People are told since childhood that they must worship and serve their parents for life no matter how badly treated by them. The logic is, parents can kill them but chose not to, and that is a divine favor, an *en*, to be repaid with lifelong servitude. There is no principle such as freedom or justice beyond submission. In a community of people so trained there must be a patriarch figure, to who the rest pledge pious loyalty. He is usually head of the largest clan in the community, also the richest man by virtue of his power. He settles disputes among other community members, who are treated like his children. In all traditional Asian communities from East Asia to South Asia to Central Asia, the tribal/community chief really owns his people. He may be a religious leader, a landlord, a warlord or all of the above. If there is a strong national totalitarian regime like a Confucian imperial house or a Saddam Hussein Baathist party, these local chiefs can be undermined or even replaced by magistrates or bureaucrats who exercise total power on behalf of the central authority. In absence of a totalitarian regime these local chiefs are indispensable in maintaining peace and order. It is impossible to have Western style local communities, which requires that each individual at least understands he is not a slave to anyone, and the courage to fight for his rights. When each community is ruled by a warlord, and there is no central military authority, political elections can not fundamentally change power dynamic. Suppose a national assembly is voted in, with each warlord represented. What can this democratically elected government do? If it tries to impose any law in any place, the resident warlord may reject. The national government becomes a joke. That was why Sun realized China had to go through those three stages: unified military rule to gain control of the whole country first, which makes tutelage possible, and perhaps a generation or two after that the thought reformed public can learn to exercise their democratic rights, or at least get used to the idea that they are not slaves.

He founded a military academy. Graduates of the academy then organized a new army, supposedly loyal not to any person according to Confucian tradition, but to the new republic under the new ideology of Three-People-ism, possibly inspired by Abraham Lincoln's Gettysburg speech "of the people, by the people, for the people", but explained by Sun as nationalism (abolishment of unequal treaties with foreign powers), political equality (not clearly defined) and economic equality (not Western style egalitarianism, but that the government must care about livelihood of the people, close to Mencius' peopleism). Whatever he intended it to mean, most Chinese took Three-People-ism as a modern rephrase of the Mencian peopleism, which implied that whoever was in power, whether a president or a congress or just the vague idea of government, the ruling elite must put people's interest first. In other words, people were still looking at their government as a Confucian father figure, with sweeping power, but a benevolent heart.

Sun died before his new Nationalist army, under the leadership of his more traditional protégé, Chiang Kai-Shek (蔣介石), defeated many warlords in its Northern Expedition and nominally unified China in late 1920's. This was somewhat like a shogun after demolishing many rivals and securing the allegiance of the rest achieved hegemony. Japanese invasion in the 1930's and communist rebellion allowed Chiang to further consolidate his power at the expense of the remaining warlords, turning into a real dictator. The Nationalist Party became synonymous with China; loyalty to the country was indistinguishable with pious loyalty to the Party and ultimately to Chiang himself. After losing to the communists in 1949 and fleeing to Taiwan, Chiang ruled the island state another twenty six years before passing power on to his son, reverting to traditional dynastic rule in all but name.

In the century or so since its encounter with Western merchants and gunboats, China tried various kinds of reform, imported science and technology, toppled a three hundred year old dynasty, cut man's braids and loosed woman's feet, flirted with political elections and a parliamentary system, only to see the experiment crumbling into chaos and then had to resort to military dictatorship to regain order. It is easy to criticize Chiang for his draconian style, but just like the warlord Nobunaga who unified Japan in sixteenth century, he had little choice but to resort to personal loyalty based on *en*. For Confucians there can be no peace without a clearly defined social hierarchy. At the top of that hierarchy there must be a stable entity that serves as its anchor and object of pious loyalty. That entity can be a person, like an emperor, or a political party, if the party can always remain in power, but it can not be an idea, such as popular consensus reflected in elections, which would represent a variable, an uncertainty and insecurity for the subjects who look for an almighty father figure to take care of them. Japan had an emperor to worship in the Meiji reform, China discarded dynastic rule but could not find a suitable replacement. Chinese reform was so much harder than Japanese also because it is a moral tradition. If constitutional rule is accepted it is taken as the morally right thing to do. And so if it does not achieve the intended objective, "for the people", then support quickly dissipates and the whole scheme collapses. Japan has no such problem. From imperial Confucianism to neo-Confucianism to Western constitutionalism, Japanese can always borrow a form, any form, to serve its military style hierarchical rule. Most of the details in terms of institutions and regulations can be swapped wholesale, because they have no moral significance whatsoever.

Though failing its initial goal of an American style democracy the Nationalist Revolution did change Chinese culture in many ways. One of the major transformations was the role of women. Abolition of foot binding was part of a larger equality movement that quickly followed similar movements in Western countries in early twentieth century. The newly educated women not only physically walked out of the confines of their homes, which foot binding was meant to prevent, they became reporters, writers, teachers and other professionals, and through their firsthand recant of the torturous treatment at the hands of traditional men, presented a convincing and morally indisputable case for abandoning the old culture. Their quest for equality still had a long way to go, obviously, but after the revolution the trend for liberation was already irreversible.

Another profound change was the induction of spoken language into written form, replacing the ancient written language that remained essentially the same in three thousand years. In the very beginning this written language was the oral tongue at the time, but over the centuries oral tradition changed so much that without years of study the average person could no longer understand written words. In the end the majority of Chinese were not only illiterate; they needed help from a local teacher or scholar to understand an imperial decree when it was read to them. Historical Confucian scholars serving the succession of dynasties also did their part to separate the pictographs from vulgar tongues of the plebian, adding moral connotation as well as aesthetic value, making it an ornate and euphemistic propaganda tool for the ruling elite, and obscure for the uneducated.

For the new intellectual elite of the revolutionary age, this ancient language was the carrier of the old culture that they wanted to demolish, as well as the barrier between their enlightenment and the population they tried desperately to reach. Many of these intellectuals went to the West or Japan and saw with their own eyes vastly different worlds and attitudes, but upon coming back they found it hard to communicate with childhood friends and neighbors. It is impossible to translate Western ideas into the old language, because this language carries with it a strong moral judgment against anything new. In promoting familiar vernacular as the new official Chinese, intellectual reformers hoped to wrestle language to their side, substituting new values for old, and forging a new vehicle friendly to new ideas and easily accessible to the uneducated.

One of the leaders of this movement was the American educated pragmatist Hu Shi (胡适). He was a moderate on political reform, focusing his attention instead on cultural transformation, which he understood to be a multi-generational enterprise. The most restrictive tendency of the neo-Confucian mind is to judge everything large and small in stark moral terms. If proposals were made on taxation, education, health care, industrial and trade polices, national versus local government, land ownership, etc., the immediate reaction of the typical Chinese would be: Will this violate teachings of our ancestors? Is this going to undermine our values and social order? Is it moral? There was a lot of debate within intellectual circles as to which course China ought to take, from capitalism to communism and everything else in between, and these debates often ended in the Mencian style, where scholars attacked opponents' personalities with the vilest language and the most vicious moral condemnation, even when their ideas were not that far apart. Without a tradition of objective reasoning like ancient Greeks, "logic" being a newly imported word and an alien concept, every point had to be made morally significant to even gain attention. It was hard to separate criticism from character assassination.

Seeing that such quarrels would never lead to any resolution, Hu advocated a pragmatic approach, namely to set aside ideological issues and focus on problem solving. He wanted people to criticize the government, apply pressure on it, incrementally correct its wrong doings and gradually establish better norms and standards, instead of trying to overthrow it. After all, several governments had been overthrown and nothing came out of it but more chaos. This approach worked in the Anglo-American tradition, where the core values of the society are conducive to rather than against modern sensibilities like individual freedom, so injustices against women and the underclass can be addressed within the moral confines of traditional values. The thirteenth century Magna Carta was a prelude to these modern developments. The same can not be said about Confucian tradition, whose guiding principles are diametrically against that of Magna Carta. Confucius argued for the king's absolute power and barons to be his slaves, rather than a compromise between the two sides on more or less equal ground, in a similar situation.

Hu's approach did not achieve its intended objective, but it was applauded by the new dictator, Chiang, because it denounced revolution. Over time Chiang silenced most of his critics, often through brutal means, save Hu himself, who became one of the only Chinese who could openly criticize the government with impunity, because of his name recognition in the United States, and also as a useful showcase of free speech to the West, which Chiang depended upon for military and financial assistance. As such Hu's "critic the government but do not overthrow it" and "piecemeal changes instead of revolutions" doctrine sounded increasingly hypocritical.

Another leading thinker of the time, the self educated Lu Xun (鲁迅), went further in examining Confucian tradition. He said words like mercy, benevolence and morality fill volumes upon volumes of Confucian classics, but upon reading between the lines he could see only one word: brutality ("man eating"). He observed that Chinese children were hardly ever happy, even from a young age, that they lost their innocence to this brutality very early. For unstated reasons he stopped short of condemning filial piety, possibly having to do with Japanese success: they are Confucian as well. The vivid depiction of average Chinese man and woman in his short novels was unparalleled in its depth and intensity. He felt the pain of the common people, but anguished as to why they do not have the courage to stand up for themselves.

That is the essence of the Chinese dilemma. People are trained to be slaves since they were born. They are docile, easy to control, content, as long as their basic needs are satisfied with reasonable security. In exchange for total subservience they expect mercy from authority. That is why when

Japanese soldiers ordered them to dig a hole and then jump in, to be buried alive, they complied, peacefully, in the hope that their total submission would bring out the merciful side of their tormentors, which was not forthcoming. But they were moral beings, and their harmlessness made their misery all the more heart wrenching. As the Nationalist elite became increasingly pro status quo and corrupt, moral conscience of the people could no longer wait for the hypothetical incremental improvement, it was desperate for a total solution.

CHAPTER 17

COMMUNISM AND THE THIRD SYNTHESIS: MAOISM

Confucians are not prone to rebellion; in fact they are averse to it. Early Chinese Communists found that out the hard way, as they tried over and over again, following instructions of Communist International in Moscow, to organize unions and strikes among industrial workers in coastal cities, waiting for the "rising tide" of revolution that never came. However, when pushed to the brink of starvation many would fight, as in numerous peasant uprisings throughout Chinese history, and the slogan with the widest appeal was "equal wealth for all". This has to do with the pyramid culture, where traditionally each peasant gets the same allotment from the ruler regardless of individual merit. Since people are not allowed to freely compete, inequality in the outcome is not deemed fair. The perception is further reinforced by the fact that wealth is always tied with power, and generated out of monopoly or exaction. As a result popular sentiment is favorable to the doctrines of Marxist economics, though it has nothing to do with Karl Marx's quantitative analysis of how an Englishman working in a nineteenth century mill was exploited by his capitalist boss.

The intellectual allure of Marxism lies in its historical worldview. Marx posited four stages of past human history: primitive communism, ancient slavery, medieval feudalism and capitalism, all serving as a prelude to the inevitable incoming socialism and finally communism. Confucianism designated the entire population as slaves, and that was what Asians felt they were. In the pyramid hierarchy everyone was owned by someone above, who had the power of life and death. Though this kind of relationship was the only one known to Asians, their born human instinct nevertheless resented it. It was a scourge that they desperately craved to rid of. Of all the great philosophers of the world, Marx was the only one to address the issue of slavery as part of natural human evolution, not only in the "ancient slavery" period (classical Greece and Rome) but also in the serfs of the medieval feudal period. By translating both "slave" and "serf"—two different ideas in European history—into the same Japanese/Chinese word, Asians could breathe a sigh of relief. Europeans of the industrial age were undeniably free, but by Asian interpretation of Marx's theory they had been serfs/slaves in the not so distant past. This furnished hope that with a quick modernization process Asians can be immediately free, just like Europeans transformed themselves from the feudal period to the industrial period. It alleviated the insurmountable inferiority complex that plagued Asians ever since invasion of the West.

Marx based social development entirely on economics, asserting that mode of production determines social culture and political system. When this theory—concluded from Western history—was applied outside the West it ran into trouble. According to its line of reasoning socialist Russia as a later stage in the social evolution must be more advanced than capitalist West, which was obviously not true. A critical but not widely recognized fact is that the "ancient slavery" of Greece and Rome, characterized by two legally distinct classes of free citizens and slaves, was not the kind of pyramid society that Asia was. Greco-Roman culture was dominated by the class of free men that never existed in Asian history. The serfs of medieval Europe were not slaves by law. Their landlords could not arbitrarily kill them the way a samurai could behead any peasant or a daimyo could order the suicide of any of his samurai. To Asian intellectuals these are just unimportant details of the theory which they are willing to bend out of shape to suit Asian reality. Japanese historians who are by no means communists in the political-economic sense (class struggle) are just as fervent believers of the Marxist historical view as their Chinese counterparts, because no other philosophy provides a comparable historical frame that makes sense to Asians.

Communism also appeals to those at the bottom end of Confucian hierarchy because it promises total equality. This not only applied to the economic underclass, such as the peasantry, but also sons and daughters of urban elites who had absorbed some Western ideas and were no longer willing to bear tyrannical ways of their parents. When the communist Red Army was lying low in a remote corner of northwest China, after the Long March (an organized flight to avoid annihilation by the ruling Nationalist troops), many youthful intellectuals and progressives went a long way to join them, abandoning comfortable material conditions in coastal cities. Some fled from marriages arranged for them by their parents. Others simply wanted to live in a community of equals, not masters and slaves.

Their choice reveals limitations of the Nationalist Revolution, which despite its initial objective and rhetoric had faded into little more than a dynastic change. To be sure many visible forms of old culture were abolished, such as the Manchurian hairstyle and foot binding, as well as title of the ruler—from "emperor" to "chairman". These changes also did usher in a new attitude, that not everything inherited from ancestors is sacred, that changes are good or at least not immoral. However, core cultural values remained, as did inter-personal relations. The five deities—Heaven, Earth, ruler, parents/ancestors, and teachers—that Chinese had worshiped for centuries were kept intact, only that ruler was now replaced by the vague idea of state (Republic of China). Traditionally state was the same as state-family of the emperor. Now in official propaganda state was equated with the ruling Nationalist Party (KMT), often called "party state". Pious loyalty was due to party state, which in the minds of the average person was just a modern way of saying the ruler's regime.

For all its exaltation of Three-People-ism, its proclamation of the three stage political transformation of China, supposedly leading to constitutional rule, for all its educational and institutional reform, for all its efforts to industrialize and modernize, the Nationalist Revolution failed to address the issue of Confucian hierarchy and Confucian culture with any consistency. By the time the Nationalist government firmly established itself, earlier revolutionary rhetoric gave way to what might be called cultural inertia. Parents still routinely beat up their grown children and treated them like slaves. The top ruler himself required his children and grandchildren to kowtow to him. Out in the streets police and officials dealt with commoners with condescension and contempt. Confucian hierarchy up and down the society, inside and outside the family, survived the revolution unscathed. The Confucian mentality, despite material and lifestyle changes, was intact. Corruption was rampant just like the old times. To get anything done one needed to bribe. Military officers jumped on the gravy train, known as U.S. Aid, in the same fashion Manchurian generals embezzled funds for ammunition. Many in the ruling elite collaborated with various mafia groups to rob and loot the helpless, and since it was military rule, criticism was often labeled unpatriotic and banned. The same culture that doomed previous dynasties was hardly shaken.

For those who managed to reach the communist stronghold in northwest China (it was remote and close to Russian border), life was totally different. The Red Army survived years of hardship, of having to fight off Nationalist attacks and find food for themselves. At first they suffered devastating defeats, losing its only power base in southeast China. In the Long March that followed, a previously lower ranking figure, Mao Ze Dong, a home grown intellectual with no ties to Communist International, gradually assumed leadership, because he was the only one who understood Chinese peasants well enough to sustain the Red Army. Their settlement in the northwest was by no means secure, and they could not afford to alienate the peasantry by taxing them with abandon like other regimes. That presented a dilemma. They needed both to tax their base and to gain support from those peasants being taxed. To compound the problem, in the eyes of the average person, rebels were criminals of the worst kind, since violations against pious loyalty (and filial piety) are the most egregious sin in Confucian morality. The masses by their indoctrination tended to keep away from rebels as much as they could. In order to survive Mao carefully studied Chinese peasant communities and devised ingenious methodologies.

A village was internally bound by family ties and personal loyalty. Usually half or more of all villagers had the same last name and belonged to the same clan, because a typical village was founded sometime in the distant past by a single family. Patriarch of the main clan—an old male—would be village chief. Every member understood his position in the village hierarchy, which was largely based on seniority in the clan tree. The chief was a Confucian father figure, domineering and controlling. He owned much of the land, which he assigned to his relatives to work on, and collected fees. The average villager saw the chief the same way a son saw his father: he "loved" him out of Stockholm Syndrome, and feared Heaven's punishment if he disobeyed.

According to communist doctrine the Red Army should just kill all landlords and divide their properties equally among peasants. Indeed some suggested just that. But that kind of dogmatic approach would have alienated the masses that the Red Army was supposed to liberate. Mao took a different approach. He would arrest the chief, set him up for a public trial, and encourage villagers to chastise him. At first villagers might be tentative. The chief, though bonded or shackled, might be able to stare them down. If this happened, Red Army soldiers would beat him, humiliate him, make him kneel and beg for life. All this was done to embolden villagers, who were prodded to participate in the "class struggle". That was often not enough for the average person to overcome the fear of violating filial piety/pious loyalty. Red Army soldiers then broadcast the new doctrine: the landlord exploited you, oppressed you, he represents a reactionary class, and it is righteous to take revenge on him.

The average Chinese was incapable of savagely beating anyone, much less taking a human life. Aside from psychological barrier of hierarchy, there was the moral barrier of mercy. The only way for Chinese to condone a killing was if the condemned was deemed immoral, and the only way for them to participate in the killing was by intense and righteous hatred, as if the condemned had just murdered one's father. Mao turned the communist doctrine of class struggle into a moral struggle between good and evil. The propertied class is immoral by definition of the new ideology. There is always pent up anger in any pyramid culture, and it can not find expression against core cultural values. That anger is caused by the master-slave hierarchy revered as universal law, the Dao. Chinese hated their landlords not because of their wealth (although they might think so), but because of their oppression. Maoism provides a moral justification for that anger. Though economic exploitation is the main focus of Marxism, deduced from its political economy, it is always mentioned with oppression in the same breath in Maoism.

Sooner or later some youth was emboldened enough to throw the first punch or kick. Once that step was taken, the individual crossed the aforementioned two cultural red lines, and fear set in again. He was beyond the point of no return. It was now in his interest to persuade others to join him, to find security in numbers. Being a leader of sorts, he would show that he was all in by escalating violence, eventually killing the condemned in a brutal manner. Along the way others would join the effort to varying degrees, constantly watching each other and struggling in their minds whether or to what extent to break away from long held beliefs. Similar struggle meetings and psychological process would reappear later in the Cultural Revolution.

This process yielded two important effects. One was that the peasants all became collaborators of communist rebels and co-criminals by law, tying their fate together. After such events peasants were afraid the Red Army would leave them. Once the area was back in government control they would be harshly dealt with, since what they did was not a forgivable garden variety crime in the Confucian book. If the Red Army had to leave, then those who were culpable had no choice but to join them. If the Red Army stayed, loyalty from the local community was guaranteed. Tax was no longer a problem. The other effect was that those who had such an experience underwent a transformation of heart. They had been suffocated by core cultural values like filial piety and pious loyalty. Once that religious taboo was thrown off the individual instantly adopted an all new perspective on life. He was not a slave any longer. The Red Army taught him that he had the right to rebel against any oppressor. Chairman Mao said "rebellion is righteous".

From the Confucian "rebellion is blasphemy" (不忠不孝, 大逆不道) to "rebellion is righteous" (造反有理), Mao's movement was truly revolutionary. Traditional peasant insurgents operated with guilt, even though they were pushed to rebellion by unbearable circumstances. An imperial regime would label them bandits and they would feel like bandits in their conscience. The Nationalist government labeled Mao's army bandits as usual, and the society by and large saw them in that light, but Red Army soldiers believed in their cause and righteousness. In their newly adopted moral doctrine they were the enlightened and truly moral, while the rest of the country were either cynically defending oppression or ignorantly believing in its validity. Their purpose transcended seizing power. For many the revolution itself was an expression of freedom. Thus from very early on true power of this "communist" revolution came from cultural revolution against Confucian values, though that was never conspicuously stated as a rationale or a slogan for lack of a philosophical/moral foundation. Most propaganda was borrowed from Marxist terminology, but the reason that it was stirring was not because of a proletariat class eager for justice, but because of its psychological suggestions of a whole new kind of character, proud, rebellious, fearless, and self-righteous, contrary to the Confucian slavish prototype. Instead of seeking justice (a Western idea), peasants simply wanted to get out of slavery (翻身做主人).

Chinese military had been traditionally incompetent, due in main to lack of motivation. Revolutionary zeal might compensate for it to some extent. But for a national army engaged in a multiyear campaign, it was still the dominating issue. Japanese solved this problem by the bushido code, a Confucian micro management scheme. Chinese never fully developed that training methodology, outside sporadic cases, because it is too cruel to put into words for the mercy minded. Western training does not address the motivation issue. Western soldiers are free men. They are there to perform a duty, for the country that is theirs. What about slaves who feel that the country is not theirs, that they are just fighting for a ruling house, for possible rewards like promotion and pay, something worth a minimum effort but not their lives? The much larger, better equipped and American trained Nationalist army lost to the communist force in a landslide, in less than three years, not for any tactical reason but because of a huge imbalance in the motivation factor.

Communism of course played a role here. Many who joined the Red Army believed in equality and democracy, which to them meant absence of master-slave relation. But they were also Chinese. Without proper guidance the relation between an officer and his foot soldiers would quickly deteriorate into master-slave, soldiers would lose all initiative, and eventually motivation, like what happened in the Nationalist army. Being a brilliant student of Chinese history Mao perceived this problem as a key military issue. He founded a system where each unit—a company, a battalion, a regiment, a division or an army corps—had two commanding officers of equal rank. One was in charge of military operations, the other a political officer, in charge of the mind. The political officer monitored the mental state of his partner as well as subordinates, and "corrected" it as he saw fit. Officers and soldiers alike spent sometime every week on political study. They typically sit in a meeting, discussing instructions from top command, current issues and general views. Every person was encouraged to speak his mind. If someone was too shy the political officer would have a chat with him in private. Through this process he knew what everyone was thinking. If he was not sure whether a particular mindset was acceptable he would ask superior political officers for guidance, not just instructions but why, for he had to understand it in order to convince his subordinates.

If he saw a problem he would have a private conversation with the individual. Suppose a soldier is beaten by his lieutenant, and he feels humiliated and depressed. The political officer would then try to persuade the lieutenant to apologize to the soldier, which is not at all easy. In a Confucian society higher ranks do not apologize to lower ranks, ever, because of the nature of Confucian hierarchy. A master must not apologize to his slaves regardless of what he did to them, or else it would upset the order. If a superior feels sorry for something he did to an inferior, he can privately give money or other materials as compensation. For a superior to apologize to an inferior would mean that the superior now lowers himself to the rank of the inferior, which is a humiliation that many would rather die to avoid, because once you lower your rank, it affects how others treat you: your former equal may now see you as an inferior. In the Red Army the doctrine is: everyone is equal regardless of rank. So the lieutenant in question is pressured to apologize to the soldier, an act which is traditionally considered losing face big time. When the apology finally comes, it is an overwhelming experience to the soldier. His parents never apologized to him, nor did any other authority figure. He never experienced anything like it. At that moment, he learns a new kind of relationship, and that he is no longer a slave.

They called each other comrades. To those who tasted its meaning the term engendered warmth. For people who realized that they had been slaves all their lives and only the Red Army offered them an oasis of liberation, going back to traditional society was unimaginable. It is important to point out that this liberation has nothing to do with freedom in the modern Western sense. In fact the Red Army was highly disciplined with strict rules of conduct. But inside the heart of each soldier the feeling of being liberated was palpable and exhilarating. Red Army officers did not have the demeanor of traditional Confucian officials, which was characteristic of the Nationalist force. All abuses both verbal and physical were effectively banned. Though it was still not quite the kind of equality in a Western society and the new culture was vulnerable to changing circumstances, for there was no principle like justice to support it, compared to traditional hierarchy it was a major improvement.

There was also a flip side to this liberation. With loyalty of foot soldiers to the communist cause secured by new found equality, Mao still wanted absolute loyalty of officers to himself. This obviously had a lot to do with his personal ambition, but there was also a cultural element, as the Red Army faced a dilemma in its organizational structure. All traditional Confucian organizations are based on the family model and are strictly hierarchical. The Nationalist Army was such an organization, where superiors could arbitrarily beat or even execute subordinates, a practice that was banned in the Red Army. But equality is not well defined in Confucianism. Why should a lieutenant obey a general if they are equal? Why should a general obey Mao? What ought to be the extent of authority? What kind of orders can be rightfully rejected? Without a moral principle like Western justice or a clear idea of the free man, it is impossible for Asians to sort out these questions. To have a command structure at all, Mao had to build personal loyalty, along the lines of pious loyalty. For that he had to resort to Confucian tactics in what was called a thought form.

Mechanism of thought reform was the same coercive persuasion technique found in Confucian family training. Mao first got some henchman to declare a state of crisis regarding beliefs of Red Army officers. According to official "findings", many were not firm believers of the communist cause, some carried with them bourgeois sentiments, some were hidden spies for the Nationalist government. Right off the bat a great number of officers were pronounced traitors, most of whom undeservingly. They were publicly humiliated and ordered to repent, which included revealing one's private thoughts, recognizing what was wrong with them, why he had those harmful ideas in the first place, how he had changed his mind through a soul searching and what he believed now, in a hope to be forgiven. Some may not be willing to admit any guilt at first, but once accused they were on the defensive and forced to confess. Pushing the neo-Confucian moral tradition to the extreme, the communists demanded total altruism (the selfless state was only a moral ideal before) in the name of the revolution. Therefore whoever was forced to confess was bound to be condemned, for no one was totally altruistic at heart, or in communist parlance, devoid of "bourgeois" thoughts. Through this process destruction of the individual was thorough. He was not only threatened with death, but having his private thoughts publicly scrutinized, his character was impugned, his dignity shattered, his self worth annihilated. What awaited him was death in shame. The push was as harsh as it could possibly be.

Just when the condemned acknowledged guilt, now that their exposed private thoughts judged by high moral standards were indeed shown treacherous, and desperation and self loathing set in, Mao came in as their savior. They were pardoned, given a new lease on life, an opportunity to redeem themselves in action. They were born again. Mao was their *en* man. The pull was equally powerful. The whole experience was so overwhelming that even a true spy for the Nationalist government would turn into a diehard Mao loyalist. In harsh reality Mao inadvertently discovered Japanese style micro management—a psychological process similar to what happens to a child in Confucian family training—and merged it with communist beliefs. After the thought reform everyone in the Red Army was piously loyal to Mao, who cleverly combined Confucian training on officers with a yearning for equality by soldiers to build a cohesive and effective force.

Though the Nationalist Army was also Confucian in culture, such cruel measures were not widely used on officers, for they violated *ren* (mercy). Indoctrination was still the main tool. Officers and soldiers were told that "obedience is the divine duty of a serviceman", discouraged from political and ideological discussions, effectively banned from the "why do we fight" debate, as part of the training for "professionalism"—a professional just does his job as required without asking why. But professionalism—a Western idea—could not be absorbed by slaves. As a result the Nationalist Army fought for salary, and was culturally no different from armies of the dynastic era: their loyalty to the top leader or to the state, if any, was fragile. Higher ranks did not trust lower ranks enough to allow any autonomy even on trivial matters. If a communist force contingent lost touch with superior command, they would find their own ways to survive and prosper independently, and still stay loyal to central authority. This allowed the communist force to expand from tens of thousands to over a million in several years, right under the nose of Japanese occupiers. If a Nationalist army contingent lost communications with superior command, they would turn into bandits never to be reclaimed by central authority again. Field commanders of the communist army had a much freer hand in their operations than those in the rigid Nationalist force, where originality and entrepreneurship could be punished for disobedience. The primary concern of top Nationalist rulers was always the loyalty issue, which was never resolved. With no cohesion and no common ideal, this force was doomed to fail, however well equipped.

While the birth of neo-Confucianism in Song Dynasty marked an effort of using pious loyalty as the motivation for serving the crown, which proved ineffective in subsequent Chinese history, the CCP (Chinese Communist Party) in the twentieth century made a whole new attempt, this time using an implicit idea—abolition of Confucian style master-slave hierarchy in the military—under the explicit Marxist banner as the rallying call, combined with Confucian training to secure loyalty to Mao, with spectacular success. Chinese version of the Communist International Anthem starts with the line "Rise up, Starving slaves!" This line alone could move mountains, when peasants felt they were truly slaves desperate for liberation. In the wars against Japanese, against Nationalists, and later against Americans in Korea, there were numerous cases of suicidal attacks, which might have been routine for Japanese soldiers but unprecedented for Chinese, who had traditionally cherished life more than anything else. For many soldiers the revolutionary zeal came from a real sense of liberation and righteousness.

However, Communist leaders ran into a philosophical dilemma trying to express such a feeling or mental state. Western philosophies on individual freedom all focus on political and economic institutions as key factors—free press, separation of powers, constitution, democracy, or economic equality—because in the West the state was the only possible oppressor. Marx analyzed the nineteenth century English worker laboring in atrocious conditions for meager pay, under the implicit assumption that if wealth was shared equally by employer and employee, then there would have been nothing else in the culture to enslave the worker. Hence the problem of social justice can be explained in economics.

That is not the case in Asia. Even if all members of an Asian society were to be equally rich or poor, by cultural forces some would still be slapping the faces of others, while the latter have to bow and kneel. Here economic inequality is one manifestation of Confucian hierarchy, and often a keenly felt one, but not its source or essence. Neither are political institutions.

After the demise of the Qing Dynasty in 1911 Western political theories were tested in many governments that came and went: constitution, political campaigns, elections, parliament, free press, and the like. But these turned out to be games played by politicians, warlords and the intellectual elite, which the average individual neither understood nor participated in. In his world he was still a slave, of parents, grandparents, employers, local chiefs, police, officials and other superiors. Neither political institutions nor economics address the culturally motivated master-slave inter-personal relation.

Hence the feeling of comradeship and equality among the Communists could not find any justification in either Western or Confucian thought. By Western definition they were not free, because they were brainwashed and not allowed to deviate from the party line. Yet these measures and restrictions were necessary to keep them from falling into traditional cultural tendencies—which they acquired from childhood family training—and become downright slaves and/or masters. The attempt to undo Confucian training is itself illiberal, but it gets the individual to a stage where he is still not totally free but feels much liberated. We may call this an intermediate stage between freedom and slavery, but this was as far away from slavery as Chinese had ever been. In contrast, Western theories though looked good on paper as they promoted free speech proved ineffective and therefore unconvincing to the majority of those who truly hated being a slave. Free speech allows Confucian theorists to proclaim that the individual must serve his parents and the ruler unconditionally, to which all counter-arguments would sound immoral in the Chinese language. Before the two thousand year old Confucian morality can be turned upside down, there is no way freedom—as the opposite of slavery—can win an argument in a free debate. The imported word freedom had to be interpreted in ways compliant to filial piety/pious loyalty to stay positive.

This intermediate stage, where the individual is no longer a slave to anyone else but does not have freedom of thought or expression, is the Communist idea of freedom and democracy. As we recall the word democracy was translated from English by Japanese, and it means literally "people being masters". The Nationalists (who later fled to Taiwan) took this term for its institutional meaning (many of their elites were educated in the West), such as elections and free press, though these were mostly for show, while the Communists took it to mean overthrowing of social hierarchy. To Japanese and Nationalist Chinese freedom is what is allowed within the Confucian framework. Parents allow their children to do certain things, superiors allow subordinates certain choices, these are considered freedom, but the right to allow or disallow these choices remains firmly in the hands of the superior, and the hierarchical inter-personal relation remains thoroughly Confucian. As a result traditions like bowing, kneeling and prostration survived or even prospered, especially in Japan. To Communists freedom means equality. Servile body languages were banned in the Mao era, often by coercive means. Parents and grown children, superiors and inferiors are no longer supposed to be master-slaves.

The choice between Three-People-ism and Communism for Chinese is not, as Westerners commonly hold, between freedom and captivity. Freedom in Western sense is simply not an option; Asians have no clue what it means. One can not practice an abstract idea without perceiving it in reality first, and Confucian family training makes that perception impossible. The real battle in the 1930s and 1940s was between two competing perceptions of freedom rooted in the different conditions of people sitting at different positions in the pyramid structure. Closer to the top of the pyramid was the educated class: government officials, business owners, professors, writers, reporters, lawyers. At the bottom of the pyramid was the labor class: peasants (70+ percent of total population) and uneducated urban labors. Real power rested in the hands of the military and its top generals. The educated elite were part of the ruling class in a broad sense: a typical large family might have different members working in the government, academia and the business world. They led comfortable lives materially. Some were rich. Their main concern was the "feudal" tendencies of some officials, who might, for example, rob business owners in broad daylight. Since unconditional loyalty and obedience was a virtue, policemen functioned like private servants to their chief, as did army soldiers to their generals. Abuse of power was rampant and out of control in many places. In order to protect themselves from arbitrary encroachment by the military brutes/warlords, they wanted a free press and even Western pressure to help keep the generals in check. For his part the top ruler depended on American military and financial aid for survival, which stayed his hand on many potential executions of political dissidents.

For the vast majority of the population, however, the pressing issue was that they were treated like slaves by landlords (clan patriarchs) and capitalists—members of the above mentioned elite group. A landlord's son might go to a modern college in a big city, and end up running a textile factory. He wanted to protect his business from unruly officials. So he forged personal ties with higher ranks, through bribes or marriage. He liked the idea of Three-People-ism, which meant the government must have mercy on its people, and he, as a member of the people, must not be trampled by officials. At the same time, he paid a despicably low wage to his workers, hired a foreman to beat them up daily, and forced them to live in subhuman conditions, which he pretended to not know, as he chatted amicably over a cup of coffee in the dining room of his Western business partner. His father did the same back home to peasants.

To peasants and workers Three-People-ism or whatever ideology the government professed was far removed from their life experience. They desperately wanted to get out from under the whip, which was waved not necessarily by the government but mostly by private property owners of various kinds. Though their predicament was nothing new, it was exacerbated by constant wars, a breakdown of social order and greed of the landlord class who found new ways to exploit the peasantry. The oppressed generally would not distinguish between a landlord who held no position in the government and a police officer, because both ranked above them in the pyramid and therefore were in position to use and abuse them. Traditional values did not give them an appeal, except to cry foul and mercy when a life was taken. The newly enshrined Three-People-ism did nothing to help either. It did not mean they could now go to court, file a lawsuit, get free counsel, and win a case. Courts were controlled by the same hierarchy and only served the higher ranks.

Hence most of the urban elite preferred Three-People-ism, piecemeal changes, and basically status quo, while peasants, workers and some youthful sons and daughters of elite families wanted to replace the social hierarchy with equality, a revolutionary idea advocated by the Communists. Neither approach would turn China into a Western state, but both would lead to improvements over the past, just in different ways. The first would expand individual rights for the urban elite, including freedom of speech, but would not in the short term do anything to liberate the uneducated majority. The second would immediately end slavery for the whole country, at the expense of individual rights for the educated class.

Staying with traditional values is easy, while embracing a new ideology takes a leap of faith. The Nationalist regime by keeping Confucian hierarchy reduced the cost of management, for the culture perpetuates itself through family training and keeps people docile. Thus the government could afford a certain degree of free discussion and criticism, because Western philosophical views will never change a psychologically conditioned mind that functions under fear. To overcome tradition, on the other hand, takes an overwhelming force. In the process the individual must undergo a shift of paradigm, a renouncement of everything he was taught to believe, which takes more courage than the average individual possesses. Only a strong collective can provide him with security to help make the plunge into mental darkness—and by traditional definition immorality—less frightening, and emotional support to complete the transformation. Westerners condemn Communist collectivism as a pure oppressive instrument on individual liberty, as it denies private property and freedom of thought. That reasoning is sound in the West, which is why Communism though invented by a German never took power there. The Chinese Communist soldier felt just the opposite. The collective was in a very real sense his liberator. He might not be literate, he could not express himself in words, but when he first experienced life in a community without a master-slave hierarchy, and equality in a much deeper sense than economics (equal wealth), the elation trumped any well articulated arguments. If it took brainwash to get to this bliss, that was an insignificant price to pay. Besides, brainwashing is nothing new to Asians; they live it everyday, at home, at work, wherever there is a superior, whenever code words like *en*, filial piety and pious loyalty appear in the conversation.

Unfortunately this feeling of liberation could not find pertinent expression in either Western or Confucian intellectual tradition. Mao had to turn to communist terminology. As a result the concepts of liberation, freedom, democracy, economic equality and social welfare all conflated into one vague idea: Marxism. This was reflected in the different interpretations of Marxism among top leadership. Some thought that abolishing all private property would be communism. Others thought that if everybody was equally rich or poor it would be communism. Still others thought that wellbeing of the masses—a welfare state—was communism. Mao being the only one with a visceral knowledge of peasants and peasant soldiers as well as a sharp insight into Chinese psyche thought of not only the above, but the absence of Confucian social hierarchy as essential to the revolution. The official CCP line claims it ended the three oppressions over Chinese people: imperialism (referring to unequal treaties signed with foreign powers), "feudalism", and oligarch capitalism. Feudalism was a term borrowed from Marxist terminology. To Marx it meant a certain period in European history, with an emphasis on the agricultural nature of its production mode, since material production technology according to him determines social culture. To Chinese it came to mean the two thousand years of dynastic rule. Thus some associated the term "feudalism" with agricultural production, others Confucianism, still others imperial rule with rituals like kowtow. Similarly capitalism was intertwined with oligarchy. The so called Chinese capitalists in early twentieth century monopolized industries by virtue of their connections to power, the same way relatives of high ranking scholar-officials monopolized salt and iron trades since time immemorial. Contrary to Marxist theory, the change of production mode did nothing to Chinese culture. Many Communists hated the new industrial elite for the same reason they hated old scholar-officials, because they represented the old culture. Others hated them because they aggravated economic inequality. But they all had to call it "capitalism" for lack of alternative terms. These disparate views under the banner of the same ideology were latent in times of war, but would gradually surface in the new People's Republic, and the inability to articulate them would have dire repercussions.

After coming to power the Communist regime completely reorganized the peasantry in the 1950's, on the military model. A traditional Chinese village is a web of hierarchical/familial relations where each member has a certain rank. Every one of the hundreds of villagers knows who ranks higher, lower or roughly equal, and treats others accordingly with appropriate body language. Mao learned from Chinese history that pure economic measures like redistribution of land would not break that hierarchy. At the beginning of many dynasties in the past the emperor would purge large and prominent families from the previous dynasty and equally redistribute confiscated land to every peasant. But in no more than a few generations clan patriarchs would always end up robbing lower ranking clan members of their property. Lower ranking members who are supposed to be slaves to higher ranking ones by virtue of Confucian ethics can not possibly hold on to their land. To permanently change this Confucian hierarchy, which Mao and other Communists called feudal/capitalist exploitation, as that was the closest Marxist term they could find, private property was banned by the state, peasants were grouped into production teams, large clans were broken up, each nuclear family was equal and responsible to the team. By the rules each member of the team was equal, man or woman, old or young. He or she was paid a subsistence amount of grain plus a bonus proportionate to the amount of labor he or she rendered to the collective. The team leader was often a young activist appointed by the party. This system basically demolished the old clan structure. It was transparent, seen as fair, and had nothing to do with seniority. It was enthusiastically embraced by the youth, who used to be the lowest in hierarchy, and now took charge of village affairs. Land reform in the countryside was energizing and popular.

Reform in the cities was much more complicated, and beyond capacity of the PLA (People's Liberation Army), which was almost exclusively made up of peasants. Those intellectuals who chose to stay on the mainland instead of fleeing to Taiwan were mostly sympathetic to the communist cause (equality), but they had a hard time adapting to the communist way. As discussed earlier, the Chinese Communists wanted to liberate the entire nation from Confucian ("feudal") slavery, but their approach was itself illiberal by necessity. City intellectuals (school teachers, journalists, lawyers, scientists and engineers), just like those who went to the Red Army holdout in northwest China a decade before, resisted government propaganda and the restrictions on freedom of speech and thought. Meanwhile PLA officers who were put in charge of education, urban planning and industrial reconstruction had no clue what they were doing. Separated from the familiar military environment where discipline was kept in part by mutual supervision, some of them began to act like traditional officials—dictators in their own sphere of responsibility. To the intellectuals this was even worse than the Nationalist regime, which at least had knowledgeable people in position and was not so rough. Discontent arose. Mao asked them to freely speak their mind, in what was known as "let a hundred flowers bloom", thinking he will get some constructive input from the experts. However it opened a flood of pent-up anger and hostility. Mao sent all outspoken intellectuals to thought reform programs in what was known as the Anti-Rightist movement, scaring and silencing the rest who were not brave enough to speak up.

Demographic makeup of the country was similar to that of the military: the vast majority were illiterate peasants and laborers, the educated elite—descendents of the scholar-official class—assumed a higher place in the pyramid. Just like in the army peasants did not need a thought reform program to be loyal. Removal of the old social hierarchy and establishment of a new state ideology espousing equality ensured their heart felt support of the new regime. Just like in the army loyalty of the educated (officers/intellectuals) could not be presumed. The thought reform program solved that problem for Mao in the military, but when the same process was tried in civilian settings in peace time, Mao was not confident or secure enough to trust its results. To be sure, all intellectuals after the push and pull process was applied to them turned diehard loyalists to Mao. The Confucian training program does not miss. But loyalty thus trained is a forced habit, not a voluntary conviction. If, for instance, Mao were to be killed in a coup, then a new round of training could have redirected that loyalty to a new leader, perhaps with a new ideology. The masses would never rise up, out of their loyalty to Mao, to topple the usurper. The danger of losing power is always greater after victory than during the war.

Mao was in a quandary. He wanted to be an absolute ruler, but he could not be an emperor, since his revolution was against the old "feudal" culture, at least in theory. Marxism does not address the issue of governance, such as who gets to be the leader, how much power he should have, the relation between him and other leaders, the scope of authority and responsibility of different branches of the government, etc. Without any guidance from the deceased Karl Marx, political practices of communist governments tend to follow old patterns before the revolution, because core values of pyramid cultures regarding the nature of human existence and interpersonal relations are integrated in child rearing practices, and those can not be changed by a revolution overnight. This is true for both Russia and China. Revolutionary leaders emerged during the war, and they became the first members of the politburo. But Marxism does not say who should be chairman of the politburo, or how much power he has over other members. Equality as a slogan and a vague idea is embraced, but in a pyramid culture it is ill defined. In the West it means everyone is equal in human rights, not in power or authority. A Western leader can have awesome power, but he can not violate human rights of any citizen. In a pyramid culture there is no such thing as a right, power and authority both mean one thing: ownership. If I rank above you it means you are my slave.

Both Russians and Chinese wanted to free themselves from slavery, and after communist revolutions they did away with the old social hierarchy. But without hierarchy there can be no authority in a pyramid culture. Stalin and Mao could not fire anyone from the politburo. The communist doctrine did not give them that authority. By cultural tradition other top leaders could not give them that authority once they embraced equality as they understood it. At first decisions were made by a simple vote in the politburo. There are problems with that approach too, especially when members are divided. There can be easily three or more different opinions on how to run the economy. Without an ultimate decision maker the politburo will be deadlocked most of the time. Moreover, by their own cultural outlook it was hard for Stalin or Mao to accept that they were equal with their former subordinates in the military.

The only way to demote a member of the politburo is to convict him of a crime, turn him into an enemy of the people, in which case he is not just dismissed but destroyed. Both Stalin and Mao had to resort to that trick, as they started calling their potential political competitors—their former comrades—class enemies, the strongest condemnation in communist terms. What can be easily and legitimately done in the West (a president can dismiss a cabinet member by a simple order) has to be dressed up as a struggle between good and evil, and turned into a persecution. In order to secure absolute power, both Stalin and Mao had to periodically purge the top ranks. It was a tragedy caused by the mismatch between Marxism—an imported Western idea assuming individual freedom—and core values of pyramid cultures. Stalin and Mao wanted to be a tsar/emperor like ruler, the masses expected them to play that role, but the new communist idea of equality stood in the way.

Once the first comrade was eliminated on false charges, there was no turning back for Stalin or Mao. If you condemn someone as a class enemy and send him to jail or worse, your arguments had better stand; otherwise you have committed a heinous crime. If you have a different interpretation of communism from your opponent, and you condemned him for that, you'd better insist on your interpretation as the only correct reading of communism for the rest of your life. Deep down in your heart, you are not that sure. The economy may not work out as you planned. As events unfold other views may become increasingly more convincing than yours. But even if new facts have proved you wrong, you can not afford to admit it—you have blood of your comrade on your hands. You have to be always correct to remain innocent. You begin to define right and wrong according to your views, and liquidate other comrades who disagree on one thing or another. As their bodies pile up, you think you have eliminated all political enemies, but you actually feel less secure. You have committed so many crimes that truth if revealed will convict you beyond a reasonable doubt. Over their long reigns both Stalin and Mao fell in that trap.

This was the main reason, among other less significant ones, that Mao could never trust the intellectual class, including those in the CCP. Peasants did not have the ability to look past state propaganda (class struggle) and see what Mao was really doing (power grab). They could not read and they did not care. But the educated person if given a look at events in the Forbidden City could easily find similarities between Mao and many traditional rulers, thus exposing the great leader to be a villain. Although the thought reform program was quite successful in securing loyalty to Mao in the short term, he could not afford to trust the intellectuals. As a group they had to be permanently vilified and prevented from ever occupying the podium again. Mao said "the more knowledgeable, the more reactionary/immoral" (知识越多越反动).

Having purged the educated, the scientifically untutored Mao made a blunder in the Great Leap Forward, when he took what he learned on battlefield and applied it directly to industrial and agricultural production. Several massive campaigns were ordered, not unlike the Qin Empire in third century BC when the Great Wall was built. Millions of people tried to forge steel in their own backyards, by melting iron kitchen ware, hoping to catch up with the U.S. in steel production overnight. Hillside forests were fallen and turned into terraced rice fields. Large scale irrigation works, aqua-ducts and canals were constructed. Roads and railways were hewed out of mountains. The spirit was so high among peasant youth that they thought they could accomplish anything if they dared dream about it. Mao not only gave them freedom from Confucian slavery, but new found optimism and boldness that were unprecedented in Chinese history. The amount of manpower they put into these gigantic projects was staggering, and no one was doing it for money. Had Mao had expert advice this enormous energy could have propelled China into the industrial age rapidly, just like Meiji Japan. Alas, Mao was overconfident in himself. Though some of these projects laid the infrastructure for modern China, from which contemporary Chinese are still benefiting, others were dubious, and some were downright disastrous.

Moreover, tired of being No.2, Mao broke off with the Soviet Union and started to act like he was the messiah. It seems that arrogance seeped in, as if victory over the Nationalists and Americans in Korea proved that his ideology and revolutionary approach could solve every problem. The Soviets consequently demanded repayment of previous loans, and China had nothing but farm products. Peasants were then ordered to work double shifts and increase production. Overzealous local leaders pledged ridiculous amounts that they thought they could produce. Next year they were taxed on the much inflated quota, leaving some twenty million peasants starving to death, and the entire country in serious malnutrition.

After all this the peasantry was still loyal to Mao, especially the youth. They might be starving but as soon as it was broadcast that knowing their plight Mao stopped eating meat, they felt guilty. It was the same psyche why Japanese soldiers and civilians despite having given everything they had, after hearing the emperor surrendered and was thus humiliated, felt guilty that they did not do enough. It is similar to Christians feeling guilty when thinking about Jesus Christ sacrificing himself for their sins. Though this was exactly what the *en* idea was designed for, nevertheless for Chinese such a degree of pious loyalty from the masses was unprecedented. Never before had *en* worked to its full potential for a Chinese ruler. It shows how much Chinese appreciated end of Confucian slavery, that they were willing to sacrifice everything for the party and the *en* man.

When carnage from the economic disaster became painfully evident, Mao took some responsibility and was temporarily sidelined from economic policy making, though he remained party chairman. Since the extent of the damage had a lot to do with zealotry and extremism on the part of the participating masses, CCP leaders who took over sought to retreat from this mass movement campaign approach to everything, as if growing crops and smelting steel were just like fighting a revolutionary war where the spirit and mental toughness was all that was needed, to more prudent governance, letting relatively knowledgeable and experienced officials manage things, at least they are less likely to make claims that are scientifically impossible. Also, collectivist rules were loosened, and peasants were allowed to keep some land and domestic animals outside the collective, as an incentive for more grain and meat production.

For a few years in early 1960's this more modest approach bore some fruits. Starvation was reduced and common sense replaced zealotry. However, the collective was weakened by lack of a common purpose. Solidarity among the masses was dissipating, so was their enthusiasm. As things began to formalize, and officials entrenched in fixed positions, traditional cultural forces naturally resurfaced. Central government made plans, but local officials had the right to interpret them and authority over the masses. Authority in the Confucian sense was not just about favoritism, nepotism and cronyism, which only depict the beneficial side of the equation, but those who disobeyed even personal and unfair demands were labeled anti-revolutionaries and purged mercilessly, just like in the old days scholar-officials would label a recalcitrant a blasphemer. CCP was really facing a Confucian dilemma. If the society was allowed to function on its own momentum, there was no chance the old culture could be broken. People—especially the young—would again feel like slaves. Most of them would be cynical and disinterested. No one would want to contribute to the state. Corruption would permeate every corner of society. The average individual would be timid, lifeless, and cowardly. Numerous attempts since the Nationalist Revolution to break this cultural mode failed, and the Communists succeeded only by practicing collectivism and brainwashing in the army. When the same approach was applied to the population at large, it worked in the short term but at a huge economic price.

Momentum of such a cultural transformation against trained Confucian instincts had to be maintained by constant collective activity and simple goals, enforced by mass movements. Forces generated therein destroyed all natural mechanisms, such as the invisible hand of the market, supply and demand, and a good deal of common sense, resulting in economic and human disasters like the Great Leap Forward. It did not take much in terms of central planning to slowly recover; all that was done was to stop these mass movements and let the market force function to a limited extent. However, without mass political movements the momentum of cultural transformation was gone, and old habits came back quickly.

Seeing signs of a cultural setback, despite economic recovery, Mao was not about to sit on the sidelines for long. He first sent in work groups all over the country in the Four Cleanups program, targeting corrupt and abusive officials, now called cadres (another term coined by Japanese). That effort predictably failed. Emperors of old all tried to curb corruption by sending inspectors to the provinces, but the inspectors were not immune from a corrupt culture, they were only human. In the 1950's Mao's political campaigns enjoyed the support of not only the masses but also his Communist rank and file. By 1960's these new cadres had replaced pre-Communist officialdom, and became increasingly the target of public outrage, and Mao's criticism. At this point most of the CCP top leadership could no longer agree with Mao. They felt obliged to the former lieutenants who risked their lives in the war and now deservedly took positions of privilege in the new republic.

Here the different interpretations of what the Communist Revolution really meant came into play. Most thought it was about abolishing private property and exploitation by capitalists. That was accomplished. Every factory was state owned, so was every commune. The factory chief was a state employee earning a salary, perhaps a former peasant soldier who knew nothing about industrial production, but definitely not a capitalist. All Chinese land, all nine million six hundred thousand square kilometers of it, belonged to the state. When everyone was a state employee and no one owned anything, exploitation by Marxist definition was eliminated. What the new republic should do next was to engage in economic activities.

But the new factory chief could still function like a traditional scholar-official, who in theory owned nothing either, as the emperor owned all-under-heaven. He could promote sycophants and punish those who dared consider themselves equal. A factory worker or commune farmer who refused to lie about production numbers—to boost the chief's career—could be labeled an anti-revolutionary and harshly dealt with, while fawning flatterers ascend fast in the hierarchy. People started to fear their superiors which in the 1950's they did not. Subservient body language was encouraged as a result—head hung low, back hunched over, ingratiating smile, a tendency to bow and weak knees.

To Mao this would be negating the revolution. Upon coming to power the CCP banned kneeling, kowtow and all other forms of prostration. Bowing was replaced by handshaking. A whole host of personal titles were abolished in favor of the single title "comrade", not because there was anything wrong with these old forms of address on paper, but in people's minds they were associated with Confucian hierarchy. For example, women's inferiority was insinuated by all the terms associated with them in traditional Chinese. There was no way to call a wife without implying that she was owned by her husband who could have additional wives and concubines. Women were desperate to end slavery at the hands of man, and if it helped for them to be called the utterly unromantic "comrade wife", so be it.

Actually for many lovers of the new revolutionary generation the term comrade was more romantic than pet names and diminutives, as it conveyed a message of mutual respect and equality, a new kind of love as opposed to the traditional pious loyalty based devotion of women to men. If the ultimate objective of the revolution was to permanently eradicate Confucian hierarchy in the family and the society, then state ownership of all property was only beating around the bushes of the issue. However, centuries of neo-Confucian indoctrination made Chinese believe there must be an overriding moral principle in the universe. Marxism for the equality it preaches gained moral high ground over many specific principles of neo-Confucianism, such as filial piety. In absence of other moral theory on the horizon, Mao had no choice but to use the inconvenient and often misleading Marxist lexicon to communicate with the masses.

Cultural transformation had always been a major issue in China since late nineteenth century. The Nationalist Revolution abolished foot binding, but soon fell to the spell of Western philosophies unfitting to Chinese reality, such as pragmatism and piecemeal changes, and the effort of transforming Chinese culture stalled. The Communist Revolution finally managed to create an equal inter-personal relationship completely alien to Confucian tradition, but suffered from the inability to articulate such equality, in part due to a key modern Japanese translation, or mistranslation rather, of the English word slave, to a term (奴隶) that in Asia referred to the kind of people who could be bought and sold: probably less than five percent of total population in the dynastic era. This mistranslation limited the idea of a slave to only a specific kind of slaves in Asian history, implying that the rest of the masses were free. It prevented Asians from seeing the true nature of the Confucian father-son and ruler-minister relationships as that of master-slave. As a result the average peasant was not considered a slave but erroneously a free man, even in dynastic times. Since most peasants had always been "free men", the newly found equality could not be defined as the absence of slavery, which left the idea philosophically indefinable and often confused with economic equality.

Equality was only understood intuitively by PLA soldiers who experienced it in the context of their military units. Mao and the CCP leadership tried to spread the idea in the only way they knew: to organize the entire country, all five hundred million growing to eight hundred million over time, into military style work units—communes, factories, schools, etc—and indoctrinate them through propaganda, with tortured Marxist lexicon. It was only partially successful and the limited success was temporary. While in the military everyone lives together which makes it impossible to have any privacy, in the civilian world workers unlike soldiers have separate homes and private lives, so do leaders of these work units. It is hard for a soldier to curry favor with his commander without being seen by others, but easy for a worker to pay a visit to the leader's home at night in secret. Military merits are highly visible and fairness of promotion practices easily gauged, there is obviously much more room for a corrupt leader to maneuver in a civilian setting. Since leaders of each work unit decided who got a subsidized flat and who did not, as well as other perks, the cultural force of subservience could easily find itself useful, making it difficult to transplant the military experience to the civilian world. Over time many communist officials became corrupt both materially and in the sense of adopting a traditional master-like posture over their employees (this domineering was called "bureaucracy", again reflecting inability of the Chinese vocabulary to articulate the nature of Confucian hierarchy).

This was the background in which Mao launched the Cultural Revolution in 1966, calling on the masses to overthrow local governments and authorities, in an effort to do away with the new class of "revisionist" cadres who simply took the place of old scholar-officials. Multiple campaigns were mounted, including "Break with Four Olds"—old ideas, old culture, old customs and old habits—to tackle Confucian culture and hierarchy, "Cut Capitalist Tails"—elimination of small amounts of private lands allowed after the failure of the Great Leap Forward as an incentive for production—aimed at total eradication of private property, and "Struggle Hard Against Private Interest/Selfishness"—clearly a neo-Confucian ideal. The desire for equality (ending a master-slave hierarchical culture), Marxist economics, and neo-Confucian ethics were all intertwined in Maoism.

In fact the poor farmers whose tails were cut off had pathetically little land and a small number of cattle, and were by no means capitalists or exploiting anyone. This extreme interpretation of Marxism came from neo-Confucian habit. Once Marxism was adopted as the official doctrine every one of its tenets became absolute truth and sacred. If private property is condemned then it is morally unacceptable. It does not matter whether one owns thousands of acres and have slaves working for him, or just a few hogs raised by himself to put meat on the table. The neo-Confucian tendency to judge everything in stark moral terms culminated in the Mao era. Even Albert Einstein's theory of relativity was condemned, because "relativity" flies in the face of absolute truth. In Chinese language the word truth—another modern word coined by Japanese—has a sense of sacredness attached to it. If anything is true it can not be relative.

As we have discussed earlier the Confucian distain for private interest is deeply rooted in the slave culture. A good slave must not have any private interest at heart, but devote his entire being to the master. This is not the same reasoning as Marx's condemnation of private property, which he thought to be an instrument of exploitation when it is concentrated in the hands of a few. But in Chinese understanding the two were taken as one and the same. Marxism in Chinese mind as the new moral ideology confirms one of the key Confucian values. In the dynastic era private interest was bad because the officials, having absolute power over their subjects, invariably exploited them for private interests. Confucianism advocates absolute power, so it has to condemn human desire (of the officials) to make something accountable for the suffering of the masses. In the Mao era private interest was bad for an additional reason, that it disrupts the collective spirit and unity, both of which are critical in maintaining that new inter-personal relation—equality—which can not be articulated in Chinese.

Protagonists of the Cultural Revolution, just like earlier mass movements, were young people, this time urban high school students. They grew up "under the red flag", in primary and secondary schools where teacher-student relationship was sometimes one step behind the revolution. Traditionally this was a master-slave relation, just like father-son. New textbooks of the communist era convey a new spirit of standing up and being one's own master. Illustrations depicted a new body language—chin up, chest out, stand tall—to replace the traditional submissive bent knees, hunched back and head hung low. Primary school students joined the Communist Children's League, and high school students joined the Communist Youth League. Membership of these organizations brought a sense of belonging and honor—you are now a successor of the brave revolutionaries. This new found pride did not sit well with most teachers (Confucius condemned pride categorically and as a quality it almost disappeared in Asia), who then used various tricks to put down their students, or put them back in their proper place, as an inferior to the teacher. Though teachers were no longer allowed to physically or verbally abuse any students, they still demanded "respect", which is a loaded Confucian term. A student could not challenge a teacher on anything, by saying "but sir, that's not how you taught us, your decision is not fair", or simply pointing out an obvious mistake. Being openly challenged by a student causes a teacher to "lose face", which in this case means upsetting the hierarchy, regardless of whether the student has a legitimate argument or not. In more traditional Confucian societies like Japan, South Korea and Taiwan, such behavior would be immediately punished verbally, physically, and administratively, under the accusation of "disrespecting a teacher". In China the teacher is equally offended by such "unruly" behavior, but he can not punish the offender if the latter happens to have a good case that stands to reason. What usually happens is the teacher remembers this insult, and seeks revenge at a later unrelated opportunity, for example by giving the trouble maker an unflattering assessment at the end of the semester, downplaying his merits and highlighting his flaws. In the end all such trouble makers get the message. There are also other ways to put down independent spirit of the entire class and show who the boss is, like giving an unannounced exam that could fail even the best students. This kind of vague and uneasy interpersonal relationship stuck half way between clearly defined Confucian hierarchy and clearly defined Western equality is quite symbolic of the entire Communist Revolution. It also adds fuel to the Chinese tradition of dishonesty—the principles they learn from school textbooks and state propaganda do not match reality. Everyone knows what is right (equality, stand up for your belief, defy authority if necessary), but everyone has to behave in a subservient manner to survive in the real world.

Suppose you are a student, a factory worker, or an office clerk, and your teacher/boss/superior makes decisions that seem unfair to you, you complain and protest, but are reprimanded, punished and threatened by your superior, there is nothing you can do to get justice. You can not move your residence or change your job/school. Even if you could you would end up with the same problem elsewhere. Communist theory is all about class struggle, and it does not say anything about how to deal with disputes between individuals of the same class, or address grievances of the average person. The Confucian tradition does not provide an independent court system, and everyone in a position of authority—a Communist official or a traditional scholar-official—naturally behaves like a master with absolute power over his subjects. You know that you are supposedly liberated by the revolution, and yet in reality, as the new generation of cadres settles in, you feel you are once again enslaved. At this moment Chairman Mao broadcasts his message, over the heads of the officialdom, directly to the masses, that it is righteous to rebel against all authorities, for they have become new masters and enemies of people. You can now openly challenge your teacher/professor/principle/local party chief, who has used his power to silence your dissent and intimidate you.

To say the youth loved Mao is an understatement. Mao was their *en* man and savior. They plunged into the Cultural Revolution wholeheartedly, ready to give all they had, and believing it was a righteous cause. Steeped in neo-Confucian moral tradition they took this to be a battle between good and evil. As a result it became much more violent than previous campaigns. Intellectuals, party officials, and all other visible authority figures, were dragged into public "struggle meetings", where they were humiliated and forced to recant their "thought crimes". Many died of mistreatment or committed suicide. Traditional Chinese would have mercy in their hearts and not be able to carry through some of the more gruesome tortures. Mao taught the new generation that they should treat comrades with "spring-like warmth", and treat enemies like an "autumn wind sweeping away falling leaves". Bifurcation of the population into good and bad was in line with Confucian tradition, with bad people now called "class enemies". Mao's revision of that tradition was to eliminate mercy (*ren*) towards enemies, and hierarchy among comrades, in other words intensifying both love for the good and hatred for the evil.

This new ideology—Maoism—further raised vehemence of moral judgment, if that is imaginable in an already fiercely moral neo-Confucian culture. When teenage Cultural Revolutionaries—the Red Guards—beat up their professors, it was with the same kind of zeal that medieval Christians burned witches and blasphemers at the stake. The same kids could shed tears for their friends and readily sacrifice for an ideal, but they had no mercy for "enemies of the people". Their cruelty in turn enraged families and friends of the victims, who might have otherwise endured persecution like victims of previous movements. Soon opposing factions emerged, each claiming loyalty to Mao and orthodox believers of Maoism. Bloody firefights broke out everywhere and small scale civil wars engulfed parts of the country. Cultural Revolution turned into terrorism and chaos.

Though Mao quickly put an end to the chaos by sending all Red Guards to the countryside to "accept reeducation by peasants", ferocity of the ideological battle hardly abated, in other words an air of terror remained. After so many political movements the core of the CCP leadership slowly arrived at a consensus in opposition to Mao's policies, as many of them were personally hurt by one campaign or another, including those who initially supported Mao's efforts. However, they could not find proper moral language to articulate their position, so they avoided ideological debates, quietly mended damages, tried to bring all sides together and the economy back. Mao called this approach represented by Deng Xiaoping "rightist restoration". Although Mao's faction was isolated in the party they continued to dominate the agenda until Mao's death in 1976, while majority of the party silently resisted. Air waves were filled with rhetoric of class struggle, people were constantly aroused to find a hidden enemy nearby, and every now and then a poor fellow was selected in each community and "struggled". Mao's words became so sacred that when he said, casually, that 95% of Chinese were good people, every work unit designated exactly 5% of their headcount as class enemies.

Without Cultural Revolution the society would have slid back into traditional Confucian mode, negating the purpose of Communist Revolution and alienating the masses who enthusiastically supported it. With Cultural Revolution all internal conflicts that might have been reconcilable in a peaceful manner were magnified, shattering social harmony. As the severity of moral judgment increased towards the 1970s, it also created an intense atmosphere, where everyone was afraid to comment on state affairs, for fearing of being labeled an anti-revolutionary, in contrast to the beginning of the Cultural Revolution, when people tripped over themselves to broadcast their messages publicly, as they posted their articles on bulletin boards, one over another, several layers thick, trying not to be buried in a sea of debates. In the end, as the Red Guards were dispersed and various revolutionary bodies dissembled, the totalitarian nature of the Confucian culture came back in a fresh reincarnation: Mao's own dictatorship.

Since early 1960's he started labeling his top comrades as rightists, revisionists, capitalists and anti-revolutionists, in short, enemies of the people. By 1970's almost all of the dozen or so top leaders were denigrated, demoted, incarcerated, tortured or killed, leaving no one in a position to possibly challenge him ever again. He was openly hailed as the *en* man of all Chinese, as in "Chairman Mao's *en* is deeper than the sea". Even the term most symbolic of pious loyalty, *banzai* (万岁, ten thousand years), traditionally reserved exclusively for the emperor, was applied to him, as in "ten thousand years to Chairman Mao". In the Cultural Revolution Mao's own political interest in purging the top ranks and denigrating intellectuals converged with the popular desire to do away with social hierarchy, and the entire official class was replaced by new activists, who arose from the bottom. The pyramid structure was smashed, leaving nothing between Mao and the masses, who were grateful for an unprecedented divine ruler, and Mao harvested their thanksgiving.

With neo-Confucian language (*en*, pious loyalty) fully used to his advantage, Mao's revolution against Confucian tradition was only half hearted. To his credit the CCP under Mao's leadership openly criticized Confucius, and identified Confucianism as an attempt to restore slavery, while in other parts of Asia Confucius is almost sacred and untouchable. But the way CCP criticized Confucius itself followed Confucian tradition: it was a broad stroke condemnation and character assassination rather than an objective analysis. Confucius was depicted as a representative of the reactionary ruling class of an "ancient slavery" society, borrowing Marxist terminology, locked in a class struggle against the more progressive landlord class of the emerging "feudal" society. Shao Zheng Mao, Confucius' rival in the private education business, who was later executed by Confucius as soon as convenient, was portrayed as a representative of the landlord class. So Confucius' crime in killing his intellectual rival, or in modern parlance a political dissident, was not because he violated freedom of speech, but because he belonged to the more reactionary class. It was the bad guy killing the good guy, the reverse would have been right. Similarly, Confucius' objection to the publication of a penal code was interpreted as that the content of the penal code was too progressive to his taste, rather than he was against transparency or the idea that a written document can have more authority than the ruler. The logic was that the working class—the ruled—could do no wrong, while the ruling class could do no right. Moral judgment rests with one's class origin, not one's conduct. As a neo-Confucian interpretation of Marxism, Maoism turns Marxist class economics into a new set of moral principles. But people are still clearly divided as good and bad, and bad people (class enemies) are treated even worse than before, now that *ren* (mercy) no longer applies to them. Moral judgment still trumps any legal code.

Like previous political movements (e.g. "let a hundred flowers bloom") the Cultural Revolution started with free and open debates on issues of social justice, and ended up in tyranny. On important matters like ideology, Confucian tradition requires an absolute truth to be established. Once that is done by the highest authority, all other views are deemed heresy and condemned, together with their proponents. Thus the debate can not be carried on in a rational and scholarly fashion, for losing it entails grave consequences. Most people would not dare participate in such quarrel. For those who do, defending your belief with your life is not a choice: you live or die with your professed belief. The other factor that makes cool headed discussion impossible is that core cultural values imbedded in the language are at odds with the objective of liberation. Suppose your boss promotes only his cronies, no matter how incompetent they are, or your teacher favors the few students who like to go to his office and report on everyone else, essentially functioning as his secret agents, and you are enraged by these practices. You want to make accusations, or at least complain publicly. But there is a Confucian value that says you must "respect" you superior. Respect in the Confucian sense means obedience, and offending a superior in any way is automatically a sin. The only way you can address the injustice without breaking Confucian tradition or sounding immoral is to raise the issue to a moral level, condemn the superior, and permanently depose him, in other words removing him from the superior position. Ferocity of Cultural Revolution was precipitated by the culture itself.

By expressing the effort of overturning Confucian master-slave hierarchy as a Marxist proletariat revolution against the ruling class, Maoism fails to define an alternative inter-personal relationship on an individual level. A high ranking comrade can no longer physically or verbally abuse a low ranking comrade, but what is the nature of their relationship? A commander must have authority to get anything done, but what is authority in absence of slavery? Marxism does not address these questions, nor does Maoism. That is why mass political movements had to be organized by Mao every few years. Once things settle down, and officials become ensconced in their positions, traditional cultural force will make them masters. It was a sad reality but no one could help it.

Conspicuously missing from the official list of Confucius' crimes were pious loyalty and filial piety. State propaganda say Confucius was trying to restore slavery but fail to mention these core slavish values at the heart of Confucianism. There may have been two considerations behind this glaring omission. Mao wanted loyalty of his people, and there is no Chinese word for loyalty other than pious loyalty (忠), with the *en* logic and corresponding psyche built in its connotations. Similarly, there is no other appropriate word for a man's legitimate love to his parents save filial piety (孝). To say that one has no filial piety to his parents automatically means he does not love them or care about them. Therefore openly condemning filial piety would encounter resistance from the masses. Whatever the reason failing to address these two words in an open and candid manner doomed Maoism intellectually, rendering it incoherent. Just as the Nationalists failed with their democratic attempt, Mao failed with the Marxist attempt, because neither of these Western philosophies addresses the Eastern problem of slavery as a core cultural value.

Maoism tries to abolish the pyramid social structure for good. It enjoys great support from those traditionally at the bottom of the pyramid—peasants and uneducated urban workers—and is generally hated by those traditionally at the upper half of the pyramid—the educated scholar-official class. However, it fails to discover the real source of that pyramid culture and what sustains it. Instead it erroneously interprets the struggle of Chinese peasantry to get free as a communist proletariat revolution. The upper half of the pyramid—the scholar-official class—is depicted as the landlord/capitalist class. Class struggle is seen as a moral combat between good and evil. When after all landlords and capitalists have been eliminated by the revolution the pyramid structure reemerges with communist cadres sitting atop, these officials are called neo-capitalists (走资派). Masses are mobilized in political movements to overthrow them over and again, once every few years. Failing to realize that the culture gravitates towards a pyramid structure by its own momentum, Maoism pinpoints self interest as the root cause of revolutionary officers degenerating into oppressors. Neo-Confucian ethics banning self interest altogether is vehemently enforced, further undermining honesty. As persecution and power struggles done in the name of the revolution become frequent and ruthless, long standing Chinese traditions of mercy and respect for privacy are seriously damaged. Politeness and moderation are gone, as well as social manners. All this sacrifice is only able to earn temporary flattening of the pyramid structure.

CHAPTER 18

A CAPITALIST DEMOCRACY?

Unlike the German war, the Japanese war did not have anything to do with race, nor was it a popular movement. There was no such thing as National Socialism (NAZI) in Japan. Japanese expansion into the continent started in 1895, when they defeated the Chinese fleet. The pacific war of 1941-1945 was just a late stage in the natural development of that long expansion, a stage that happened to coincide with the European war. In the decades long process imperial Japanese army officers in Manchuria often acted on their own initiative to provoke and conquer, when their superiors were quarrelling in parliament over foreign policy. This was not a case of field officers taking liberty in tactical moves within the scope of a larger predefined mission. What drove these officers and soldiers was the *en* that they felt they owed to the emperor, and the desire to repay it, which served as the highest principle. More land added to the emperor's possession would surely please the throne, and enhance the position of the army within the government. Japanese emperors since Meiji had cleverly stayed low key, leaving important decisions to the ministers. This predictably resulted in fierce infighting among different factions, each trying to outdo the other in its contribution to the throne, much like in the old days samurai competed for their lord's favor on who was more loyal, "I have a better plan and can do a better job than the next guy, if not I'll commit suicide". It was under such a mentality that the army, the navy and industrial leaders sought expansion on the continent and pacific islands, often in absence of a preconceived plan agreed upon by the government as a whole. Had it not been stopped by a foreign power this expansion would have continued forever, in ever increasing pace, because there is no logical end in repaying *en* or fulfilling pious loyalty.

In the American occupation that followed the war, general McArthur made the wise decision of keeping the entire administrative apparatus, saving Japan from potential chaos. Had they adopted a de-NAZI-fication program like they did in Germany, Japan would have ended up like post Baathist Iraq. A pyramid society needs a hierarchy to stabilize. Demolishing the structure without quickly replacing it with a similar one leads to an unstable situation. It is not a power vacuum that can be filled by elected politicians, because, in short, a pyramid culture only works by coercion, not by persuasion. If the elected politicians have brute force (military, mafia/militia, religious organizations) under their command, they can assume positions high in the pyramid, in which case the elections are just a rubber stamp on their de facto station, otherwise they would have little power regardless of what office they are elected to.

The American command also kept the Japanese emperor as a symbol of the nation, while depriving his powers, accentuating the point that he is human, not divine. Western understanding of breaking up dictatorship regimes centers on separation of secular and religious powers, but this has little relevance in Confucian states. Here emperor worship (pious loyalty) is conceptually and psychologically the same as filial piety. Everyone knows their parents are real people, not superhuman gods, yet they worship their parents anyway, because they have no choice. It is Stockholm Syndrome. The emperor can walk around the streets, shake hands with the plebian, and show them he is only five feet tall with glasses on. None of that matters. If the state requires everyone to worship him, everyone will. Worship in the context of filial piety and pious loyalty is not a choice made by free individuals, it is an ethical code forced on them since childhood. As we have shown in Boxer Syndrome, the ruler can deliberately appear weak and vulnerable, and it would incite intense devotion. Being divine in the Confucian sense does not mean omnipotence, omniscience or omnipresence; it is entirely secular, it means ownership of the worshiper.

Events surrounding the Yakusuni Shrine clearly demonstrate Western incomprehension of Confucian culture. All Japanese military servicemen who died in the war were enshrined as gods. Prewar propaganda films showed Japanese soldiers swearing not to come back alive when assigned to the front. American administrators knew that the shrine was an important instrument in the Japanese war machine, and they intended to demolish it. But they could not do it because religious freedom had to be protected. In the end they only barred the Japanese government from funding or directly controlling the shrine, in line with separation of church and state.

What is worshiped in the Yakusuni Shrine is the idea of pious loyalty (忠) exemplified by loyal servants who died for their master. The master can be a warlord of old, an emperor, or the state. That is not important. How the shrine is funded is also irrelevant. The key is whether or not pious loyalty as the ultimate Japanese principle is condoned by American authority. By leaving that shrine standing and allowing Japanese to worship there, the American administration essentially answered that question in the affirmative. Americans failed to understand that after being through Confucian training in the family and in schools, Asians can no longer be free, with or without political elections. There is no such thing as religious freedom in Asia. People who suffer from Stockholm Syndrome can not choose what they believe. They may join any church, but the dominating belief in Asia is Confucianism, and it is not a religion in the Western sense of the word. Pious loyalty and filial piety imply coercion. The shrine as a symbol of pious loyalty signals to Japanese that they must remain obedient and devoted to state authorities, in other words their core cultural values are intact.

One of the consequences is the dispute today between Japan on the one side, China and Korea on the other, surrounding the issue of fourteen Class A war criminals being enshrined, and the fact that Japanese political leaders keep paying tribute there. On the Chinese side there are two kinds of different complaints. Those with historical knowledge can not forgive the atrocities committed by Japanese soldiers on harmless civilians. The Chinese governments (both the Nationalist party in Taiwan and the Communist party on the mainland), on the other hand, object to the invasion itself. They want to obscure the fact that most Chinese at the time did not mind the invasion as much as the inhumanity of some Japanese soldiers, trying to frame it as a nationalistic issue rather than a humanitarian issue. The governments of course dominate the agenda and their message is the one conveyed to Japan.

If invasion is the main charge, Japanese can rightfully claim innocence, as most of them do. Invasion of foreign countries if ordered by the state is not against Confucianism. The average Japanese soldier simply followed orders in observance of pious loyalty. Whether the order was to invade China or commit suicide was not their choice. Unless pious loyalty as a virtue is overturned, they did nothing wrong. On the contrary, had they disobeyed, they would have committed the ultimate crime in Confucian terms. The fourteen Class A criminals did not have their own agenda, they were serving the emperor just like everyone else, only that they happened to be in important positions. Some initiatives were indeed taken by them, but they did it in the interest of the crown. Should Japanese in the future stop serving their state? Should they shun positions of responsibility? As long as pious loyalty remains a virtue, Japanese will see those war criminals as heroes. One officer who was not convicted at the trial and lived to his natural death regretted not being convicted, because otherwise he would have been a god. It is impossible for Japanese to perceive any guilt in this matter, and the dispute turns into a psychological game of which country ranks higher than the other.

From the Confucian perspective Japanese are consistent, Chinese and Koreans are not, if we leave aside the issue of inhumanity against innocent civilians. Had Japan succeeded in permanently annexing China, Japanese ruling would have been accepted by Chinese, just like Mongols and Manchurians of the past. Confucianism does not discriminate against any race, whoever manages to rule with stability gains Heaven's Mandate. Japanese are vilified only because they failed (成王败寇). Pious loyalty is extolled in China and Korea as well, where the masses are indoctrinated to blindly follow orders and serve the state. China threatens to invade Taiwan. If that war occurs, and China fails, Chinese will find themselves in the same situation.

After the war American legal experts drafted a new constitution for Japan, supposedly securing human rights for all Japanese. Having foreigners write your constitution is itself absurd. A constitution written by Americans in English can not possibly be accurately translated into a Confucian language, Chinese or Japanese. Philosophically, the Western idea of human rights is irreconcilable with Confucianism, which defines human being as a servant, a slave. One is born with a debt of life to his parents and to his ruler/state, which he must try to repay with a lifetime of absolute obedience and devotion. The American written Japanese Constitution prohibits involuntary servitude, but Confucianism demands it. How do Japanese square the conflict?

The answer is they don't. To a people who have always been slaves for their entire history a constitution is utterly meaningless. The only kind of law they can understand is concrete rules that tell them what they can and can not do. The Meiji Constitution allowed Japanese far more social mobility than before by abolishing hereditary ranks, hence it was enthusiastically embraced by vast majority of the population as a breakthrough of individual freedom. The postwar constitution did not have nearly as great an impact on the Japanese mind. Aside from a few labor activists, who were deemed lefties and quickly put down by the regime with American acquiescence in an emerging cold war against communism, Japanese by and large lived in fear and trepidation, eager to obey commands from all authorities. They felt lucky just to survive. In its history of warfare members of the losing side either die or become slaves of the winning side. In fact right before the end of the war the emperor proclaimed that all one hundred million Japanese were prepared to die (一亿玉碎). Far from it for them to be in any mood to demand rights, something alien to them in the first place.

In 1952 official American occupation ended with signing of the San Francisco Treaty, some chaotic political jostling ensued in Japan, and in 1955 national election was won by a coalition of conservative parties merged into one—the Liberal Democratic Party—and it has essentially ruled Japan ever since. For one party to win election after election five decades in a row (with only one short lived interruption) would be an anomaly, even an impossibility in the West, but upon a closer examination of the Japanese system, one would be surprised if it did not turn out that way.

Core cultural values remained the same after the war—filial piety and pious loyalty. For the average Japanese worker his employer is his parent, a higher ranking parent than his biological ones. The company functions like a Confucian parent, caring and controlling. High school and college graduates basically have a one time career choice for their entire lives. Once they select a company to join, they are essentially pledging loyalty to a parent, an *en* man, a master. Quitting a job or jumping ship is considered disloyal, a cardinal sin frowned upon by the society at large. Other reputable companies would not take a disloyal person regardless of how competent he is at his profession. To tighten up loose ends, housing is deliberately made out of reach for a young worker without help from his employer, which typically pays the down payment and guarantees the loan after some ten years of service in the firm and "good behavior".

Parent-son relationship is not just recognition of hierarchy; there is a strong emotional undertone. To develop that tie, companies draw on the same traditional methodology, time tested from samurai training to modern education, adapted to the corporate setting. For the first few years the novice is assigned menial chores, regardless of his education background or experience. Shuffling papers, running errands, cleaning toilets, he is an assistant, a secretary, a personal aid, a housemaid, and a janitor all in one, to his direct superior, who is a more concrete parent figure than the company. The novice is frequently scolded or beaten, and must learn to take these abuses as a norm, if he hasn't learned that in school. Most boys after high school are docile characters by virtue of earlier training, but the more relaxed college environment tends to bring out the long suppressed carefree side of some, maybe even rekindle a little defiance, having not been slapped in the face in four years. Girls in companies are destined to not last long, as their job is to find a mate and retire to be full time moms.

A superior carefully watches facial expressions and body language from each of his apprentices, paying special attention to those who show the slightest sign of resentment. Some horses are harder to break in than others. That is normal. But in the end a good trainer will break everyone of them. When fear dominates their mind and absolute obedience is secured, it is time to give emotional pulls, to show the caring side of a parent. "You are promoted, young man, and I'm so proud of your achievements." The first few years of training has little to do with technical knowledge needed for the business operations of the firm, but everything to do with making sure that every employee is a loyal servant ready to give himself up for the company, a soldier qualified in his mental state and devotion, as modern workers are treated as "corporate soldiers" modeled after the samurai, and more recently imperial troops.

From the perspective of an objective observer, this is involuntary servitude. Through the eyes of the employee, however, the company is a benevolent parent who is so kind to get him a home, not to mention a secure job for life; that is an *en* he can never repay. Such feelings grow as the employee climbs the corporate ladder, which is largely based on seniority, for lack of a better choice. In ancient times performance could be easily measured by counting dead enemy soldiers, but in a modern setting, particularly in a corporation, individual performance is hard to gauge. It often involves subjective personal judgments on the part of a supervisor, which in Confucian culture will not come even close to being fair, for the same reason a parent finds it hard to objectively evaluate the abilities of his children—he usually favors the one who is emotionally closest and most dependent on him, the most fawning of them all. Promotion by seniority can lead to declining performance, as is the case in the state run sector of China, but the merciless nature of the Japanese tradition preempted that problem. In a more lenient culture like China, seniority means that as long as one does not make any major mistake, he can walk up the ladder with or without real credit. In a harsh culture like Japan, one has to function like a samurai just to stay alive. In other words the baseline requirement is very high for every individual, making it impossible for the whole enterprise to fail due to lack of effort.

Of course that does not mean individuals with exceptional contributions are not promoted beyond their age. The person who invented color TV obviously leapfrogged many of his seniors. But by and large a Japanese employee would say he belongs to the college graduation class of which year, and based on that you could guess his rank, regardless of which company he works for, with ninety percent accuracy.

Corporations so structured to provide a family like atmosphere and transparent rules offer a sense of security that is otherwise sorely missed by Asians, demanded by their core cultural values of lifetime responsibilities to serve, but without any rights whatsoever. To Japanese the system is fair. Not fair in the Western sense because they are subjected to involuntary servitude, but fair in the sense that everyone is subjected to the same treatment. After getting used to it, they do not even realize it is involuntary, or servitude, just like in the family, abuses by the father are first resented and feared, then after the Stockholm Syndrome sets in, they become acts of benevolence and love. He beats you because he loves you—this is widely accepted by Asians.

If the major corporations conspire to trap their employees in lifelong involuntary servitude, is there any other opportunity for the Japanese individual to escape it? Suppose I am a diehard independent whose spirit somehow miraculously survived school and family training (my parents may have been absent all my life and my teachers incredibly incompetent). I can not stomach what a lifetime job with a big business would require of me, I want to open a restaurant, be a small business owner, and I am lucky enough to have inherited enough money to do just that. Now all I need is to learn some culinary skills. Finding a willing mentor is not easy but fortunately for me, my father used to know such a person, to whom I go for an internship. The first thing the master would try to establish, just as any teacher/employer/supervisor would do, is the Confucian parent-son relationship between us. He makes me do all the chores around the clock, push me beyond what my body can physically take, scold and beat me up at every turn, humiliate me with every possible phrase he can muster, in short, put me down and let me know that I am completely at his mercy, which he has none. I hate his guts. But I can not quit now if I want to keep my dream alive. So I swallow every abuse, turn my anger into energy, and release every bit of it in kitchen work. I practice every little skill until my arms are numb and then five hundred times more. I work myself to such an extent that when I come home every night I fall immediately to sleep. Then every morning, at the order of my master, I shout at the top of my lung to redouble my efforts today, swearing to overcome whatever difficulty that lies ahead.

After a period of such torturous training I exhibit noticeable difference. Upon hearing a command I shout "hai!" (Yes sir!) and quickly spring into action, spirited and energetic. When cursed or slapped in the face I shout "hai!" in acknowledgement of wrong doing and gratitude for the teaching.

I no longer even think about humiliation or my dignity, I am selflessly devoted to the learning process. Seeing that I am mentally ready, my master finally teaches me how to make the best dishes he is known for. He could have taught me that on the first day, but there are two reasons he did not. First, as every competent Japanese teacher/master would explain, is that one needs the right mentality when approaching a career or anything else of importance. Running a good restaurant is not just about secret recipes and culinary skills. I have to treat it like a battle the way samurai did. I have to clean my mind of everything that has motivated me so far, such as to live independently or to get rich, focus on the job at hand, to the extent that there is nothing else on my mind beyond cooking and serving, and go at it with reckless abandon, regardless of pain, injury or death. If there is even a tiny bit of dust on the floor after I cleaned it, it means my attitude is not right, I am not taking it seriously, and I am not "sincere" enough. If the color of my soup today is slightly different from yesterday, it means I am not there yet, even if customers can not tell a difference. Perfection is not an aspiration; it is a requirement short of which I am sure to be judged a failure. The second reason, never stated but almost always present in the mind of a teacher/master, is that without abuse I would not appreciate the *en* bestowed on me by him—without a hard push the pull loses much of its intended effect. When I finally make a dish that gains his approval "you have passed", after all that ordeal, my feelings have completely changed. I am no longer angry at him. I now look at the restaurant business, or even my life, with a new perspective. I have acquired the ability to concentrate on anything I set my mind to, and in that concentration itself I find the meaning of life. I could be cutting carrots, mopping floors, or should I change career, doing anything else, and in that moment my mind is in such a state of emptiness that I feel liberated from all concerns of this world. I started off with some "selfish" motivation, such as to avoid lifetime servitude, but ended up indifferent to the original objective. Now I can work anywhere on any job. Of course in the back of my mind I know I have been forced into this new mentality, but that humiliation is too painful for me to revisit. I know resistance is futile, so I might as well adopt this new outlook and tell myself it is voluntary. For all practical purposes I am a changed man, more suited to survive in this society. My teacher/master is in a real sense my *en* man. I look back at this experience and all sorts of feelings well up in my mind. I am moved by my capacity to endure and survive desperation, and grateful for the new stronger me that is ready for any challenge/humiliation. My teacher/master asks me to never forget how I feel at this very moment.

Japanese are not particularly good at articulating feelings, but most everyone has experienced such trainings and understands the power of that feeling, a mixture of self pity, gratitude, devotion and accomplishment. It is an indispensable cog in the Japanese machine. In virtually every profession the trainee has to go through a similar process, after which he becomes a reliable and dedicated soldier. Working on automobile and electronics production lines, the soldier's single minded attention to detail is not a forced effort on a daily basis. No one can force himself ten hours a day for thirty years, not even the Japanese. It is a trained habit, a state of mind that they can get in and out of at will. To say Japanese live the spirit of Zen is not overstating the case. That state of mind is forced through a process of harsh training within the context of Confucian hierarchy. The whole procedure is fully controlled and the end product is fully exploited by that hierarchy.

With such ubiquitous Confucian trainings, individuals are guaranteed to function like standardized nuts and bolts in a machine. For the whole country to operate smoothly like a well oiled engine, corporations can not be independent from each other or from the state. The idea of the corporation mirrors that of the individual. In the West the individual is a legally free and independent entity, so is the corporation. The individual's private property is protected by law, so is that of the corporation. In a Confucian state the individual is a servant to the state, so is the corporation. There is a hierarchy between individuals, so there is one between corporations. Ownership of property is not a right but a privilege granted by the state conditionally. As a servant to the state a business' fortunes depend on its relationship with the government, which defines its position in the hierarchy.

Large businesses are organs of the state, high ranking members in the business hierarchy. Their operations, then, do not follow the laws of free market, the "invisible hand". For example, in its early days Toyota as a private business was financially bankrupt. The government decided that Japan needed its own automobile industry, so it settled all of Toyota's debt and gave it favorable loans, practically grants. This established a relationship where the government is the *en* man to Toyota, which means in the cultural sense, in everyone's mind, the state owns Toyota, regardless of who on paper owns what percentage of it. Appointments of board members and top executives, as well as major decisions concerning the company, are all prerogatives of the government, even though on paper it is not a state-owned business. Other large businesses follow the same pattern. In the end all major corporations and banks own each other, forming an entangled web of mutual dependence, and they are all directed and controlled by the state.

Over time the line between major corporations and the government becomes blurred. Suppose I am a government bureaucrat. I have worked in the Transportation Ministry for decades, since graduating from university. My job is to help all Japanese auto makers compete against foreign rivals. To that end I have to coordinate their research efforts and regulate domestic competition, so that they function as members of a team rather than enemies. Maybe one of them is not doing well and needs financial assistance. I must investigate the situation and determine the cause. None of them is allowed to go bankrupt, but incompetent management must be weeded out of the system. Since I hold their purse strings and have considerable influence recommending top personnel changes, I am obviously a superior figure to these companies. Meanwhile, within the Transportation Ministry, I have established an *en* man status to my protégé and other younger subordinates. When I retire from the administrative branch of the government, I can either run in elections and become a party politician, or "descend from heaven" and land a cushy job in one of these auto makers, or do both, in that order. Now as a corporate executive or board member but also a senior to the new generation of Transportation Ministry bureaucrats who owe me *en* for their career, I can order the government to do what is good for my corporation. The relative ranking between government and big business is no longer one sided; it depends on where the senior person is.

Politicians follow the same inter-personal relation pattern that has remained essentially the same since lord-samurai days. Members of a party all owe pious loyalty to the party or faction leader, who is their master. Sometimes several factions within a party manage to fight to a standstill, in which case there are several masters. In either case any member of a party can scarcely afford to be independent of all masters. He must pledge pious loyalty to one of them. These masters decide who gets on the ballot in the next election.

A Japanese political party is not primarily about a political philosophy. The Liberal Democratic Party is neither liberal nor democratic. It has no constitution or any broad objectives/philosophy agreed upon by all its members, other than Confucianism of course, which is shared by all parties. It is essentially an interest group organized in a Confucian family structure, just like any other organization in Japan. Once it obtained power in 1955 it began to function like a parent throughout the Japanese society, and it is extremely difficult to vote your parent out of office.

There is a major difference in mentality between a Japanese voter and a Western voter. Let's say residents in a small Western town want to build a dam. As long as they are willing to pay for it they can go ahead and do it. The local mayor may help in legal and administrative issues, but residents would not feel that they owe him a huge favor—that's his job, if he does not do his job why is he paid? Latent in this logic is the assumption that doing something to help themselves is well within citizens' rights. Japanese on the other hand do not have any rights. Here is the relevant article from the current Constitution: (Article 13) Their right to life, liberty, and the pursuit of happiness shall, to the extent that it does not interfere with public welfare, be the supreme consideration in legislation and in other governmental affairs.

This is essentially the same as the Meiji Constitution, where citizens are said to have all kinds of rights, subject to "law", except that "law" is now replaced by "public welfare". Of course the government decides what "law" or "public welfare" entails, which means a right is not a right to Japanese, but a privilege conditionally granted by the government. Reflected in the mindset, the individual is always afraid to do anything that is not specifically permitted by the government, for fear of violating "public welfare". If you do not know whether something is permitted, usually it is not, since everything is regulated in Japan. A college student wants to find a place to study at night. He steps into an empty classroom, sits down and reads his books. By common sense he did nothing wrong? Incorrect. He must first obtain permission to use the classroom from school authorities.

If Japanese residents want to build a dam, they need permission from authorities, and that's where the mayor comes in. It is now 1955, and the town voted for LDP, which won national election. The mayor, an LDP member, obtains permission from the national government, controlled by his party. The project is completed successfully. Now local residents owe him an *en*, because without him, they would not have been able to do anything. A trivial matter from the Western perspective brings about a parent-child bond between the mayor (the parent official) and citizens (children subjects). As that bond strengthens over numerous such projects big and small, pious loyalty/filial piety from citizens to the mayor is expected and secured. Come next election it is unimaginable for local residents to vote for another candidate—betraying your parent is the most serious crime in Confucian ethics.

In any election the voter is not objectively examining two candidates. He has an emotional bond with the incumbent, even if the latter did not do a good job at all. A parent can abuse his children, but loyalty due to him is unconditional. Once that bond is established it is almost impossible to break. When the incumbent retires his son can sometimes take his place and assume the same loyalty. For the voter to cast his vote for a new guy, from a new party, he must first overcome the guilt of betraying a father figure, even if he has all the reasons in the world to do so. This is, in a nut shell, why the LDP once in power kept getting elected over and over again.

Politicians, bureaucrats and big business develop close personal relationship and loyalty along the same *en* based logic. Suppose I am elected to the diet, after my long career as a bureaucrat in the Transportation Ministry, whose new leaders are my protégés and former subordinates. I then naturally become a member of the transportation committee in congress, legislating for the auto industry. The new leadership in the administrative branch are loyal to me, and as their parent figure I would take care of their interest and be their advocate in congress. The auto industry trusts me because of personal loyalty, and I make sure they tell their employees to continue to vote for my party, the LDP. Over time all the key bureaucrats in major industries and government agencies become LDP members or at least have personal ties to the party.

Unchallenged power inevitably corrupts. After 38 years in power, the LDP suffered its only defeat in national elections in 1993, following a corruption scandal of immense proportions. But the opposition party that won the election found it impossible to successfully run the administrative branch. They had never been in power. They had no personal ties with anyone in the Japanese machine. All key personnel in the bureaucracy and big corporations were loyal to the LDP and many of them refused to cooperate with the new ruling party. After a short failed stint the perpetual opposition returned power back to the LDP, and it has remained there ever since.

Regardless of what the constitution says, power in Japan rests with these three branches: big business, government bureaucracy and politicians. All three are controlled by the LDP, tied internally through personal *en* based relations, as members of the elite frequently travel the bureaucrat to politician to corporate board member lifecycle. Underneath them the entire country is trained to obey orders and devote themselves to the state in every profession, selflessly and unconditionally. There is social mobility, as the elite are selected from university graduates, regardless of birth, though sons born into elite families get the first chance.

Since the time of the samurai Japanese have always been under close and strict control, though head cutting has been replaced by numerous rules, both written and unwritten, and all kinds of punishment of varying degrees. Each rule or punishment is less severe than those of the old times, but the collective effect of all the rules and punishment is no less suffocating, leaving no escape routes. Japanese mentality has not changed at all in the hundreds of years that saw various different forms of government come and go. Except for trivial matters Japanese do not make choices of action based on moral conviction or personal preference, they do not see themselves as independent entities free to make their own choice, instead they try to recall all the rules applicable in a given situation and look for a course of action that would not violate any. Fear, forced habits and collective liability syndrome still dominate their behavior patterns. Choice is limited to things like the taste of food.

In 2004 three young journalists/aid workers went into Iraq, ignoring government warning that it was a dangerous place, and were subsequently kidnapped by some insurgents, who demanded Japanese troops to withdraw from Iraq. The Japanese government privately negotiated for their successful release, allegedly paying a ten million dollar ransom. Upon returning home the three walked into a nation of hostility. A cabinet member called them "reckless", another law maker labeled them "anti-Japanese". The prime minister criticized them for bringing trouble to Japan, and the government billed them for some of the expenses incurred during their release. The whole nation unleashed its revulsion at these three, in newspapers, TV shows, and internet discussion forums. Some openly called for their heads. They were trapped in their homes, not daring to venture out. No Japanese was happy that three of their fellow citizens (including an 18 year old kid) were finally home and safe after a nine day ordeal in the hands of terrorists; most wish they had been killed in Iraq. It was the same hatred Japanese have always had on anyone who disobeys rules or causes trouble for the collective, a common sense in Japan, and a clear demonstration of collective liability syndrome.

One of the unwritten rules says that superiors can physically abuse inferiors, such as slapping their faces. This is evident in businesses, government, schools, homes, everywhere in Japan. The Japanese mind would take all rules like this as a given without ever questioning. No one, no elected politicians, Western educated legal experts, professors, constitutional lawyers, would ever think of it as a human rights violation.

Recently there was a major accident in the subway system, where dozens of passengers were killed. The company that operates those trains requires drivers to perform with robot like precision. Every train must be on time at every station, with a margin of no more than a few seconds, and stop exactly where it's marked, with a margin of no more than a few feet. Underperformers are subject to retraining sessions, a process similar to those outlined in this and previous chapters. One driver was so scared of such programs, that he desperately wanted to make up for the minutes he lost adjusting his train back and forth in the previous station trying to park it precisely where it was supposed to, and in so doing far exceeded speed limits, resulting in the disaster. In newspapers and other media outlets Japanese commentators did not criticize the training program, but condemned the profit seeking of the company. By this logic a company that seeks profit inevitably pushes its employees to extremes. Private interest remains the root of all evils in the Japanese mind.

To call this system a capitalist democracy would stretch both words far beyond what they mean in the West, unless we redefine capitalism as commercialism, and democracy as merely voting. Japan could abolish all elections, and declare that all private properties ultimately belong to the state, and the country would function exactly the same way, without missing a beat. The same can not be said about any Western democracy. Japanese still see this world in stark hierarchical terms, and still believe that inferiors must obey superiors unconditionally. Just like four hundred years ago, they still view the world as an amoral battlefield between the strong and the weak, and government as an amoral interest group, not fundamentally different from the mafia, which is why the nationwide mafia organization—a political/business/crime entity—is perfectly legal in Japan, boasting more than one hundred thousand members, with its head democratically elected.

Chapter 19

A NEW ERA

With Mao's passing in 1976 and particularly Deng's ascension to power in 1978, the Cultural Revolution was officially over, along with persecution done in the name of ideological struggles. Sooner or later top leaders were going to realize the Maoist approach does not work. Having to conduct mass political movements once every few years is just not sustainable. For one thing, no one had any incentive to work. Profit seeking was banned not only as an action but also as a thought. Everyone had to profess total selflessness. Lying was mandatory to survive, and it became a habit even more so than the old tradition warranted. "Language crimes", a relic of the dynastic era, made a full come back. One could be jailed for misspeaking in public or misspelling in any form of publication. Standard of living dropped to new lows. The whole country was constantly teetering on the edge of starvation. To prop up its image the regime filled newspaper pages with grossly exaggerated production numbers. But privately they knew they faced a bleak picture. Something had to change.

Yet it was dangerous to try to overturn Maoism as the ruling ideology, for that would have split party ranks and plunged the CCP into domestic strife. Deng had no choice but to shelve all ideological debates and concentrate on the economy. He started with dismantling the commune and allowing some profit seeking in agriculture. Within just a few years national food production rose dramatically, so did living standards in the countryside. Nationwide starvation was no longer an imminent threat. Moreover, a few "window cities" were granted tax exempt status to attract foreign investment, mainly from Hong Kong and the overseas Chinese community. Under the broad objective of modernization, likened to crossing a river, Deng was trying to find a way by "groping the stones (at the bottom of the river)", in his own words.

Initial reaction to the new approach was overwhelmingly favorable. People of all walks of life felt suddenly loosened up. No more political movements meant people no longer had to confess their sins and impure thoughts to the party regularly. Some started saying things they did not dare say, such as complaining about miseries of the Red Guards generation, who followed Mao's orders enthusiastically, only to be forced to spend their youthful lives in the countryside. Others started doing things that would have landed them in labor camps just a few years before, such as opening a small restaurant, a private business. There was a general relief that the era of fierce inter-personal struggles was gone. They no longer had to look over their shoulders or fear that one of their friends or relatives would report to the party what they said in private. To most Chinese it was like being liberated once again. Deng was hailed as the "chief designer" of a new modern China and enjoyed tremendous popularity in the early 1980s.

Behind the short term apparent success was a time bomb. Deng's silence on the issue of principle presumed a continuation of Maoist beliefs, if not Maoist practices. His pragmatic approach of shelving all moral/ideological discussions and concentrating on the material side of things came at a time when equality as the highest value had staying power in Chinese minds and Confucian social hierarchy was largely destroyed by decades of political movements. The communist belief was still intact. People were generally moral and responsible. Crime rate was extremely low. Corruption was rare. However, the new economic policy by allowing profit seeking was morally/ideologically subversive to the widely held communist ideals. CCP propaganda written in textbooks contradicted new government policy. In Deng's words the state should "allow a portion of the population to get rich first", implying that eventually every Chinese will get equally rich. But this half a sentence is a rather haphazard and irresponsible way to statecraft. Which portion should get rich first? Who picks the winner? By what rules? How to ensure fairness? The entire country was groping stones. But Chinese civilization had always needed a state ideology that defined right from wrong. Although at the end of the Mao era the country was tired of ideological struggles and eager for a time out, in the long run it could not be held together without a principle. Deng's approach amounted to a delay of inevitable reckoning.

Top ranking officials let themselves get rich first. In this new half baked economic system, where factories were still owned by the government and run by despotic party officials, but market mechanism was introduced, there was a total disconnection between management and responsibility.

In the Mao era everything was planned and controlled from the top. Now factory chiefs had more leeway in pricing their products, but they were not required to make a profit, since part of their production was still sold on fixed price to other state owned sectors. Coexistence of two pricing systems—planned economy and market economy—generated easy opportunity for corruption, and many cadres made the most of it. To them the end of political movements meant finally it was time for the ruling elite to get its loot, just like in the dynastic era. This is our dynasty, our fathers fought with their lives for it, all spoils naturally belong to us—sons and daughters of revolutionary leaders—was the mood.

Peasants as a group benefited from relaxed rules on free entrepreneurship, as reform started in the countryside first. And they did not have to do much in order to do well. In an age when meat was in short supply, and the entire country was equally poor, raising chickens and hogs could make one a rich person, now that they were allowed to sell these in free markets. Because there were no established commercial channels in the private sector and no rules to go by, price gouging was rampant and inflation ran wild. It got to the point where a street peddler of salted eggs would make ten times more money than a rocket scientist, who could not survive on his salary alone, and had to find menial jobs like sewing pants to feed his family. In 1987 hyperinflation triggered panic buying in cities, and for urbanites—intellectuals, factory workers and low ranking bureaucrats—financial security that had been taken for granted for so long was ruined, as well as their sense of fairness. University students could not find peace in their hearts to continue their study when they saw their future—the professors—could barely put food on the table.

By spring 1989 these tensions exploded on campuses and streets of Beijing. Students demanded an end of corruption and return to fairness. This was the generation who grew up during the Cultural Revolution, when Chairman Mao told them that no human authority was higher than principle, "to rebel is righteous". They thought they were defending a high principle—equality/fairness—which was what they had been taught since primary school, thus serving the revolution. They were also trying to save the country from corruption and decline, which is in line with pious loyalty. These two objectives—communist principle and pious loyalty to the state—were combined in Maoism, and the students were sincere followers of that doctrine, which was why they dared challenge the highest authority for an answer.

Hard questions were presented before the Deng regime. Does the new hybrid economic system mean core values of the revolution including equality are overturned? If so, what is the new value system? There is little evidence from Deng's writings that he dwelled upon philosophical/ideological questions. Obviously he was more of a doer than a thinker. Perhaps he thought material development, such as modernization and rising standard of living, was the only way to stabilize the country in the long run, and the true purpose of the revolution. Or perhaps he did not care, he simply wanted to rule in whatever way was practical. In any event equality/fairness did not seem an important value to him, as he remained unnerved by the growing discontent over corruption. Mao's interpretation of the communist revolution was mainly cultural. Chinese were fearful, docile, that was why they were unable to resist foreign invaders or fight abuses of domestic ruling class. Mao wanted them to fear nothing, to stand tall, and to have a rebel spirit, always ready to topple oppressive superiors. By stepping away from that theme, but without giving an alternative, Deng left the cultural and moral issue in limbo. Faced with open challenges from the youth, top CCP ranks could not agree on a response.

Not able to get a straight answer from the regime after repeated requests, student protestors turned their attention from corruption and equality issues to democracy. The term means "people being masters" in Chinese. Cultural Revolution reinforced that idea. When Red Guards followed Mao's call to overthrow all authorities, they did feel they were masters of their own domain, as they brought down high ranking officials in the national government and local party chiefs alike. Decades of mass political movements and revolutionary propaganda removed some of the fear that naturally comes as a result of Confucian family training for the younger generation, especially when they found themselves among a rebellious crowd, preparing them to boldly claim the role of masters of the country. Most students were not seeking national elections or other democratic institutions (they had no way of knowing how democracy works in the West), but they insisted on the idea of people—the masses, not a few party oligarchs—being masters.

The prolonged protest that spread to all other major cities—virtually wherever there was a college—presented a dilemma to the regime. CCP itself started off as a student movement back in the Nationalist era, and in its textbooks all historical rebellions, from peasant uprisings to strikes to protests, were exalted as heroic acts against oppression, while ruling regimes that brutally put down these protests were condemned with the harshest language. Rebellion against a corrupt regime was always right, and the CCP after Mao was certainly corrupting. Deng could not offer any straightforward rebuttal to the charges. Had the CCP condemned this obviously righteous student movement, it would have negated its own legitimacy. On the other hand, knowing the moral nature of the national debate and dire consequences of mass movements, Deng had no room to compromise. His own son was a millionaire, one of the first in 1980s China. By communist doctrine he had already crossed the line. Admitting wrong doing would have meant stepping down from the throne and possibly into prison, or worse.

By then Deng's pragmatism was exposed for its lack of a moral paradigm. Pragmatism by itself can not be the foundation of a culture. There must be basic principles. Traditionally these have been mercy on the part of superiors and fear of authority as if fearing gods on the part of inferiors. Maoism undermines both. It divides the population into good and bad, just like before, but along class lines—95% are poor therefore good, 5% are rich therefore bad. There is no mercy on the bad, or enemies of people. Among good people equality is the highest principle. Authorities are not to be feared. If they try to enslave subordinates they ought to be knocked over as class enemies. Deng did not explicitly endorse either view, or present his own. He did not want to back down, yet he could not openly challenge Maoism. In the end he fabricated some bogus charges on the movement and ordered a bloody crackdown.

As tanks rolled into TianAnMen Square and machine guns opened fire in Beijing streets, the question of where Deng was leading the country was answered in action rather than words. CCP effectively proclaimed might is right. The fact that Deng never addressed the issue of social justice even after the massacre sent the strongest message that the days when the average person could use the Little Red Book (quotations from Mao) to challenge authority are forever gone. However problematic and intellectually dubious, Maoism had been the only weapon in the hands of the masses against despotic party officials. The peasant soldiers who opened fire on protestors were too ignorant to realize it, but without equality as an overriding principle, and without rebellion as an option, Chinese had no more recourse against oppression, and the fate of the peasantry was going to take a nose dive.

Whatever Deng thought of his reform, the TianAnMen debacle took away many possibilities as to what direction China could go, and painted the CCP into an ideological corner. By Maoism merciless force can only be used on class enemies, and it is hard to call those twenty year old college students enemies of the people. This crime can not be easily explained away under the current communist doctrine, and since it was widely recorded overseas, the CCP can not destroy all evidence and rewrite history. Having committed the ultimate crime in its own book (suppressing the people that it is supposed to serve), the communist party has lost its legitimacy established by Mao's popular revolution. Its claim to power has to be justified some other way, and the CCP has been trying to find a rationalization for its own existence every since.

The only way this massacre can be justified is to go back to Confucianism, in other words from Mao's "rebellion is righteous" back to the Confucian "rebellion is blasphemous". But that is easier said than done. Decades of communist indoctrination can not be washed away overnight. Confucianism as a moral construct has little appeal to the current generation of Chinese, who can not accept total servility as the ultimate virtue. If it is to be reestablished openly as the new state ideology anytime soon, its moral reasoning will likely come under fire, and the inevitable heated ideological battle will be more than the top leadership can handle.

The CCP anguished in ideological impasse for a decade before Western capitalists offered them a way out. Eager to take advantage of low cost labor, multinationals successfully lobbied for globalization of Western economies, and moved their manufacturing facilities to China en mass, providing capital, technology, management and market for a Chinese economy that had struggled to take off on its own momentum. In 2005 foreign businesses accounted for more than half of the entire Chinese economy. With a huge foreign currency reserve and a still growing trade surplus, the Chinese currency is stabilized, pressured to appreciate even, compared to the hyper inflationary 1980s. Chinese economy has to follow the same export driven growth model of other Asian countries (Japan, South Korea, Taiwan, Hong Kong and Singapore), mainly because the pyramid culture does not afford the bulk of population—lower portion of the pyramid—enough security to spend their savings and sustain enough domestic demand for a self-sufficient economy.

With rising standard of living and more opportunities in a vibrant economy people's attention is turned away from ideological debates, and the CCP quietly changed the official doctrine. It now bases its claim to legitimacy on GDP growth, the fact that it brings welfare to a large number of people, particularly educated urbanites—the same scholar-official class that is influential in national debates or indoctrination effort. Welfare can be tied in to the Mencian idea of peopleism (also inherited by the Nationalists and now the Taiwan government in their Three-People-ism). With new found legitimacy the CCP can start the process of seamlessly switching from a Maoist paradigm to a traditional Confucian paradigm, although a strenuous intellectual arm twisting is unavoidable. The first step came a few years ago in the theory of "three representatives". It states that the CCP represents "the most advanced culture, the most advanced production force, and the interest of the majority of Chinese people". The last item of the three is meaningless, but the first two items signal that the party is abandoning the revolutionary role of leading slaves to overthrow their masters, and the class struggle rhetoric. CCP now represents the most advanced—a code word for the educated elite, the new scholar-official class. With one simple trick of semantics CCP now switched sides, from representing the peasantry (bottom of the pyramid) to representing the scholar-official class (top of the pyramid).

And the pyramid structure is quickly reemerging in China. Everyone knows the growing gap between rich and poor. But unlike in the West, where even the poor have human rights, in Asia there is mercy but no such thing as a right, and the poor can not escape the fate of slavery. Although peasants are the ones working on assembly lines for foreign businesses, they are not benefiting much from China's economic boom. For sure few people are starving these days, and there are plenty of jobs, but workload for the average peasant labor has increased, working conditions worsened, free education and basic healthcare largely gone. To the average peasant family taxes and fees add up to more than their agricultural income, in other words their net income would have been negative, if they did not send most family members of working age to factories in the cities, leaving the old, underage, and sick in the countryside tending farm work. They can not move into cities either, as they can not afford the now sky high commercial housing there (urbanites have bought their flats with state subsidy). Moreover, they are often mistreated on the job. In government run construction projects they frequently go months without pay. Some jump from high rises they just built, out of desperation. In foreign businesses, almost all of which managed by Chinese and other Asians, they are routinely abused verbally and physically. Two years ago a South Korean business owner forced all her Chinese employees to kneel in front of her as a sign of submission, which drew some attention in national media. To traditional Confucians like Japanese and Koreans, kneeling for a superior is no big deal. But for Chinese coming from the Mao era, it is a precipitous decline in their social station and self esteem. As they gradually get used to bowing, kneeling, and prostration (body language abolished in the Mao era), as well as abuse, their status as slaves are increasingly accepted as the new norm.

Meanwhile things are looking up for intellectuals, government bureaucrats and the new urban business elite—many of whom are former government officials. Education is no longer free. Tuition helped raise income level for professors and teachers alike several fold, not to mention fast increasing government funding for higher education and research. Bureaucrats saw their pay raised ten fold or more, under the slogan "high pay prevents corruption". Officials "buy" large state enterprises, under the newly imported Western term MBO (management buyout), at a nominal price arbitrarily set by themselves, with money borrowed from state banks, and then sell these assets at market price. Many of them got into the real estate business, where they basically removed many city residents, often by force, with a token compensation, and built skyscrapers on top of confiscated land. If anyone challenges their practices, the now well paid professors will defend them, with Western economic theory. "Growth and development trump everything else", they say, "If we had democracy, like India, it would have been hard to build anything, since residents would reject." A new class of ruling elite emerges from the new system or at least the new reality if it can not yet be called a system. Social structure has largely reverted to that of dynastic times, except that a single ruler is replaced by a clique of oligarchs.

Educated urbanites and illiterate peasantry live in two different worlds, though they often meet in city streets. Peasants hate urbanites, but they have to come for jobs. Urbanites look down on them as if they are lowly animals. Occasionally a tragic death of some overworked peasant worker would make the nightly news. A few intellectuals may be stricken by their wretched conditions, and are willing to risk a lot in championing their cause, but most simply do not care. Part of that indifference has to do with cowardice. Part of it has to do with rapidly declining social morals. Part of it is a sense of entitlement: I am higher in the hierarchy, this is the way it should be. Part of it is a strong distain for the ignorance of peasants: if you hate this regime, why do you keep sending your sons to the military?

Had this been an earlier era, there would have been a major revolution in the countryside by now, led by someone like Mao. Modern means of communication and tight control made possible by it have prevented local protests from developing beyond the local level. Besides, this is no longer the 1920s; the government has machine guns, tanks, fighter planes, and nuclear bombs. However, rising malcontent does present an opportunity for the Maoist wing of the party that has recently lost influence. Thus the second step of CCP ideological transformation came last year in the theory of "harmonious society". As we have seen from Japanese history, harmony is an amoral principle used to justify harsh rules.

By now the CCP has completed the ideological preparation of a cultural shift from the traditional moralistic outlook to a Japanese style amoral worldview. Its new propaganda reflects the Japanese interpretation of Confucianism, where peace, order and harmony justify every measure undertaken by the state, with no moral principles given. Both *ren* (mercy) and equality have been discarded. Deng's delay of moral debates is to be made permanent by moving to an amoral culture. What is left to happen for the new ideology to fully take hold is for the masses to become amoral.

And that process is well underway. Tired of Maoist ideological/moral struggles, which were often cruel, and unable to openly debate issues of social justice, also told by Western evangelicals of capitalism (commercialism) that equality means communism and is wrong, a message encouraged by the current CCP regime, educated Chinese now think they have finally understood what the West is all about, which is what Japanese found out in the Meiji era. Categorical abandonment of moral judgment is enabling Chinese to freely engage in scientific research, commercial profit seeking, as well as various kinds of recreational activities, including previously forbidden pleasures. In the Chinese mind to Westernize is to be promiscuous, to assert one's own interest without regard for others, to have no shame, and to try to get away with whatever one can. The urge to liberate oneself from the suffocating traditions of the past, manifested in the form of core cultural values, combines with the inability and/or lack of freedom to openly and objectively examine those values, to give birth to the trend of amoralization. The only success in slave traditions of the world—amoral Japan—will ultimately be the model for all Confucian states, and possibly all pyramid cultures.

Amorality aside, servility perpetuated by traditional family training must also be restored to its glory for the whole system to work, and the CCP propaganda has not been idle on that front either. Key words like filial piety are now all over the airwaves, in talk shows, TV series, and school textbooks, while stories of poor peasants suffering under the landlord's whip have disappeared. In the Mao era students swore to the flag to fight for the communist ideal, now they swear pious loyalty to the country, often expressed by the new term "patriotism". The young used to grow up learning that the principle (equality, fairness) is higher than any human authority, now there is no principle other than pious loyalty to the country. Without directly tackling the issue of whether rebellion is right or wrong, the propaganda machine quietly but forcefully reinserts core Confucian hierarchical values.

In Japanese movies and TV series the ruling class—emperors, shoguns, daimyos, modern corporate bosses—are usually good guys, though not necessarily main characters of the show, who are most likely paragons of pious loyalty, selfless and brave warriors, servants and corporate soldiers, while selfish—anyone with the slightest consideration of self interest—and cowardly servants are the bad guys. In the Mao era the entire Chinese history was deemed immoral, now it is proudly presented as a splendid civilization. In movies back then the ruling class—emperors, scholar-officials, warlords, landlords, capitalists—are invariably the bad guys, rebels and revolutionaries are the main characters of the show, while the masses are the supporting cast, who may be passive and timid in the beginning, quietly enduring abuses and oppression, but finally, encouraged by the spirit of the rebels and moved by their sacrifice, joined the rebellion, be it a peasant uprising or the Communist Revolution. Now TV shows frequently feature historical figures from the dynastic era, with suggestive servile body language. Rulers are good guys again, unconditional devotion by loyal servants is glorified, and motivation of the servants is now professionalism—a professional has no moral concerns, he fights for the state because he gets paid. Chinese culture looks increasingly Japanese.

Contemporary Japanese child rearing practices have not changed much over the past decades, and schools continue to play a critical role. For Chinese, home is still the primary training ground. As the world is becoming more interconnected than ever, many parents are increasingly reluctant to use brute force. Those who have immigrated to the West learned that it is illegal, sometimes the hard way. Some who live in large cities are sensitive to their global image, and try to change habits that are frowned upon in the West. Child abuse has entered their vocabulary, though the term is not clearly defined in Asia. To most people it means excessive use of violence. Just how much is excessive depends on who you ask. Regardless of individual opinions the trend is towards less violence.

However, a changed approach does not mean a changed objective. For most Chinese parents the only reason to have children at all is still to train them into loyal servants to be used in retirement (养儿防老). Filial piety is still unchallenged, and psychological manipulation remains the same, only that now actual violence is often replaced by threat of violence, which is usually enough to scare a kid. The same logic of *en* is still universally accepted—children owe *en* (divine favor/original debt) to parents because the latter feed them, and they must repay that debt with lifetime devotion. Chinese/Japanese language books on child rearing focus almost exclusively on subjects such as how to make your kid smart, or how much TV time should be allowed, avoiding discussion on the purpose of child rearing, as that is always implied. They are essentially tool books on how to turn out a smart and healthy product in the modern world for the purpose of parents. Asian kids may have the same physical skills or even share the same popular culture as their Western counterpart, but remain psychologically Confucian.

Confucian parents want their child to remain dependent on them. They let him/her know that they are the highest authority. There are typically few rules in the house and definitely none binding on them. The child is not allowed to make his/her own decisions; everything big and small has to be decided by parents. Siblings fight everyday, over toys or something else, and parents will be the arbiter every time (rules will take away some of their authority). They make their judgments based on which child is emotionally closer to them at the moment. As they grow up each kid learns that everything depends on their parents' favor, which the child can not afford to lose. To drive that point home parents do not hesitate to threaten with abandonment or withdrawal of love. Sooner or later children figure out that the only way to win parents' love is by total submission. They learn to fawn. They develop Stockholm Syndrome. Parents enjoy the ingratiating smiles, the jealousy between siblings for their love, the clever maneuvers to get closer to them, to be the favorite kid. These mind games go on throughout the entire childhood, and very often carry over into adulthood. It is not uncommon for two adult sons, each married with their own families, to fight for favor of their aging parent, not for inheritance or anything material, just a continuation of the psychological game, in which the parent gets to play the ruler.

How can a person who grows up in such a power dynamic understand what a human right is? His parents have never given him any security. Their love has always been conditional. Since the days of a baby he knows his survival in this world depends on his acknowledgment of being owned by them, and his obedience or emotional devotion to them. His value lies entirely in his service to them. In school he is trained to treat the state just like a parent. Official propaganda idolizes pious loyalty. If he does not observe filial piety or pious loyalty, he is seen as worthless by the society and ostracized. His understanding of the "self" is a total slave with no independent value. As he goes into the real world he carries the same logic and psyche acquired from family and school experience. The society is an enlarged family with a similar structure. Everyone plays the role of a child to his superiors and the role of a parent to his inferiors at the same time.

In such a pyramid structure many common Western social ideas can not find any parallel. What, for example, would a "stakeholder" mean in this society? One might be tempted to say that anyone who has property is a stakeholder. But that is not how they feel. As they themselves in theory belong to the state so do their properties by implication. Of all the well-to-do in China, no one is safe from potential prosecution, as most of their wealth comes from "grey income"—something that is strictly speaking illegal but since everyone is doing it few are actually prosecuted. In the more mature "capitalist" country Japan, though blatant violations of property rights are not seen, the position of any individual, including his life, not to mention his wealth, is still conditioned upon "proper" behavior, which includes total submission to superiors. The Western sense of a stakeholder implies a free man, an idea that does not exist in Asia.

In terms of achieving the intended social objectives envisioned by Confucius, Japan is the Confucian state par excellence. Rituals of propriety and hierarchy (*li*) are so well trained they are practically second nature to Japanese. Westerners may wonder how a Japanese man can be both obstinate and submissive, both brave and timid, both honest and deceptive. Well, these are different traits required of a slave in different circumstances. Consider the following scenario. You are advising your master on certain actions to take. You have carefully examined the case and devised a plan in his best interest. He on the other hand, due to ignorance or not being able to see beyond immediate gratification of his senses, is about to take a course of action that will in your judgment put himself in harm's way. A Westerner in your position would think that he has done his job and withdraw; after all it's the master's decision to make. But a Confucian wouldn't quit. He is obligated to try, even at the risk of losing his own life, to talk some senses into the master. So you must insist with death defying courage, with love and devotion in the face of your indignant master, for you have nothing but his interest at heart, and that selflessness makes you righteous. However you are not trying to impose your will on your master, you are discharging your duty as a loyal servant to protect him from his own unwise judgment. You submit your body, mind and soul to him. You are at his beck and call. But you are not a blind follower of instructions. You are a thinking machine, on his behalf, for his interest, even at your own expense. Your character is a combination of strong will and weak knees, only that your will is not your free will, but an extension of your master's will, since your mind belongs to him just as your body does.

Chinese are indoctrinated the same way. The only difference is that most of them are cynical. However, Japanese style training manifested in modern business practices have over the last few decades spread all over Asia, first to the "Asian Tigers" (South Korea, Taiwan, Hong Kong, Singapore), and now into mainland China. Current Chinese economic boom, just like that of the Asian Tigers earlier, has a lot to do with learning and mastering Confucian business management techniques, invented and perfected by Japanese in the forms of strict hierarchy and codes of conduct. Face slapping in the workplace is no longer news, though not yet a common practice. Sooner or later Japanese corporate culture will completely conquer China, just like it has already conquered other Asian economies. Japan has blazed the only successful path in the Confucian world; other states are bound to follow. Having undertaken two revolutions and largely failed to reform its ancient culture, China has given up the revolutionary approach, and now found the groove laid by Japanese one and a half centuries ago.

Some say the twenty first century will be a Confucian century. In this globalized economy that may very well become true. If the state is the ultimate authority (a prevailing view in the world) and the ultimate measure of success, then Confucian states have a perpetual advantage over other kinds of states, because they need not adhere to any principle (especially when mercy is downplayed), and pious loyalty to the state is a core cultural value, ensuring cohesion that is not easily maintained in a free society. However, the rise of Confucian culture is not necessarily a blessing to human freedom. If forced love and loyalty are taken as true, if Confucian psyche and practices are accepted as normal and good (i.e. loving, worshiping and identifying with the oppressor; voters feel like helpless children and elect caretakers—parent officials—instead of representatives; freedom is defined as privileges granted by an almighty government; core cultural values trump human rights, etc.), then freedom may prove forever unattainable to Asians.

Just like twenty five hundred years ago when Daoism was born, Asians still feel like inanimate objects being moved or used by superiors or other incontrollable forces. Their survival strategy is to accumulate every bit of security they can gather: saving money, training loyal and skillful children, forging connections with higher ranks, avoid standing out from the crowd, staying obedient to superiors, etc. For all their economic spectacles, Asians continue to struggle, to find security, courage, self identity and unconditional love, to understand freedom and justice, to acquire the body language and psyche of Western people, to break free of suffocating social conventions, to cope with anger precipitated and denied of an expression by core cultural values, to put the best face on a tortured soul.

REFERENCES

1. The Book of Lao (道德经), translated by Arthur Waley
2. The Book of Rites (礼记), translated by James Legge
3. The Analects (论语), translated by Arthur Waley
4. The Book of Mencius (孟子), translated by James Legge
5. The Book of Xun (荀子), translated by Burton Watson
6. The Book of Han Fei (韩非子), translated by Burton Watson
7. Sources of Japanese Tradition, compiled by WM. Theodore De Bary
8. Studies in the Intellectual History of Tokugawa Japan, Masao Maruyama, translated by Mikiso Hane

Printed in the United States
59825LVS00004B/74